The Downsizing of America

The Downsizing of America

Carlos Ramirez-Faria

Manas Publications
New Delhi (INDIA)

MANAS PUBLICATIONS
(Publishers, Distributors, Importers & Exporters)
4858, Prahlad Street,
24, Ansari Road, Darya Ganj,
New Delhi - 110 002 (INDIA)
Ph.: 23260783, 23265523 (O); 23842660 (R)
Fax: 011 - 23272766
E-mail: manaspublications@vsnl.com
Website: www.manaspublications.com

ISBN 81-7049-276-9

Rs 695/-

Typeset at
Manas Publications

Printed in India at
Nice Printing Press, Delhi
and Published by Mrs Suman Lata for
Manas Publications, 4858, Prahlad Street,
24, Ansari Road, Darya Ganj,
New Delhi - 110 002 (INDIA)

To Milena,
sans phrase

Contents

Acknowledgements

Even though this book covers a short period in "real time", so to speak, it is inserted in a vast historical context. In this sense, it has been long a-borning and I have so many debts it would take a great deal of space to enumerate them, as would expanding on the debts which I feel I must acknowledge here. Without the interest and boldness of Vivek Garg this book would not have been published, and I cannot thank him enough. My sincerest recognition to the Indian friends who have extended to me their friendship and help: professor S.P. Ganguly, Kunwar Narain, M.S. Joshi, Siddarth Varadarajam, and Parvez Dewan. I owe so much to Kaldone Nweihed that this mention barely suffices, but it must do, as must also this posthumous mention of Ignacio de la Cruz. What knowledge and training I possess derive in a great part from my acquaintance and intellectual commerce with Luis Brito Garcia, Colin Lewis, John Lynch, John Fisher, Peter Worsley, Leslie Bethel, Leslie Wolf-Phillips, and Amiya Kumar Bagchi. During the time I spent in the Philippines, many people took an interest in my historical work but three people were particularly encouraging: Ramon K. Ilusorio, Teresita Alcantara, and Josie Lichauco. In the matter of unconditional support, Carlos Diaz Sosa, Olga Gonzalez, and Meri Benmergui are in a special category of their own. It was Ian Jacboson who permitted me to do the groundwork for the wider historical cradle of this work by giving it a sense of editorial purpose. Joseph and Lynn Moorhead determined the special course that my writing took after a certain point in my life. No book on history is devoid of politics and in this one they are so entwined that at times they may seem indistinguishable, but then the same can be said of history and any other discipline, for, when all is said and done, history is the ultimate arbiter of knowledge. At one time or another, I have had as practical political mentors Domingo Alberto Rangel, Jose Vicente Rangel, and Teodoro Petkoff. To close arbitrarily, I must mention John Pinfold who introduced me to the internet "at the creation"; Rafael Araguren has stood by me through thick and thin in all my affairs; Asutosh Roy patiently went through the manuscript minutely and offered helpful suggestions; and Rajesh Prasad crucially assisted me in giving this book its shape, for whose deficiencies I take full responsibility in all respects. To all, my deepest thanks.

1

Overture on Terror

The downsizing of America is not a denial of its power or its achievements. It starts by accepting the American thesis of American exceptionalism, the proposition that America is like other countries but better, much better. The trouble with the thesis is that it just doesn't work. In 1970, the Uruguayan revolutionary Tupamaros kidnapped and executed Dan Mitrione, an intelligence attaché in the American embassy. This was generally considered to have been one more egregious example of communist brutality. The Tupamaros claimed that their victim had been teaching the Uruguayan military torture methods. Americans teaching Latin Americans how to inflict pain? It turns out that it probably was true.

American exceptionalism has many grounds but three are crucial: the economy, democracy, and freedom of expression. The dollar has been taking such a beating that it induces suspicions about the road that American capitalism is following. It is more likely that the American currency is going through a cycle and that it will rebound, as it recently has been doing. But its present vulnerability before an upstart like the Euro, among other contemporary developments, demonstrates that the American economy is no longer the high-and-mighty, unassailable fortress that it was until sometime back. With the election of George W. Bush with less than a majority of popular votes in 2000, American democracy showed that it is not a peerless model for the planet. And the record of the 9/11-traumatized American media has been so deplorable in terms of reliability that it is hardly possible to speak of a recovery. It used to be that veracity was their value of values. Today, if you believe the headlines in the American press you will probably be out of touch with reality.

Ultimately, the downsizing of America is its insertion in history, just like any other country, which is what this book attempts by placing the period from 1989 to the present in a world-historical context. Objectively, of course, this is undeniable. But the American-begotten thesis of American exceptionalism is that the USA is a peace-loving country, that it goes out of its way to respect human lives everywhere, that it is there when it is urgently needed anywhere in the world, that it is the paragon of freedom of expression, and that it is the country in the world where any individual is more likely to obtain judicial redress. All these claims are either false or exaggerated. Many could probably say that only unpardonable naivety would have allowed such affirmations to pass. But it can also be said that for many objective observers American exceptionalism, with some modulation, was essentially right. This point of view became astigmatic when President George H.W. Bush plunged America into the senseless maelstrom of war on terror. This introduction is not so much like a symphonic movement (as its title obliquely suggests) as like the anticipatory sounds of a symphony orchestra before the maestro climbs to the podium.

(1) The bipolar world

The interaction of the constants of history—the lust for power and immanent forces such as economic improvement, judicial redress, and religious freedom—has on the whole been beneficial to mankind. The world has gone from multipolarity to bipolarity to unipolarity. With the advent of the Second Iraqi war, we are back again in a multipolar world.

Arguably, the greatest achievement of mankind was the defeat of Nazi Germany. World War II itself, especially the barbarity of the Nazis, was a nadir for the human race. But in hindsight its consequences have generally been good, among them the practical repudiation of racism and the principled denial of despotism. The figure of crimes against humanity was first expounded at the Nuremberg trials.[1] These lessons,

1 On 8 August 1945, a war crime tribunal was empowered to judge captured Nazi hierarchs. It sat in Nuremberg. On 1 October 1946 it handed down eleven death sentences on the most visible members of the Nazi government and party. Goering killed himself just before the time of his hanging. It is widely believed that an American officer he befriended obtained for him a cyanide capsule. There followed four more Nuremberg trials that judged physicians, execution squads' commanders, judicial functionaries and judges, ministers, and other Nazi leaders. In all, 24 executions were carried out. The Nuremberg trials lasted until 13 April 1949. "The Nuremberg trials: chronology" (www.law.umkc.edu). Telford Taylor, *The anatomy of the Nuremberg trials* (1992)

like all historical processes, have been slow in getting through, but they have done so much more quickly than, say, the rise of the West or the acceptance of its values by rest of the world.

The bipolar world also emerged from World War II. Nuclear warfare was the fastest military revolution in history, so potentially devastating that it was never actually implemented the way, for instance, artillery was. If in the first drawing of a rudimentary cannon about to be fired the cannoneer stands away from it in fear and mistrust, the technology of nuclear weapons was never an object of fearful ignorance but of panicky rationality. The USA had a monopoly on nuclear terror for approximately four years.

The USSR might have been the most inefficient agglomeration of scientific know-how and vast economic resources history has ever produced, but when it was determined to achieve something, it did not matter that along the way it also missed achieving countless other things. This inefficiency was underpinned by extremely undemocratic practices, which were used to make the inefficiency over, but prosperity, the only thing that could have validated Soviet tyranny, was the one thing it could not provide. It was this disparity between the much it could do and the immensity it could not that eventually led to its collapse and the emergence of the unipolar world.

(2) A deeply flawed "new world order"

The unipolar world was accompanied by great hopes and great calamities. Since it was the USSR that caved in leaving America as the main world power and the USA was a democratic, prosperous, and generally trustworthy nation, world perspectives appeared rosy. The Soviet Empire had disintegrated and the fears of nuclear conflict were quickly dimming.

Between the fall of the Soviet Empire and the disintegration of the USSR, the USA led a large coalition of states in what can only be described as a "just war". The Gulf or First Iraqi war was just because it defeated gratuitous aggression and taught an unscrupulous tyrant a lesson it was hoped he would not ever unlearn. It was also just because once it attained its goal, the liberation of Kuwait, it stopped literally on its tracks rather than provoke more destruction and unnecessary civilian deaths. Saddam Hussein was a brutal dictator who did not hesitate to sacrifice his own people for his ambitions. It did not take him long to forget the strapping he got.

Arab despots have the seemingly magical power to convert utter defeat into victory, which is like turning dross (not even lead) into gold.

But at the time Saddam Hussein was foiled and humiliated, things looked so good that American President George H.W. Bush could get away with a bit of wizardry of his own about the coming of a golden age for mankind, a "new world order", as he put it. And he deserved all the credibility he got. He steadfastly and successfully opposed Congressional support for the inflammatory Israeli policy of founding Jewish settlements in Palestinian territories, thus showing that America was a fair-minded super-power, one which could be trusted to lean even on its closest allies if they misbehaved or exaggerated.

Even as the USSR dissolved itself, tacitly conceding its Cold War inferiority, American bragging was muted. The USA was not going to lay into a fallen foe in the time-sanctioned manner of conquerors. There was some crowing among article-writers, usually bad historians, and especially in Hollywood, which simply will not accept that Russians can be anything except villains, but officially the USA acted with magnanimity and only threw its weight around by encouraging the North Atlantic Treaty Organization (NATO) to expand and enlist former Soviet satellites for no apparent strategic reason.

The darker aspects of the unipolar world, or more properly, the calamities that the fall of European communism brought with it, were visible almost immediately. Like all contemporary processes, these calamities, and the unipolar world itself into the bargain, have been brief. Communist societies were diseased but, as with those maladies which have long incubation periods, the symptoms did not start showing until long after the causal agents began operating. The root of the disease was psychiatric and consisted basically in having to live routinely in a real world which contradicted daily what was officially being said about the achievements of communism.

Like the role-modeling USSR, other communist economies were very inefficient, not quite as inefficient as most underdeveloped countries, but much more inefficient than those of comparable capitalist countries, like, say, communist Poland and capitalist Spain. When the USSR disbanded, during its disorderly transition from a centrally controlled economy to a chaotically, de-centralized (though hardly liberal) one, social conditions in its component parts rapidly degenerated: real incomes fell abysmally and insufficient or backward social services either broke down or disappeared entirely.

One of the myths about communism concerned its presumed totalitarian character. In each country where communist tyrants ruled (the prototype for the latter was of course Stalin and his personality cult), communist ideas and attitudes were supposed to suffuse every social interstice and even to dominate the minds themselves of individuals. Totalitarianism had also been predicated of Nazi Germany, yet Germans recovered very quickly from pervasive Hitlerite propaganda and control.

A famously erudite professor, Karl Wittfogel, became fashionable for a time with a book, titled *Oriental Despotism*, published in the 1930s but useful for Kremlinologists and assorted pundits during the Cold War to explain that Russia was like it was because it was not really European but Asian. Actually, the best illustration of totalitarianism was Wittfogel himself and the way he brought his vast erudition to bear on one single, obsessive idea. In a nutshell, Wittfogel's argument was that despotism originated in agrarian societies that required "hydraulic works", like irrigation canals, to overcome unpredictable weather patterns. This type of works involved the dragooning of collectivities by despots. The peasantry surrendered all their political rights to such despots in order to survive. Many historians, however, have claimed that Asian despotism was nurtured in the steppes where people were not agrarian at all. Others dispute outright the phrase "oriental despotism" itself. The force of Wittfogel's thesis lay in the huge number of historical references that its author could muster.

When communism began collapsing in Russia, it turned out not to have been as totalitarian and homogenizing as all that. Russian entrepreneurs, most of them previously as red as Lenin, showed as marked a vocation for inegalitarianism as the truest blue American CEO. Russians in general developed in short order such a fondness for democracy that on three successive occasions, when they were going through the hellish transition from stifle-all communism to grab-as-grab-can capitalism, they resisted both illegal and legal communist lunges at power. The break up of the USSR itself showed not only that communists took to inequalities as if born in ancient régime France, but that in fact the USSR itself was so permeated by inequalities and by untotalitarian differences that it spawned states that went from (1) the relatively developed, such as the Baltic republics, to (2) those in which high development was a feasible but gradual process, such as Russia, to (3) those which were very underdeveloped, in a station not much better than that of low-income non-communist countries.

The diseased condition of communist societies became truly morbid in Yugoslavia. If communist despotism had failed to make the USSR cohesive, an impossible task made to look simple from a totalitarian perspective such as Wittfogel's, it not only could not integrate a much less complex political formation such as Yugoslavia—constituted after all by Slavs with a common national history going back to the end of World War I—but it created so many divergences and nestled so many accumulated ethnic hatreds that people looked on in disbelief at the sheer barbarism of the sequels to Yugoslavia's dismemberment. Yugoslavs themselves seemed to grasp the inevitabilities that non-Yugoslavs could not fathom. It was as if Oedipus knew that he would end up knifing his own eyes and went ahead and killed his father and married his mother.

It took the world, still largely and willingly and happily unipolar, three years before it realized that in Bosnia and Herzegovina were being re-enacted Nazi atrocities that had supposedly been buried nearly half a century ago. It got so bad that even when the UN intervened the atrocities increased, for the killings in Srebernica and Zeta occurred after Blue Helmets had been deployed.

When the Kosovo crisis came around, America and Western Europe were inured to Yugoslav political irrationality and acted accordingly. The bombing of Serbia by NATO and the evacuation of Kosovo by Serbian forces might well be considered the high point of the unipolar world. Even Russia, which in an ancestral Slavic reflex did not approve of the punishment inflicted on Serbia, had to accept the fait accompli and secured self-attributed occupation rights in the airport at Pristina, the capital of Kosovo.

Both the Bosnian and the Kosovar wars are too easy to blame on Serbia and specifically on its former ultra-nationalist president Slobodan Milosevic. It is not likely coincidental that in Russia and in Yugoslavia communism both dissimulated and encouraged social tendencies which in public it strenuously disavowed. In Russia, as in the rest of the USSR, communism was supposed to have created the ultimate egalitarian society. But it hadn't at all. In Yugoslavia, not as hardline egalitarian as the USSR, communism was supposed to have integrated a country that remained profoundly divided. Both societies were sick at their cores not because of anything that their citizens were but because of the lies that communism foisted on them.

(3) Encouraging footnotes and fatal flaws

Insofar as the unipolar world, united behind America, coped with these dangerously ailing societies, it too, like the constants of history, was favorable to mankind. Better yet: the unipolar world seemed to be striking a balance between the lust for power and the aspirations of humanity as a whole. Even the historical footnotes of the unipolar world-text were encouraging.

When Augusto Pinochet, the former Chilean military dictator and rightist executioner, was incarcerated in England, albeit in comfy surroundings, the effect on human rights advocates was electrifying. For once in world history the rallying cry could be heard: "Tyrants beware!" There was to be no more despotism in the world. Well, not quite, but would-be despots had better think twice before siccing their myrmidons on the politically defenseless. America was ready to take the lead wherever and whenever mass murder or famine or any of mankind's scourges could be prevented. As to world poverty and international inequalities, America again, this time as the guardian of free trade, Minerva and Mercury to the globe, was the example to follow. Who could deny the benefits of financial globalization? Who would be foolish enough to try to swim upstream of the river of history?

Unfortunately, it wasn't only post-communist societies that were in trouble. Elsewhere, the American-led unipolar world was flawed in too many ways. UN-sponsored American troops landed in Somalia, which everyone knew was starving because night-in, night-out television showed skeletal Somali children. This intervention was another historical footnote, as thrilling in its way as the one on Pinochet. The American presence in Somalia was the acme of humanitarianism. Here was the world's greatest nation sending its soldiers to a God-forsaken, warlord-ridden place to prevent human beings from dying of hunger. However, not all Somalis were starving and those that weren't were not pleased. They rather liked their homegrown warlords. To complicate matters, American soldiers began getting involved in the local, Kalashnikov-based politics. With the downing of a helicopter in Mogadishu, a city bristling with snipers and machine-gun-mounted vans, American soldiers were beset and killed. Their bodies were dragged along the streets by mobs. President Bill Clinton wisely chose to withdraw American troops and left the Somalians to their own devices.

The Somali incident was one in a chain of terrorist attacks on American forces overseas and on American diplomatic missions. There were other signs that the world had not improved that much with the collapse of the USSR, even that perhaps, oh unthinkable of unthinkable, the bipolar world was more stable, or less problematical, than the unipolar world. The exultation that had accompanied the dismantling of the Berlin Wall was not followed by the fast and easy economic integration of backward East Germany into "miraculous" West Germany. To this day, the formerly separate nations have not achieved an economic "common denominator" and federal Germany is now a less cohesive, recession-prone country compared to when it did not include "democratic" Germany.

The Third World had not been made any less unstable either. The incredible stories about the incompetence of the Congolese dictator Mobutu

Sese Seko were shown to be all too true when his 32-year-old regime caved in very quickly before what was practically a feint from an unknown opposition leader, the corpulent and hairless Laurent Kabila, who obtained backing from Rwanda and Uganda. Once in power, Kabila made such a hash of Congo's politics and foreign relations, and the country became so disunited with internal and external warring factions, that central authority, tenuous before, evaporated like a muddy puddle under the equatorial sun. Kabila was assassinated and succeeded by his son. The Democratic Republic of Congo has become basically a phantom country, ramshackle and deadly, a not uncommon condition in Africa's tragic contemporary history.

In Indonesia, the cronyism and nepotism of Suharto, the country's strongman, had become so nauseating that Indonesians forced him out of power. In a famous photograph, Suharto stands suited up looking with fondness and fatherly pride at his grown offspring dressed in Indonesian costumes and striking various poses. The daughters look demure. All of them were involved, directly or indirectly, in multi-millionaire projects requiring state patronage. One of the sons was later charged with complicity in murder. Since Suharto's ouster, Indonesia has had four presidents but more ominously it has become a country prone to crises and home to a bourgeoning Islamic fundamentalist movement. It seems to be stabilizing after years of turmoil and an insurrection in Atjeh, which is apparently winding down after the catastrophic tsunami of 2004.

The Indian-Pakistani conflict over Kashmir became outright local war when Islamic irregulars occupied the heights of Kargil and were dislodged by India with considerable casualties. India and Pakistan had both detonated atomic bombs. In 2002, India mobilized in Kashmir over alleged Pakistani laxness in suppressing terrorist organizations. The possibility of nuclear war only gradually dissipated.

But the most unstable of all the world's regions is still the Middle East, a condition it arguably has been in since 1949.[2] The Vietnam War,

2 The history of wars and insurrections in the Middle East (from the eastern Mediterranean to Iran) includes: the first Arab-Israeli war (1948-1949), the Suez crisis (1956), the Six-Day war (1967), the expulsion of the PLO from Jordan (1970-1971), the 1973 or Yom Kippur war, the Lebanese civil war (1975-1991), the theocratic revolution in Iran (1979), the Iraq-Iran war (1980-1988), the First Intifada (1987-1993), the Gulf War (1991), the Second Intifada (2000-2004), the Second Iraqi War (2003). Large and small foreign interventions in Lebanon have been numerous. This is not counting many internal upheavals, revolutions, and the countless acts of mutual hostility between Israelis and Arabs.

which was considered highly de-stabilizing by the USA, did not turn out that way. Middle Eastern instability is in a way comparable to the condition of the Near East from the start of the Crusades in 1098-1099 to their virtual defeat in 1187. Today's instability has not lasted as long but, unlike the Crusades, it is not only regionally conflictual but also globally divisive and a constant source of international tensions.

Israel had been establishing settlements in Arab lands ever since the annexation of Gaza and the West Bank. This policy was low-key and discreet but after Menachem Begin's election it took off with the constant encouragement and support of Ariel Sharon. Palestinians in the occupied territories were smoldering about Israeli encroachment and they staged a mostly stone-throwing insurrection, called the Intifada (shaking off), that Yitzhak Rabin, then minister of defense, ordered crushed expeditiously with barely restrained use of force. The Intifada began in Jabaliya in the Gaza strip with the knifing of an Israeli and the subsequent deaths of four Palestinians in a car accident. At the time, the PLO and its leader, Yasir Arafat, were based in Tunisia. Israel/Palestine antagonism was standard fare during the bipolar world but unipolarity did not improve things.

Seven years or so after he got an international thrashing in the Gulf War, Saddam Hussein, despite his country's evident weakness, started acting defiantly again by expelling the UN monitors of Iraq's disarmament. Since American and British warplanes regularly attacked Iraqi military installations, there was not much of an international fuss over the dictator's obduracy. Foolhardy might have been a way to describe his attitude. But Hussein's behavior in general has probably got to be considered in the context of Palestinian resentment of Israel, which has the unanimous backing of Arabs everywhere.

The number of Israeli settlers in the West Bank had ballooned to around 200,000, nearly a tenth of the Palestinian population, when the Second Intifada began. This new conflict was characterized by the use of suicide bombers and it was much more difficult to put down than the first one. It was still going full blast when, on 11 September 2001, Islamic fanatics hijacked and slammed airliners into the twin towers of the World Trade Center (WTC) in New York City and into one side of the Pentagon.

America's indignation had never reached such high pitches. President George W. Bush, son of the previous Bush, was determined to get even. Osama bin Laden and his Al Qaeda (the base) organization were behind the terrorist attack on the USA—soon referred to as 9/11—the largest-ever perpetrated against any nation. Osama bin Laden, a personage with a certain physical resemblance to Dickens' Fagin, was the "guest" of the fanatical Taliban regime in Afghanistan, where he holed out with his people in the rough borderlands with Pakistan. Kabul refused Washington's peremptory demand that bin Laden be handed over to USA authorities. The resulting War on Afghanistan was the last concerted military action carried out under unipolar American leadership.

Though not actively as in Kosovo, NATO supported the invasion. Already present militarily in Tajikistan, Russia (formally the Commonwealth of Independent States) backed the USA, as did Uzbekistan, from where supplies were funneled to the so-called Northern Alliance, formed with the last remaining resistance movements within Afghanistan itself. The force of American aerial firepower, the same that had made the Serbians back down in Kosovo, fell on Taliban strongholds. The Taliban regime quickly collapsed. Not for nothing have Americans always made space in their history books for the "Don't Tread On Me" flag, which depicts a poised-for-attack rattlesnake and was proposed in 1776 in South Carolina as the flag for the commander in chief of the American navy. But the main target of the war, the capture of Osama bin Laden, was not accomplished.

(4) Bush's "axis of evil" suffered from an unfortunate oversight

President Bush the younger had inaugurated his administration with two specific foreign policy doctrines: one, to construct an anti-missiles shield around the USA, and two, to do so against the "axis of evil" represented by Iran, Iraq, and North Korea (hence, really a triad). Afghanistan was an unfortunate oversight. The high-tech shield idea was somewhat discredited by 9/11. Bush could hardly consider victory in Afghanistan retribution enough for having been wrong footed by terrorism. The Afghan war's dubious results did not compensate for the loss of lives and the havoc in New York and Washington. "Closure", that egregiously sound-bitish coinage of newsmen covering the vigils on the southern shore of Long Island after the 1994 TWA crash, was simply not there.[3] Another target for American fury was needed. That's when Iraq and "war on terror" came up. It was the beginning of the end of the unipolar world that had seemed so promising barely a decade before. And its consequences dealt a mortal blow to the thesis of the historical exceptionalism of the USA, the land where life and fairness were supposedly sacrosanct and where torture was a word translated from other tongues.

3 Closure means to close, as a sale. It was not usually applied to finding body parts or attending executions. In the sense of recovering bodily remains, it could stem from the question of the MIA (missing in action) in Vietnam.

Despite nearly unanimous global opposition, including that of traditional allies like France and Germany, the USA got the UK and Australia to form a military coalition for a war against Iraq. The Australian presence was symbolical. British Prime Minister Tony Blair took his role as Bush's second in command very seriously, even to opening fissures within his own Labor Party that have not closed. Polls in Britain were against the war until it started and then the bandwagon effect set in. The sequels of the war have made opinion swing back against involvement in Iraq. In Australia, polls followed the British pattern.

Various reasons were alleged for attacking Iraq: that it was a menace to world peace, that if Saddam Hussein was not overthrown Americans would be fighting terrorists in their streets, that Iraq was manufacturing nuclear, chemical, or biological weapons of mass destruction (WMD), that Saddam Hussein was tyrannizing his own people, and that Iraq probably had something to do with 9/11. The last point was insinuated through a hypothesized link between Hussein and bin Laden. Not one of them was convincing. Basically, Bush had made Iraq part of the "axis of evil" and America still had some evening up to do for 9/11.

The military results of the war were foregone conclusions. Even so, the Second Iraqi War was singularly inconclusive, not unlike the War on Afghanistan. Iraq was defeated, but subsequent Iraqi resistance to American occupation has been so ferocious that it could hardly be said that the country was subjected. The USA had won a war but what it gained from it was a popular insurrection it did not commit the military means to quell. If what America wanted was closure, it wasn't about to get any, especially if what closure had concretely come to mean was revenge. The New York City towers were gone forever. The accomplices and backers of the perpetrators of the deed were being tracked to the ends of the earth. The USA had fought two victorious wars against unfriendly states, yet the global, unipolar American leadership was shattered. Especially, there were no indications that America was even near to having won the war on terror. At the root of this dilemma was the concept itself of "war on terror".

(5) Terror as a weapon of state

There is to start with a distinction between terror and terrorism. Terror is an emotion. It is what we feel before the real or imagined imminence of death. Terror can be shared by passengers in a bus in a terrorism-prone area who hear a loud bang or by prisoners confronted by snarling dogs. The state uses terror as an instrument for waging war.

The First World War was a paroxysm of terror. No one disputes the expression "Nazi terror". And Japan was terrorized into surrender by two atomic bombs. A country that was prepared to commit collective hara-kiri, whose military had given brutality and ruthlessness new dimensions, was actually frightened into submission, because here was something that made suicide ordinary, even trite, and voided of meaning the idea of fighting to death. You did not fight under the shadow of an atomic mushroom. You just died. The "something" that made Japanese militarists quake in their boots had all the earmarks of terror.

Terror unnerved the Japanese militarist state. That happened under extraordinary circumstances. Normally, states take terror in their stride. Civilization did not break down despite the carnage of World War I. There were some mutinies, but there was always abundance of cannon fodder. Waves of soldiers were waiting to follow the waves that were mowed down by machine guns. As a result of World War II, Germany lost its power to terrorize but it did not lose its nationhood, or the qualities, such as efficiency and genius for organization, that had made it so terrorizing in the first place. It only channeled them differently and Germany earned by other means the laurels it had forfeited in war. Japan was tacitly absolved of its terrorizing excesses when Emperor Hirohito, the personification of Japanese aggression, was allowed to keep his throne through the simple expedient of a "humanity declaration", basically the public avowal that he was not a god, which apparently many Japanese believed.[4]

From a common social perspective, terrorism is the pursuit of anarchy by violent means. The most lethal individual act of terrorism was undoubtedly the assassination by the Serb fanatic Gavrilo Princip of the heir to the Austro-Hungarian empire, archduke Francis Ferdinand, a deed which set off World War I and cost tens of millions of lives. Up to the present and from the heyday of political assassinations in the last third of the 19th and the early 20th centuries, terrorism has been associated with social aberration. Besides the Habsburg crown prince, the Spanish prime ministers Juan Prim y Prats (1873) and Antonio Cánovas del Castillo (1897), Russian Tsar Alexander II (1881), American Presidents James Garfield (1881) and William McKinley (1901), French premier Jules Ferry (1893), Italian king Umberto I (1900), Serbian king Alexander Obrenovic (1903), Russian prime ministers Plehve (1904) and Stolypin (1911), Portuguese king Carlos I (1908), and Greek king George I (1913), all were also victims of assassins, most of them anarchists

4 On the atrocious treatment of prisoners by the Japanese, see, among many works, Eric Lomax, *The railway man* (1996); Herbert P. Bix, *Hirohito and the making of modern Japan* (2000)

or implacable enemies of established social order. The most senseless of this sort of murders was that of empress Elizabeth of Austria-Hungary who traveled a great deal because she was never quite psychologically stable after the suicide of her only son prince Rudolph. On one of her trips, she was spotted by an anarchist and butchered with a knife for no reason other than their being accidentally together on board the same ship.

Joseph Conrad, a genetic conservative (if such a thing were possible), tried to grasp the mentality of the anarchist in two of his novels *The secret agent* (1907) and *Under Western Eyes* (1911), but what he really expressed was his amazement and perplexity. And it wasn't just because of his conservatism. Conrad was trilingual: his native tongue was Polish but he wrote in French and in English. He served for decades in the British merchant marine and attained the rank of captain. In his view of life, discipline and courage were the two greatest virtues. But he wasn't a racist, unlike W. Somerset Maughan who wrote the ultimate statement of racism in a short story called "The yellow streak", in which a trace of Asian blood could manifest itself in acts of cowardice.

The state is the defender of law and order. It is on the state that devolves the responsibility for containing and eliminating the enemies of society and the terrorism that the fair-minded and unprejudiced Conrad so deplored. There is a kind of irony involved here. Since in war states inflict terror on one another but states are the legitimate barriers against anarchy, then war cannot coherently be a form of terrorism. War is a condition that authorizes the use of all state weapons, except those that, like poison gas, could turn against its users. Since war is not terrorism because it is the doing of states, then whatever the Nazis and the Japanese did in World War II cannot have been terrorism. Wherever the Germans and the Japanese went, their main concerns were to maintain law and order and to repress terrorism. The city of Nanjing and the villages of Lidice and Oradour-sur-Glane were subjected to systematic, sadistic slaughters to cow terrorist enemies of law and order.[5] British Air Marshal Arthur Harris demolished Dresden gratuitously. He couldn't very well be blamed when German cruise missiles and rockets were hitting London.

5 A Nazi jurist once said in 1933: "it is necessary to have a new respect for the term terror in the penal code". Lidice was suspected of harboring anti-Nazi terrorists. In 1942, after Reinhard Heydrich was assassinated, Nazis killed all its inhabitants. Only a few children adopted by Germans survived. Oradour was a French village from which shots were fired on a retreating SS unit in 1944. The SS, fanatical Hitlerite police that doubled as army units, turned on the village, locked its inhabitants in the church, and set it on fire.

In war between roughly evenly matched opponents, terror is a zero-sum game in which there is usually a winning side at the end. Terror is one of the many instruments of state power, but terror is the life-and-blood of terrorism. The state's use of terror is obviously a form of terrorism, but unlike non-state terrorism, the state has means at its command other than inflicting terror and it will never admit that it engages in terrorism. From the state's perspective, its struggle against terrorism is not considered as terrorism against terrorism but at most as terror against terrorism.

Terror as a political weapon is much too profuse in our times for enumeration. State-sponsored terror, as in Syria or in Turkey, usually triumphs. The Alawites were the minority in Syria from which the rest of the population used to hire its servants. But the system was not that rigid. The Alawites infiltrated the armed forces and took power. When other Muslims tried to overthrow the Alawites, these went from house-to-house in Hama killing indiscriminately, some say 10,000, until people were cowering. Kurds became terrorists in Turkey, which answered in kind and more. Sometimes, state terrorism doesn't win, as in Timor or Sri Lanka. In America, state terrorism was finally curbed by laws guaranteeing Blacks rights. In Brazil, there are no statistics, as there are in America, as to the proportion of blacks killed by the police in relation to the rest of the population. In Latin America, local whites have always had the social and psychological "moral" cushion of over-all mixed ancestry, which allows governments to say: "Discrimination? Goodness me, no! That's in the USA."

(6) Social terrorism

Contrary to Conrad's visceral detestation of terrorism as gratuitous mayhem, terrorism has causes. Since in a struggle between the state and terrorism the state usually has the upper hand, terrorism could be said to be the tactic of choice of the "underdog". The word "underdog" has the curious, even contradictory, connotation of respect for law and order. It also evokes the quest for some kind of equity or justice. Justice is a difficult concept, so difficult in fact that, apart from legality, it is utterly incoherent, except in art, and here it is a fiction. "Underdog" is usually applied to a law-abiding individual or group of individuals seeking to overcome a situation of disadvantage by legal means. A widely shared view is that the most play an underdog can be allowed is some justified deviousness. But terrorism against states almost invariably involves the killing of "innocent civilians" and this is not in the nature of the basically decent if somewhat abstract "underdog". In America an underdog is so tame and so utterly un-terrorizing that even a presidential candidate can go around claiming that he is an "underdog".

There is a darker side to underdog. The Jewish politician and terrorist Vladimir Jabotinsky once put the case for the underdog in these terms: "When the Arab claim is confronted with our Jewish demand to be saved, it is like the claim of appetite versus the claim of starvation."[6] One of the historical prototypes of the underdog was anything but a tame, slightly rebellious, but basically law-abiding citizen. Spartacus was the Thracian gladiator who made powerful Rome tremble. An uprising of the unwashed cannot but be destructive. When peasants revolted in Tsarist Russia, they butchered landowners and destroyed country houses full of paintings and books. Evidence that the rebellious Roman slaves were not savages lies in that they did not slaughter their hostages, maybe because they also were not suicidal and hoped to obtain clemency (they didn't).

Roman slaves and Russian peasants were both underdogs and terrorists. On a basic level, then, underdog terrorism is the use of terror against states, which can also, therefore, be called anti-state or social terrorism. The state's struggle against terrorism is not against terror per se but against social terrorism or, put another way, against the use of terror in a cause that can be as historically justified as the state's upholding of its authority.

For a state to declare war on terror, apart from the patently unwinnable challenge to the most basic feeling that the prospect of death provokes, is politically like denying a fundamental part of itself, which is nonsense. By any standard, the state's use of terror is at least controversial, and states go to great lengths to avoid the charge of terrorism. But in reality the use of terror is terrorism. In this sense, the state can be as guilty of terrorism as its enemies. In a rational world, the state should admit that through the use of terror it places itself in a reprehensible situation. This would lead to a dangerous reasoning. If I admit that I am not totally in the right, then obviously I am partly in the wrong. But this of course the state will never concede. For the state, its application of terror is not terrorism but just the opposite. It is the defense of authority and order. Since war is a prerogative of states, war on terror is an absurdity. Waging war on terrorism is another proposition altogether, for however much it may be based on valid social grievances, terrorism is subversion, and this, no matter how terrorizing it may itself be, the state cannot allow.

(7) History is not "just": it is just as it is

Social terrorism has as lengthy a history as state terrorism. If we count the times that early state-formation was frustrated by brutish

6 Geoffrey Wheatcroft, *The controversy of Zion* (1996), p.177

recalcitrance, perhaps its history is even longer. Anti-state terrorism is a fact of all times. If the antiquity and frequency, and occasional successes, of social terrorism are anything to go by, it is as legitimate and as valid as the state's use of terror, with the difference that terror has been, is now, and always will be primarily a weapon of the state.

History presents another phenomenon that goes hand in hand with social terrorism. Actions produce reactions. Unlike what the Hindu doctrine of *karma* teaches, historical actions do not have inevitable and commeasurable consequences. Messenia, the source of Helots (slaves) for Sparta, was under Spartan tyranny for centuries. When Sparta declined, Messenia by then free, the rest of Greece did so also. The traffic in black slaves is a crime that was never expiated. Arguably, the Germans paid for the near extermination of the Hereros in south west Africa with their defeat in World War II, but this hardly fits a pattern of cause and effect.

History is a bad teacher because it does not re-enact itself in exactly the same way and consequently it has no indisputable lessons to impart. Tyrants rise and fall, but each tyrant has his peculiarities. Terror breeds terror, but it always breeds it in different circumstances. Yet there is no mistaking the validity of a wide action-reaction pattern in history. Basically, unless you rid yourself of all your victims, these will come back to haunt you.

For centuries Hurrians and Hittites fought in Anatolia. The Hurrian Mitanni kingdom contributed to the downfall of the Old Hittite Kingdom (ca1500 BCE), but eventually the Hittites strengthened and so weakened Mitanni that the Assyrians could defeat the Hurrians and blind all its fighting men in one eye (ca1250). The Hittite empire fell to unknown aggressors (no doubt Hurrians among them) in a campaign of terror that left chaos and darkness in its wake (ca1200). When the Hittites tried to make a political comeback as the Luwians, the Hurrians of Urartu wiped them out (ca700).

The Crusaders were Christians who underestimated Muslims. They were up their knees in gore after they captured Jerusalem (1099) but in the hill of Hattin Saladin smoked them out, hunted them down at will, and had his holy men execute the Christian knights who survived (1187). Muslims were doing their own underestimating when Afghans invaded northern India, killed all the Buddhist monks they found (the last survivors of their religion in its birthplace), and tried to suppress Hinduism (12th century). The antagonism between India and Pakistan—not to mention the killings before, during, and after Partition—is the legacy of centuries of clashes and stalemates.

27 Overture on Terror

The Ottomans oppressed, impaled, and slaughtered their European subjects. Not of course all the time and Turks were not spared when Europeans were on the offensive. Dracula, after all, was not a Turk but a Valachian Christian prince.[7] Ottoman oppression of European Christians is probably the main reason why Turkey still has a long way to go before being accepted by the European Union (EU). Some contemporary European leaders have made it clear that Turkey's Ottoman past has not been forgotten. In the 19th century, Muslim Bosnians ferociously resisted attempts to reform local administrations, which would have benefited the Christian population.[8] Ottoman antecedents in the Balkans were certainly not for nothing in the savagery that went on in Bosnia and Herzegovina and in Kosovo.

There are countless equally pertinent examples: Tamils hounding Sinhalese and Sinhalese terrorizing Tamils, Turcomans enslaving Russians and Russians slaughtering Turcomans, Bismarck's Reich dictating terms in Europe and Germany losing its sovereignty, and so on.[9] In all cases, "collective memory" was crucial—the story of Jewish resistance to death in Masada, like that of the Muslim killing field at Karbala (680), was told by survivors—and as long as there is memory, there will always be the possibility of retributions.[10]

History cannot speak any clearer than this. Terror is ingrained in history. Democracy cannot be the excuse for more terror. Terror only

---

7. Vlad the Impaler, son Dracul and ruler of Valachia at various times from 1448, made the Ottomans the object of his fury, to no avail for the territory became vassal to the Ottomans in 1462.
8 On Turkey's application to join the European Union, the German Helmut Kohl and the Dutch Wilfred Martens declared in 1997: "The EU is a civilization project and within this civilization project Turkey has no place." George Castellan, *History of the Balkans* (1992), pages 214-215
9 Ceylon became independent in 1948. Prime Minister Solomon Bandaranaike (1956-1959) promoted the use of Sinhala as the national language of Ceylon and Buddhism as the national religion. Tamils were discriminated and in 1981, in retaliation for killings of policemen, government troops went on a rampage in Jaffna and destroyed the showcase Tamil library in the city. In 1983, there were anti-Tamil riots, badly contained, and the Tamils launched a savage armed separatist movement known as Tamil Tigers, led by Vellupillai Prabhakaran. The Tamil Tigers became adept at suicide tactics. These were first terrifyingly demonstrated by a terrorist called Captain Miller, who in 1987 stormed into an army camp with a truck filled with explosives blowing up himself and 40 soldiers. On Turcomans, see Peter Hopkirk, *The great game: the struggle for empire in Central Asia* (1990).
10 Under the Herodiads, Judaea fell into a state of disarray culminating in the first Jewish rebellion, which began in the reign of Nero (54-68) and lasted from 66 to 73. The Jewish rebels were known as Zealots. They occupied the hilltop of Masada where they resisted Roman legions for two years.

works when it annihilates, but history knows of only a few minor, even dubious, "total" annihilations (the Hatti, the natives of the Bandas, the Patagonians, the Hereros).[11] Before history, the worst atrocity could have been the extermination of the Neanderthals by modern humans, but the thesis that there was interbreeding has not been conclusively discarded.[12] The rule of thumb in history is that if people are tyrannized and abused by other people, they will retaliate if they can.

Come-uppances and historical vengeances are not "justice". History is not "just". It just is as it is. Historiography divides history into periods delimited by significant events. Although some periods, such as the Renaissance, are international, some are pertinent only to specific countries or regions, such as the English Commonwealth or the French Revolution. Historians make estimates of relative rights and wrongs within such spaces of time. These judgments can but need not be consensual. They are seldom unanimous. The post-9/11 years can be considered a discrete period in contemporary history. American foreign policy during this time evoked mixed reactions. War on Afghanistan was understandable and justified, but when America veered to military aggression against Iraq there was an avalanche of world condemnation.

There is a way to combat terrorism and that is to remove the causes that make it possible in the first place. If states themselves provoke social terrorism but refuse to recognize its legitimacy, then they are in a no-win situation, perhaps not in the short-run but certainly as time passes and no redress is forthcoming. The best example we have today of this dilemma is the Israel/Palestine problem. Israel has smothered the Second Intifada, but no objective observer could say that the causes of Palestinian, Arab, and Islamic terrorism have been eliminated. Terrorism can be self-defeating, which is what may be happening now to Islamic extremism, but the possibility of the resurgence of the terrorist threat to Israel is going to go on indefinitely as long as the hostility, even the mutual hatred, between Israelis and Palestinians persists. Since in this encounter Israel is the state and Palestinians are the social terrorists, then somehow, in some manner, at some time, for the conflict to cease Israel will have to make reasonable but real concessions.

---

11 From the Dutch East India Company's headquarters in Batavia, Java, the Dutch, commanded by the ruthless Jan Pieterszoon Coen (1618), carried out a master plan to monopolize the spice trade of the Moluccas. For this, they had to oust the English, who already in 1601 were in the Bandas, a tiny archipelago that produced nutmeg. The Dutch went about it rationally if not scrupulously. They chose Ambon as their center after they massacred a British post there (1623) and they exterminated the Bandanese they did not need, which was the bulk of the population.

12 James Gorman, "Nostalgia for Neanderthals", IHT, March 13, 2003.

(8) As war on terrorism, how does the Second Iraqi War fare?

In the light of these historical considerations and arguments, how does the Second Iraqi war fare? Let us assume that despite the overuse and misuse of the phrase it was not a "war on terror". It was a war on terrorism then. President Bush himself has admitted that a war on terrorism is unwinnable even as he insists that the war against Iraq was justified. But was it? All the arguments used to wage war on Iraq have proven to be limp. Perhaps the only one that still has a leg to stand on is that Saddam Hussein was a tyrant. But the most candid opinion, one that expresses common sense pure and simple, is that Iraq was not the only dictatorship in the world, far perhaps from being even the worst one. At least it kept the country together, it protected its cultural heritage, it promoted science, and it had an independent judiciary (except in political matters).

In the world at large in which Saddam Hussein was defeated and captured and treated like a common felon, many other deplorable things had happened or were happening. In Arabia, millions of residents had no legal rights and could be deported at the whim of autocratic authorities. It was known that torture was routinely applied in Egypt and Syria. Pakistan had become a military dictatorship, which initially at least, probably abetted the nuclear proliferation that had been going on during previous regimes. Myanmar was a notorious violator of human rights. Iran, contrary to America's wrath, was a complex theocratic democracy.[13] Thailand had become a democracy barely a few years before and when Muslims rebelled in the south of the country the military reaction was so brutal that over 80 protesters were suffocated when stuffed into vans. In Indonesia, Timorese separatism had excited the ire of the Indonesian military resulting in 10,000 or more dead. In Colombia, rightists and leftists were engaged in reciprocal butcheries. Jail conditions in some Latin American countries are so hideous that riots frequently produce hundreds of dead. Despite evidence to a limitless number of possible judicial miscarriages, executions in the USA were being carried out regularly. In China, the total of executions year in year out is in the thousands, and some for economic crimes that in America would warrant short sentences in minimum-security establishments.

---

13 Iran has the most complicated system of checks and balances of any country in the world. It has a president and a supreme leader. An Assembly of Experts, elected for an eight-year term, chooses the supreme leader, who has more power than the president. The Council of Guardians, half of whom are named by the supreme leader and the other half by the Majlis or parliament, monitors elections. The experts are all Shiite clerics. The system was designed to make Iran democratic but also theocratic. Political change in Iran must begin with the Assembly of Experts.

One particularly feeble argument for the Second Iraqi war was a presumed Iraq-al Qaeda or Hussein-bin Laden link. This is the claim that most makes one doubt American good faith about the war. It cannot have been known to any intelligence analyst short of a total dimwit that the Baath party, being anti-religious, is inimical to Muslim fundamentalism. Secretary of defense Donald Rumsfeld sought the Iraqi alliance for Reagan precisely because Hussein was seen as a bulwark against the religious fanaticism of Iran.[14]

Nobody denies that it was bin Laden's al Qaeda that financed and organized the destruction of the twin towers. It has been said over and over that bin Laden fought in Afghanistan with the Taliban and that when he returned to Saudi Arabia he found foreign, specifically American, troops stationed in his country, which to Muslim fundamentalism is sacrilegious.[15] What is not repeated over and over is that bin Laden and al Qaida have always insisted that they also back the Palestinian cause, that in fact it is this particular issue that is usually placed at the top of their complaints against the West and, again specifically, against America. After its various military victories over its neighbors, Israel's only avowed enemy among Arab countries, its only military threat (albeit remote) was Iraq. In this sense and this sense alone alone can it be said that there was an Iraq-al Qaeda connection and that is feasible to find a theoretical connection between Iraq and the terrorist attack on America.

In what sense was the Second Iraqi war successful as a war against terrorism? The answer here is a categorical zero. This absurd and

---

14 The inter-Arab, secularist, and socialistic (but not communist) Baath party was founded in Damascus in 1932 by Michel Afleck, a Christian, and Salah al-Din Bittar. It was influential among students and young military officers. Baath became the most important political force in Syria with the coup led by Col. Faisal al-Atasi in 1954. In 1963, Syria's unstable politics were somewhat steadied through a coup by nationalist, leftist officers led by Col. Salah al-Jadid, who purged the founders of Baath, still intent on Arab unity. In 1963, the Iraqi government was presided by Abd as-Salam Arif with the Baathist Col. Ahmad Hassan al-Bakr as prime minister. Arif kept Baath on a tight lead and relations were established with Kuwait. In 1968, the army and Baath took over and formed Revolutionary Command Council: al-Bakr and Saddam Hussein ruled in tandem. In 1970, Baath gained power in Syria, but ironically this created a rift between the Baathists of Iraq and those in Syria, even though in both countries Baath was secularist, left-leaning, and military-based.

15 Muslim fundamentalism throughout this work refers to a set of beliefs, among which three figure prominently: (1) Shariat or Muslim law is superior to all other laws, (2) jihad (war or hostilities against "infidels") is justified, and (3) women have practically no legal rights.

illegitimate war not only did not put a brake on terrorism but it made Iraq itself a hotbed of terrorism whereas before it was a despotic state that used terror to cow internal threats to itself and, not insignificantly, against the possibility of its dismemberment by religious differences and ethnic antagonisms. The First Iraqi war had already dismembered part of Iraq with the creation of an autonomous Kurdistan.[16] The Second Iraqi war did not put an end to a terrorist threat to America, which remains in place from Muslim fanaticism the world over: it merely completed the work of dismembering and destroying Iraq. As at the same time the war took place Israel was snuffing out the Second Intifada, the only gainer from the Second Iraqi war, as war on terrorism, was Israel.

In the rest of the world terrorism has become rampant, but it is at this stage also becoming as wildly incoherent as the Second Iraqi war. It is thrashing about in search of any target of opportunity and killing people needlessly. In Iraq itself, the national insurgency against the American occupation sometimes veers into the worst sort of political sadism as when it kills workers from poor nations in order to make rich America smart, which is tantamount to a political endorsement for Bush, the man who got the circle of violence going in Iraq. It is, in an unwitting or an obtuse way, an ex post facto justification of the Second Iraqi war as war on terrorism and it is an indirect betrayal of justified Arab grievances against Israel. The only valid political lesson that such morbid terrorism holds is that the permanent state of instability in the Middle East has entered an irrational phase that will probably be getting worse with time.

The Second Iraqi War is arguably the most de-stabilizing single event in recent world history. Politically, nothing fundamental has changed in the rest of the Middle East. Social terrorism is potentially more lethal now than it was before the war. It is possible that neither

16 Kurdistan is the conventional designation for the territories embracing southeastern Turkey, northeastern Iraq, and northwestern Iran where Kurds, who are Sunni Muslims and speak Indo-Iranian languages, are a majority. Kurds, whose total numbers are estimated at some 25 million, also inhabit to varying degrees of density entire areas and pockets in central and northeastern Turkey, northern Syria, Georgia, Armenia, and Azerbaijan. Some historians identify the Kurds with a people mentioned by Xenophon in the early 4th century BCE. The Ayyubid dynasty founded by Saladin in Egypt (12th-13th centuries) was of Kurdish origin. But Kurds never coalesced to form a state. The main obstacle to statehood has been that Kurds inhabit territories where other people have become politically dominant whereas they have been disunited by a mountainous topography and by dialectical differences. Kurds speak two related but mutually incomprehensible languages.

Intifada nor "Saddam Hussein" have been totally eliminated. There are historical grounds for this supposition, one being that Israel is still considered by most Arabs as a hostile enclave. In the wake of the Second Iraqi War, Arab hostility (and international antagonism) towards Israel is climbing historical heights. The eventual denouement could be some kind of modus vivendi, or it could be more of the same violence that we know. But the most dangerous result has been the possibility of nuclear proliferation in Iran and in North Korea and American impotence to do much about it except complain.

(9) The resurrection of multipolarity and its nuclear subtext

It could be argued that the action-reaction pattern is obsolete in a unipolar world and that together America and Israel can foil the worst attempts at retaliation that Arabs can muster. This proposition depends on a narrow definition of "unipolar". Compared with the Cold War, yes, America is the dominant world power. But after the Second Iraqi war, the world does not seem quite as unipolar as before, certainly not as it was during the War on Afghanistan, when the USA led and the world followed. There existed a trio of pre-requisites for unipolarity, which America then fulfilled. The traditional system of links with other countries was intact. The UN was respected as the ultimate legitimating forum for military action. And the American economy had the strength to sustain the dollar as the reserve currency of choice for the rest of the world.

The Western alliance, which stood through thick and thin during the Cold War, has been sundered. Russia and China separately have nuclear capabilities to match America's: sufficient bombs and missiles, not parity of destructive power, is all that is required.[17] Russia and China were opposed to the Second Iraqi War. Not only then did the war on Iraq alienate some of America's formerly unconditional anti-communist allies, but it has turned the clock back by antagonizing former enemies with whom America had been burying strategic hatchets. There is little likelihood that America will be engaged once

17 "With the Cold War over, the USA and other countries were trying to defuse the arms race with global cooperation. As a sign of the new openness, the Energy Department began declassifying millions of ideas and documents about nuclear arms, and even encouraged weapons scientists to share unclassified computer codes with their foreign counterparts...On September 25, 1992, a nuclear blast shook China's western desert...From spies and electronic surveillance, American intelligence officials determined that the test was a breakthrough in China's long quest to match American technology for smaller, more sophisticated hydrogen bombs." "The Making of a suspect: the case of Wen Ho Lee", *The New York Times* (NYT), 4 February 2001.

again in "cold wars" with its former enemies. But its reckless foreign policy has placed it at a disadvantage in dealing with nuclear proliferation and it must rely on China to bridle North Korea and probably on Russia to moderate Iran, which could become the worst challenge that Israel has ever faced, not necessarily in the sense of a threat to its existence, but as an irresistible force for negotiating Israel/ Palestine differences. To add more piquancy to strategic speculation, should Israel try to take things in its own hands, as it did when it blasted the Iraqi Ossirak nuclear plant, the unlikelihood of a revival of former Cold War enmities could become an instantaneous world-shaking probability.

Part of the strength of unipolar American leadership was that it had the sanction of the United Nations (UN). America is ambivalent about the UN whereas the rest of the world has few reservations about the fact that, as some one in the USA put it, it is "chock full of foreigners". Willy-nilly, American unipolar international authority derived from the "foreignness" of the UN. But in the Second Iraqi war the USA demonstrated that it was willing to act on its own regardless of UN opinion or sanction. This was also true of the Vietnam War, but the world then was bipolar and the UN itself was divided whereas when Bush initiated his campaign against Iraq, the UN Security Council was still willing to accept an American unipolar world. By so contemptuously disregarding the UN, the USA has forfeited one of the mainstays of unipolarity.

America's unipolar role also depended on its ability to impose economic policies for the world. Globalization is founded on the belief that capitalism is good for the world and that the more freedom for financial flows the more prosperity for all people. It turned economic imperialism on its head. Globalization hasn't been knocked off its perch. But the US is no longer calling the shots. Under the guidance of President George W. Bush, the American economy is showing a syndrome of most disquieting, unglobalistic symptoms. A noticeable protectionist bent accompanies fear of competition and huge deficits in all macro-ledgers (trade, current account, and fiscal budget) are making for a currency so weak that it maintains its prestige because other countries do not want to devalue their reserves. The American economy has faced disturbances like these before, but not of such magnitudes and all occurring at the same time. And most significantly, whereas the USA had no credible economic rivals before, it now faces some serious competition.

There is the European Union (EU), which functions as an organic economic whole despite fracture lines that have appeared between the older members and the slew of new members from Central and Eastern Europe. The economic EU is starting to seem like the real paladin of globalization. In a recent World Trade Organization (WTO) meeting, while America hung back, the EU offered to dismantle its system of agricultural subsidies, which undermine the ability to compete of efficient developing countries like Brazil. Even *The Economist*, which would rip its tongue out before it badmouthed the USA, is talking of the Euro as a real alternative to the dollar as the reserve currency of choice. Many observers are now daring to say that the world monetary system, what is often called Bretton Woods II, is undergoing a spontaneous revolution.[18]

And then there's China and in the near future India. In the space of two decades China has bolted from being the poorest country on earth to become its most dynamic economy, with so much demand and growth, real and potential, that, for one thing, it carries along with it economic heavyweights such as Japan and South Korea, and for another, its problem is not how to keep up growth but how to prevent growth from getting out of hand.[19] America is still the biggest national economy and it will probably go on being so for a long time, but it no longer has the clout to tell the world the way it should or should not go as it has felt free to do in the past. Thus, with two legs broken (traditional alliances and the UN) and a third (world economic hegemony) wobbly, the table of unipolarity can no longer stand up, or it could but through such a precarious balancing operation that it would only make it seem unsteadier.

(10) The capsizing of unipolarity leaves American exceptionalism high and dry

The USA bungled its leading role in the unipolar world through its ill considered, gratuitous, and contradictory war on terror. Its iron alliance with Israel compromises its role as the paramount, impartial world leader. But perhaps more damaging of all is that these circumstances justify a highly critical look at America's self-proclaimed exceptionalism.

18 Bretton Woods was an international agreement in 1946 to stabilize major-currencies exchanges using as standard a gold price set by the USA at $35 an ounce. Many complications, particularly the vertiginous rise of the price of gold during the oil crisis of 1973, led to a system of floating currencies in which the dollar itself, instead of gold, was the parameter.

19 In a review of *China Inc.*, by Ted C. Fishman, William Grimes wrote: "The numbers are staggering. From 1982 through 2002, the U.S. economy grew at an annual rate of 3.3 percent...China's grew at an annual rate of 9.5 percent...In 2003, [China] bought 7 percent of the world's oil, 25 percent of its aluminium and steel, almost 33 percent of its iron ore and coal and 40 percent of its cement." IHT, 12-13 March 2005.

There were perhaps never sufficient grounds for that claim but, through contrasts with the poor historical performances of other countries and other parts of the world, it could seem as if America had indeed been begotten to lead mankind. The darker aspects of its past were ignored.

With the end of the Cold War in America's favor, the Soviet past seemed more somber, but the savagery of the American Civil War, American terrorism against Native Americans, against Blacks and other minorities, the long history of American war atrocities, were dimmed into insignificance by the brightness of its glories. Then Bush the younger came along with a moralistic chip on his shoulder. The American unconditional alliance with Israel was partially responsible for 9/11. War on Afghanistan was amply justified, but war on terror was sheer arrogance and political alienation. Bush and his retinue not only did not fit the mold of American exceptionalism, but seemed intent on shredding to pieces any semblance of such a thing. The Second Iraqi war and all the rot it produced was the catalyst for a cold, pitiless look at America. Ironically, then, a war against tyranny and a "crusade" for democracy have backfired so badly that the USA has lost its footing on the historical high ground and it is not likely it will ever recover it.

American exceptionalism implied that the USA, though unavoidably part of history, was not quite part of history in the way other countries were. This historical motif is a constant in the events since 9/11. Americans victoriously hoisted historical flags in Afghanistan (as if the Afghans knew what in the dickens they were doing). Bush the younger at one point justified his reckless foreign policies by arguing, essentially, that facts were facts and that he gladly conceded historians the rights to revisionism. There was here the implication that he didn't give a hoot about history. Subsequently, he changed his tune and arbitrarily assigned the USA the historic role of world promoter of democracy. He implicitly claimed that this was America's God-given mission and that he was only an instrument in carrying it out. But the reality is just the opposite: what Bush did in Iraq, and not coincidentally, Ariel Sharon in Palestine, has been to try to yank their countries and their policies out of the context of world history. This has had the reverse effect that if before you did not swim with America you were swimming against the mainstream of history, if you try stroking side by side with America now you will be facing a very strong opposite current.

This book, then, argues that American exceptionalism is an unsustainable myth. It reaches this conclusion after a historical narrative of the principal world events during a core time frame from 1989 to the present. However, it assumes a world-historical perspective on this process and tries to contextualize the present as far in history as circumstances allow or permit. The USA fumbled the ball as leader of the unipolar world when it embarked on its misguided war on terror. And it did it so badly that it opened itself to criticism from practically all quarters.

In principle, this flow of opposition need not have involved America's past, which, needless to say, contains incomparable periods of grandeur. However, too many things have been handled so badly by the Bush administrations that there are grounds for going into the past and revising the image that America has of itself, formerly shared also by much of the world. This book is basically about how the flow and counter-flow of international relations provoked this revision and about how they damaged irreparably the pride of American exceptionalism. To do so, it takes up as crucial themes: (1) the crisis of the unipolar world (it develops themes summarily mentioned in this introduction); (2) the background to the different historical processes going on in the years from 1989 to the present; and (3) the "multipolar world" that is now emerging and its multiple implications.

2

Reagan's Proxy Wars might have set the stage for 9/11

There was a brief pivotal period in the recent past when the world seemed to be on a roll. It was also America's greatest moment, one it had been preparing for since the great humiliation of the Vietnam War. After the war, America had two rebounds: one away from the filthy-mouthed and confrontational Richard Nixon to Jimmy Carter—President Gerald Ford's term of office, fairly or unfairly, is usually perceived as an interlude—and another from the well-meaning Carter to the assertive Ronald Reagan. Nixon, the man who really began to temper the Cold War, does not deserve his ill-repute, but he will live with it in history for a long time to come because of his typification as a ruffian, nowhere better than in Herblock's cartoons. In one of the most famous, Nixon emerges from a sewer with an angry alley-cat look and a five o'clock shadow while a group of smiling, naive-looking people wave acclamatory signs. Considering that it was under Nixon, much-derided for his profanity and paranoia, that the United States established relations with China, nuclear detente was achieved with the USSR, and the Vietnam War ended, not only the United States but the world is in debt with a man who was forced to resign from office accused of conspiring to cover up, or even of himself inspiring, a minor felony.

Despite the historical importance of what it had achieved in foreign affairs, the Nixon administrations were nerve-fraying. Ford was emollient but it couldn't very well be denied that he was Nixon's legatee. The Vietnam War, at that point the biggest collective trauma in American history, was over and the USA was at peace, except of course for its permanent, non-violent confrontation with the USSR. There was no need for the sort of aggressive leadership that wartime requires. America did not feel that it deserved the rebuff it got in trying to defend freedom in Vietnam, but the values it had fought for were real enough.

(1) Tired of intrigues, the American electorate turned to a God-fearing humanitarian

In the immediate Post-War, the USA had been on a war footing of varying intensity during the Berlin crisis and during the Korean War.[1] After Korea, America was on the qui vive to counter communist moves anywhere. It was not at war, but it could not elude the knowledge that it could be at any time. This was stressful for a society, like America, in which individual human lives are considered sacrosanct and in which information is doled out freely day after day, on either count not the case of the USSR. But this did not mean that Americans were willing to accept Soviet aggressiveness passively. For most Americans, including most of the media, the transition from Stalin to Khrushchev was not originally observed as particularly significant. The pent up bellicosity began to be released in Vietnam. It had a lot of space in which to expand until it was burnt out in 1973. The world peace that then began was much more real (except in Afghanistan) than the tense period from 1948 to the 1960s escalation in Vietnam.

Tired of intrigues but confident in its moral righteousness, the American electorate turned to a God-fearing humanitarian from Georgia, Jimmy Carter, who tried to engage America in a world-wide human rights campaign. Carter was to Nixon what an antacid is to bile. But it wasn't a question of renouncing war for conciliation or of backing off from confrontation.

The USSR in its own way was becoming conservative. It seemed to have a stake in peace. America still embraced the domino theory—the belief that if you let one communist slip by a hundred more will do so (although this effect could also be feared of other enemies of America)—but it wasn't about to get involved in another war in a far away tropical land any time soon. Every sane strategist by then knew that in any given nation the forces for conservatism and continuity were generally stronger

1 There were actually two Berlin crises. One was the Soviet blockade of Berlin in 1948, which was foiled by an airlift and suspended in 1949. The second Berlin crisis occurred when in 1958 the Soviet leader Nikita Khrushchev announced that the administration of East Berlin would be turned over to East Germany, the communist counterpart of the Federal Republic of Germany. Theoretically, this could be interpreted as a unilateral abrogation of the Post-War agreements over the control of Berlin. William Taubman, *Khrushchev: the man and his era* (2003), makes much of this, but it is highly unlikely that East Germany would have been able to do anything about the status of West Berlin or that the USSR would have allowed things to get out of hand. The over-all status of Berlin remained unchanged: a Länd or state of Federal Germany in its western part and the capital of East Germany in its eastern sector.

than revolutionary drives. For a time it didn't seem that way because the height of the Cold War and "revolutionary" third-worldism came about during the same Post-War decades (1950s to 1970s). After Vietnam, America perceived a more stable world, one in which it could exert its economic and moral advantages rather than its military might, and Carter embodied ideally this perfectly reasonable attitude.

(2) From the tsarist yoke to Camp David

Carter's greatest triumph was undoubtedly the Camp David accord. In rough historical terms, the origins of Israel are to be found in Zionism and in the Holocaust. Zionism brought east European Jews to Palestine. Nazi genocide gave this migration full moral right, the kind it would not have had with simple, garden-variety anti-Semitism. Discriminations and "ethnic" antagonisms are common social phenomena in any society. In Europe, Jews were particularly mistreated during the Middle Ages, especially for a time during the Crusades, but they had been gaining legal ground and acceptance. The most critical area was the part of Russia known as The Pale, a wide swathe of land on either side of an axis from Vilnius to Lviv, and here persecution occurred principally in rural areas, although pogroms were not unknown in the cities. In a mainly Jewish city such as Odessa a pogrom was more like an assault by the authorities on the civil population.[2]

---

2 There is evidence that starting in the late Middle Ages Jews were settling in large numbers in the area which later was known as The Pale, the region of dense Jewish habitation in the 19th century whose axis ran from Vilnius in Lithuania to Lviv (Lvov) in the Ukraine overlapping to eastern Poland and western Russia. At the time of its settlement, it was lightly peopled by Lithuanians and Poles. It has been argued to explain the density of Jewish settlement in The Pale that at least part of it can be attributed to the Turkic Khazars who converted to Judaism sometime in the 8th century north of the Caucasus and lost political cohesion in the 11th century when they were vised between Russia and the Byzantine Empire. However, this argument depends on the premise that the many millions of Jews that occupied The Pale during the 19th century could not have been the result of natural reproduction and this entails that Jews were less reproductive than other nations, not a very plausible supposition. Other important cities in The Pale were Bialystok, Lublin, and Vitebsk. Although not in The Pale in a strict sense, cities such as Odessa, Lodz, and Warsaw were significantly Jewish. Most of the great Jewish Hollywood moguls were originally from the Pale. Marc Chagall was born in Vitebsk. The literary Nobel Prize winner Isaac Bashevis Singer was born in The Pale. Usually when Jews were born in Poland, such as Israeli Prime Minister David Ben Gurion (original name David Grün), it was The Pale that was meant. The extermination camps of Belsec, Sobibor, and Treblinka were near Lublin. Together they accounted for at least 1,750,000 Holocaust victims, hundreds of thousands more than in Auschwitz. On this see Henry Friedlander, *The origins of Nazi genocide* (1995).

The tsarist yoke was heavy enough to make millions of Jews immigrate to America during the 19th century and the early 20th century. Even so, there were still many more millions of Jews in Russia than those that immigrated. It is likely that as many or more Jews remained in The Pale than the huge mass that left. The Nazis, mainly in eastern Poland and the western USSR, carried out the persecution and cold-blooded extermination of Jews, usually placed at six million. Reliable estimates are that just over three million Jews died in extermination camps after the "final solution" was adopted in early 1942.[3] The bulk of the rest was the result of gory massacres carried out by special Nazi units and their many collaborators in other nations—notably in Croatia and Lithuania—starting with the invasion of Poland in 1939.[4]

It was from these tragic circumstances that European Jews gained uncontestable rights to a homeland, to a country of their own, in the eyes of America and of a significant part of the rest of mankind, especially the part that lived in the more culturally advanced nations, including after World War II Germany itself. The masses and generally the oligarchies in the economically and educationally less advanced nations couldn't care less, the masses because they were too busy surviving and the oligarchies or upper classes because, if they had no compassion to spend on their masses, they certainly weren't going to generate some for Jews.

(3) British imperialism decides to cut its losses

One section of humanity that was neither sympathetic nor indifferent but actively hostile to Jews was the Arabs. Jews had settled in their midst without being invited. The country the Jews claimed was the land for which the ancient name of Palestine (Philistia) had been revived after

3 The conference of Nazi bureaucrats convoked by Heinrich Heydrich, Himmler's right-hand man, at Wannsee, a suburb of Berlin, on January 20, 1942, is often cited as the place and the moment when the "final solution" to the "Jewish problem" was adopted. Considering that the Holocaust had already begun, what happened at Wannsee was that all previous "niceties", such as deporting German Jews to Poland, were set aside and the killing juggernaut was put into full operation in the German Reich, in Poland, and in Ostland.

4 When in June 1941, the USSR was invaded the Holocaust started in earnest. Genocide went into high gear. But was it genocide? It was undoubtedly the killing of Jews by Germans, but genocide is the extermination of one race by another and neither Jews nor Germans were a race. In fact, the Jewish Holocaust was the killing by Nazi and Nazi-led Germans of a people, mostly poor and rural, who practiced the religion called Judaism.

World War I.[5] Emigrating Jews were not millionaires by any means, but they did not lack for funding when it was needed. The kibbutzim movement, the epitome of Jewish austerity and reciprocal help, was not exclusively born of necessity—although there was a strong economic justification for it—but of a desire for "rooting in". The kibbutzim or Jewish collective farms were leased from the Jewish National Fund, which was financed by rich Jewish contributors in Europe and America.

British administration in Palestine blew hot and cold about Jewish emigration, but there is no doubt that Jews were closer culturally to the colonialists than were Arabs. They also were harder to deal with, hence they got more respect. When, before World War II (1936-1939), the Arabs staged a revolt, the British repressed it harshly. They hung some Palestinian ringleaders and gradually brought the rest to heel. The spiritual leader of the Arabs, the grand mufti of Jerusalem, Amin al-Husayni, sought asylum in Berlin. When, in the immediate Post-War, the Jews were in open contempt of British restrictions on Jewish migration to Palestine, the British tried hangings and Jewish resistance hung a British sergeant back as a warning. The British learned they were vulnerable. They laughed off a Jewish terrorist threat to the King David hotel in Jerusalem and their headquarters were blown to bits. Zionists claim that they warned well in advance of the impending explosion. As veteran imperialists, the British knew when to cut their losses and handed Palestine to the UN.

(4) Zionism had powerful sympathizers among Stalin's slavish hierarchs

The Arabs could do nothing to get out of the situation that had been created in their midst and so they had no choice but to brave it out, both within Palestine itself and in the countries around Palestine. Militarily, it was almost irresistible to think that weight of numbers plus the weapons the Arab states had amassed would suffice to overwhelm the Jews and either subject them to Arab rule or expel them. But the Arabs were mistaken on two counts: one, it wasn't bare numbers that counted but discipline, training, and morale; and two, they had only achieved real independence after the war and they did not possess that big an arsenal.

---

5 The original Philistines are only known from the *Bible*. Philistine archaeological sites have not been productive or revealing. The name Philistia is of Greek origin. The Roman province of Judaea was renamed Philistia or Palestine by Hadrian (117-138), who caused the Jewish diaspora. Under Islam, Palestine was considered a part of Syria. To the Crusaders, Palestine was the Holy Land. The Ottomans did not create a province of Palestine. Palestine was mandated to Great Britain after World War I.

There was a third crucial influence and it was that the Arabs did not see or did not want to see that the Jews had unlimited financial resources on which to draw whereas most Arab states were very poor and had little international credit. There were some nouveau riche Arab nations but they were not generally willing to underwrite unrestrictedly a war on Israel. When the showdown came, the Jews were better supplied. They outfought the Arabs and Israel was founded against the intense but powerless opposition of all its neighbors, Jordan and it's small but steel-hard British-trained Arab Legion being the only exception in an unforgiving list of military shortcomings.

Upon its creation, Israel was recognized instantly by the USA and the USSR. In fact, Soviet official recognition anteceded America's. Armaments for Israel's war of independence arrived from Czechoslovakia with the blessing of the USSR. This seeming quirk of Soviet foreign policy needs to be fully appreciated when it is taken for granted that Stalin had another Jewish holocaust among his plans prior to his death. The case for this conjectured piece of Stalinist mayhem is far from proven and Soviet recognition for Israel could signify that Zionism had powerful sympathizers among Stalin's slavish hierarchs.[6]

Other explanations especially that Stalin himself miscalculated about where Israel's loyalties in the future would lie seem close to the nonsensical. They depict Stalin as a political moron, which, whatever else he might have been, and we ignore, he certainly wasn't. Despite the support they received from the Soviets, Israelis knew that the lifelines for their survival led to New York rather than to Moscow. It didn't take long for the political waters to run in their natural channels, which meant that Israel became a firm ally of the USA, and more likely vice versa (an argument equally applicable to west European countries), and that the Arabs in the "frontline" against Israel sought Soviet support. American partiality towards Israel, which was stronger unofficially than officially, assuredly had to do with the international orientation that Egypt took under Gamal Abdel Nasser.

To heap troubles upon defeats, the Jews applied terror liberally and Palestinians fled of their own volition or were expelled by Jews.[7] Those that fled ended up in refugee camps in Gaza, Jordan, Lebanon, and

6 Simon Sebag Montefiore, *Stalin: the court of the red tsar* (2003)

7 The most famous Jewish raid—according to Arab sources, there were 34 attacks in all and they started at a place called Sheikh Breik—was against the village of Deir Yassin where the Jewish terrorist organization Irgun killed 250 civilians on 29 April 1948. Menachem Begin, the future Israeli prime minister who negotiated the peace with Egypt, led Irgun.

Syria, mainly in the first three. Gaza was an Arab enclave that resisted more than from Egyptian military capability from Jewish restraint. It wouldn't have looked too good if a people that had barely escaped extermination in Europe were itself to inflict on another people a policy of outright destruction, which is what expelling a hundred thousand Arabs into the Sinai would have seemed. Jordan retained the West Bank through its ability to interdict a Jewish advance on East Jerusalem, whose capture was a primary Jewish objective. The least militant of the Arab states, Lebanon, had no choice but to accept Arab refugees, but it did so without the intention or the means to integrate them into what already was an unstable, multicultural society. Thus were engendered the conditions for one of the longest and most complex conflicts in history.

(5) The Arabs' pride of numbers

Neither Jews nor Arabs spent much energy in trying to accommodate each other. The Jews that had created Israel were not refugees from Nazi barbarism. They considered themselves a people (Sabras) who had been living in their proper homeland for a long time. Their leaders were mostly not born in Israel, but a core of citizenry was native. Sabras felt they had claims over the land as good as or better than those of Arabs. Tel Aviv, then Israel's only significant urban center, was wholly Jewish, initially a suburb of Arab Yaffa but later a city in its own right. Sabras considered Israel a state among states, with all the appurtenances of sovereignty, and not just a refuge of last resort for the destitute, even if they were Holocaust survivors. The Holocaust was a justification for statehood, a powerful one, but with or without Holocaust Jews were prepared to fight for Israel. The Holocaust gave Zionism a dignity and an ethical sense above "arguments" from strength or force. But Israel was essentially a state and states do not have moral consciences.

Arab states for their part now had a pair of irresistible reasons to oppose Jews: the existence of Israel itself and the Palestinian refugees, which proportionally were a diaspora comparable to the original Jewish one in the sense that there were more Palestinians evicted from their original homes than Palestinians who still possessed homes in the former Palestine, now mostly Israel in territorial terms. Additionally, and most erroneously, the Arabs still believed that they had the upper hand, still because of their far greater number than that of Jews, and also because with the inception of the Cold War they felt confident that they could redress the logistical disadvantages that they had in comparison to Jewish resources. The Israeli-Palestinian conflict was another process that ran conjointly with the Cold War and the third world process. It was through third world support that the General Assembly of the UN declared Zionism to be a form of racism.[8]

(6) The Suez Canal crisis

Because of innumerable prejudices, from those with long cultural antecedents to those which surfaced in the day-to-day coverage of issues by the media, America might have perceived Israel as a democratic underdog surrounded by hungry wolves, but that was hardly the case as could be observed, if one wanted to observe objectively, during the attack on Egypt mounted by France and Great Britain in connivance with Israel. The Egyptian nationalist dictator and Arab-world culture hero, Gamal Abdel Nasser, nationalized the Suez Canal, whose management required only mid-level administrative skills. In an unwarranted imperialist start, Britain went into war mode persuading the French, resentful because of the hard time they were having with Arab-backed Algerian nationalists, to accompany them. Harassed in its territory by fedayin (the Arab name for commando meaning literally one who dies for one's country) and uncomfortable with the constant threats emanating from Egypt, Israel went along with the invasion plan of Suez. The disingenuous ploy was that Israel would invade the Sinai and British and French paratroops would land to separate the contenders.

The UN condemned the aggression, but it was American President Dwight D. Eisenhower, the architect of the Normandy invasion and of the final assault on Germany in World War II, who brandished the stick that made America's allies back off. British Prime Minister Anthony Eden was discredited. The French 4th Republic was itself already so discredited by its inherent political instability that another crisis more or less didn't really matter much. But in Israel, where David Ben Gurion was prime minister, there were no internal counter-effects and instead Israeli anti-Arab resolve was strengthened.

---

8 "15 years ago in this month the United Nations passed Resolution 3379 equating Zionism with racism. It was an outrage then. It still is. Resolution 3379 not only slanders Zionism—the national liberation movement of the Jewish people—and the State of Israel it created, it also gives license for anti-Semitism". This charge by the American Jewish Committee, from an ad placed in the NYT, on 12 November 1990, is also a good illustration of the dilemmas raised by the "anti-Zionism equals anti-Semitism" argument. Zionism is a political movement. Anti-Semitism is a racialist attitude. But Zionism can be racialist. A great many Israelis, Zionists by definition, are as racialist about Arabs as the most rabid white supremacist in America is about blacks. The implication in the American Jewish Committee ad is that only Jews can be honestly anti-Zionist, because anti-Zionist non-Jews are ipso facto anti-Jewish.

Despite Egypt's vulnerability, Nasser claimed victory, which made Arabs unrealistically delirious. Egypt assumed an exaggerated bellicose stance. Some argue that Nasser had no choice, but he certainly did nothing to calm superfluous passions. When the Egyptians took steps to close the access to the Israeli port of Eilat, on the Gulf of Aqaba, Israel struck at its neighbors and in six days had taken Jerusalem and the West Bank, Gaza, and the Golan Heights. Somehow, Nasser claimed another victory but he died in 1970. His successor, Anwar el Sadat, was a man with a different mentality. He did not have Nasser's charisma, but his mind was less cluttered and he could think with more clarity.

(7) The Yom Kippur war

Sadat had one objective in mind: to recover the Sinai. Nasser's successor knew that he could not force the USSR to attack Israel and therefore he also understood that it was only with the support of America that he could engage Israel in negotiations for the return of the Sinai, where the Israelis were entrenched as if in permanence. The Israelis had also occupied the Hurghada enclave on the Egyptian coast of the Red Sea, which they used as a beach resort. Israel had taken big and small chunks of lightly peopled Egyptian territory, which Egypt could lose like the Palestinians their homeland if it did not act decisively and soon. But to attain its goal, which in essence was negotiating peace for land, Egypt had to carry out a radical international re-alignment.

Sadat asked the Soviet military advisers to leave Egypt and adopted a neutralist stance, but one that militarily left Egypt out on a limb. To justify this breaking of international political molds, Sadat also had to prove his ultimate commitment to the anti-Israel, pan-Arab cause, and he had to do some vindicating of Egyptian fighting ability. The events of the 1973 War, often called the Yom Kippur War, appear to indicate that Sadat was not entirely confident in ultimate victory, so in a sense he waged a war he knew or suspected he was going to lose because he wanted to prove that Egypt was not a loser. Strangely, but not that strange in the Middle Eastern context, his politico-military strategy worked very well for Egypt, although not so well for Sadat himself.

Allied to Syria, the Egyptians caught the Israelis with their guard down. They crossed the canal and advanced well into the Sinai, where Egyptian land forces halted and formed a defensive line. Close observers of these events tend to coincide with the view that Israel's arsenal was significantly depleted and that to mount a counter-offensive Israel needed American supplies badly. President Nixon provided them whereas Egypt, no longer freely aided by the USSR, had to try to contain the inevitable

Israeli counter-attack with sharply lower military means. Israeli forces led by Gen. Ariel Sharon, the promoter of the Jewish settlements in Palestine, drove the Egyptians back across the canal and cornered them in the city of Suez, at the southern entrance of the canal, until the late 1980s a visibly war-ravaged city. Israel could have advanced towards the Egyptian capital. Fighting went on in the desert between Suez and Cairo and for many years afterwards the former battlefield was littered with tank carcasses. The Israelis also initiated an advance on Damascus from the Golan Heights.

(8) For the sake of Israel, Kissinger takes the USA to the brink of atomic war

Although the Soviets had been expelled from Egypt, they did not relish virtual American hegemony through Israel in the entire Middle East, where the USA already counted with the support of Iran. The USSR told Israel to halt its offensive. It is often said that the nearest the world came to a nuclear conflagration was during the Cuban missiles crisis. However, it could be argued that the danger of nuclear war was greater when Nixon's secretary of state Henry Kissinger, presumably with Nixon's approval, placed American forces on a world-wide nuclear alert in response to the Soviet warning to Israel. In this case, there was no actual physical face off as there had been in the Atlantic Ocean in 1962, but war surely would have been an option if Israel had continued to move in on Egypt and Syria. A truce was negotiated by which the Israelis withdrew to the Sinai and far away enough from the canal to permit its peaceful re-opening.

Sadat was reviled by Syria for not following up on the Sinai offensive. Syria also complained that when Egypt halted its advance it had left the Syrian forces in the lurch and imperiled Damascus, the Syrian capital. The Israeli line of occupation in the Golan Heights is not far from Damascus, certainly a much more attainable military target than Cairo. Israel's main objective however was the greater menace that Egypt represented.

What would have happened if the war had gone on is anybody's guess, but there is little doubt that the Egyptian situation was critical. Sadat had not revealed all his strategic cards to the Syrians, but it is not fair to say that Egypt did not do its best to beat Israel. For the moment Sadat's strategy was going roughly according to plan. He initiated peace overtures to Israel, which were not successful until he made his what-more-can-you-want trip to Jerusalem and an encounter with Israeli Prime Minister Menachem Begin. Even then there was no breakthrough, for

Israel was not in a conceding mood. The counter the Palestine Liberation Organization (PLO), Isreal forces were raiding deep into Lebanon.[9] The process was at the point where ground was broken but nothing had been planted, let alone anything harvested, that President Jimmy Carter stepped in.

(9) Carter gets himself a winner

Carter was already two years into his administration and his approach to foreign relations, crucial to an understanding of his presidential and post-presidential careers, was not going down well in Congress or among the media and the public. Americans are proud of being tough-nosed about foreigners, unless they perceive them, as they paradigmatically do Israelis, as being very much like themselves. Outside of that, they have little patience with abstract principles, and what Carter was proposing was to put principles above calculations on what conforms or does not conform to common perceptions of American interests.

Carter wanted to discriminate between democratic and non-democratic practices the world over but some of America's allies in developing countries were not democratic at all. So who cared? Sure, democracy was a good in itself, but what mattered was that to each his own. If you missed the democratic boat, then you had no one else to blame but yourself and it wasn't in America's interest, much less was it its duty, to help democracy along anywhere. Of course, presidents were allowed to sound pious about such things, but taking themselves too seriously was definitely a public opinion hazard. Besides, Carter had already caved in to a dictator when the USA signed with Omar Torrijos of Panama the canal-reversion treaty, which was evidence that Carter did not make democracy a pre-condition even for such a monumental give away of American property.

In the negotiations between Egypt and Israel, however, Carter got himself a winner. People might still consider Jimmy Carter a nerd, but it is difficult for any one to deny that his intervention in this issue was decisive and beneficial all around. Speculating about might-have-beens is about as useful as making predictions on the basis that things do not change over the short-run. But it is possible to argue that had Egypt and Israel not made an enduring peace the course of world history could have been much more hairy than it has been in the last decades. And what Carter achieved was a real peace. He brought Sadat and Begin

9 There were major Israeli incursions into Lebanon in 1968, 1970, 1974, 1976, and 1978. There was full-scale invasion and occupation in 1982. The Israeli army was engaged in Lebanon until 1985.

together in Camp David and he kept them under such constant pressure—Begin called Camp David an "elegant jail"—that the two leaders finally did achieve agreement. By way of contrast, and as proof that history is recalcitrant to remakes, President Bill Clinton adopted exactly the same tactic, perhaps with even more persistence, to force Ehud Barak and Yasir Arafat depose their differences, but in the end he had nothing to show for his efforts.

The Camp David Accords were essentially an exchange of Egyptian recognition of Israel for Israeli-occupied land. As the ultimate architect of the peace process, Sadat was generally denounced in the Arab world and a frigid no-comment was the best that he could hope for from any Muslim state. Sadat was assassinated by fanatical military during a national day parade under the lenses of the world's television cameras. His killer was an officer, Khalid Islambouli, who, after firing a deadly burst, looked inside the presidential box to see if Sadat was totally dead, and fired another burst. The following year Israel returned the entire Sinai to Egypt. Despite initial high hopes, the relations between Egypt and Israel soon became chilly, but the two nations share a common interest in not breaking the peace negotiated in Camp David, even though on occasions it has been hard for Egypt to countenance what Israel was doing.

The Camp David Accords included an Israeli commitment to promote Palestinian self-rule. But there was no one present in Camp David from the Palestinian side, and before the accords were signed, Israel had already undertaken something that went against the spirit of Camp David. Early into Begin's tenure, Israel had begun a colonization or settlements program in Palestinian territories (Gaza and West Bank) under the supervision of the extremely anti-Palestinian, outspokenly anti-Arab Sharon, famed in Israel for his raids outside Israel and the same Sharon who encircled Suez during the Yom Kippur war.

(10) Somoza, Inc.

In other foreign places, events for Carter and America were either mishaps or outright disasters. Nicaragua, a country in Central America, had a turbulent history, which was nothing remarkable in itself. Its capital Managua was the result of a compromise between "liberals" entrenched in Leon and "conservatives" in Granada. It was as a player in these rivalries that the American adventurer William Walker made himself dictator in Granada in 1856-1857. Walker could not have done it without the financial largesse of Cornelius Vanderbilt, the future railroad tycoon who wanted a stable Nicaragua as a transit way between the eastern USA and California.

Walker was driven out of Nicaragua by a coalition of Central American forces (mainly Nicaraguan and Costa Rican). During his roller-coaster career, which had begun in Baja California, Walker had twice been apprehended by—more likely he had twice taken refuge with—American constabularies and twice he had been acquitted by complaisant juries on the charge of violating neutrality laws. On his last adventure, this time in Honduras, Walker, by then forsaken by Vanderbilt and acting on the strength of his notoriety, ended up seeking protection in a British gunboat, whose captain did not like filibusters and handed him to the Hondurans, who promptly put him in front of a firing squad.

Under a strong ruler, José Santos Zelaya (1894-1909), an exception to the rule, Nicaragua had the grandiose but feasible project of cutting a canal between the Caribbean Sea and the Pacific Ocean. Its route was the deep-water San Juan River to Lake Nicaragua. The actual cutting was to be done in a short section between the lake and the ocean. The British were listening.

At the time, the USA was putting a lot of money and work into digging the Panama Canal, which had been started by Ferdinand de Lesseps, the builder of the Suez Canal, whose company went bust in part from fraud and mismanagement. The republic of Panama, an American protectorate, had been founded at the instigation of Philippe Bunau-Varilla, a French engineer with de Lesseps who refused to let the Panama Canal idea die and awakened American interest in it. When Colombia, the South American country of which Central American Panama was a province, refused to grant the USA land rights to construct the canal, the Panamanians (barely 300,000) declared independence and Colombian troops were prevented from intervening by an American blockade.[10]

The USA did not see with benevolent eyes Nicaraguan, not to mention British, competition. Alleging law-and-order considerations, it made Nicaragua a colonialist dependency from 1912 to 1933. From puppet president Diego Manuel Chamorro, the USA obtained exclusive rights for itself if any canal-building was to be done, which of course was a sure warranty that none would be. The American occupation of Nicaragua was harassed by guerrilla leader Augusto Cesar Sandino, which was no worse than a few mosquito bites on the imperialist giant, and when the Marines finally evacuated Nicaragua they made sure that their law-and-order man, Anastasio Somoza, possessed the means to dispose of Sandino, who walked eyes wide open into a trap that Somoza

10 D. McCullough, *The path through the seas: the creation of the Panama Canal 1870-1914* (1977).

set for him. Sandino was assassinated and Somoza later ruled as dictator, directly or through straw men, for 20 years until he himself was killed by a Nicaraguan poet.

The elder Somoza was succeeded by two of his sons, first Luis and then Anastasio Jr., but an underground Sandinist movement had developed and with considerable though not unanimous popular support it came fighting into the open. The Sandinists were leftist, possibly armed by the Cubans, and Carter could have supported Somoza, Inc., which was what the regime amounted to in practice, and in America only a fraction of a tiny minority would have reproached him for it. Instead he chose the anti-dictatorial, non-imperialist stance of letting the chips fall where they may. They fell in favor of the Sandinists who were quickly welcomed by Castro and Nicaragua virtually joined the international communist cause. One of the cultural highpoints of Somoza, Inc., was a witless ditty, which went "Managua Nicaragua is a wonderful place". After over four decades of darkness, the Sandinists couldn't have been worse, and more likely they would be doing their country some good by following the Cuban model of social welfare. This wasn't meant to be.

(11) Khomeini taped sermons that were the Iranian equivalent of platinum discs

The mainstay of American Middle Eastern policy was the Central Treaty Organization (CENTO), whose two pillars were Turkey and Iran. In the oil-saturated Arabian or Persian Gulf region, nearly half of which was Iranian shoreline, the USA had placed all its marbles on the stabilizing influence of the progressive if tyrannical Iranian regime. Even idealistic Carter had in good conscience to praise Shah Mohammed Reza Pahlavi, Iran's dictator-king. The Shah was sincerely modernizing. But he was an exhibitionist and he was despotic. He and his wives, the ravishing but barren Soraya and her successor, the lovely and impeccably sophisticated Farah Diba, were the main dish in any given edition of the garishly illustrated Spanish weekly *Hola*, which slobbered over royalty and entertainers and was the almost inevitable recreation for hardworking Spaniards during and after the Franco dictatorship.

The Shah's despotism was a vice bred by power, for in private the Iranian monarch was such an amiable person that he had practically been forced by the Central Intelligence Agency (CIA) to defy and unseat the Iranian nationalist politician Mohammed Mossadegh. Although he made a great deal of Iran's origins in the ancient Achaemenid Empire, Mohammed Reza Shah was only the second ruler of the Pahlavi "dynasty", which had been founded by his father, Reza Khan, a military man who in 1925 had overthrown Ahmed Shah, the last of the Ghajar dynasty.[11]

Whether in a democracy, or in a crumbling state such as Russia in 1996, but especially in a dictatorship, rulers are wont to ignore what is happening in the nations over which they rule. This happens less in a democracy where there are polls and the media editorialize freely, but the president of the USA, or those exceptional individuals who aspire to power in America, do not have the same perspective on the world around them as does the "common man", which is why now and again you have poll-busting electoral upsets.

In the case of Iran, the Shah was totally shielded from reality that his subjects detested him and were enthusiastic about a cleric with perhaps the most terrifying frown in history and a look from out of darkened orbits that was the closest humanity has come to a Medusa stare. This cleric was the ayatollah Ruhollah Khomeini, a fierce enemy of the Shah for his "un-Islamic" modernizing ways who had been exiled to Turkey, from where he subsequently moved to next-door Iraq.[12]

Sunni is the form of Islam most Muslims accept. Khomeini, like most Persians, was a Shia Muslim. Shia-at-Ali, or the party of Ali, one of Muhammad's sons in law, appealed to Persians because, although they converted to Islam, they resented Arabs, and Arabs were, and today still are, mostly Sunni. Iraq, whose population is mainly Shia, expelled Khomeini to Paris, where he taped searing, sanctimonious sermons that in Iran became the equivalent of platinum discs.

(12) The ayatollahs were on a hanging binge but insisted on calling Carter the "president of Satan"

For no particular cause other than the accumulation of resentments, Iran went on a huge collective riot in which the masses lost their fear

11 Nadir Shah, a Turk from Khurasan, defeated the Afghans, expelled them from Persia, and occupied Herat and Kandahar in 1736. Strapped for cash, Nadir Shah attacked Kabul, invaded India, and sacked Delhi (1738-1739). The occupation of Afghanistan ended with the assassination of Nadir Shah in 1747. Persia disintegrated. Afghanistan went independent under Ahmad Shah Durrani. Nadir's blind grandson, Shah Rokh, ruled in Khurasan and Esfahan. Karim Khan Zand ruled in Shiraz. When Karim died (1779), Agha Muhammad Ghajar (Qajar), a warlord from the north whom Karim had managed to restrain, went on a ruthless campaign that led to his assassination in 1797 but also resulted in the reunification of Iran in 1794. The capital had been moved to Tehran in 1788.

12 The honorific title of "ayatollah" means "sign of God". Although the other clerics who have held ruling positions in Iran are often also called ayatollahs, some historians prefer to apply to them the title of "hojatolislam".

of the repressive secret police, SAVAK, and the Shah was forced to abandon Tehran and his throne. There was some political opposition to Khomeini but the government could not contain the Islamist impetus and the first modern aggressively Islamic fundamentalist state was born.

The Ottoman Empire, for instance, was Muslim and aggressive in its early period, but it had a system called millet through which each religious community had its own head and retained jurisdiction in certain areas of social life, mainly within the scope of what is known in the Western world as civil law. Religious toleration in fundamentalist Iran is almost inconceivable, although there are many Sunni Muslims, who cannot simply be banished; and other religions, including perhaps even Judaism, survive by being totally inconspicuous. Needless to say, no sooner had the Shah fled his country, officially on vacation, and (after some dithering) Khomeini had been acclaimed as national leader, than Iran abandoned CENTO and rejected its alliance with the USA.

Carter now showed weak knees and in a useless gesture of conciliation with the ayatollahs, who were attacking America and handing down death sentences with the abandon of a Robespierre, at first refused asylum to the fallen and ailing Shah.[13] This was as if Carter had disemboweled his own foreign policy showing the contradictions at its gut. Just as this honest American president could not deny that the Somoza dictatorship was reprehensible, so he could hardly blame the Iranians for getting rid of a tyrant and his minions, who had gone far beyond torture in their methods. But this meant that the USA was in the most uncomfortable position of having to ingratiate itself with its enemies. In the case of Nicaragua, the name Sandinist, an anti-American cry of defiance that resounded over Latin America, said it all. In Iran, Khomeini lost little time in calling America "Satan", a very distorting perspective indeed and one which had to be particularly disturbing to Baptists, themselves prone to denunciations of Satan and among whom Carter was a lay preacher.

To make things more difficult for the American president, not only was he called the "president of Satan", which Carter most certainly wasn't (precisely the opposite is what he wanted to be), but when the USA finally granted a visa for hospitalization to the dying Shah, Khomeini's zealous oratory, which, like Castro's in Cuba, was exercised continuously,

13 The chief Iranian hangman, Sadegh Khalkhali, bragged: "I killed over 500 criminals close to the royal family, hundreds of rebels in the Kurdistan, Gonbad, and Khuzestan regions, and many drug smugglers. I feel no regret or guilt over the executions. Yet I think I killed little. There were many more who deserved to be killed but I could not get my hands on them." IHT, 1 December 2003.

incited young Iranian fundamentalist revolutionaries to seize the American Embassy and sequester its some 60 occupants in contempt of all rules of diplomatic conduct. The American government was forced to canel its visa to the Shah for the sake of the lives of its diplomats. The Shah, who had made it a point during his reign of having himself photographed restraining people trying to kiss his hand, was generally shunned in the West and he ended his days in Egypt. His tomb and a memorial plaque can be seen in the Al Azhar mosque in the center of old Cairo.

(13) Saddam Hussein sneaked up on the world because everyone was looking at Iran

The man responsible for Khomeini's expulsion from Iraq was Saddam Hussein. Iraq's population was divided roughly into 70% Shia and 27% Sunni (the rest being mostly Assyrian Christians). The scission between Sunni and Shia occurred in Iraq, at the battle of Karbala, south of Baghdad, where the Umayyads, who established the caliphate or the successorship of Muhammad in Damascus, killed Hussein and his partisans in a massacre so thorough that, according to legend, only one person, Ali, Hussein's sickly child, survived to tell about it.

Hussein was Caliph Ali's son. The 7th century details are murky, but there were three caliphs after Muhammad: Abu Bakr, Umar, and Uthman. Ali either was the fourth caliph or claimed during the period of the first three successors that he was the one and only caliph, in part because he was married to Fatima, daughter of Muhammad. The Prophet had many children and Abu Bakr and Uthman were also his in-laws. Sunni Muslims accept the tradition of the first three caliphs but Shia Muslims insist that Ali was the one and only caliph. Shia's history after Karbala is somewhat shadowy for not caliphs but imams kept the Alid tradition alive and the succession of the imams is itself imprecise there being further sub-traditions involving seven, twelve, and even hidden imam (not unlike Judaic messianism).[14] The important point politically is that Shia has survived to our days not only as a religious tradition but as a political force, crucial

14 Shiites, the Muslim partisans of Ali and Fatima against the Umayyad caliphs, held to their own line of succession from Muhammad in the figure of the imams, of whom Ali and his sons were considered the first three. The Shiites split after the death in 765 of the sixth imam, Jafar ibn Muhammad (also sometimes identified as Jafar al-Sadiq). A minority accepted the succession of his son Ismail, hence Ismailites, with whom the "visible" succession of imams ended and a line of "hidden imams" began. These Ismailites were therefore also called Seveners. The majority of Shiites recognized another son of Jafar, Musa al-Kazim, and a line of imams until the death of the twelfth imam, when they too adopted the hidden-imams doctrine. These Shiites came to be known as Twelvers and are the vast majority of Shiites today.

in Iran and important in Iraq. Khomeini, in sum, was deported by Saddam Hussein, himself religiously unzealous but of Sunni origin, because, with his compulsive sermonizing, the Iranian cleric was making Iraq's Sunni rulers nervous.

The year that Khomeini and the Shia ayatollahs took power in Iran, Saddam Hussein had become president, in reality sole dictator, in Iraq. This fateful event went virtually unnoticed in America and the world because, in regard to the Middle East, every one was looking at Iran; and America in particular was fretting over the unmerited imprisonment of its diplomats in the embassy compound, where insolent Revolutionary Guards kept them in jitters with their taunts about "Satan" and "the great Satan".

Hussein, a pistol-packing, conspirational politician, had climbed to power through his leadership inside Baath. The Baath ruler of Syria was Gen. Hafez el-Assad, who emerged from very lowly social origins through the Syrian air force academy. Ironically, his call for a political union between Iraq and Syria did not make for Baathist solidarity but for quarreling between the two countries and their separate Baath parties.

America's collective mind would soon be concentrating on still another crisis, one that, though less painful to Americans from a heart-felt patriotic perspective, was a humiliating strategic slap from the USSR, for Americans the real "great Satan" on the loose in the world. It occurred in a country so remote and backward that it would have crossed no one's mind that it could be the base for a devastating terrorist attack on New York City itself.

(14) Afghanistan or nationalism avant la lettre

Afghanistan has an ancient history as complicated as its land-locked, arid, mountain-frazzled geography. It was the gateway and sometimes the original base for invasions of the Indian subcontinent. The country was peopled in pre-history by Indo-Iranians. The Afghans were linguistic cousins of the Persians, the ancestors of the modern Iranians, but the Persians were closer to civilized Mesopotamia than Afghanistan and it was in Persia—the designation originally of a region north of the Persian Gulf and later of all of Iran—that an Iranian empire first emerged. Greater Persia extended to western Afghanistan, which to this day is still Persian speaking.

Roughly starting in the 10th century CE, eastern Afghanistan was mostly ruled by Muslim Turks from the lands between the Syrdarya and the Amudarya rivers (Transoxiana), originally from the great Eurasian steppes. In the 11th century and after, Afghans conquered northern

India and ruled it from Delhi. In the 13th and early 14th century, Mongols used Afghanistan as the staging area for attacks on the Delhi Sultanate. Eastern Afghanistan and the Mughal Empire (16th century) were consubstantial. When the Mughals, probably Turks who claimed Mongol imperial descent, were strong the Persians were kept at bay, but when the Mughals declined the Persians swept in. There were local Afghan dynasties, but Afghanistan did not acquire some sense of national identity until the mid-18th century when the Durrani dynasty de-linked its affairs from those of Transoxiana, Persia, and northern India, except for linguistically Persian Herat with a history of its own connected as much to Afghanistan as to Persia.[15]

But Afghanistan was not an unified, centrally ruled kingdom: the historical background and the topography stood squarely in the way of that. Afghanistan had three great cities: Kandahar, Kabul, and Herat. There were other less important towns but most Afghans were scattered in valley bottoms, where rivers seasonally swell, and were grouped into villages divided into clans. Kandahar was the original Afghan capital, later moved to Kabul. The British tried to dethrone Afghanistan's most formidable monarch, Dost Muhammad, only to discover that to conquer Afghanistan would require more money than the revenues that the country could ever yield. Dost Muhammad was restored but even Afghan kings could not control their own unruly countrymen.

British India was obsessed by Tsarist Russia, whom it could envision plucking Afghanistan like a ripe plum. This fear was what settled the issue of Herat, which the Afghans obtained with British backing against the claims of Persia, too close to Russia for British comfort. Normally tantamount to British protectorship, a British resident was imposed on Kabul by threats and military feints. Unfortunately, the resident's arrival coincided with that of lean, underpaid Afghan soldiery, who loped off the British envoy's head and paraded it around central Kabul. This was an ancient Eurasian tradition that was codified in Latin as: "Si inimicus caput hominis in palo miserit" (put your enemy's head on a stick). It

15 In 1709, Kandahar became independent of Persian rule. In 1716, the Afghan rulers of Herat, known as Abdalis and as Durranis, also rejected Persian domination. In 1722, the Afghan Mahmud attacked the Persian Safavid dynasty, defeated and killed Shah Soltan Hoseyn, and occupied Esfahan, the Persian capital. The Turco-Iranian Nadir Koli Beg of Khurasan defeated the Afghans and expelled them from Persia crowning himself Nadir Shah (1729). He occupied Herat (1732) and Kandahar (1738). Nadir Shah gained the Durranis of Herat to his side. When Nadir Shah was assassinated in 1747, Ahmad Shah Durrani (also Ahmad Khan Abdali) formed an independent Afghan state with its capital in Kandahar, which extended from Meshed to Kashmir and from the Amu Darya to Sind (southern Pakistan).

only signified primitiveness, like scalping, usually associated with North American Indians but practiced also by the ancient Indo-Iranian Scythians of southern Russia.

The British invaded Afghanistan again and, after going on a vindictive rampage in Kabul, handed power to one of Dost Muhammad's descendants and exited as graciously as possible. They thought they had persuaded the Afghans to let them run their foreign affairs. Most Afghans were also Pathans, speakers of an Indo-Iranian language known as Pashto, and British India had annexed so much Afghan territory that there still are more Pathans in Pakistan than in Afghanistan. The Afghans not only rejected British tutelage but they also raided the lands in British India where their fellow Pathans lived and which the British had renamed Northwest Province, a designation that Pakistan, for obvious reasons, later retained. The British contained them but despaired of ever colonializing such an unruly people. It could be said that Afghanistan, as backward a country as you could imagine, was also as nationalistic and as jealous of its sovereignty as any 19th century western European state, a spanner in the works of any general theory on nationalism, its origins, and its characteristics.

(15) Kabul was mere backdrop to the passions seething in the villages

The contemporary history of Afghanistan is completely incomprehensible if it is narrated only with a view to what went on in Kabul, which is about the farthest that Afghanistan ventured into the 20th century, although in this limited sense it didn't do badly at all and pre-civil war Kabul, even communist Kabul, is remembered as a lively, handsome city with spacious avenues, important cultural institutions, and impressive public buildings. The Afghan capital was inhabited by a sophisticated population avid for modernity, blessed by nature with lovely views and a good year-around climate. Kabul was definitely atypical, yet the tragedy of all of Afghanistan could be seen in the unmistakable grief of the native curators of the Kabul museum when, heads bowed in regret and shame, they told of the depredations of the Taliban authorities. Better, they seemed to express, a century of communism than half a decade of religious obscurantism.[16]

The last king of Afghanistan, Mohammad Zahir Shah, encouraged reforms after World War II and the country tried to strike a balance between communism and capitalism, although commercial relations

---

16 Paul Watson, "The Taliban war on art: culture axed to oblivion", IHT, 24 November 2001.

leaned heavily towards the USSR. Afghanistan has borders on the former Soviet republics of Turkmenistan, Tajikistan, and Uzbekistan. A Loya Jirga or grand assembly sanctioned a constitution and elections were held for a House of the People and a House of Elders. Politics were polarized between modernizers and Islamic traditionalists, but it did not appear from outside of Afghanistan, or even in Kabul itself, as if the country had such an inexhaustible reserve of the fundamentalist energies that later surged. Even the traditionalists (Jamiyyat e Islami or Islamic Brotherhood or Society) had their base in the theological school of Kabul university. The radical modernizers were either in the Khalq (people) or the Parcham (banner) parties, offshoots of a parent Marxist organization, the People's Democratic Party of Afghanistan (PDPA).

Mohammad Daud Khan, a general turned politician and a cousin of the king, also the central figure of Afghan politics for decades (when he mostly had a conservative tint), expelled king Zahir Shah and declared a republic with Parcham support. In another Loya Jirga, a new constitution was adopted. Daud ruled with royal relatives and cronies and Khalq and Parcham united in opposition.

Kabul was in the grip of political upheavals and Daud and his family were assassinated. The coup organizer was Hafizullah Amin, who obtained military support, but Nur Muhammad Taraki as leader of the PDPA dominated the government that emerged. The Khalq and Parcham factions began feuding, thus weakening the government, which was getting heat only from the Islamists in the absence of political rivals. A certain sign of growing radicalism and creeping anarchism was the assassination of the American ambassador, Adolph Doubs. Gradually and without making world headlines, rebellion in the countryside was spreading and the army was giving up positions. The decades old political process in Afghanistan was something of an urban drama with Kabul as stage and backdrop. Rural Afghanistan, which before appeared to have zero weight in the country's affairs, began to emerge as the bull-necked rival of pro-Soviet radicals.

(16) Afghanistan was the last twist to the USSR's hangman's knot

Hafizullah Amin, who disclaimed subservience to the USSR, overthrew Taraki and had him executed. Another radical, the one closest to the Soviets, Babrak Karmal, head of the Parcham faction, fled to the USSR, which, at his behest, invaded Afghanistan and eliminated Amin. Karmal became nominal head of government, that is, a Soviet puppet. While America wallowed in impotent anger over Iranian brutality, the Soviets, led by secretary general Leonid Brezhnev, seemed to have effortlessly added another satellite to their empire. What no one could foresee at the time was that the Soviet invasion of Afghanistan did not constitute a strategic victory for the Soviets but the last twist to their own hangman's knot.

Carter's reaction was immediate. Given the sequence of events from the Soviet invasion to 9/11, it is possible that, like the British, the American president might have over-reacted. Condemnation of the invasion was forceful and unequivocal, disarmament negotiations with the USSR were suspended (although Washington and Moscow announced separately that they would abide by the results achieved), and relations fell to the coldest of Cold War temperatures. The USA refused point blank to participate in the Summer Olympics, which in 1980 were celebrated in Moscow. But however vigorously Carter acted, his previous foreign policy record, plagued as it was by vacillation and by inherent contradictions, did not support the platform on which he wanted to stand and challenge the USSR. In the media he was sometimes portrayed as a blubber-lipped, gap-toothed hick. To find a comparable level of contempt, one would have had to go back to some of the dirtiest 19th-century American political campaigns.

The coup de grâce to Carter's re-election hopes occurred when American commandos botched a rescue operation inside Iran so badly that it could have seemed like a tragic script for a Keystone Cops short. Most damaging for Carter, his exemplary moral stance had been weakened too glaringly for him to start acting like the tough guy in a dangerous neighborhood. The USA was also suffering from inflation due to new spikes in oil prices, although Carter's administration handled the problem better than other developed nations. Carter, who had no problems with being called a liberal, gave liberalism a "bad image" and Americans, who had long before forgotten that it was liberalism that had helped them or their parents through the Great Depression, happily and even tauntingly began to boast of their conservatism. This was so marked that women voters, who had been predictably conservative, began to act like liberals in contrast with their illiberal men. Carter could be called the last successful, as well as the most unsuccessful, representative of traditional American liberalism.

(17) It never crossed a liberal's mind that an actor could become president of the USA

Ronald Reagan, a competent if unexciting actor, but a real-to-goodness Hollywood professional with dozens of movie credits, had started way back in his life as a liberal but had evolved towards extreme conservatism, especially when he became a much appreciated corporate spokesman and lecturer. This placed him in a position to make a complete switch from acting to politics. He did it so skillfully that he served two terms as governor of California. In office, he was true to the widespread conservative standard that prescribed spending cuts, less social subsidies, more reliance over all on the virtues of economic entrepreneurship and on private, strictly voluntary giving.

Professional politicians, Nixon and Ford, twice defeated Reagan when he lunged for the Republican presidential nomination. But Reagan went on talking, softly, with impeccable diction and clarity, about toughness and other American values. He praised success and contemned losers. He was unashamedly for the happy ending. He did not avoid a show of vanity and claimed the right to ostentation.

When Carter appeared to be stumbling badly, Republicans finally caught on: the majority of the American voting public wanted chin-forward conservatism and was no longer ashamed of being considered illiberal or even anti-liberal. Reagan was so prototypical of the conservative that he was the obvious choice as the opponent to the prototypical liberal Carter. At election time, Reagan trounced Carter and liberals couldn't believe what was happening. Naturally, being liberals it never crossed their mind that an actor could actually be elected president of the USA, the highest public office in the world.

Reagan as president was loyal to his beliefs as he was consistent in his advocacies. Domestically, he was constrained by the liberal proclivities of the federal government, which hadn't been tampered with even by Richard Nixon, the archconservative who wasn't. Reagan's economic creed was that granting the affluent tax breaks was the best incentive to the production increases which would generate the taxable income to compensate for the budget deficits that his tax cuts created in the first place. As investment growth was supposed to generate employment, his argument was not as circular as it sounds, but even his vice-president, George H.W. Bush, called Reagan's reasoning "voodoo economics", for every one knew that fiscal measures to stimulate growth took time and deficits are short term. Reagan got his tax cuts markedly skewed towards the wealthy, but deficits increased and later, as president, Bush was forced to reverse some of Reagan's tax cuts in order to make fiscal ends meet.[17]

(18) Rambo was the model for a long list of Hollywood fantasies about Americans wreaking vengeance on sadistic Orientals

Reagan called the USSR and its dependent states the "evil empire". This came straight out of the 1977 film hit *Star Wars*, but Americans

17 Steven R. Weisman, *The great tax wars* (2002), p. 361

did not see anything frivolous or shallow about the simplification. They found nothing startling either in Reagan's admiration for the movie character Rambo (played by Sylvester Stallone) a Vietman war veteran superman and the model for a long list of masturbatory fantasies about American heroes wreaking revenge on sadistic Orientals, although the germ for the genre was the cloyingly patriotic *Deer Hunter*, the 1978 Michael Cimino movie.

Reagan also initiated the American male's infatuation with the Three Stooges, which was a defiant affirmation, like being a conservative and the hell with liberals, that there were fun things in life that one need not be ashamed of just because the pretentious called them, or used to call them, low-brow. Reagan arrived at the White House but he did not renege of his Hollywood background and instead put it center stage and used it to bolster his popularity, for America has always taken movies very seriously and fawning on stars and fixating on celebrities have always been acceptable collective traits. The harmful extreme in these practices is stalking and attacking the objects of awe and admiration and Reagan did not escape the hazards of being the greatest super-celebrity ever when he was shot at and almost killed by a deranged would-be assassin. Unlike the assassination of Kennedy, there were no politics involved in the attempt on Reagan's life.

Reagan had been married to an actress, Jane Wyman, who had a better reputation in their field than he did. Critics and Reagan himself considered that his best acting moment was his secondary role in the film *King's Row*. Wyman said that one of the reasons for their divorce was that she got tired of watching reruns of *King's Row*. One of the perks of celebrity status is showing off and Reagan and his second wife, a former starlet who believed in astrology, put on a lavish round of celebrations after the oath-taking that had few if any precedents in American history. Again unlike Kennedy, who had sidelined, and alienated, such showbiz supporters as Frank Sinatra and Sammy Davis jr., Reagan went out of his way to demonstrate that he was proud of his affiliation with the movie industry. Thus, "evil empire", which most anywhere would have elicited sniggers, in America, and coming from Reagan, seemed a natural thing to say.

(19) SDI against "evil empire"

The problem with "evil empire" was that it meant nothing whatsoever. Did the "empire" include communist China or just the Soviet Empire? If both, why not "evil empires"? If both also, there was an implicit distortion of historical facts, for the USSR and China were not allies but rivals, and how could you have evil opposing itself? If that was the case, then you had evil schizophrenia, which could be good or bad depending on whether it went berserk and self-destroyed or tried to destroy America. Was "evil" meant in a sense that excluded redemption? Did "evil empire" embrace any one the world over who adopted a more analytical, less smug view of history, or God forbid, actually found some thing to admire in Soviet history, if only its indispensable role in the destruction of Nazi Germany? And if "evil empire" was accurate, then how could the USA, presumably its angelical foil, have any truck with it? It would have been as if Gabriel had been over to Lucifer's for lunch.

Reagan backed up his characterization of communism with the Strategic Defense Initiative (SDI). The SDI consisted in the development of a missile system that could knock attacking missiles out in space. This was promptly and inevitably dubbed "star wars". Some conservatives allege that the movie tagging was critical and derisive. It has the ring of the tabloid, which is usually conservative, and besides Reagan virtually asked for it by using the meaningless but decidedly Hollywoodesque "evil empire".

The project immediately flew into a flack field. The most reiterated criticism said it was unfeasible and a waste of money. And some of the tests that were carried out did seem clownishly inept, like the Three Stooges in outer space. As to the real possibility of its achievement, in view of foreseeable technological advances, it seemed more foolish to deny than to accept it. But when Reagan first announced it, the SDI sounded like a reckless, self-righteous, and de-stabilizing policy, a guzzler of money that could have been better spent, say, NASA. There was a string of reasons why SDI made anti-nuclear activists jumpy.

(20) The trouble with arms races is that it is impossible to define "enough"

The first two atomic bombs were dropped on Japan by American planes in 1945. The USSR had the bomb four years later. The USA developed the hydrogen bomb in 1952 and the USSR tested one in 1953. Thereafter, advances in weaponry followed on the heels of each other. In the case of missile technology, responsible for the carrying of nuclear bombs, the USSR bounded ahead of the USA when it sent into orbit the first artificial satellite, before America even lobbed a much smaller device in an up-and-down run in a rocket with less thrust than the Soviet one.[18]

---

18 Taubman insists, in op.cit. that the USSR never had an edge in ICBMs over America and that it only seemed so from Nikita Khrushchev's bragging and blustering.

Both countries were obsessed by what was known as "first-strike capability", or victory in one nuclear onslaught, so they went into massive bomb-building programs. Since bombs needed means to transport and drop them, they also started producing "strategic bombers"—very long-range with a capacious belly—and more menacingly, because bombers were fast but still sub-sonic, intercontinental ballistic missiles (ICBM) which could fly at over 30 times the speed of sound.

In principle, you can have too many of a certain weapon, but the United States and the USSR could not know exactly what were "enough" atomic bombs and missiles, because they had to be prepared to withstand a first strike by one on the other and be able to retaliate in kind, that is, wreaking the same or more destruction than a first strike occasioned. Nuclear strategy went on looking for the mythical advantage that would give one side the edge over the other.

There were many kinds of strategic missiles by then—ICBMs, mid-range missiles, even "tactical" atomic weapons—but they all went from surface to surface. Why not missiles that were accurate enough to stop a first strike? To make the strategist's task virtually unsolvable, ICBMs, which originally were placed in static launchers or silos, could also be placed in submarines (SLBMs), or moving platforms, which, if nuclear powered, could remain undersea for long periods of time and go anywhere undetected. Sub-launched missiles made targeting missile sites impossible. There already existed a technology by which one ICBM could divide into many separate nuclear warheads and these could be aimed at different targets. These were the MIRVs or Multiple Independently-targeted Re-entry Vehicles. This did not invalidate the concept of anti-missile missiles, but at the time the technical problems of coping with MIRVs and SLBMs were daunting.

The nuclear arms race was not without costs and every bomb test spewed into the atmosphere clouds of radioactivity that, every one agreed, could eventually result in dangerous contamination. A crucial point was that, since nuclear tests were carried out by the USA and the USSR in their own territories, these countries would be the first to suffer the consequences of radioactive fallout. For these very valid reasons a treaty was signed in Moscow for a partial test ban, which later was voluntarily converted to a total ban. The UK had suspended testing in Australia before then, but the French went on making tests in the South Pacific, provoking official protests (New Zealand was especially critical) and the active opposition of the environmental organization Greenpeace.

The ban on testing was not accompanied by a ban on manufacturing, so basically being on the earth was beginning to feel like living next to an unlicensed fireworks factory, where an explosion could occur some time. To dissuade copycats, the Nuclear Non-Proliferation treaty was subscribed by a large majority of states. By that time, the USA and the USSR had such an overabundance of nuclear weapons and ICBMs that no matter what defense strategies either country adopted, nuclear war would eventually result in reciprocal annihilation. The two super-states had so much destructive power that even in the eventuality of a surprise attack by either, the attacked party still had the means to inflict destruction on the other.

(21) SDI versus MAD

When this reasoning became the subject of public debate, it was also realized that it was better to be in such a situation than in one in which one country had the advantage, which anyway was not likely to happen. This approach to nuclear strategy was called Mutually Assured Destruction or MAD. In America it is associated with the name of Robert McNamara, a former auto industry chief executive and Kennedy's secretary of defense, but in the USSR no one in particular hogged the credit, so it is more likely that MAD was just another name for common sense. MAD became official with the signing of the Anti-ballistic Missile Treaty (ABM), a strictly two super-powers or bipolar affair.

After that, the next logical step was to implement arms limitations, perhaps arms reduction. These negotiations were called Strategic Arms Limitations talks or treaties (depending on the results). There was a SALT I during Nixon's second administration. There were the SALT talks during Carter's administration which ceased the moment the Soviets invaded Afghanistan. The MAD equilibrium was not affected. When Reagan came up with the SDI against the evil empire, which however "evil" was still an empire, not only was the USA repudiating MAD, but the project was from start to finish a contravention of the ABM. Reagan gained for himself the admiring epithet of "great communicator". Although his adversaries said that all he did was read screen prompters, it would be foolish to deny Reagan's formidable eloquence, which he used to promote the SDI. It took a surprising chain of events in the USSR not to dissuade Reagan but at least to break the impetus of SDI, which was so beset that it was losing it anyway from its own deficiencies.

This public airing of strategic issues, which in every other country in the world would have been kept in unbreachable darkness, was one of the reasons why America, whatever its faults, was the exemplar of an open society. The USSR occupied the opposite extreme. In between there were gradations in openness and it was not inconceivable, for example, that in Britain such issues could be raised in the House of Commons. Besides,

Reagan deserved more credit than his critics gave him, because he did a masterful job of clearing the way for the SDI by previously throwing at the Soviets gauntlets for new SALTs and for an outright scrapping of intermediate-range nuclear forces (INF). In this range (between 500 and 5,000 kilometers), the USSR had a clear preponderance. Warsaw Pact INFs covered Western Europe and faced only a French deterrent, which other Europeans did not consider as reliable as an American one. The Soviets did not accept the American challenges.

(22) What America learned from the Vietnam experience

There was another area in foreign affairs in which Reagan showed himself unarguably astute and truly the most formidable adversary that the USSR, stagnating under the leaden leadership of secretary general Brezhnev, had ever faced. If the USA learned something from the Vietnam War it was that in the third world it was better to fight by proxy than to get involved in actual combat. The USSR had been the ultimate victor in Vietnam because it committed not one soldier to that war. Also, the Vietnamese were scrupulous about keeping it a strictly nationalist war and they never accepted, or for that matter needed, non-Vietnamese volunteers, except those with propaganda potential or value, which ironically more often than not were Americans themselves, the actress Jane Fonda being the most notorious case.

This incidentally taught Americans another lesson, which was that it didn't pay to be too active against your own country's wars, right or wrong. This lesson was learned so well that activism against the Second Iraqi war was so discreet that jingoist journalists had a hard time finding celebrities to pillory for being against arguably the most blatantly imperialistic war that America has ever fought. And the Democratic candidate, John Kerry, a Vietnam veteran who openly opposed the Vietnam War, had a terrible time getting over what could be called a "Jane Fonda complex". Incredibly, what the Soviets apparently drew from Vietnam was not a cautionary lesson but some besotted sense of their invincibility in third world countries.

The fight-by-proxy strategy was immediately applied by the Reagan administration in Nicaragua. There was no scarcity of Nicaraguan enemies of the Sandinists, and they weren't necessarily only former Somoza supporters or discharged soldiers. The latter-day Sandinists, like their idol, also walked into a trap: because their victory came from the muzzle of a rifle and because Cuba, the only Latin American state to challenge the USA successfully, was being an enthusiastic supporter, they lost sight of the fact that in the Western Hemisphere, as the Guatemalan leftist politician J.J. Arévalo put it, it was the American shark chasing sardines, Nicaragua being among the sardines. In brief, the Sandinists were not being accommodating, domestically or internationally, and the USA was not even disposed to be accommodating. It was eager to conspire. But instead of sending in the Marines, like Presidents William H. Taft and Calvin Coolidge had done, Reagan's administration began financing openly the anti-Sandinist Nicaraguan guerrillas that came to be known as Contras.

The Sandinists had only a short period of relative internal peace in which to apply their revolutionary program before they became embattled, and not just by the Contras, but by the USA itself, which, to make sure that the Sandinists were really hurting, air-dropped mines in the main Nicaraguan ports. This was pure, unashamed bullying. But it shouldn't have come as a surprise to any one, least of all to Sandinists, and anyway it was done, honestly, in the name of democracy, for in Nicaragua there was none. The Sandinists like Castro might have won any election, but they were, also honestly, and stubbornly, opposed to free elections.

(23) Grenada was a pushover but Beirut only seemed like one

Reagan did not always approach international issues with the indirection he adopted towards Nicaragua. The tiny Caribbean island state of Grenada came to independent life under a labor leader, Eric Gairy, whose party was named GULP. Gairy knew how to begin strikes but not how to end them. Under British colonial administration, Grenada became a competitor in the spice trade and was given the nickname of the "nutmeg island". It also had some top-class tourism, although its beaches are not spectacular.

Maurice Bishop, the leader of the opposition and founder of the New Jewel Movement, which was more leftist than GULP, deposed the junketing Gairy and took power effortlessly. Apparently, Bishop was not being revolutionary enough for his constituency, which included hardened Castroites. Although it wasn't clear exactly what his opponents wanted to revolutionize, Bishop was overthrown and killed. Cubans were in view in the island constructing a big international airport, long enough to land Russian MIGs, when American forces parachuted in and in one day or two corralled the communists, expelled the Cubans, and settled in for two more years, when they left Grenada with an elected government.

Beirut, the setting for another direct American military action, had a less than happy conclusion. During its inter-war League of Nations mandate, France sheared off Lebanon from Syria. After sundry constitutional arrangements to accommodate Muslim, Druze, and Christian Maronite interests, it granted Lebanon independence at the end of World War II.[19] During the first Arab-Israeli war, many Palestinians fled to Lebanon, where the miserable conditions of refugee camps bred strong anti-Israeli activism. President Camille Chamoun, a Maronite Christian, tried to lead Lebanon into the Western camp and away from Arab entanglements, but this was moving against the tide of events. When the nation exploded in protests, Chamoun asked for American help and President Eisenhower responded with Marines. Chamoun made some political concessions defusing the situation and leading to American evacuation. This was but a prelude for the hurricane to come.

(24) The PLO overreached in Jordan and got a good licking

The PLO was an umbrella organization originally sponsored by Egypt and other Arab states to oppose Israel. For them, it was just one expression of a shared foreign policy. The PLO has never associated itself officially with terrorism. Even at the height of the Lebanese civil war, when it was rare not to engage in terrorism rather than the other way around, the PLO avoided sending any indication that it was involved in or condoned terrorism. The PLO always claimed that its fighting men were soldiers engaged in war with other, specifically Israeli, soldiers. After the Yom Kippur or Six-day war, when Yasir Arafat, leader of the militant Al Fatah faction, which had distinguished itself by destroying Israeli tanks in Karameh, Jordan, took over the presidency of the PLO, he made Jordan its base. Jordan's population had been more than doubled by the Palestinian refugee influx and the PLO felt that it had the right to intervene in that country's domestic affairs.

One of the most active Palestinian terrorist organizations was the Popular Front for the Liberation of Palestine (PFLP). In September 1970, the PFLP simultaneously hijacked a Swissair DC8, a TWA Boeing 707, and a BOAC VC-10 and forced them to land in Dawson air base near Amman. It tried to hijack an El Al flight. Deterred by tight Israeli security, it did manage to hijack a PAA 747, which it directed to Cairo. All passengers were released and the empty planes were exploded and burnt for the benefit of world cameras. The provocative actions of the PFLP and other terrorist groups led to a confrontation between King Hussein and the PLO. Hussein declared martial law.

---

19 An Ismailite branch, known as the Druzes, survived in the Levant. Although not strictly Muslims, Druzes, whose name derives from a Turkic divine named Mehmet al Darazi (10th century), incorporate some fundamental Islamic beliefs in their creed. The Maronites accept the primacy of the papacy but their liturgical language is Syriac and their priesthood is allowed to marry. Their immédiate head is called the patriarch of Antioch, although he resides in Beirut. The name Maronite comes from the 4th century monk St. Maron.

Jordan's Arab Legion could be as efficient against Palestinians as it had been against Jews and it crushed a PLO insurrection. As a consequence of these events, Black September, a particularly nasty Palestinian terrorist faction, was formed and gained world-wide notoriety through various sensationally shocking actions, including the assassination of nine Israeli athletes taken hostage in the Munich Summer Olympics in 1972. As classic terrorist shockers, to the multiple plane hijackings and the Munich massacre must be added the capture in October 1985 of the Italian cruise liner Achille Lauro, where a paralytic Jewish passenger was killed and flung overboard in his wheelchair. This was the doing of still another terrorist group, the Palestine Liberation Front.

Jordan's King Hussein did not intend to destroy the PLO but to get it off his back. That the PLO and states like Egypt and Syria were agreed on their enmity towards Israel did not mean that they were fighting the same war. The PLO claimed to be the official government of the Palestinian people and did not accept other sovereignties over itself. Egypt and Syria would have made the PLO an agency of their foreign offices at the slightest opportunity, which is why the PLO, after the Jordanian debacle, chose divided Lebanon, an important refuge for the Palestinian diaspora, as its military base. Arafat himself established his offices in Damascus.

(25) The PLO again tries to get itself a country

In Lebanon, the PLO re-constituted its combat units and soon had those fighting fit. The Lebanese army had been active against Palestinian commandos, but its effectiveness was severely constrained by Lebanon's multi-religious composition. Even though they were as Arab as the Palestinians, Maronite Christians were not particularly sympathetic to the Palestinian cause, and the Muslim Arabs, fragmented into Sunni, Shia, and the semi-Muslim Druzes, were as concerned about not being put upon politically by the Maronites as they were about fighting Israel. The Lebanese internal security problem was now aggravated by the nearness of the PLO command, which was also leaning as hard as it could on Israel. There were frequent Israeli reprisals in southern Lebanon. All of these difficult circumstances finally led to out-and-out civil war.

The civil war in Lebanon was mainly between Christians and Muslims, although as it evolved in a crazy-quilt fashion Muslim militias fought each other and Christian factions jockeyed, often violently, for power. As a rule, Druzes and Palestinians made common cause and the Maronites usually stood alone. Beirut was divided into Muslim west Beirut and Christian east Beirut by a no-man's land (formerly Allenby street) where any one who ventured could have his brains shot out. As it became overgrown with vegetation it was known as the "green line". As the civil war intensified the PLO was actually close to winning and taking over the country. Now, in theory this sounds, and it sounded then also from a distance, as if it would have been the ideal solution to the Palestinian problem: a country where Palestinians had a decisive voice, from which they could exert pressure on Israel and perhaps arrive at some sort of cohabitation arrangement in Israel/Palestine.

Various important obstacles stood in the way of a process of this sort. They were all of equal importance. Israel already had a foot in southern Lebanon and it would have opposed Palestinian supremacy in the rest of the country. Negotiations were probably out of the question for both sides. Within Lebanon, although the Palestinians showed more mettle than the other factions, the opposition to Palestinian hegemony would have become formidable, not only from Maronite Christians, who considered that they were Lebanon's own, but also from other Arab Muslims. It was only after the close shave with the Palestinians that Lebanese Shias, Sunni, and Druzes really organized their fighters into small separate armies.

The Palestinians were on the offensive when President Suleiman Franjieh, a Maronite, sought and obtained Syrian intervention shortly before he left office. For Syria, Lebanon was more than a strategic weapon against Israel. Syria considered Lebanon to be historically an amputated part of it. It could probably have more easily adjusted to the permanent loss of the Golan Heights, itself an unthinkable, than to forfeiting its influence over Lebanon to the Palestinians. An Israeli invasion would make Syria's military situation more fraught. In brief, a Palestinian hold on Lebanon would have de-stabilized the Middle East more than it was and would have generated greater tensions towards regional conflict. Thus it was that to tacit though not unanimous Lebanese approval, Syria invaded Lebanon and stopped the Palestinian offensive. It was one occasion when Israel and Syria saw eye to eye, without even hinting at such a thing.

(26) "Peace for Galilee"

The Syrian military presence was deliberately weak and it was concentrated in the Bekaa valley in eastern Lebanon, which lies astride the Beirut-Damascus road. A ceasefire was agreed, which degenerated into worse fighting between the multiple factions. This favored PLO anti-Israel operations. Israel invaded southern Lebanon and a 6,000-man multinational force under UN auspices (Unifil) was stationed on the Lebanon side of the Israel-Lebanon border. It was, and still is (now much reduced), largely ineffectual.[20] The Israelis also formed the core of what later became the mainly Christian Southern Lebanon Army

20 New Zealand Ministry of Foreign Affairs and Trade, *United Nations Handbook 2001*.

(SLA). When the ayatollahs came to power in Iran, they sponsored Hizbollah and other anti-Israeli Shia organizations. Hizbollah is still active in southern Lebanon, although this is mainly due to its role as collective representative and defender of the Lebanese Shia population.

Syria began to flex its muscles in Lebanon by first installing SAMs in the Bekaa valley, which obviously were meant to deter Israel. At the same time, fighting between the PLO and Israel in southern Lebanon, but overlapping into Galilee (northern Israel), was taking on the character of a small war. It was as a result of these circumstances that, under the supervision of Sharon, now in his character as Israeli defense minister in Begin's cabinet, Israel launched its full-scale invasion of Lebanon designated Operation Peace for Galilee, including as one of its targets the destruction of Syrian missile sites in Bekaa. Syria rose to the challenge with its air force, which was engaged by the Israelis in a gigantic dogfight covering 2,500 square kilometers and involving hundreds of supersonic fighters on both sides. The Syrians lost 90 aircraft. Their air forces were shattered.[21]

The Israeli army, known as the IDF (Israeli Defense Forces), advanced to west Beirut, which was put to siege. As the main Israeli objective was to eliminate the PLO, a multinational force (MNF)—American, French, and Italian troops amounting to some two brigades—was allowed to land in Lebanon in August and evacuate thousands of Palestinian fighters from Beirut to Syria and Cyprus. Its objective accomplished, the MNF withdrew.

Bashir Gemayel, the Maronite leader who, as "official president" of Lebanon, was blamed for Israel's invasion, was assassinated. His brother Amin succeeded him. Despite the PLO evacuation, there remained in west Beirut the camps of Palestinian refugees, and these were bristling with resentment and arms. The IDF occupied west Beirut. Shortly after that, the Falangists, a Maronite militia, went at sunset into the crowded Sabra and Shatilla refugee areas. The Israelis provided flares and observed operations from nearby buildings. At dawn it was found that the Falangists had left behind a massacre, which is estimated at 2,000 victims. The Falangist leader Elie Hobeika was blamed for the slaughter, although he denied that he was anywhere near the camps. The killings must also be put in the context of innumerable atrocities committed by all sides wherever there was fighting in Lebanon.

Sharon was forced to resign the defense ministry although not from the cabinet. When Belgium approved a universal human rights law,

---

21 The webpage www.geocities.com/Capitol Hill/Parliament/2587/war.html is a reliable narrative of the Lebanese civil war. It contains a bibliography, but no references.

Sharon was accused before a Belgian tribunal. The jurisdiction claimed by Belgian legislators led to legal suits against President George W. Bush and Prime Minister Tony Blair over the Second Iraqi war. Israel disdained the proceedings. Afraid that Belgium might be getting in above its head, its prime minister, Guy Verhofstadt, announced that the law would be modified to apply solely in cases of Belgians victims of human rights abuses. Hobeika was killed in an explosion in 2002.

(27) What the PLO learned from the Lebanese civil war

From the Palestinian perspective the Lebanese incident was an enlightening defeat. The PLO was diminished as a fighting force. Arafat must have begun to realize that the uneven war the PLO was waging against Israel could not be won. He was faced with Sadat's dilemma, but on a far greater level of complexity. Sadat represented a sovereign state. But Arafat represented an aspiration, which was tainted by social terrorism. How could Arafat go about disarming Israeli antagonism and engage the enemy in negotiations?

International terrorism was discredited. To declare the end of hostilities with Israel would have been like laying down arms and Arafat would have lost prestige in the PLO itself. There was one card he could still play which was that the UN had recognized the PLO as legitimate representative of the Palestinians. It took Sadat six years to bring Israel around to negotiations. For Arafat, the process lasted twice as long and the results were nowhere near close to what Palestinians expected.

The Israeli intervention was getting mired in the Lebanese fighting. It was taking casualties without eliminating the threat to Israel. In these unpropitious circumstances, another MNF, composed like the previous one, landed in Beirut to separate the Israelis and the Lebanese. At first hopes were pinned on peace for Lebanon through the MNF, unrealistic considering its small size, but soon Muslims began to see Americans again as the enemy because of their key alliance with Israel. A van loaded with explosives rammed into the American Embassy leaving 63 dead, including 17 Americans. The Iran-backed Islamic Jihad claimed the deed.

Arafat was feeling pressure from the Syrians for not having ordered the PLO to fight to the death in Beirut and he left his Damascus offices for Tunisia barely escaping an assassination attempt. Syria was stepping up its efforts to get things in hand in Lebanon. This highly devious and bloody process would take nine years. It began with the formation of a National Salvation Front (NSF). Gemayel was tacitly accepted as Lebanese president, although the parties to the front—Muslims, Druzes, and Syria itself—controlled much more of Lebanon than he did. Syria encouraged a scission within the PLO, the Abu Musa faction, and fomented aggression against Arafat loyalists.

The IDF began phasing down its occupation of Lebanon, first out of Beirut and south to Sidon. Fighting between Druzes and Christians was at its peak during this period. On 23 October 1983, a terrorist drove a truck around in circles in a parking area in front of the USA barracks in southern Beirut. He was gathering impulse for a dash against the American military compound. The heavy vehicle crashed and smashed its way over various obstacles and was detonated next to the barracks. The detonation, which has been called the "single largest non-nuclear explosion" in history, killed 241 USA servicemen (mostly Marines). Shortly afterwards a lesser explosion devastated the French barracks producing 58 fatal military casualties. Syria is thought to have had a hand in both attacks, in part because of the sophistication of the bomb targeting the American troops.

His signature coif unruffled, the tip of an index finger resting on his ultra-thin lips, a look of mild distress in his eyes, Reagan saw the mess and prudently ordered withdrawal. American politicians had just learnt another lesson: rather than take politically damaging casualties it was better to lose face, even if the baddies went unchastised. Nine years later in Somalia, Clinton reacted exactly the same way as Reagan had in Lebanon. You couldn't win them all and the bottom-line was that if Americans got the shaft in Beirut they gave it to the Cubans in Grenada. The French and Italians also evacuated Lebanon and the Israeli incursion proved so costly and unproductive that it was terminated.

(28) The USA recruits a snarling partner to help in Afghanistan the sort of people it hated in Iran

The greatest and most successful proxy-war America backed was in Afghanistan and not against Russian proxies like the Cubans but against the Russians themselves. When the Soviets invaded Afghanistan, they did so because this country's radical regime, inherently unstable, was under threat by scattershot Muslim traditionalism based in the countryside and its numberless villages. By then the Iranian ayatollahs had made Islamic fundamentalism famous—or infamous depending on your perspective—but certainly forceful enough to have a global impact.

The Afghan traditionalists were your Iranian fundamentalists writ large. Basically, they wanted their women in purdahs or burqas (baggy head-to-toes black dresses with vertical slits to see through); they did not want them in schools or in the professions or in government; they wanted sharia law at its crudest (stonings and maimings); and they wanted the letter of the Koran respected in all things. In lieu of universities they preferred madrasas (religious schools). Above all, they did not want foreign atheists crossing them, and the Russians in Afghanistan were both foreign and atheists.

The majority of Afghans were still living in more or less medieval conditions, save for modern guns, and they couldn't have driven the Soviets out of Kabul any more than they could the British almost exactly a century before. But unlike 1879, when the British did not have to contend with the Russians themselves, Soviet-occupied Afghanistan no longer bordered on British India but on sullen and pugnacious Pakistan.

The reason for Pakistan's snarling temper was that shortly after World War II British India had been partitioned along roughly religious lines, Hindus in India and Muslims in Pakistan. But the partition was not achieved peacefully. There were countless Muslims in India—India still is the third largest Muslim country in the world (after Indonesia and Pakistan)—and there were countless Hindus in Pakistan. In the messy Partition process, most if not all Hindus fled to India and many Muslims to Pakistan. To get to their respective destinations, Muslims and Hindus were crossing each other's paths and when they did mayhem often ensued.

Partition involved the greatest movement of populations in history: 10,500,000 in Punjab, half going to India and half to Pakistan. Another million went through the same anguishing ordeal in Bengal. The estimates of fatalities in the clashes between the migrating masses (mostly in Punjab), as well as in chaotic rioting in cities, is between 200,000 and half a million. The most devastated city was Lahore (ceded to Pakistan), where a population of half a million Hindus and Sikhs was butchered or forced to emigrate. There were reciprocal slaughters at a basic community level. Calcutta and New Delhi were hard struck by the violence. Lord Louis Mountbatten, the last British viceroy, can be faulted for the haste in which Partition was decided and carried out. Calcutta, where Muslims lived in large numbers under British rule, was so badly torn by religious riots that Mohandas K. Gandhi, the Mahatma or Great Soul of Indian politics, went there expressly to fast, the most powerful weapon in his moral arsenal, and exert pressure on the warring communities. He managed to temper the carnage. Upon his return to Delhi, he fasted again for India to allot to Pakistan the agreed part of their previously common treasury and he was shot dead by a Hindu fanatic who felt he was giving in to Muslim demands.[22]

22 G.D. Khosla, *Stern reckoning: a survey of the events leading to and following the partition of India* (1948); Dominique Lapierre and Larry Collins, *Freedom at midnight* (1975)

Among the complications of Partition one derived from the time of the first British invasion of Afghanistan. The British had an alliance with the puny-looking but strong-willed Ranjit Singh, the ruler of Punjab, against Dost Muhammad, the Afghan emir. Many Sikhs were part of the invasion force. After Ranjit Singh died, his successors were no match for the British, who annexed the Punjab. The British never lacked for either Hindu or Muslim accomplices to aid them in their gradual subjection of India. In the Punjab it was the Hindu general Gulab Singh who helped them and was rewarded with the dependent throne of Muslim Kashmir. During Partition, his descendant, Hari Singh, had to face a disorganized Pakistani attempt at annexation. He fled to the Hindu part of his kingdom, where he ceded all of it to India. Indian troops were airlifted and they contained the Pakistani invasion force, which at first was mainly a levy of undisciplined Pathans lured by the prospect of looting.

That was hardly the end of it. India allowed elections in Kashmir, which Muslims as often as not boycotted, but it refused to permit a plebiscite on Kashmiri preferences and Pakistan charged that Indian politicians were holding Kashmir hostage. Kashmir includes Jammu, which is majority Hindu, so the Indians could claim that they were not intruders in the state of Jammu and Kashmir. Pakistan was not about to fall for that line of argumentation. Kashmir could be partitioned as all of British India had been, but the Indians were not disposed to concede any Pakistani points.

(29) A schizoid Pakistan stands on the sidelines cheering Chinese aggression on India

Indians and Pakistanis were at war in 1965 and in 1971. Both times Pakistan lost. In 1965, India had to beat off a Pakistani tank offensive in the Rann of Kutch, a desert in Gujarat (northwestern India). In a second round Pakistan tried to choke the corridor to Kashmir, but a concerted Indian land offensive towards Lahore put the Pakistanis on the defensive. In the air the Pakistanis had an ace, M.M. Alam, who in one minute flying a Sabre jet made five Indian kills (Hawker Hurricanes). The Indians had a heroic infantryman who single-handedly destroyed three Pakistani tanks firing rockets from the shoulder before being gunned down. Pakistan underestimated India's pluck and saw its forces whittled down to size.

In 1971, East Pakistan rebelled against West Pakistani rule. East Pakistan was really eastern Bengal. West Pakistan was composed of various provinces, Punjab being the largest in terms of population, and the name Pakistan was an invention: either an acronym of Punjab-Afghan province-Kashmir-Sindh or a composite word meaning "land of the pure". The first etymology, which would give a handle to Afghan claims on northwestern Pakistan, doesn't sound quite right.

The East Pakistanis spoke Bengali and the West Pakistanis different tongues, mainly Punjabi and Urdu. East Pakistan was the principal foreign-exchange earner for the nation through its jute exports, but central political power was concentrated in West Pakistan and East Pakistan believed it was not being given the consideration it deserved. When West Pakistani reprisals provoked an exodus of East Bengali refugees into India, the Indian armed forces intervened and smothered West Pakistani military resistance. East Pakistan became independent Bangladesh.

Jawaharlal Nehru, the first Prime Minister of India, was a socialist in the sense that he believed in rigid economic controls, although he also favored huge private consortia to aid the government in industrializing India. He did not get very far with those policies and India is still wrestling with bureaucratic and other vices acquired during its infancy. Nehru was also one of the original founders of the so-called non-aligned movement promoted by Tito of Yugoslavia. India was a democracy and it had a thin Western cultural veneer. During and after British colonialism, Indian middle classes have spoken English as a second and sometimes even as a first language. India's neutralism or non-alignment consisted in an informal alliance with the USSR, which was India's principal arms supplier.

Pakistan was solidly with the west as a member of SEATO and CENTO, a somewhat schizoid position as it placed it in both the Middle East and South East Asia. But it would have been with the West under any circumstances if only to spite India. Pakistan was so obsessed with the Kashmir issue that it made an alliance with China when Chinese-Soviet relations were strained to the breaking point. When the Chinese attacked India to occupy a barren portion of Ladakh (Aksai Chin) over which they had built a highway between Tibet and Xinjiang, Pakistan stood cheering on the sidelines.[23]

(30) The Afghans did to the Soviets what the Vietnamese had done to America, with a significant difference

Pakistan was drifting towards fundamentalism even before the Iranian revolution. Not surprisingly, when the USSR invaded Afghanistan and the Americans decided on war-by-proxy, Pakistan eagerly became the middleman between the USA and Afghan guerrillas. A more ideal situation could hardly have been imagined for Pakistan, who in one deal strengthened its hand against India through the American connection, undermined India's principal arms provider and long-term ally, and struck a blow for Islam. On the other hand, the USA couldn't have found a

---

23 Parvéz Dewân, *Ladakh* (2005), p. 362.

better partner to needle the Russians than Pakistan, whose military intelligence service was imbued with Islamic mystique and, because of the continuing low-intensity conflict in Kashmir, was adept at cross-border infiltration. This marriage made in Paradise would turn out to be the cause of America's worst nightmare. By the time all its weirdness was revealed, including such a monumental failure of intelligence as can hardly be imagined, America had made Pakistan a major partner.

The objective of the original American-Pakistani alliance was to bloody the Russians so much that they would admit defeat and evacuate Afghanistan. This was in general terms much like what the Russians and Chinese did to the USA in Vietnam, with a significant difference for the future of Afghanistan and of the world.

In Vietnam, the independence movement got its real start against the Japanese occupation. There is some irony in that Japanese colonialists, unlike the French, usually made a show of favoring independence movements in the countries they occupied. This was not as hypocritical as it sounds. The Japanese installed a spurious independent government in the Philippines, where they were detested. But they armed an Indian division, led by the nationalist S.C Bose, and they gave Sukarno, a genuine independence leader, enough space to formulate principles for an Indonesian state. The difference in the Japanese attitudes towards the Philippines and towards Indonesia lay in that the Philippines as a whole was a major Japanese military base—and even so, there were many Filipino resistance movements—but the Japanese occupation of what until then had been the Dutch East Indies was much looser, almost peripheral, and was designed basically to ensure the supply of natural resources, especially oil.

What the Japanese occupied in Vietnam were the French dependencies of Tonkin and Annam (north and central Vietnam) and of Cochin-China (southern Vietnam), hence theoretical possessions of Vichy France, a German puppet but formally a Japanese ally. The Japanese occupiers didn't even go through the motions of fomenting independence, until the very end of the war.

The Vietnamese communists acted on their own when they founded the Vietminh independence movement and when they formed their own clandestine armed forces. The latter were under the command of Gen. Vo Nguyen Giap, but the supreme and undisputed leader of the Vietminh was Ho Chih Minh, once a street photographer in Paris (among many diverse occupations). When their homeland surrendered, the Japanese in Hanoi handed over power to the Vietminh. The Nationalist Chinese who accepted the local Japanese capitulation ratified this.

When the metropolitan French returned and tried to re-impose colonialist rule in Vietnam, they faced, in the north at least, one independence movement under the direction of one leader and a unified resistance command. In Afghanistan, armed resistance to secularist, leftist rule had begun before the Soviet invasion, but after the Russians arrived it became like "a thousand points of light", except that these lights were more like the torches of a lynch mob, and they did not follow one leader but many different warlords.

(31) In hindsight America's meddling in Afghanistan might have been an ill-considered strategy

Even though Americans were the paymasters, it was the Pakistanis who smuggled in and apportioned the weaponry. After the Iranian gantlet, the Americans had reasons to be suspicious of fundamentalism, but not necessarily of Pakistani fundamentalists. They reasoned correctly that power politics provide stronger motivations, on the whole, than religious fanaticism. This turned out to be true when Pakistan supported America in the War on Afghanistan, but, in view of the events leading to 9/11, it could have been considered an ill-conceived strategy.

For the purpose of striking at the Russians, the Pakistanis did not have to show favoritism, so arms were allotted to all the Afghan resistance factions. Renowned for their marksmanship, the Afghans had become adept at the use of the famously effective Soviet-designed Kalashnikov automatic rifle. This weapon is so uncomplicated that it was replicated in hundreds of workshops in northwestern Pakistan and in Afghanistan. First used in World War II, the Kalashnikov is the weapon of choice in warring countries all over Asia and Africa, but nowhere does it have a stronger association with a people than with the Pathans of the Pakistani Northwest Province and of southern and eastern Afghanistan. Afghan logistic competence did not rise much above the Kalashnikov and when Afghan fighters were given weapons even as lowly as mortars they handled them as they would a live grenade or a lit stick of dynamite. After short but intensive field training, they overcame their initial apprehensions and became quite proficient at downing Soviet aircraft with shoulder-held SAMs, perhaps the deadliest infantry weapon ever devised.

The Russians were barely holding their own in the cities, but even approaching Kabul airport Soviet military transports had to do zigzag patterns to avoid getting hit by SAM snipers that it would have taken battalions to chase down in the surrounding hills, and during the entire Afghan war the Russians never committed on average more than 100,000 troops. Americans were so cocksure about their anti-Soviet strategy in Afghanistan that they even financed the printing of fundamentalist texts for distribution in Afghan-controlled areas as educational aids and morale builders. They were basically catering to prejudices and passions that hardly needed encouragement, perhaps on the advice of their Pakistani allies and bridge-builders.

(32) On Muslim fundamentalism, America was burning both ends of the candle

Of the proxy-wars waged by the Reagan administration the one that required the greatest secrecy and bristled with most possibilities for cross-purposes and other pitfalls, and pratfalls, was the one undertaken on the side of Saddam Hussein against Iran. Iraq and Iran had been at odds for control of Shatt al Arab, the natural channel formed at the confluence of the Tigris and the Euphrates rivers.

Shatt al Arab flows for most of its length in Iraq, where Basora or Basra, one of Iraq's largest cities, lies on its right bank. However, for the last 75 kilometers or so before it empties into the Arabian or Persian Gulf, the left coast of the waterway had been occupied by Iran, to which it had been ceded by the Ottoman Empire in the 19th century. The Iranian island of Abadan in this section of Shatt al Arab is the site of what once was the largest oil refinery in the world. In theory, Iraq had sovereignty over the channel but in practice Iran shared in this sovereignty. The ambiguity arose because in the 1930s and 1940s American and British oil interests, as they operated equally in Iran and Iraq, were not particularly finicky about the frontiers between the two countries.

At the time when the Shah was standing tall and Iran was considered a crucial American ally, the Iranian government denounced the treaty that gave Iraq formal sovereignty over Shatt al Arab. Because of Abadan, Iran wanted the boundary moved to the thalweg (the middle of the river). The Iraqis were pressured through military help for rebellious Iraqi Kurds and the dispute was patched up with the recognition of Iran's claim.

In the early stage of the Iranian revolution, the ayatollahs, led by their revered Khomeini, dabbled in inflaming the Middle East with their Islamic fervor, as was the case of Hizbollah in Lebanon. Iranian Shia militancy did not inspire confidence in nearby Arab countries that saw in Iraq and its leader Saddam Hussein a shield against Iranian subversion.

The Iraqi dictator decided to cut the Gordian knot of Iran-Iraq relations by attacking and invading Iran. Hussein did not know the wasps' nest he was meddling with. The Iranians were at the acme of their revolutionary fervor. If they had defied the USA out of sheer bravado, no presumptuous Arab despot was going to cow them. Since relations between the USA and USSR had deteriorated to very unfriendly levels because of Afghanistan, this was also a good time for radical regimes of whatever hue in developing countries to ripple their biceps. Thus began the curious circumstances in which a fundamentalist regime in Iran felt emboldened against the USA at the same time, as fundamentalism in Afghanistan was still a real policy option for America. Stranger combinations were shortly to follow.

(33) A Shia Iran and a Shia Iraq were about the worst domino game America could play

If the Soviets miscalculated in Afghanistan, Iraqi aggression against Iran was not a miscalculation but a phenomenal blunder. Iraq's longest and most irregular border is with Iran. For much of its length it follows foothills or mountainous areas in which Iran commands the heights. Iran had three and a half times the population of Iraq. Much of it was young and passionately devoted to the thundering Khomeini. Iraq was not significantly better armed than Iran. It did have poison gas and its dictator and the male members of his family were not finicky about the means of coercion they used. But all in all, Iraq was at a disadvantage and this soon began to show.

Dislike and mistrust of Iran ran high in the American government and these attitudes bred fears. During the Cold War the possibility of "falling dominoes" was never far from American strategic thinking, basically because Americans simply do not trust people who are not in their same league of economic development or as attached as they are to democracy. The fear was that Iran would turn the tables on Saddam Hussein and instead of Iraq getting full possession of Shatt al Arab, Iran would get possession of Iraq, which was conceivable, and if Shia Iran and Shia Iraq acted jointly, why, it was not unimaginable that the entire Middle East would be subverted and that it would rise like a huge sandstorm against the West. The USSR could not fail to try to take advantage of such a situation. The Soviets would then of course win the Cold War and conquer the world. The line between the "not unimaginable" and a real threat is not wide in these cases.

Besides, whether the reasoning was sound or not, America could not stand around with its arms folded while a part of the world went to pot, especially a part whose own pot was already brimming with oil. There was also the matter of not losing face, which throughout the Cold War was as important to the two superpowers as any strategic consideration. The usual reason alleged for American interventions in the third world was that people there, especially in Asia, did not like losing face and so America, who, with the USSR, was a great face-saver, had to act in such a manner that it did not lose face. Since losing face is simply a matter of not giving in and since America has given in only seldom in its history, then the losing-face reflex is more likely American than Asian and still more likely universal than specifically either American or Asian.

The upshot was that the USA decided that it was to its advantage to side with Iraq against the detested Khomeini and his revolutionary guards and so Donald Rumsfeld, a trusted Reagan aide, was dispatched to Iraq various times until he finally met Saddam Hussein personally. Whatever their personal rapport might have been—Rumsfeld probably had to dissimulate a lot, but no one really knows at this point—the two finalized a low-key but very consequential alliance of convenience. Iraq and America established diplomatic relations. More importantly, the USA began to feed Iraq satellite-gathered intelligence on Iranian troop movements, by which means Iraqi numerical inferiority in the war was discounted.

(34) America was engaged in three proxy wars and sometimes its right foot didn't know where the left foot was treading

If ever an American president followed Theodore Roosevelt's advice to speak softly and carry a big stick, it was Ronald Reagan. Through the incongruous understanding between a ruthless Arab dictator and the world's greatest democracy, Americans got off the rocks that had been weighing on them since the Iranians had sequestered their diplomats, one of the major disrespects inflicted on a great power in the Post-War. The secrecy involved in these operations was not without perils.

America was then engaged in three proxy-wars: in the Middle East, in Afghanistan, and in Central America. Covert operations by their very nature tend to create situations in which one hand might not know what the other one is doing. Or feet might stumble over each other. Financing for them is not usually above board. And this was what had been happening when the Iran-Contra scandal came into the open. Given its "banana republic" status, Nicaragua did not excite American rancor the way Iran and the USSR did. Grenada had not either, so basically Reagan had acted decently in sparing Grenadians the trials of a tyrannical, Cuban-type regime, although American intervention was undertaken less to spare Grenadians anything than to humiliate Castro.

Reagan's White House was not given carte blanche by Congress in Nicaragua. But the Sandinists had to go. The administration had been making profits selling arms to Iran in order to liberate hostages in Lebanon. This already was somewhat dodgy but it was humanitarian, hence not unethical. Not so unimpeachable complications arose with the disposal of the profits. That was when John Poindexter, Reagan's security adviser, and Col. Oliver North, his operations man, came up with the stranger-than-fiction scheme to use them to finance the Contras.

The arms deal with Iran did not square with the rapprochement with Iraq and it favored the unsavory ayatollahs, but the armaments involved were not large enough to offset the aid that America was giving Iraq. Thus America was both undermining and aiding one enemy, Iran, to sabotage another enemy, Nicaragua. From another angle, it was being complicit with a big menace, if strategic fear of Iran was to be taken seriously, in order to get rid of a mere nuisance such as the Sandinists.[24]

From the perspective of the Second Iraqi war, American cynicism in the Middle East could be accounted for as evidence that the USA had picked Iraq as the lesser of two evils. Events would show that it was the wrong choice, but also that once it was made the USA stuck to it even when it could have backed off and prevented bad from becoming worse. Whatever the margin for honest error, though, the seeds of the Second Iraqi War, and of the Gulf War and even 9/11, were sown when America consecutively gave its backing to two dictators: the Shah of Iran and Saddam Hussein of Iraq. The shah's fall led to the end of Iranian friendship with America and this made it possible for the USA to befriend Iraq, Iran's enemy. Assuming American support, Iraq began acting up and America garrisoned Saudi Arabia. Fundamentalists, Osama bin Laden foremost among them, took umbrage at the presence of American troops in Arabia precisely at a time when the Israeli-Palestinian conflict was beginning to boil over. It must be said that as Hussein consumed a lot of Iranian fundamentalist zeal, at first he was probably not seen by the USA and especially by his Arab neighbors as a bad investment.

---

24 Poindexter surfaced in headlines again in July 2003 when it was reported that he was proposing in the Pentagon a "futures market in terror", the idea being that whoever predicted a specific terrorist act which came to pass would stand to make a profit. The scheme was considered shocking and Poindexter resigned his post as advisor. Terrorist attempts are of course often unsuccessful. The obvious flaw in Poindexter's idea was that terrorists themselves could predict terrorist acts, attempt them anyway standing out of the way, and get paid for it into the bargain. Some Wall Street commentators didn't think it was such a bad idea but that it needed polishing.

3

The Inexplicably Inevitable Rise of Gorbachev

The world might have started on its brief roll when Michael Gorbachev became secretary general of the Communist Party of the USSR (CPSU).[1] To an external observer his ascent could not have seemed very promising. Stalin died on 5 March 1953. Officially he died from a stroke. It is possible that his death was induced. There can be little doubt that medical assistance to the Soviet despot was crucially delayed. As Stalin lay dying, Lavrenti Beria, head of the NKVD, did not dissimulate his glee. Or perhaps he lived in such fear and was so relieved that his reaction was a nervous reflex.

After a funeral procession characterized by mass hysteria and deaths by suffocation and trampling in crowds, Stalin's heirs opted for what seemed like an inevitable and sensible solution: collective leadership. Georgi Malenkov became prime minister, technically chairman of the council of ministers, and Vyacheslav Molotov and Beria deputy prime ministers. Nikolai Bulganin occupied the important post of minister of defense.

Stalin had been secretary general of the politburo of the central committee (CC) of the CPSU. The politburo was the standing committee of the CC. After a party congress in 1952, Stalin enlarged it and renamed it presidium, but he did not otherwise modify its authority.

Despite their republican and egalitarian posturing, communists have been the most intense devotees of political pomp and ceremony in our times, perhaps in history, which in effect has made them inaccessible

1 The account of the Gorbachev and the Yeltsin years (to 1996) is significantly based on David Remnick, *Lenin's Tomb* (1993) and *Resurrection* (1997).

and pretentious as rulers. In keeping with his parody of proletarian simplicity, Stalin, who like Hitler never wore medals, gave up the post of secretary general of the party around the time, before World War II, when he had become not just the party leader but the absolute autocrat of the USSR. He put himself at the top of the list of party secretaries, hence inferentially the first secretary, but in principle the equal of the others or at most a primus inter pares. That was of course pure stagecraft and every one from Stalin down, in and out of the USSR, knew who was the boss, as the Chinese knew unmistakably that Deng Xiaoping, a mere chairman of a military committee, was at the top of the pecking order in his country during the time he held that post. With Stalin dead, Malenkov also occupied the rank of first secretary.

(1) The peasant who let the genie out of the bottle

The perspectives for collective leadership in a country where the cult of personality had been deliberately made a religion-substitute were not very good. The collective leaders turned on Beria, either because they felt relegated by him or had real evidence that he was conspiring to make himself dictator. Beria was acting as if he was the boss and, curiously enough for a pervert who reputedly serially raped unconscious women, he initiated the process of de-Stalinization by opening some gulag exit doors. His hatred of Stalin was perhaps greater than that of the other members of the party presidium, possibly because he had to bear more than the others with Stalin's omnipotent insolence.

Beria was arrested and executed and so were his closest associates in the following three years, which suggests that there was more to his dispatch that mere moral scruples about Beria's role as Stalin's executioner.[2] These purges were the last publicly acknowledged political executions in the USSR. About a country so given to secrecy and arbitrary methods, however, it would be unpardonably disingenuous to believe that extreme abuse of authority ceased when Beria was eliminated.

Even with this upper-echelon purge, collective leadership did not survive for long. The person who emerged as the main wielder of power, Nikita Sergeyevich Khrushchev, was at first not even in the forefront of

---

2 To close the cycle of terror in the late 1930s, which, though naturally unpublicized in Soviet media, was so vast that it was beginning to give Soviet society the twitches, Stalin dismissed Nikolay Yezhov as head of the NKVD. He replaced him with Lavrenti Beria, and this man, who was considered in the 1940s and the early 1950s as the epitome of communist terror, actually toned down the Stalinist terror, although he kept the machinery in place and in mint condition. Orlando Figes, *A people's tragedy: the Russian Revolution 1891-1924* (1996); Robert Conquest, *The Great Terror: Stalin's Purges in the Thirties* (1973);. Simon Sebag Montefiore, op.cit.

Stalin's successors, even though he was part of Stalin's inner circle. He frog leaped over all the other CPSU secretaries and, displacing Malenkov, was officially ranked first secretary, formally the same as Stalin had been.

Khrushchev was the son of peasants, but his father also worked as a miner and Khrushchev preferred to think of himself as of proletarian origin. He and his wife, Nina Petrovna, could have been, as they say, chosen by central casting for the part of Russian mujiks. But Nina Petrovna, Babushka face and all, was a party activist who originally had an educational edge on her husband. Later, as communist boss of Ukraine, Khrushchev showed a keen interest in agriculture. He was as communist as they came and he sincerely believed that planning could beat a free market any day.

He had big projects for the USSR and he did not want interlopers. He overhauled the NKVD, Beria's vipers' nest, which was renamed KGB (committee for state security), ironically the designation under which it became most notorious in the West despite having been much more murderous under its previous avatars. Khrushchev launched the policy known as "virgin lands", or the plowing of steppe lands in Kazakhstan and western Siberia to expand cultivated acreage in lieu of increasing the productivity of existing farmland. Collective leadership was formally maintained, although Malenkov's substitution by Khrushchev as top party leader indicated that there was agitation in the Soviet corridors of power. But Stalinism as a political system of one-man despotism was dead. Khrushchev gave it a funeral oration in his so-called secret speech to the 20th Party Congress on 25 February 1956.

(2) Khrushchev sends Malenkov to Ust-Kamenogorsk with the unlikely excuse that he was an "anti-party man"

In Soviet history, this political document rivals in importance with "Lenin's will" (1922-1923), perhaps the most renowned and useless denunciation in history. Stalin, the object of Lenin's criticism, edited Lenin's words for other communists, and even if he hadn't, Lenin's complaints were probably too late and so mild—Stalin was described as "impolite"—that they would be one of history's great comic anti-climaxes if Stalin's crimes weren't so enormous. It is on the basis of that farcical document that Lenin's admirers have built a drama in which Stalin plays the villain even as understudy during Lenin's brutal dictatorship.

If Lenin was only moderately scolding, Khrushchev went to excess, for not content with revealing Stalin's use of sadistic state terror he also tried to depict him as a coward and a quitter, specifically when Germany attacked the USSR, and that wasn't something even the most phobic

Kremlinologist was about to swallow. Khrushchev's intervention in the 20th Congress also came out in favor of peaceful co-existence with capitalism, which had been Malenkov's tune and, ironically, one of the reasons for his demotion.

As in empires throughout history, Soviet policies were never without significant consequences. Khrushchev's denunciation of Stalin was especially influential on events that followed, although the ultimate causes of those events were rooted in previous Soviet imperialism. Hungarian communists tried to chew off the Soviet lead around their necks. For a few days they got away with hustling out and executing political police, but Soviet tanks rolled into Budapest and the restored communist regime inveigled and later executed Imre Nagy, the leader of the Hungarian insurrection and a former communist prime minister. Not for nothing Stalin had given the Ukraine a border on Hungary. When Polish communists also became so recalcitrant that they would probably have opposed a Soviet invasion. Over Moscow's discontent, the reasonably nationalistic, but still communist, Wladislaw Gomulka became Poland's leader.

Khrushchev consolidated his authority by dismissing Molotov, Malenkov, and Lazar Kaganovich at one go from the party presidium with the unlikely excuse that these men, life-long Bolsheviks and apparatchiks, constituted an "anti-party group". Malenkov had survived his first defeat but this time he was completely ousted from power and ended up managing a hydroelectric dam in Ust-Kamenogorsk, somewhere in Kazakhstan. Molotov was posted to Mongolia as ambassador, later named Soviet representative to a UN agency in Vienna. Kaganovich, originally a Jewish cobbler and later one of Stalin's henchmen, was given the lowly task of managing a cement plant.

But Khrushchev was no despot, perhaps mainly because he did not have Stalin's absolute hold on the party. Bulganin was kept on as prime minister and even accompanied Khrushchev on junkets, until he too was retired by Khrushchev. Anastas Mikoyan, a genial Armenian, also palled around with Khrushchev and made friends for the USSR abroad. He was adaptable and survived Khrushchev's downfall.

(3) A thaw that was more like an Indian summer

Khrushchev on the whole was well intentioned but he was not one to weaken party control. After his denunciation of Stalin there was a period, known as the thaw, when free expression was given some leeway. Ilya Ehrenburg, usually conventionally Stalinist in his writing, was the one who first used the image, explicitly represented in a Russian period film, of winter ice melting into a clear spring brook. But Boris Pasternak's *Dr. Zhivago,* which was crude about the infancy of communism, did not find a publisher in Russia and a communist editor first printed the novel in Italy. Pasternak was awarded the Nobel Prize for literature. Given a choice by Soviet authorities between rejecting it or travelling to Stockholm and not being allowed to return, he chose to remain in Russia. Pasternak's experience was the model upon which the samizdat "industry" was created and flourished: officially unprintable works were chain-copied, circulated within the USSR, and smuggled out of the country, where some were published, others not.

Soviet censorship had a devastating effect on a gentle patriot such as Pasternak, who did not survive his disgrace as a bona fide Soviet author for long. In the case of the bilious Aleksandr Solzhenitsyn, the recoil was horrendous. Solzhenitsyn's novelette "One day in the life of Ivan Denisovich", about living conditions in a Siberian labor camp, was published through Khrushchev's personal intervention. Solzhenitsyn, a one-time officer in the Red Army, was fed up with the political persecution of freedom of expression and he began to write furiously denouncing the Soviet system. With his galloping boldness and Khrushchev's forcible retirement, his lengthy, over-written works went unpublished. Khrushchev had probably supported him in the first place because Solzhenitsyn is not entertaining, hence did not seem likely to get a wide and durable following, but his testimony on the Stalinist prison system was the ideal literary pendant to Khrushchev's secret speech. "Denisovich" sold in the millions.

Via samizdat and foreign publication, Solzhenitsyn gained a big following abroad and he too won the Nobel Prize. Placed in the same disjuncture as Pasternak, he too declined emigrating. His voluminous *Gulag Archipelago,* a denunciation of the vast and complex Soviet system for detaining, mistreating, and liquidating political dissidents or any one the regime did not like, appeared in the West and the Soviet authorities raised a hue and cry. Solzhenitsyn was arrested, his citizenship was annulled, and he and his family were exiled. Reading Solzhenitsyn had become almost dutiful in the West, and the writer, who also now could collect his Nobel Prize money, was a wealthy man and could afford to live in splendid, almost paranoid isolation in Vermont, which he did until after the dissolution of the USSR.

(4) Mao thought that Khrushchev was an upstart and Khrushchev thought that Mao was barmy

Khrushchev's supremacy was beset by problems, some of them of his own creation, but by no means all. Mao Zedong had established communism in China mainly with indigenous resources. The USSR welcomed him, but it had not always been unconditionally supportive of Chinese communists. Before World War II, the Comintern, the Soviet organization for the promotion and coordination of revolutionary movements everywhere, had urged on them an alliance with the Guomindang, the party of Chiang Kai-shek, a nationalist who hated communists. Stalin was then calling the shots from Moscow. The original Chinese communists were city-bred, but Mao himself had rural roots although he had a good urban education. The Chinese city communists' obedience to Comintern instructions resulted in their slaughter in Shanghai and Canton. The Shanghai massacre was the subject of André Malraux's novel *Man's fate* (1933), once basic reading for fellow-travellers, which consisted in the last thoughts of a communist activist before being fed to a locomotive furnace.

Despite previous slights, Mao Zedong was willing to defer to Stalin as the leading figure in international communism, but not to an upstart like Khrushchev, who in turn believed that Mao's pretensions were barmy. Communist leaders, like mafia dons, were punctilious about ceremonials and Khrushchev and Mao were looking at different claims for precedence. Given that it was the USSR that had atomic bombs, and that it was Mao who had written that power comes out of the barrel of a rifle, Khrushchev had the better arguments, but China had the biggest population in the world and numbers had made a difference in Korea.

In any event, relations between the USSR and China went from bad to worse until the break was consummated with the Soviets packing up their blueprints and engineers from Eastern Europe abandoning their jobs in construction and industrial projects. China was then in the middle of a mind-boggling economic crisis because of Mao's absurd "Great Leap Forward"—a steel mill in every village—and the Soviet withdrawal came like an earthquake after a typhoon. Mao's leadership was so patently incompetent that he effaced himself, but only long enough to get military support and to plan the Great Cultural Revolution, in which young people were incited to attack and destroy anything that smacked of order, intellect, or tradition, sometimes even to torture and kill. That youth took to such directives with so much gusto is an indication that William Golding might not have been far from the truth in his depiction of children in the novel *The Lord of the Flies* as naturally cruel and barbarous.

Mao's Cultural Revolution was the model the Khmer Rouge imitated in Cambodia, except that they cut to the chase and just tortured and killed in the millions.[3] Nobody initiated a crusade to save Cambodia

3 Ben Kiernan, *The Pol Pot regime* (1996).

and it was only when the Cambodians began a piecemeal penetration of Vietnamese territory that the Vietnamese invaded Cambodia and overthrew the Khmer Rouge, a purely strategic move that was much denounced by the USA and China.

(5) Castro was Spain's hex on the USA

Fidel Castro occupied Havana on 1 January 1959.[4] Unlike traditional Latin American government-over throwers, usually called revolutionaries, who until then had been content with overlooking such peccadilloes as torture and political murder, Castro inaugurated his regime with hundreds of drumhead-trial executions. In some documented cases, Castro's men practiced mock executions either as a means to obtain information or as chastisement for crimes that fell short of requiring a full execution. The legality behind all these measures was not at all clear.

It was self-evident that Castro was different—he acted very much like a Bolshevik—but, as he was not overtly contradicting the impression that he was democratic and reformist, no one suspected the hatred he bore America, which was obsessive. The origins of such an attitude are not hard to find in Latin America where leftism has always entailed basic Leninist anti-imperialism, inseparable from the closest to an empire in the Western Hemisphere and that is of course the USA. In the case of Castro, the detestation of the USA could be traced also to his Galician father who emigrated to Cuba precisely at the time when the Americans were gratuitously and systematically demolishing the shreds of empire that remained to Spain, and with that a great deal of Spanish pride, which can never be underestimated.

Soon after attaining power Castro veered to communism and America helped him to stay in power by encouraging the Cuban middle classes, the only ones that could mount an effective opposition, to flee to Florida, and by organizing a weak invasion of Cuba that was easily quashed. Latin American hearts beat in unison over what seemed like a well-deserved vengeance for resentments as recent as the CIA overthrow of the moderately leftist government of Jacobo Arbenz in Guatemala.

Just as his speeches, which could last ten hours or more, transcended anything in the history of declamation, so Castro wanted to transcend Latin America, and for that he made a firm alliance with the USSR, which under Khrushchev was actively recruiting allies in the third world. Khrushchev's greatest blunder in foreign affairs—and the USSR, like America, made some whoppers—happened when he tried to install medium-range missiles in Cuba that would open a nuclear flank next

4 Tad Szulc, *Fidel: a critical portrait* (1986).

door to the USA. Howard Taubman contends the whole scheme was Khrushchev's invention to get even with the USA for perceived humiliations inflicted on the USSR, but it is likely that Castro, who had the USA breathing down his back, had as much a say on the matter as Khrushchev did.

The myriad Castro-sympathizers in Latin America, not to speak of Cubans themselves, might have asked why Cuba could not do what it wanted to defend its sovereignty from American aggression, which was the excuse for the installation of the missiles; but from an American perspective having a nuclear threat in Cuba was tantamount to letting yourself get slapped around without lifting a finger in self-defense. The missiles were still in their crates, more were on the way in freighters, and the emplacements for them were till empty, so before things got out of hand, President John F. Kennedy took the nerve-jangling decision of telling the Soviets that their ships would be intercepted and impounded on the high seas, with the implication that further retaliations could follow. The Soviet ships turned back before reaching the American naval blockade line and the missiles already in Cuba were all taken back to the USSR.

The missiles crisis was on the whole constructive for both sides. The Kennedys, the president and his brother Robert, had negotiated with the Soviet ambassador Anatoly Dobrynin the removal, after a decent face-saving lapse, of American Jupiter missiles, of the same medium range as those destined for Cuba, from their base in Izmir, Turkey, which is what soon occurred. The USSR obtained American guarantees that Cuba would not be invaded, which, as the USSR had invaded Hungary and was still to invade Czechoslovakia, is not as cursory or offhand as might sound. And the missiles crisis was so hair-raising that the two superpowers signed the nuclear test ban treaty, a certain sign that both sides knew that they had been playing with matches in a gasoline depot.

But the USSR had, any way you looked at it, given in over Cuba and Khrushchev's colleagues in the presidium were keeping a tally against him. There was no pretense at collective leadership although there wasn't a Stalinist-type cult of personality either. When agricultural production, the platform on which Khrushchev had risen, took a beating, his rivals began to plot. That they had to maneuver with stealth but could actually maneuver without being exposed and disposed of demonstrates how tyrannical the USSR still was but also how far it had left Stalinism behind. Then the plotters struck. They summoned Khrushchev from a vacation in Abkhazia and confronted him with a list of charges in which it is hard to say which was the most damaging. He was accused of being dictatorial and letting a personality cult develop, but as this was to happen again in the 1970s, it is more likely that Khrushchev was the victim of political ambition, the lust for power that activates history, which in the USSR after Stalin was dissimulated with the cheesecloth of collective leadership. The anti-Khrushchev coup was an instance of collective leadership, but only to put itself in reverse, so to speak.

(6) When people in the former USSR wax nostalgic, they think of Brezhnev

Leonid Brezhnev, who took over the post of first secretary, headed the group that deposed Khrushchev and banished him to a dacha outside of Moscow. Aleksei Kosygin was the new prime minister and Nikolai Podgorny president. The KGB was in on the move. The present consensual version of the results is that Kosygin became the most influential member of the new collective leadership. But Khrushchev was set aside by the CC of the CPSU, not in the presidium of the Supreme Soviet, or in the council of ministers, and during the 23rd Party Congress, Brezhnev was elected secretary-general, which had been Lenin's and Stalin's rank, certainly one or various notches above first secretary. If Kosygin was indeed the top man in foreign affairs, as is often claimed, it was a precarious perch and the fiasco of Czechoslovakia was his undoing.

Initially without a veto from Moscow, Alexander Dubcek, the Slovak head of the Czechoslovak party, began to introduce reforms, which soon went far beyond de-Stalinization and Khrushchevism. This was the process variously known as the Prague Spring and as "socialism with a human face". It was like telling Soviet leaders that they were, to say the least, sourpusses frozen in time.

The Warsaw Pact, the Soviet counterpart to NATO, was put in motion and its communist neighbors invaded Czechoslovakia. Only East Germany and Romania abstained. The Germans did so probably because it would have smacked of a re-enactment of Hitler's destruction of Czech sovereignty. And Romania under Nicolas Ceausescu was taking a "neutralist" stance, much reported in the West, but as Ceausescu was an unreconstructed Stalinist, only a pantomime. Kosigyn lost his job to Brezhnev, who after that really did promote such a cult of himself that even today when people in the former USSR wax nostalgic about communism they usually have Brezhnev in mind. Brezhnev's consolidation of power took about as long as Khrushchev's, but when it was completed he was more securely in command. Again, Brezhnev was no Stalin and it was he who signed the SALT with Nixon, the first real attempt to reduce nuclear arsenals.

(7) As it led to the downfall of communism, Afghanistan was far worse than Khrushchev's adventurism in Cuba

When Brezhnev died, anyone could tell even from photographs that he was a semi-corpse being carried about or being held up by the people around him. In a very literal sense, "minders" is the word that comes to mind. But when he committed his greatest foreign policy blunder, the Soviet invasion of Afghanistan, Brezhnev was fully aware of what he was doing. As it led to the downfall of communism, Afghanistan was far worse than Khrushchev's adventurism in Cuba.

Brezhnev had a reputation for laziness and he tended to delegate, hence he probably encouraged initiatives within conventional Soviet canons. But he was surrounded by mediocrities. Afghanistan was such a predictable error that it is hard to understand how it came about in the first place. The invasion was delusional. The Russians might have been fooled by Afghanistan's lack of jungles. It is almost inconceivable that they did not realize (1) that Afghanistan's dry, rugged mountains were as formidable barrier as jungles for control of a country and (2) that SAMs would be as effective against their aircraft as they had been against American warplanes. Afghanistan was a mistake compounding such a vast quantity of previous errors that the Soviet system was literally cracking under the load, but this was not yet apparent even to the most percipient of Kremlinologists.

While Brezhnev was dying, Yury Andropov quit his post as head of the KGB to devote himself to the coming scramble for power. He was so good at it that when Brezhnev was finally pronounced officially dead, his peers chose him secretary-general. Because of Afghanistan and also because the Soviets had deployed the intermediate range SS-20 missiles, the Cold War was gusting again. Reagan was in the White House lambasting the USSR and its "evil empire". More effectively, he bucked the trend towards disarmament and increased America's defense spending. To counter the SS-20s, Pershing and cruise missiles were stationed in Germany. In sum, a new arms race was on. But it wasn't exactly as before. No country could win a nuclear war, no matter how many more missiles and bombs it added to its already existing arsenal, so it was that Reagan sought the advantage of the SDI.

Andropov lasted fifteen months as Soviet leader before dying from kidney failure. His successor, the even more infirm Constantine Chernenko, lasted eleven months before succumbing. Both Andropov and Chernenko were not exceedingly old when they died, 70 and 74 respectively, but they were in bad health. Their colleagues knew it, so in promoting first one and then the other they were apparently following a Buggins-turn rule.

(8) One of the most influential men that ever lived might not have known exactly what he was getting into

Among the other members of the presidium one stood out over the lot: that was Mikhail Gorbachev, also at 54 the youngest in the group. Already before Chernenko's demise Gorbachev had impressed Margaret Thatcher, the normally dour British prime minister, an anti-communist Boadicea even before Reagan came on the scene. Gorbachev had also already enunciated the two ideas that were to be the guiding principles of his tenure as Soviet leader: glasnost and perestroika, the former meaning "openness" and the latter "re-structuring". These concepts derived their impact not from themselves, but from their context. Their essential lack of originality was more than compensated by their novelty and their incongruence in a society that had prematurely old, ailing conformists for leaders. So how could Gorbachev have made it to the top?

Glasnost went against the grain of the policies that had victimized Russian intellectuals, notably Pasternak and Solzhenitsyn (but there were countless more), although these policies were hardly limited in application to men of letters. Perestroika was even more antithetical to Soviet values because it struck at the fundamental economic model that had prevailed in the USSR since the revolution: public ownership of the means of production and state allocation of resources according to "compulsory" economic plans. The plans, during the Stalin period, were elaborated for periods of five-years. They were coercive but, except in fancy and propaganda, their goals were never attained.

The surprising thing is not that Gorbachev succeeded Chernenko, but that he could do so with the help of men of whom the least one could suspect would be the remotest sympathy for more social openness and for the re-modeling of the Soviet economy. Gorbachev's political background was impeccable and in hindsight it is possible that Gorbachev himself did not comprehend the full implications of the ideas that he was promoting, so that it is also possible that Gorbachev, one of the most influential men that ever lived, might have achieved his eminence without knowing or wanting what he was getting into. Be that as it may, Gorbachev did not come out of a void: his reforms, which resulted in the destruction of the USSR, had to have some grounding in Soviet history.

(9) Gorbachev does a reverse Castro on the CPSU

Despite his titles, Brezhnev was probably more figurehead than any previous Soviet leader. He was the embodiment of Soviet society and especially of the CPSU. When Soviet archives are finally opened, it might be found that Brezhnev was a spokesman rather than a leader and that he was given his rank because the other Soviet hierarchs did not grudge it to such a mediocrity. Towards the end of his life another consideration might have come into play and it was that who would envy or feel inferior to a person who was more dead than alive.

During the Brezhnev years, there always loomed, almost above his boss, another figure, and one that was abhorrent to any self-respecting Western intellectual. That man was Mikhail Suslov. He looked big, but especially, with his intense, unfriendly look and his eyeglasses, he had the air of some one who thought very seriously about things and was not tolerant of opposition. Suslov was universally acknowledged as the Rottweiler of Soviet orthodoxy. In the USSR, his thinking was of the right sort and whoever did not think the way he did, and came to the attention of others, was sure to get into big trouble.

It was under Suslov's guidance that the procedure of branding and treating dissidents as mentally sick came into full and dreadful operation. In America, by contrast, even the certifiably insane were being released from asylums through the use of tranquilizers, although one of the results of this program was to increase the number of the homeless. Confinement in a psychiatric ward certainly beat Stalinism, to be sure, but at the time it seemed like the height of political impudence, almost as bad as being sent to a labor camp.

Suslov made his first impression by being particularly boisterous against maverick Tito. Within the collective-leadership arrangement, he backed Khrushchev but later dumped Khrushchev to promote Brezhnev. Gorbachev ascended within the party with Suslov's good will. In view of what Gorbachev later did, which was to flout everything that Suslov stood for, this could indicate various things. It could be that Gorbachev was hypocritical. Because of the circumstances of Soviet politics, he had to be such a master dissimulator that he managed to do a reverse Castro. After he was firmly in control, the Cuban dictator claimed that he had always been a communist.[5] Since Gorbachev did a comparable but inverse turnabout—from communist to libertarian—it was conceivable that he might have been a crypto-capitalist from the beginning of his career, although, unlike Castro, he has never made such an admission.

It is possible to dissimulate an intense dislike or a profound disagreement, but you can hardly keep up an act like that for years without revealing some inkling of the truth. It could be that in the mare

5 When Edward R. Murrow did a long distance interview of Castro in Cuba, he presented him as a reformer or a democrat. Castro, who spoke halting English, answered the cheery Morrow with moroseness so palpable that he felt obliged to explain it as fatique.

magnum of Soviet political sameness Gorbachev's eloquence was like a beacon of Marxist reformism. This would also explain how after Suslov died, at about the same time as Brezhnev, Gorbachev became the leading light in the presidium under Andropov, who is often cast as his patron. Gorbachev not only retained that position during Chernenko's tenure but also improved on it so much that fellow presidium members, and future detractors, Yegor Ligachev and Nikolai Rhyzkov, helped him on the way to the top. But if Gorbachev had so much support from Soviet reactionaries, and then he went and did the opposite of what they believed in, he couldn't have been speaking his true mind during his ascent to power, and what we have is the psychological problem of how it is possible to keep up such a two-faced act for so long. There is yet another possibility.

(10) The USSR was committed to ideals that it flouted with day-to-day regularity

There was an "ideological" counterpart in the USSR to American political democracy, social openness, and economic liberalism, and that was the humanist side of the Marxist state that could reiterate the old revolutionary mantras of liberty, equality, and fraternity even in the shadow of Stalinist sociopathy. However monstrous its aberrations in practice, Soviet communism always made a pretense of legality and especially it always claimed to stand for Marxist humanism. The USSR was supposed to be the "workers' paradise", but even more pointedly it avowed noble principles such as social justice, anti-racism, the equality and brotherhood of mankind, and so on.

The USSR, for example, founded a university in Moscow exclusively for students from the third world. It was named in honor of Patrice of Lumumba, the slain first leader of the independent ex-Belgian Congo. Patrice Lumumba University still exists. According to one version, the idea for the Nuremberg trials began at Yalta when Churchill proposed the summary execution of 50 top Nazis. Stalin countered that it should be 50,000 and Roosevelt toned that down to 40,000. Churchill got angry and left the informal meeting with Stalin trotting after him to say he was kidding. But as the Soviet armies entered Germany they formed courts to justify the execution of Nazis and the other Allies were forced to accept the principle of trials rather than outright executions.[6]

For Gorbachev, that what the USSR did was pay lip service to humanitarian principles might have mattered less than that the principles

6 Leon Goldensohn, *The Nuremberg Interviews*, edited by Robert Gellately (2004). Pp.vii-xiv.

themselves were never questioned. Soviet society was committed urbi et orbe to the ideals that were buffeted and trampled on a daily basis within itself. It was this kind of intellectual sophistry that gained for the USSR the on-and-off adhesion of a man like the agonizing French philosopher Jean-Paul Sartre, one only in a roster of fellow-travelers the world over that rivals in length Leporello's catalogue in *Don Giovanni*. In other words, Gorbachevism, often simply reduced to glasnost and perestroika, could have been not only a response to failure but also a spontaneous assertion of the much-trampled but still living ideals that made communism so appealing to so many millions all over the world, despite the gulag and despite the ban on travel and despite the overall political despotism.

Even if Gorbachevism had some ground in Soviet society, it was still subversive and Gorbachev still had to dissimulate if he wanted to achieve anything. During the time when he was making the pronouncements that caught the world's attention, he often spoke in a sybilline, sometimes seemingly incoherent and even ungrammatical manner. He wasn't the only one who in his time had to waffle.

President Eisenhower was not the most brilliant of elocutionists when he gave press conferences. In his racially conciliatory phase, Malcolm X also seemed to have this problem about making direct, easily graspable statements. It is one thing to be fully committed to the Soviet system and it is another to have to simulate commitment to a system you want to transform top to bottom from within. Eisenhower could not have been supreme commander of allied forces in Europe during World War II, president of Columbia University, and chief executive of the USA if he did not think capably and possessed the eloquence to communicate his thought. His biographers attribute his difficulties with phrasing to the trying circumstances in which he had to govern, the height of the Cold War (Stalin only died in the third year of his presidency) and the beginning of the civil rights movement prominent among them. Followers of Malcolm X expected their man, who knew the uselessness of permanent confrontation, to go on bating whites. Like Eisenhower before and Gorbachev afterwards, Malcolm X had to sound radical and send unradical signals at the same time. To put it in a homely way, try having to praise a dish you heartily dislike.

Intellectuals, who tend to see too many sides to an issue, seldom make good politicians, who always have to sound firm on issues or they equivocate and sound incoherent, although intellectuals are not safe from this trap, which makes them doubly handicapped: they cannot sound firm like politicians and they tend to equivocate like politicians but without the rewards (or discomforts) of politicians. Yet despite the ambiguities and incoherences, Gorbachev held his audience and got important people to give him a leg up, almost, one could say, in open defiance of their own interests.

(11) Perestroika was not about throwing out the communist baby with the capitalist bathwater

Besides Gorbachev did not want to undo everything that had gone before him or that was there when he got to the political pinnacle.[7] The Soviet system was capable of spectacular successes. Some of its war technologies were as good as America's. Before Reagan's SDI, the Soviets had experimented on its feasibility. When the USSR concentrated its resources, it could attain specific, sometimes awesome, goals, but this meant sacrifices in other sectors. In America economic freedom and entrepreneurial initiatives are the means by which the system performs at peak and policy goals do not interfere with over-all economic innovation and growth. If the Soviets had been capable of erecting an anti-missile shield they would not have hesitated, which means that they knew how weak they were. This makes Reagan's choice of terrain on which to challenge them a stroke of genius.

Gorbachev did not mind forfeiting the Soviet empire. But he did not pursue the dissolution of the USSR. Perestroika meant reform, radical reform, but it did not imply throwing out the window the entire communist economic system. He was not the only one who knew that it needed re-structuring.

The post-war history of the USSR can be told in terms of successive efforts to improve its economy, which is not without irony for Marxists claimed that economic realities determine the social "super-structure", such as judges sentencing according to economic interests, and a communist society in principle was beyond such a skewing of legality because it had no particular economic interests to benefit. It is true that in America government has been and often still is partial and supportive of big business, but if the Soviet leadership had constantly to be tampering with underlying Soviet economics, then obviously capitalism was the steadier of the two. Nevertheless, since the Soviet system worked, and sometimes did so extremely well, it did not seem on the surface to justify its total abolition. That it had been decaying for decades could not be denied either, and the leaders of the USSR had to know this first hand. Gorbachev certainly did and he also said that he knew how to reform it, which might be what made him interesting, especially as there was no reason to think that he wanted to go beyond tampering in the usual ways.

---

7 Mikhail Gorbachev, *Perestroika: new thinking for our country and the world* (1987).

(12) If you granted economic freedoms, why not abolish the CPSU and the KGB?

Khrushchev probably owed his ascendancy over the CPSU to his ideas on how to improve the Soviet economy. The "virgin lands" policy was the first significant measure he took once in power. Long before that, it was evident that economic centralization was burdensome and inefficient. Under Stalin, who ruled the USSR like an anthill, it didn't much matter. But his successors, even Beria but especially Malenkov, were concerned about consumers. Khrushchev replaced the economic ministries with "economic councils", which were more numerous than the ministries and permitted some independent management. It was less complicated to make coherent plans in one region or in one sector of the economy than in bureaucratic offices in Moscow where the signals received were at best over-optimistic and at worst completely unreliable, and in general so voluminous that it was impossible to sort them out.

Politics aside, the crucial difference between the Soviet and the American economies lay in that every American businessman was like a Soviet economic bureaucrat but working for his own benefit with the advantage of reliable information to make decisions of restricted scope in comparison with the entire economy. These traits of course meant that the American businessman was not like a Soviet bureaucrat at all, but they did imply that a Soviet insider could potentially function like an American businessman, which is, all things considered, what eventually has obtained.

In a further measure of economic de-centralization, Khrushchev went to the wolf's lair and created within the CPSU itself different sections for agriculture and for industry, which normally would have been anathema to orthodox Marxists. Khrushchev had smooth sailing until the agricultural sector faltered and, as he had already made a raft of other mistakes, an opposition united against his unorthodox ways toppled him.

There followed economic changes, which are often attributed to Alexei Kosygin, but they basically consisted in a reversion to the situation before Khrushchev's timid reforms, mainly the absorption by the central ministries of the economic councils. What Soviet leaders either refused to believe or believed but were afraid to act upon was that tinkering with economic institutions alone would not do the trick. Real change if it was to come had to be systemic, but that involved striking at public ownership, and this was of the essence in communism. They also had to concede some measure of economic freedom, but if this was granted, why not just abolish the CPSU and the KGB and all the other means of coercion?

(13) In the system created by Lenin and Stalin, Gorbachev could get away with making vague but loaded statements

Curiously, despite the previous record of economic incompetence—the USSR on its own couldn't even mass-produce a decent small automobile—the Brezhnev years, during which experimentation was set aside and orthodox Stalinist economics prevailed, were considered prosperous. The CIA accepted along general lines Soviet statistics on economic growth and even on occasions revised them upwards. This presumed Soviet prosperity seems like a conundrum as impenetrable as how it was that the USSR, burdened by Stalinist terror and limping from a depleted officer corps, with inferior armed forces and a second to third rate economy, could resist the full might of Germany and go on to crush its enemy utterly.

One explanation for victorious Stalinism is that the situation of the USSR when the Germans invaded wasn't as dire as it might seem. Most of the officers liquidated were those recruited by Trotsky from the old Tsarist army and Stalin counted with a group of extremely competent generals that had risen from the ranks during the revolution. These men, at one time known as the "military opposition" (Kliment Voroshilov was the most politically prominent of the group), more than compensated for the losses in the purges. They showed, especially marshal Georgi Zhukov, although others were on the same level of military proficiency, that they could not only match but also out-general the Germans.[8]

In the case of the literally unbelievable Soviet economic growth during the Brezhnev period, it is more likely that what the USSR actually achieved was an offsetting of population growth, low in Russia itself, to barely sustain a dreary standard of life. With the system it had been saddled with by Lenin and Stalin, the people of the USSR would never be able to opine freely or to travel abroad or to entertain hopes of improving their economic situation. They could if they succeeded at communist party politics, but this was not something within the reach of the average consumer. It was against this background that Gorbachev could get away with making intelligent observations about Soviet society and offering changes that could be expressed in loaded but vague concepts, which is only what glasnost and perestroika at first were.

That Gorbachev became party secretary general with the support of people who would later try to overthrow him and eradicate the changes he introduced indicates the host of ambiguities that were at play at the

8 Antony Beevor, *Stalingrad* (1998); Harold Shukman, ed., *Stalin's generals* (1993)

time. These people were attracted to Gorbachev and it cannot have been merely because of his eloquence or his charm. They were willing to accept reforms that did not overstep a certain boundary. What Gorbachev initially attempted were measures of the superficial sort that had come and gone before. He must have known that they were going to fail but he couldn't push the USSR towards radical change from one day to the next. He was bolder on the political and the international fronts than in the economic field.

A catastrophic incident showed that one of the really hopeless problems under the Soviet system was management. In the worst accident in the history of atomic-power generation, one of the nuclear cores of a gigantic plant located in Chernobyl, Ukraine, melted producing a detonation. The effects of Chernobyl, whose uncontrolled chain reaction released radioactive energy forty times as great as the Hiroshima and Nagasaki bombs together, are still being felt (although recent findings are that the efects of the radiation are beginning to die down). Although not in the form of an atomic mushroom, the explosion blew off the steel ceiling of part of the plant. Soviet engineers first covered part of the Chernobyl building in a leaky, concrete "sarcophagus". There are now plans for a huge hangar-like arch of steel, twelve meters thick and one hundred meters high, to be slid over the gigantic, radiating pile of twisted steel, concrete, debris, and dust.[9] Chernobyl could and should have been interpreted as a symbol of the difficulties, the entrenched, day-to-day incompetence of the system, that Gorbachev would have to face during the following years, but he had a tendency to underestimate opposition to his policies, perhaps because he figured that if he had been able to carry with him hidebound communists on an adventure that could only have seemed abhorrent to them, he was not likely to encounter greater or more dangerous obstacles.

(14) The convergences of unlikes in our times

One indirect way to ease the economic burden on the Soviet system was to start mending the old Cold War fences, which had been transgressed badly under Brezhnev provoking strong rebuke from Carter and an aggressively anti-Soviet attitude from the soft-talking but unsubtle Reagan. After becoming top Soviet leader, Gorbachev met Reagan in Geneva. Reagan was already committed to the SDI, but he and Gorbachev agreed on the initiation of new START talks. The easy, cordial relationship between Gorbachev and Reagan illustrates a curious tendency in international affairs during the last decades of the 20th

9 Guy Gugliotta, "A 20,000-ton steel shell will enclose the damaged Chernobyl reactor", IHT, January 1, 2003

century. It is what could be called the convergence of opposites and is probably strictly conjunctural.

Some convergences between unlikes were inevitable. When De Gaulle decided that for the good of France it was better to let Algeria go, he had no choice but to accept the Front of National Liberation, which united all anti-French opposition, as interlocutor. During the Portuguese revolution, the radical officers running it, who wished to be shot of colonial wars, had only to leave the field to existing guerrilla movements. Here likes converged, but Portuguese de-colonization was a rushed affair, in the case of East Timor a virtual abandonment. When P.W. De Klerk wanted to finalize apartheid in South Africa there was no credible counterpart other than Nelson Mandela and the African National Congress. De Klerk and Mandela grated on each other despite being "on the same side". In these cases, a political stalemate was resolved through the unavoidability for parties at opposite ends to meet and basically for one of the parties to make a renunciation of power.

But peace between Israel and Egypt was made between political contraries, Begin and Sadat, who did not renounce to anything basic and had the alternative of not meeting at all. It was during the administration of Richard Nixon that America reconciled itself to the fact that communist China was not going to go away. Nixon's political career began with a cynical anti-communist smear campaign in a California senatorial contest against the overly polite liberal Helen Gallagher Douglas, whose husband, the actor Melvyn Douglas, had made a great hit with the film *Ninotchka,* a very funny satire on Bolshevism. Although it was hardly the prelude to a great friendship, Nixon even visited Mao in Beijing. It was also Nixon who signed SALT. But it was during the liberal Carter administration that Brezhnev provoked America most inconsiderately by invading Afghanistan. After this Soviet blunder, it was only to be expected that Gorbachev had to be the seeker and the very conservative Reagan the courted. Basically, then, what these convergences of contraries demonstrate is the primacy of impersonal processes over the individual actors on the historical stage.

(15) As the USSR sank into crisis, the USA was ready to boom

After Geneva, there were three other meetings between Gorbachev and Reagan: in Reyjavik (Iceland), in Moscow, and in Washington. In Reyjavik, Gorbachev tried to dissuade Reagan from pursuing the SDI, still more evidence of Soviet weakness, but he did not get anywhere, although the SDI was downplayed in the remaining Reagan years and during Bush's administration.

By then, the Cold War was becoming less chilly. The relations between the two superpowers were much less abrasive. Nuclear terror was circumscribed by the MAD equilibrium with now the substantial difference that America and the USSR were no longer on a fully adversarial footing. In other respects there was progress on disarmament. Gorbachev accepted the INF (inter-mediate range nuclear forces) treaty spurned by Brezhnev, eliminating the Soviet SS-20s and the American Pershing missiles. It provided for mutual inspection. In all, both sides destroyed over 2,500 missiles.

In perhaps the most significant move to ease the Soviet economic situation, and to improve relations with America, Gorbachev put an end to the invasion of Afghanistan after the mostly Russian troops engaged there had taken some 20,000 casualties. Above all, that Reagan and Gorbachev were able to click on a personal level showed that America was definitely not a vindictive empire gleefully kicking a falling adversary, or at least, at that point, an adversary that, cuts and all, was proffering a friendly hand.

Gorbachev's mending-fences policy was as successful as his efforts to repair the Soviet economy were unavailing. Perestroika at first took the form of measures to lubricate bureaucratic stiffness and to stimulate productivity, but in the Soviet system there were just so many things that could be done in that respect and by the time that Gorbachev arrived there were hardly any left that had not already been tried. Gorbachev must have seen this and his idea of perestroika surely went further than just reform within the conventional communist mold. That he knew exactly how far he was disposed to go is another matter, which eventually was taken out of his hands anyway.

What perestroika basically achieved was a loosening of central control over the huge Soviet industrial empire. This had been tried with the economic councils introduced by Khrushchev. But these councils were still responsive to central planning and perestroika did not compensate the losses of central authority with alternative mechanisms. Since perestroika wasn't capitalism either, its immediate impact was a dramatic fall in the state's revenues. It is also possible that the wild capitalist seeds that eventually sprouted in Russia were already sown during the perestroika period, when in situ management realized in essence that it could get away with murder and began considering profitable options either immediately available or in the near horizon.

By way of contrast, at the time when the USSR was experiencing all sorts of crises, America was entering the greatest economic boom in its history, one that continued into the 1990s and that ended only at the beginning of the 21st century. Gorbachev and those, and they must have been thousands, who helped him up the greasy pole, had to understand that America was so far ahead of the USSR in economic performance that their own country was slipping into underdevelopment by comparison. Gorbachev did not introduce perestroika as a personal whim. He did not meet a solid wall of opposition, because others beside him knew that central planning and much of the communist paraphernalia had to be discarded in one way or another. Economic liberalism was gaining ground all over the world. The idea that state burocracies were the most appropriate means for economic development was rapidly becoming passé.

(16) Yeltsin out - Gorbachevs Gorbachev

If his economics were hazy, Gorbachev knew slightly better the political ground he was treading and where he wanted to go, although in the end for him it turned out that it was precisely in the area of politics where he most erred. Gorbachev placed himself in various dilemmatic situations. His program for reforming the USSR in a radical manner was made possible through his ascent within a party that was by nature anti-radical-reform. On his way to the top Gorbachev had allies who were of his bent of mind, notably Aleksandr Yakovlev, who was his media advisor and a cornerstone of glasnost. But he also initially had on his side tepid reformers such as Ligachev, and in the same central committee session from which he emerged as secretary general the party, he also chose Andrei Gromyko to be president of the USSR. Gromyko in his prime was a scowling cold warrior whose face American newspapers loved to print as a living symbol of countless Soviet vetoes at the UN.

Gorbachev came up the party hierarchy from his base in Stavropol, an industrial city in southern Russia, with the tacit support of counterparts such as Boris Yeltsin, the communist boss of Yekaterinburg (then Sverdlovsk), the Urals region city where Tsar Nicholas II and his family were assassinated by Lenin's command. It was Yeltsin who, on superior orders, razed the Ipatev House, where the killings took place. Yeltsin in some manner must have contributed to the rise of Gorbachev, who had Yeltsin in mind when his main concern was to consolidate his position within the party. Yeltsin was brought by Ligachev from Sverdlovsk to head the party apparatus in Moscow. He was made a non-voting member of the presidium.

Yeltsin's re-assignment in the party organization was another of Gorbachev's dilemmatic situations, for when push came to shove the newcomer to Moscow turned out to be more radical than the secretary general. Even before this became notorious, Gorbachev already knew that he had a rival in Yeltsin. Ligachev, who later claimed Gorbachev was deceiving him, orchestrated the removal of Yeltsin from his Moscow post and his expulsion from the presidium, which as Yeltsin was practically an arriviste, was probably not hard to achieve. Gorbachev did not oppose this maneuver. Yeltsin, already known as an offence-taker, was powerless but resentful.

(17) A plethora of useless countervailing executive powers

Despite his pre-eminence in the most tyrannical political party in history, Gorbachev was honestly committed to glasnost. His closest advisers, which, besides the media reformer Yakovlev, included his foreign secretary, the Georgian Eduard Sheverdnaze, were openly favorable to political reforms. But an observer of the USSR at the time could not have said that there was a communist groundswell for perestroika. At the 19th party conference—a different type of venue from the party congresses—Gorbachev relaxed the party's grip on the Soviets, or the parliaments of the constituent parts of the USSR, which previously could not have had a grain of sand lifted without getting communist-party authorization. All soviet delegates were still communists, so it was only a minimal degree of democratization. Even so party stalwarts resisted it.

In October 1988, Gorbachev was elected chairman of the presidium of the Supreme Soviet. This presidium, different from the party presidium, was a collective presidency. Its chairman, theoretically, was on a par with the offices of president of the USSR and of prime minister or chairman of the council of ministers, which was selected by the presidium of the Supreme Soviet. The position that counted for most was still secretary general of the CC of the CPUS, from among whose members those of the party presidium were chosen. The secretary general was ipso facto the chairman or president of the presidium. These posts and institutions were all, more or less, reduplicated in each of the Soviet republics, Russia being of course by far the largest, the most populous, and the most politically important of all.

In no state in history have countervailing executive powers been more numerous and more intricately organized than in the USSR. Even an expert can be baffled by the profusion of secretaries, chairmen, and presidents over bureaus, secretariats, committees, presidiums, and soviets. Yet in no state have such institutions been hollower. Under Stalin it was the man who made the post. After him, the rule of thumb to identify the person with the most clout was who held the post of first secretary or secretary general of the CC. The CC itself was nothing next to the politburo—what Stalin had renamed presidium—which was the real power-wielder. Ultimately, should doubts linger, the two great communist dailies, *Pravda* and *Izvestia*, would reveal over and over who was the real boss, just as reading North Korean propaganda rags you could hardly mistake the "sun who rises in the east", Kim Il Sung, with anything other than the absolute, indisputable Alpha male, whose destiny could be nothing less than embalming or mummification.

A Latin American communist working as copy editor in North Korea once had the audacity to call Kim "old fatty" in a letter to a fellow communist. He must have been either gullible or dull to think that letters were private in North Korea and for his irreverence he was sentenced to an indeterminate term of imprisonment, from which a compatriot who had connections in the Kremlin rescued him. Even with these antecedents, his correspondent later accepted an invitation to visit North Korea and defended his tour by mumbling something about General Motors and its publicity department. And so it went with communists.

In post-Stalinist Russia there had been two occasions when government power seemed to be in competition with party power. On both—when Khrushchev crushed his rivals in the party presidium and when Brezhnev dismissed Kosygin—the party was victorious. It was standard Soviet practice to denounce losers as "anti-party", communism being the ultimate legitimizer. But in 1988, Gorbachev was pulling off the amazing trick of actually having the party relinquish voluntarily its monopoly on power. His campaign culminated when he obtained changes to the constitution of the USSR adopted under Brezhnev ten years before. Elections were held for the Congress of People's Deputies in some of which there was more than the usual official communist candidate. Gorbachev was elected president of the USSR. Yeltsin sneaked in as a lowly deputy from Moscow.

(18) The disintegration of the Soviet empire

Things were moving at centrifugal speed, yet they might have appeared not to be changing that much. The grand sounding Congress of People's Deputies was not the ultimate legislative body in the USSR. It was more in the nature of a huge electoral college from which emanated the grander sounding Supreme Soviet, and this was more in keeping with traditional communist mystifications. Gorbachev chose a communist party hack, Gennady Yanayev, as his vice-president. The presidium of the Supreme Soviet was still in the hands of party-men.

The situation that obtained was extremely curious and lent itself to diverse hypotheses all of which appeared to be unlikely. Either Gorbachev was leading the despotic CPSU party to its doom with its acquiescence, or the party actually believed that Gorbachev was not serious about glasnost and perestroika, or Gorbachev was the only remarkable man in a sea of such mediocrity that he could do whatever he wished without serious opposition. This last hypothesis raised the question of whether Gorbachev himself might not have been just another mediocrity, the least mediocre of all.

Well, Yeltsin was not a mediocrity, and as events showed, if Gorbachev thought that he was leading the blind, he was more than half blind himself. One thing that can be said for certain is that he did not have a blind spot for the Soviet Empire. It had been unsustainable before. If backward Afghanistan had given Russia a bloody nose, a revolt of the satellites could lead to a situation comparable to a political black hole. Even before perestroika, it already cost a mint the USSR could not afford to maintain a bloated military. With economic decentralization and public revenues dropping sharply, Gorbachev not only was willing to let the satellites go: he sought the opportunity to do so, even though he knew, as every one else also did, that if they went it would be as far as they could from the USSR.

At the start of 1989 the world was still bi-polar and the USSR was far from an open, democratic society. Gorbachev had begun changing the secretive, repressive nature of Soviet governance. Then political events that affected international communism started actually happening at such a rate that Sovietologists and related experts were left in a state of complete amazement and incomprehension.

The Soviet empire started to disintegrate when the Sejm, the Polish parliament, chose a non-communist prime minister. The Hungarian communist party dissolved itself. East German tourists, who were usually prevented from crossing the border between Hungary and Austria, were let through and allowed passage in their wheezy Brabants as refugees into western Germany. Without Soviet military support, which Gorbachev withheld, the communist boss of East Germany, Erich Honecker, was toppled and the Berlin Wall was exultantly dismantled. Bulgaria entered a period of unrest, which resulted in its de-communization. Riots in Czechoslovakia were put down and for a time it seemed as if the most audaciously liberalizing of the communist satellites would resist the anti-communist surge, but then, literally from one day to the next, the country simply dropped communism altogether. The last holdouts were Nicholas Ceausescu and his wife, who jointly ruled Romania like a family property, and other communists assassinated the terrified couple.

(19) The Soviet bear could still bare its fangs

There was a nimbus of ambiguity surrounding Gorbachev and his reforms, for it was hard to believe that the CPSU would allow itself to be led willingly to the block. Yet the party, though still in power, was suffering back-to-back reverses. It lost local elections with some regularity, which was unheard of before Gorbachevism. The most galling blow was purely doctrinaire. Part of Stalin's charade about power in the USSR was that the article in the constitution that established the party's legal supremacy was shelved deep into its text. In the 1978 constitution it was made the sixth in order of appearance, a whiff of political legitimization that would have been superfluous under Stalin. In 1990, the entire article was excised from the constitution.

In the agitated times that Russia was entering, the Soviet constitution had the merit of providing quick amendments. This gave legislative sanction to the multi-party politics that were already in the offing, although Russia has yet to develop a functional multi-party system both in the sense of some programmatic clarity and of sufficient public membership or support, as if Russians after the experience of many decades of one-party rule were inherently incapable of believing in parties of any kind.

Notwithstanding the actively tolerant attitude of the changing Soviet state, it also occasionally bared its fangs as if saying "don't taunt or provoke me beyond endurance". Soviet troops had intervened in Georgia to crush separatism. Gorbachev wanted above all else to safeguard the Soviet federation. Any threat to it would have been the political straw to break his tolerance. Next, it was Azerbaijan that started acting up and Soviet intervention was again forthcoming. But the biggest challenge to the integrity of the USSR came from Lithuania, one of the small Baltic republics, which also included Latvia, linguistically related to Lithuania, and Estonia, whose linguistic affinities are with Finland.

(20) On the whole, the Paris Peace conference did respect the principle of the self-determination of nationalities

The three Baltic States became de facto independent when the Bolshevik revolution was powerless to prevent German occupation of formerly Tsarist provinces. At the Paris Peace Conference of 1919-1920, their independence was covered by the principle of the self-determination of peoples. Although it is often said that this goal, part of American President Woodrow Wilson's program for post-war Europe, was regularly flouted at Paris, the evidence rather points to that it was not.

As a result of the Paris Peace Conference (also erroneously called the Versailles Conference), Estonia, Latvia, and Lithuania were formed as ethnic republics. Albania, Bulgaria, Greece, and Romania already existed as such. The Yugoslavs constituted a kingdom from similar Slavic ethnic roots. The related Czechs and Slovaks formed Czechoslovakia.

Austria was formed with Germans. The Austrian southern Tyrol was ceded arbitrarily to Italy. There were many Hungarians outside of Hungary. Poland was constituted mainly with Poles, except for German Danzig, which was ceded as part of a Polish corridor to the sea. Memel, another German city, was ceded as a Baltic port to Lithuania, but soon afterwards was declared a free city. The most flagrant violation of the self-determination principle was the inclusion in Czechoslovakia of the Sudeten Germans, and this case, which is used by some British historians to explain Hitler's electoral appeal, occurred because this German population had been for centuries part of Bohemia.

Of the former dependencies of the Tsarist Russian empire, the Caucasian and Transcaucasian provinces and the mainly Turkic central Asian Russian annexations were eventually constituted as separate Soviet republics, formally federated over-all with Russia in the USSR, though still under the tight political leash of Russia and the CPSU. Of the republics that gained independence from Russia, only Poland and Lithuania could boast of ancient independent histories and after World War II the USSR did not absorb Poland, a big chunk of land, but incorporated much smaller Lithuania.

(21) Why Lithuania was the first Soviet republic to bolt

Though ethnically characteristic, Estonia, Finland, and Latvia had been over time under Swedish, Polish, and Russian rule.[10] But Lithuania was formed as an independent pagan duchy in the 13th century, more powerful than Russia, then under Mongol hegemony. In the 14th century,

10 Latvia was taken and Christianized by the Livonian Brothers of the Sword, a German military order, during the early 13th century. In 1561, Latvia was annexed by Poland. In 1629 the entire country passed to Sweden. In 1721, as a result of warfare with Sweden, the Russian tsar Peter I the Great was awarded Latvia. Under Russia, Germans remained in economic control but the Letts developed their own culture. In 1918, Latvia acquired its independence. The Livonian Brothers conquered the territory of Estonia in the early 13th century. It became part of the commercial network of the Hanseatic League. The Livonian Brothers merged with the Teutonic Knights in 1257 but kept their own theatre of operations. Upon the dissolution of the Knights (1525), the territory of Estonia was shared out between Sweden and Poland. It became wholly Swedish in 1629. In 1721, Russia acquired Estonia in the same circumstances as Latvia. Estonia remained Russian—Estonian revolutionaries were instrumental in the Soviet takeover of power in 1917—until it achieved independence, together with Finland, Latvia, and Lithunia, in 1918. In the 13th century Finland was occupied by Sweden and in 1581 it was made a grand duchy. In 1808-09, Russia wrested all of Finland from Sweden, but allowed it a great deal of autonomy. During the Russian Revolution in 1917, Finland, including Karelia, declared its independence.

the duke of Lithuania, Jagiello or Jogaila, became king of Lithuania and Poland and took the Polish-Latin name of Ladislaus. This federated kingdom, through which the Lithuanians were Christianized, held its own against the Tatars and in the 15th century against the Germans established in the Baltic shoreline from Prussia—the former east Prussia, today mostly in Poland—to Estonia.

However politically precocious, Lithuania was still the junior partner in the dual-kingdom arrangement and in the 16th century it was considered to be part of the kingdom of Poland. For this, however, the Polish monarchy paid the price of having to put up with the abuse of nobiliary privileges, the greatest of which was the liberum veto, or the requirement for unanimity in all decisions of the Sejm. As the nobility represented a relatively high percentage of its population, Poland was, all in all, the most democratic kingdom the world had ever known, a condition that put it at a disadvantage in relation to powerful autocracies such as Russia and Prussia.

The internal lack of cohesion, for which the Lithuanian land-owning nobility bore some responsibility, resulted in the successive partitions of Poland, which ceased to have independent existence in 1795. Russia annexed the Polish heartland. In the first partition, 23 years earlier, it had already absorbed Lithuania. By then Lithuania had known over five centuries of independent existence or of near-sovereignty under one crown, which was not the case of either Latvia or Estonia. Finland was not independent either although it was the province to which Russian autocracy granted the greatest autonomy.

All these nations had kept their traditions alive. In the case of Lithuania, this was so marked that it attracted the special attention of linguists, ethnologists, and even of Prosper Merimée, the French writer enamored of the "European exotic". Merimée set one of his better-known novelettes (*Carmen* being of course his most popular work) in Lithuania. Called *Lokis*, it is a variant on the werewolf theme involving bears.

Given this dense national background, it's not surprising that it was the Soviet republic of Lithuania, the descendant of the ancient duchy of Lithuania, founder of the kingdom of Poland-Lithuania, that in March 1990 declared its independence from the USSR, the first Soviet republic to do so. It was also where KGB troops most reverted to Stalinist type during the taking by force of a television station in Vilnius, the Lithuanian capital. There were fourteen civilian casualties. This incident is the one big stain in Gorbachev's otherwise impeccably libertarian credentials.

(22) There were three processes going on in the USSR and they were going in different directions

Gorbachev was indecisive about economic liberalization. When it was too late to change tack, he probably realized that too rapid a conversion from communism to any type of non-communist order would be chaotic. This was already happening in a spontaneous way.

As he was also intent on preserving the USSR, which he saw as coming under threat from various directions, Gorbachev began to shy away from the implications of his own reforms. This meant backtracking towards reliance on the CPSU and its dinosaurs. Now, this in itself was already impracticable. There were three different processes going on at the time in the USSR and they were not heading in the same direction. One process was what Gorbachev and his group wanted to see happen. The other process was what went on in the CPSU. And the third process consisted in what was happening in the country.

Gorbachev undoubtedly wanted to democratize the USSR. He also wanted its economy to be more efficient. But he never doubted that, whatever happened, the USSR, or some reasonably democratic, decentralized facsimile, should subsist. One thing that Gorbachev did not envision or desire was the sort of economic and institutional free-for-all that later came about under Yeltsin.

Although he was out of the political running when this came about then, Gorbachev represented everything that the "shock treatment" that Russia was made to undergo wasn't. He was a gradualist. He believed in the efficacy and the need for institutions and regulatory laws. He wanted what anti-Stalinist Soviet sympathizers desired: an USSR endowed with freedom of expression, courts that upheld due process, liberty to travel. Gorbachev's commitment was not to frantic, uncontrolled change but to orderly, constitutional evolution.

Gorbachev wanted to emasculate the tyranny of the CPSU, but within the system in which he had ascended and over which he for a time presided, the party was practically the only federal institution that did not in itself involve direct legal coercion. The party was ultimately coercive through its domination of the state, but people were not forced to join the party: they simply realized that if they wanted to improve their condition in Soviet society they had to join the party. What Gorbachev probably wanted was a docile but not monopolistic CPSU that would help to keep the USSR together as a close federation of democratic states.

(23) Gorbachev was pro-democracy, but democracy could lead to separatism, which was what he most dreaded

There were various ironies and vicious circles at the heart of Gorbachevism. He wanted to use the Communist Party as an instrument even as he himself was blunting it, thus very quickly rendering it useless. The instrument itself, which still had influential people in all spheres of government, was reluctant to be used. When Gorbachev saw that things were getting out of hand and sought party support, the party was too weak and too suspicious of him, so in desperation it tried to eliminate Gorbachev and only succeeded in putting itself out of commission.

Gorbachev was pro-democracy, but democracy meant self-determination, which meant separatism, and that was what Gorbachev most feared and made him consent to the use of undemocratic means such as the military suppression of separatisms. He wanted gradual economic reform but he was provoking economic spontaneous combustion and whittling away at the fiscal resources necessary to achieve his goals. After Vilnius, where Gorbachev demonstrated that the USSR had not entirely lost its grip, he realized that in order to keep separatism at bay he had to use persuasion based on Soviet legitimacy. Gorbachev was hubristic in his confidence in his own powers of persuasion.

In the spring of 1991, he sponsored federation talks among the Soviet republics certain that they must have believed, as he did, that in unity lay strength. But the other republics were not keen on a union in which Russia remained the super-republic. Under CPSU rule at least each republic had its own relatively autonomous dictatorship. Under a democratic federal state, there were no guarantees that the power of local bosses would be upheld and respected. Free elections and the other appurtenances of democracy could erode regionalism and, horror of horrors!, The Russians, who were everywhere, could actually become rulers of the non-Russian republics by democratic means.

(24) Collectivist greed was well and good but capitalist greed was a system-threatening clone

What was happening in the CPSU when Gorbachev, still the party's leader, was going about promoting his visions? During Gorbachev's rise in the presidium and at the time he was named secretary general, the party cannot have but known that there were going to be reforms. Gorbachev and his fellow presidium members had access to the same information about the USSR. It was the fear of stagnation and decay that had lifted Khrushchev to the top and that had made Kosygin the activist pole during the first period of Brezhnev's stewardship.

Even as separatism strengthened, Gorbachev went on with his talk of making the USSR a better place while still being the good old USSR. Perhaps up to a point Gorbachev thought that this was possible, but in the end the Soviet system was so constructed that removing a few bricks could make the building start collapsing. Gorbachev removed more than a few bricks. In fact he was dismantling the system's communist-party foundations.

The real communists, and not the wolf in sheep's clothing that Gorbachev must have seemed to them, were obviously not happy over this turn of events. The party was the overseer of the Soviet legacy and it could flirt with superficial reforms but not with anything even remotely resembling capitalism. And what party men observed was the return of undisguised capitalist greed. Collectivist greed was well and good and communist bosses had not gotten to where they did without greed. But capitalist greed meant the end of the world as they knew it. Confident in his eloquence and in his firm commitment to the USSR, and also surrounded by men who did not openly challenge him, Gorbachev had no idea what the real communists were about.

Yeltsin for his part had risen within the Russian Supreme Soviet to the head of the presidium, which he couldn't have done without the support of the Communist Party, then still the only party in Russia. Even so, like Gorbachev, he too must have felt that the support he was getting had no major strings attached. Unlike Gorbachev, he quit the party altogether, which might indicate that he believed that his communists were more committed to him than they were to their Marxist beliefs or to the values that the party stood for. Thus it was when Yeltsin selected a vice-president his choice fell on Aleksandr Rutskoi, who had not been a communist hierarch but who was still a communist with an uncapacious stomach for reform. Later, what Rutskoi had to take from Yeltsin was more than enough to give him indigestion.

Yeltsin's constraints in choosing the Russian vice-president indicated how much things had changed over the previous years. Gorbachev had chosen Soviet vice-president Yanayev from within the CPSU. Rutskoi had been a general during the Afghan war. Yeltsin selected a communist but one with a background outside traditional CPSU echelons. Despite the changing circumstances, both Gorbachev and Yeltsin misjudged in their choices of vice-presidents.

(25) Liberty lies in deliberately limiting your options

So if both major leaders of the Russian historical counter-revolution were committing big errors of judgment, what was the real situation? For one thing, the foundations for grab-as-grab-can capitalism had already been laid. The process of granting greater autonomy to state enterprises in all sectors of the economy had probably been upping the level of self-interest of the managerial class to a situation in which plans were made independently of central control and the least any economic executive was considering was a return to Soviet authoritarianism. As there were no laws or guidelines for such a transition, the improvisations that appeared spontaneously were determined strictly by profit-making calculations.

The USSR, and vast Russia in particular, had already de facto adopted capitalism, not simultaneously with capitalist legality and institutionalism, but at its most rudimentary, even savage, level, where, say, England had been during the Industrial Revolution or America in the last decades of the 19th century. And even then the comparisons are misleading, for private ownership was the ultimate basis of capitalism and in Russia control of assets was what counted, for no one really knew who owned the productive enterprises or the banks or the agencies that provided services like export and import.

As enterprises became less accountable to central ministries in Moscow, a crucial additional point was that the resources to pay for policing society were becoming scarcer. Under the Soviet system, the means for coercive social control, as distinct from the instilling of socialist beliefs, were generously financed. There were hierarchies among law-and-order bodies and there were informers everywhere. Informing was a duty under Stalinism. Above all, coercion and propaganda created certainties about society and the state that both the police and the population shared. This made the work of policing easier, because it was generally recognized as legitimate and useful. Nevertheless, legal coercion was applied in a state which regularly denied all basic liberties, or doffed its hat to them and used convoluted arguments to show that the denial of liberties was really the greatest form of liberty.[11]

The paradox of arguing for the contraries of self-evident principles was not unknown to Plato in his *The Republic*, where even philosophy was suspect, or to religious figures who denied the self-evident delights of life for the sake of bliss in another life. Although mostly based on legends, Jacobus da Varagine's *Golden Legend* depicts the extremes to which Christian saints were supposed to be willing to go in withstanding pain to obtain paradise. St. Lawrence, who was grilled alive, tells his

11 Perhaps no history of Stalinism illustrates better this excruciating paradox than the book of the Rusian historian Roy Medvedev, *Let history judge* (1989), precisely because Medvedev, though implacable to Stalin, was a convinced, if at times sceptical, Leninist, which means that he believed in the an "ideal" form of communism based on Marxist humanism.

tormentors: "Turn me over. On that side I am done." Philip II's palace of El Escorial has the layout of a grill in honor of St. Lawrence.

Every set of ethical beliefs is ultimately based on the argument that liberty lies in deliberately limiting your options. Epicurus, the philosophical prototype` of the hedonist, was a dainty moderate. On the other hand, the crudely hedonistic Marquis de Sade attributed to his villainous characters such "pleasures", like coprophagy, as normally you would have only in low and dirty nightmares.

In the USSR, self-sacrifice and devotion to socialism did not seem to bring a more abundant society any closer, a society, for instance, that did not have to pen its members in because it knew that comparisons would be disadvantageous to it. The leaders of the USSR knew better than its ordinary citizens how unpromising the prospects were. From the widest social perspective you could attain, which was the view from the presidium, the economic results of Soviet certainties were not as soundas expected.

(26) When social values are questioned, the police lose moorings

The deterioration of policing favored another emerging social trend. Even under Brezhnevian conformism, perhaps especially because of it, there was a Russian criminal class that went unreported because the Soviet system did not allow such things to be known. The USSR, where everything—goods, services, displacements—was rigorously controlled, and consequently doled out or permitted in restricted doses, was made to order for bribery and for illegal activities of all conceivable sorts. There were probably embryonic mafias everywhere, some very likely quite respectable-seeming, the equivalent of white-collar crime under capitalism.

Some have compared the Communist Party itself to a gigantic mafia, although this is carrying things too far, for individuals such as Gorbachev or Yeltsin had ideas about the good of society. They were not mafiosi or even the shrewd criminal types morphed into legitimate businessmen in books and films in America (though usually not to the extent of being made to seem sincerely philanthropic or of having serious social concerns).

Gorbachevism was not only reformist: it was also questioning, and when social values are questioned, the police lose moorings. If tyrannical Soviet legality was not rock-solid, as the whirlwind of changes in the USSR was showing, and there was no peremptory, short-term substitute for it, then laws could be openly flouted. And after all, wasn't the Soviet system itself quite unscrupulous about applying or not applying its own laws depending on its conveniences? This day-to-day, variable, unstable situation was plowed and fertilized ground for criminal activities and for police corruption. As police services declined, there arose the need for parallel security services not for society at large but to defend the profit-making turfs that were being staked out. Under Gorbachev there was not so much a breakdown of law and order as the strengthening of the forces that existed in Soviet society which could lead to or encourage such a breakdown.

Another shocking aspect of the new reality was that the USSR was visibly disintegrating. Russia was inheriting much of what the USSR still had. It was "acquiring" the USSR but trying to be different from it. Gorbachev was attempting to contain separatism with negotiations and high hopes about a voluntary, democratic federation. The Baltic States were recalcitrant even to such an arrangement, which was why the repression in Vilnius had been so heavy-handed. But most of the inertia was coming from what Gorbachev thought would be the pillar of this Phoenix-like federation of autonomous, democratic, and willing member republics. This was Russia itself and on this Yeltsin knew far more than Gorbachev.

(27) The USSR was neither an union nor Soviet nor socialist

Yeltsin was the realist foil to Gorbachev's idealism. When he climbed to the top of the presidium of the Russian Supreme Soviet, he had a law passed giving Russian laws priority over Soviet laws. This gave precedence to the Russian constitution over the Soviet constitution. They were probably then not that different so the gesture might not have seemed a big menace to the federation process that Gorbachev was promoting. But from a strictly legal point of view, Yeltsin's move implicitly contested Gorbachev's authority. That Gorbachev retained his membership in the CPSU while Yeltsin renounced his broke another disciplinary bond between the president of the theoretically superior USSR and Russia. The latter was still officially the Russian Federated Soviet Socialist Republic, part of the USSR, but, paraphrasing Metternich, the USSR was no longer a union, and it was damned near neither Soviet nor socialist.[12]

Despite the exemplary punishment of Lithuanian independentism, Latvia, its Baltic neighbor to the north, went independent in March 1991. In June Yeltsin was elected president of Russia, which, since the Russian constitution already superseded in Russia the Soviet constitution, made him at least the legal equal of Gorbachev, and in Russia his superior in point of real power.

---

12 When the allies against Napoleon were remaking the map of Europe in 1815, the Austrian chancellor Metternich said that the Holy Roman Empire was neither Holy nor Roman nor an empire.

Things were not that desperate for Gorbachevism, as they might have seemed from perspectives such as that of the Russian government. The USSR still existed. It was legal and it had the steadfastness that comes from a long history and the respect that this commands. Furthermore, the federation talks for a constitutional, orderly transition from the USSR to its democratic re-incarnation were going on and by July 1991 a federation treaty was ready. It was discounted that the Baltic republics would want to remain within the new federation, but compared to the Ukraine, the second largest Soviet republic, they were expendable; and it did not seem likely that the other republics, which were economically dependent on Russia, would recklessly choose to break away and go their uncertain independent ways. As to Russia itself, despite his resentment of Gorbachev, Yeltsin did not openly challenge his authority. He probably would have become very unpopular in Russia if he had taken up the cause of the dissolution of the USSR, and in the USSR at large Gorbachev was still the highest constitutional authority.

Even with the problems that were rising and growing like thunderclouds on a hot day that Russian summer, Gorbachevism was a promising alternative for the USSR. On paper it was the ideal solution, the means for the USSR to become capitalistic very gradually, to foment democracy in a climate of open and unhurried debate, to bolster democratic law and order, in brief, to spare the USSR the rigors and the aberrations of another revolution, one in which pure greed and social disintegration went rampant. The project was more dreamy than feasible and it depended on the vision and the abilities of one man, Gorbachev, who had a tendency to overestimate the control he had over social and political processes, probably a reflex from the time, which had been most of his life, when what the CPSU wanted went.

(28) If Iraq had a claim on Kuwait, then Turkey had a claim on Iraq

If the 1980s were trying for the USSR, for America it hadn't all been beer and skittles. President George W.H. Bush's relations with Gorbachev were also good and the meetings of the two leaders in Washington and in Moscow were ratifications of the understanding achieved in the previous years. But Iraq, America's protégé against theocratic Iran, was becoming something of a liability.

Despite American support for Iraq in its war with Iran, the Iranians captured the Kurdish Iraqi town of Halabjah and were on the road to Kirkuk. The Iraqis counter-attacked and Hussein dealt with the Kurdish problem in summary fashion through the use of gas that left 5,000 civilians dead. In the end, after huge casualties on both sides, no one gained an inch of the other's land and a ceasefire was agreed. Because the USA still could not overlook aggressive Iranian fundamentalism, still anti-Satan and also very anti-Israel, relations between the USA and Iraq remained friendly, which might have had to do with what later happened.

The USA had not been the only supporter of Iraq in its confrontation with Iran. Saudi Arabia and Kuwait had extended to Iraq large loans, which Iraq wanted written off. The creditors were pressing their claims when oil prices were sliding. Alleging a flooding of the oil market, Iraq invaded Kuwait, abolished the local regime (itself not notably democratic), and proclaimed Kuwait's annexation as Iraq's 19th province.

The basis of these actions, which at first sight seem arbitrary, was that Kuwait had been a dependency of the Ottoman governorship in Baghdad. By secret treaty, the British extended their protection to Kuwait later. The situation was anomalous. If Kuwait was Bedouin or nomadic territory that British colonialism converted into an artificial state, well, so was much of Iraq. The border between Syria and Iraq was mostly the handiwork of British and French imperialisms after World War I. Turkey only very grudgingly renounced its claim on Mosul and northern Iraq. And its renunciation extended to all Arab lands including Kuwait, so that Iraq's argument that its claim to sovereignty over Kuwait stemmed from the Ottomans could also mean that Turkey still had a claim on Iraq. Iraq did not see it that way. The grave international crisis the Iraqis provoked gave president Bush the opportunity to lead America in its first magnificent exercise of leadership in the emerging unipolar world.

Hussein was served notice by neighboring Arab states and by the USA and other Western powers to evacuate Kuwait. Of Iraq's Arab neighbors, only Jordan, for commercial reasons and out of political prudence, maintained relations with Iraq. When there was no compliance, Iraq was bombarded heavily and its forces were easily vanquished, but not before Soviet-designed Scud rockets in the hundreds were flung at Israel and at Saudi Arabia. Resistance collapsed when a high-tech American bomb was aimed so perfectly that it penetrated the air vent of a bomb shelter for Iraqi functionaries and their families killing all its occupants.

President Bush restrained the invasion short of Baghdad and Hussein remained in power as repressive as ever. But unlike his son twelve years later, Bush did not want to entangle his country in a situation from which he did not know how to extricate it and would inevitably provoke high Iraqi collateral losses. The Gulf War was international, swift, and decisive. It was not an aggression but a merited retaliation on an aggressor. It accomplished what it had to and the winners themselves decided that it was not theirs to meddle in the internal affairs of Iraq beyond restraining its ability to wage war. Interdiction zones, where Iraq was enjoined not to fly or engage in threatening military activities, were established in northern Iraq and south of Baghdad. Iraq was also forced to comply with an UN inspection program to deter the development of WMD. Oil sales were drastically curtailed, permitted only for humanitarian and reparation-payment purposes.

(29) Tiananmen

As in Russia, there were clouds in the firmament elsewhere. The biggest country in the world, China, still had a rigid communist political system. But there too change was in the works. Hua Guofeng, a supporter of the Cultural Revolution, succeeded Mao Zedong. At the head of a military committee through which he had supreme though not absolute power, Deng Xiaoping went on the offensive. For the sake of communist legitimacy and continuity, he blamed the Cultural Revolution on the "gang of four" who had surrounded Mao.[13] However, Mao's widow scotched any illusions about her husband by claiming in high-pitch at her trial that nothing moved in China without Mao's willing it.

Soon Hua Guofeng was out and China had embarked on a rectification campaign in which party secretary general Hu Yaobang represented the most liberal tendency. Southern China, especially the province of Quangdong and its capital Quangzhou (Canton), experienced extraordinary development through their special economic status. Economic growth was so vertiginous that between Hong Kong and Quangzhou there sprouted practically overnight a one-million-plus metropolis named Shenzheng. Statistics show that this once tiny hamlet has the highest disposable income per capita of any other Chinese metropolis.

The much less repressive post-Mao climate engendered democratic hopes, which, upon Hu Yaobang's natural death, were expressed in popular manifestations led by students in Tiananmen Square, the center of Beijing. When troops and tanks intervened causing a massacre—then Prime Minister Li Peng took most of the blame for this—illusions were rudely shattered. China would go the way of market reforms but at its own communist-party determined pace and for the foreseeable future there was to be no democracy outside the party.

---

13 Lin Biao was army chief as well as the compiler of *Quotations from Chairman Mao*, better known as "The Little Red Book". In 1971, he apparently tried to overthrow Mao and was killed in an airplane crash out in Mongolia fleeing to the USSR.

(30) The PLO bows to the inevitable but Israelis were skeptical

During Israel's invasion of Lebanon, prime minister Begin had resigned and given way to a fellow former independence fighter and also Likud party member, Yitzhak Shamir. By then Israel was fully committed to the settlements policy, mainly in the West Bank. Labor came back to power with Shimon Peres. After the inconclusive Israeli invasion of Lebanon was finally terminated, Israel created a buffer zone in southern Lebanon, where it claimed the right of intervention for self-defence, and armed the SLA (South Lebanon Army) to patrol it.

Shamir became prime minister again. Jewish settlements by then involved a population movement of over 150,000. Settlers were enticed by comfortable, low-price homes, and tax breaks. In the West Bank, fabulous hill-top vistas were common.[14] Gaza, flat and dry, was not the sort of real estate Israeli militants preferred--although various of the Gazan settlements were like sea-side subdivisons--and consequently the settlements were much fewer there. By the sea Arabs in the occupied territories were smoldering over Israeli intrusions and they staged the mostly stone-throwing First Intifada.

Israel was bent on obtaining the financial underwriting, which amounted to the political sanction, of its settlements policy. The American Congress, whose members are very appreciative of campaign contributions and of the Jewish vote, was all for it. President Bush was not of that opinion, which he resisted and finally defeated, and even bragged of having done so.[15] To say that he was not the favorite of pro-Israel lobbyists would not be exaggerated, but that a Republican incumbent, such as Bush was in 1992, lost the election because of lack of financing would be going too far out on a limb, as far out as making the usual claim that he was defeated mainly because he had to cover Reagan's legacy of deficits with tax increases.

Bowing to the unavoidable, which was, as the Lebanon conflict had shown, that Palestinians could not gain political objectives by violent means, the PLO had recognized the right of Israel to exist and renounced the use of terrorism, although this did not necessarily mean that terrorist organizations that were recognized by the PLO also accepted Arafat's policy. Yitzhak Rabin became prime minister in agreement with Peres, his foreign minister, about the possibility of dealing with Arafat and the PLO for a peaceful solution to the Palestinian problem.

---

14 Tim Golden, "For Palestinians, land is shrinking", IHT (July 5, 2002)
15 Wheatcroft, op.cit., pp.318-319

After preliminary talks in Madrid, Peres initiated the Oslo negotiations. An interim agreement had been reached by September 1993. Rabin and Arafat signed it in Washington in Clinton's presence and the same signatories ratified it in Egypt. The Washington treaty (usually subsumed under the name "Oslo accords") involved Palestinian self-rule in Gaza and the West Bank over a period of five years. Initially, the Palestinian Authority (PA), as the interim government of the future Palestine was called, would be ceded all of Gaza and Jericho in the West Bank. Palestinian self-rule would be gradually increased in the West Bank and it was left for a final phase to determine the exact extent of Palestinian sovereignty. Arafat arrived in Gaza and set up the PA, which organized its own police force. Another symbol of statehood was the inauguration of an international airport. Arafat, Peres, and Rabin shared the Nobel Peace Prize in 1994.

Two years later, somewhat dodgy elections ratified Arafat, who did not lack for political enemies, as president of the PA. In particular, Hamas and Islamic Jihad were violently opposed to the Oslo accords and these clandestine organizations began a sustained campaign of terrorism against Israel. Islamic Jihad had origins as obscure as its organization. It was possibly a cover name for terrorist cells that acted on their own, true to the name jihad or holy war, which can means almost anything. But Hamas was another thing. Previous to the First Intifada, its predecessor was a benevolent, mutual-help Palestinian association, vaguely related to Muslim Brotherhoods in other countries (not necessarily peaceful everywhere), which Israel thought could be a counterweight to the PLO. During the First Intifada, members of the Palestinian Muslim Brotherhood created terrorist Hamas, an acronym for Harakat al-Mukawamah al-Islamiyya (Islamic Resistance Movement), which after that never looked back to its original purely charitable activities.

Hamas became Arafat's sworn enemy once he signed the Oslo accords and it did all it could to frustrate his authority as president of the PA. The differences between Hamas and Arafat are so pronounced that during the Gulf war, when Arafat backed Iraq, Hamas declared for Saudi Arabia. Given Hamas' grass-roots in Gaza, Arafat had to deal with it if not gingerly at least in a manner that did not alienate popular support for the PA.

(31) The Taliban and the Bamian Buddhas

The Soviet evacuation of Afghanistan did not have a happy ending. The country fragmented into warlordships in permanent conflict with each other. In effect there was no central authority. Gen. Mohammad Najibullah, former head of the secret police, had replaced Karmal as head of the PDPA and as prime minister.

There was an unsteady coalition of mujahidin in which the most prominent figure was Burhanuddin Rabbani. A fundamentalist movement based in Kandahar and inspired by the ulema or mullah Mohammed Omar joined the civil war. It was named Taliban (roughly seminarians) and it did not seem very formidable in comparison with seasoned guerrilla fighters, but it had the backing of Pakistan and attracted volunteers from other Muslim countries. The Taliban gradually took over most of Afghanistan. Kabul fell in 1996 but the north was not entirely reduced. The Taliban instituted a regime of fanatical religious terror, beginning with the evisceration of Najibullah, whose corpse was put on display. According to some cynical veteran observers of Afghanistan, Najibullah was a torturer that just might have deserved his end. But the Taliban regime was easily one of the most benighted and, as it turned out, dangerous and self-destructive that the world has seen. In 2004, by way of contrast, it was announced that the Najibullah government had stored and protected many of the treasures of the Kabul museum from Taliban fury.

In an act denounced the world over as cultural barbarism, the Taliban destroyed with cannon two huge Buddhas—one 53 meters high—carved on a rockside in Bamian. These Buddhas, possibly as old as the 3rd century, were invaluable testimonies to the cultural links between India, Central Asia, and China forged by the Kushan Empire, itself an intriguing blend of Greek, Indo-Iranian, and Indian cultural traditions, the likely source of the branches of Buddhism that grew in China and Japan.[16] The

---

16 The part of Afghanistan known formerly as Bactria (north east Afghanistan) was home to the Kushan kingdom, empire, or dynasty (all three designations are used by historians). The Kushans, who lasted from the 1st century to the 5th century CE, were the inheritors of a tradition of realistic Hellenistic carving. The Kushans (Chinese Gui-shuang) descended from the Yuezhi or Tokharians, Indo-Iranians who in the late 2nd century BCE dislodged the Saka or Asian Scythians from Bactria and forced them down to India. The organizer of the Kushan state was king Kujala Kadphises (ca50). The greatest Kushana king was Kanishka (ca100), whose rule might have embraced a vast territory from the upper Oxus (Amudarya) river to Varanasi (former Benares). Kanishka was a Buddhist and is reputed in Buddhist tradition as one of the four greatest rulers with Ashoka of Magadha (active 3rd century BCE), Menander of Bactria (ca150 BCE), and Harsha of Kanauj (7th century CE). Kanishka was the sponsor of a Fourth Buddhist Council held in Kasmir in which Mahayana doctrine was formalized, particularly the Bodhisattva ideal involving the compassionate vow to save all sentient beings. It is from Kushana that Buddhism and associated artistic styles spread from Afghanistan to the rest of Central Asia and, via the Silk Route, to China and its cultural area, including Japan. Among other things, paintings of Buddha probably began in Bactria and caves around Bamian contained many of them, most of which were defaced by the Taliban.

Taliban were in effect trying to reverse or even obliterate not only what, in their view, went against their primitive and futile version of Islam, but even the historical process as it had happened before the rise of Islam. Ironically, it was in a country so gripped by intellectual darkness that was forged the plot that struck devastatingly at the most enlightened, the most tolerant, and the most advanced country in the world.

(32) The world outlook was for mostly blue skies

If Gorbachev's spectacular command of the stage of world history during the dissolution of the Soviet empire seemed to indicate the start of a promising new world, then the Gulf War, less than two years later, must be considered its culmination. A short period of glory indeed! But this is known with hindsight. At the time, the world outlook was mostly for blue skies after some clouds had burst and the winds were scattering the rest, all in all reminiscent of the post-storm music in Beethoven's Pastoral.

The USSR was reforming itself. The Soviet transformation from totalitarianism to something resembling democracy was being accomplished in a manner that could only be called juridical. Democracy was on the upswing. Economic liberalism had demonstrated, as brightly as the sun on a clear summer day, that it produced more wealth and distributed it better than any centrally controlled system. Devised to accelerate growth with a minimum of social privileges, command economies actually enshrined inequality inside a steel cast.

Despite its missteps and its often-dubious motivations, America after all was generally telling the truth and Marxists were not only inveterate liars but also they made a virtue of lying. The tropical mists that enveloped the third world, like miasmas from the Siberian tundra passed through a filter of burning charcoals, were dissipating. The third world itself was a mirage produced by a malarial fever. It represented nothing but inefficiency and economic backwardness and political presumptions, which could turn very dangerous, as when Cuba offered itself as a base for Soviet missiles.

Whatever the causes, the weakening of the USSR meant power for the USA, but one could allow oneself to believe that it was mainly a victory for fairness, for all sorts of equities within nations and between them. American values became the standard of all standards. After all, if America was the greatest nation ever, if it had bested the USSR in the Cold War, then this must have had something to do with its open, democratic society and the economic freedoms it cherished. Yet this outcome had been possible because America was the greatest empire the world had ever seen.

4

The Uses of Empires

Empires are political formations that have played major roles in world history. Empires have cores from which they expand usually to embrace different peoples. Empires, therefore, are big. They were often associated with civilizations. Ancient Egypt was an empire that was formed by combining different areas of the Nile river valley, including its delta. The Semitic Akkadian Empire had its core in central Mesopotamia but extended west to other Semitic lands. It was the antecessor of the Assyrian and Babylonian empires. These ancient empires disappeared but it was upon their achievements that subsequent empires were built.

The Persians created the Achaemenid Empire, which was in its time the largest empire that ever existed. The Achaemenids were the only dynasty that ever managed to embrace all of the Indo-Iranians except those that remained nomadic in Eurasia. But the civilization of the Persian Achaemenids has left only vestiges. One of those vestiges is the community of the Farsis or Parsis in Mumbai. The Parsis fled from Islam in Persia and kept alive the Zoroastrian religious tradition. A Parsi family, the Tata, was a mainstay of Nehru's program of development economics in India.

The Greeks created the most influential civilization in history, but the only empire they built, the Alexandrian Empire, was ephemeral, vainglorious, and anti-climatic. Hellenistic civilization was a consequence of Alexander's political impact in Greece but its achievements are secondary to the heights attained by Classical Greece. At this time, at the other end of the globe, the Chinese formed their first empire, again, as in Egypt, in the sense of unification. Eventually China would rule over many other nationalities. It still does, so that it is, like Russia, an imperial republic. Politically and juridically, the culmination of Classical Greek civilization was the Roman Empire, whose legacy was Western Civilization.

Like pre-Alexandrian Greece, India was always too recalcitrant for empire building. Hinduism survived and is still going strong without the benefit of empire. The empires Hindustan has had—Maurya, Gupta, Delhian, and Mughal—were very unstable. Before the British, the Mughals came closest to unifying the entire Indian subcontinent, but this lasted barely a score years. The British Empire, as well as the other colonialist empires, was the long-term inheritor of Charlemagne's empire, which was the successful but partial re-animation of the principles that underlay Roman imperialism.

(1) Bulwarks of civilizations

Some empires existed solely as cradles or bulwarks of civilizations (foundationally religious). Although ethnically and linguistically Greek, the Byzantine Empire survived in Rome in the east. It developed a religious tradition of its own, Orthodox Christianity, but it was beset at its core by enemies on all sides, Turks and Slavs in the Balkans, Persians in the east, barbarians from the steppes (usually Turks), Normans and Venetians from across the sea. The attacks from Italy were particularly resented and tended to consolidate the Orthodox patriarchate in opposition to the Catholic papacy.

Islam was a purely religious empire. The name of god and a canonical body of scriptures can be invoked to legitimize anything. Christianity had from its inception a hierarchical priesthood with a pope or a patriarch at the apex separate from lay authority. The rejection of a supreme religious arbiter was validated by force with the Reformation and its political consequences. But even most Protestant churches accept the concept of hierarchy and of ecclesiastical authority independent of political claims on religious sanction. In Islam, any political or military leader could aspire to legitimacy through the reading of his name in the kutbah or Friday prayers. Caliphs, or the theoretical successors of Muhammad, were political keepers of a religious tradition rather than purely religious figures themselves. In the matter of legitimacy, the Chinese expeditiously came up with the concept of a "mandate of heaven", which was eo ipso conferred on a triumphant political or military leader. In theory, only the virtuous could attain that accolade, but who was to contradict a winner? Islam was doomed to fragmentation by its theocratic nature, but while it lasted it weakened the rule of Constantinople.

More than a bulwark, which was the role of the Byzantines, the Germanic Holy Roman Empire was an aggressive drive of western

Christianity against the Slavs and the Balts. The latter were obdurate in their embrace of their pagan customs. The Holy Roman Empire exterminated the Borussians, a Baltic people, and founded Prussia, the most militaristic of its offspring. The also Baltic Lithuanians and the Slavic Poles contained the Germans. Once the impetus of the Holy Roman Empire was spent, the Habsburg Empire, another of its offshoots, took over its role as bulwark, but against the Ottomans.

(2) Habsburgs and Ottomans fought each other for centuries but their empires died as allies

The Ottoman Empire was an attempt to reconstitute Islam but with a military base in the Balkans. By the time it arose, the Persians had long before vindicated their historical identity by passionately embracing Shiism. The Ottomans conquered Constantinople in 1453. For some reason now mostly forgotten—probably mnemonic—this date was often used as the reference for the end of the Middle Ages.[1] As the Middle Ages is a category that has no counterpart in the history of islam, it manifests a very Eurocentric perspective.

Constantinople fell to the Turks because it refused to bend its knee to Rome. On occasions it feigned that it did. But it never changed. The Christian church did not start with pre-fabricated dogmas. But among church fathers there was a consensus that Jesus Christ was both man and God. The first schismatic was Arius, who defended the rudimentary idea that Jesus was the son of God, a sort of lesser god (Arianism). This simple belief appealed to the pagan, polytheistic Germans, among whom it had much currency. Nestorius refined Arius' idea and argued that in heaven God and Jesus were fused as one but on earth Christ had definitely been only a man. What these speculations addressed was the inconceivability of God on earth.

This also troubled eastern theologians, who argued that Christ's nature was solely divine. This is what became known as monophysitism. Rome rejected this outright but the doctrine never lost its appeal in Constantinople. To try to soften the edges of monophyisitism, the Eastern Church conceived monotheletism, which argued that what Christ retained while on earth was the divine will. This did not improve matters. What ultimately were involved were politics, for Constantinople could not accept the supremacy of Western Europe. The conventional date for the break between the churches is 1054. The Eastern or Greek Orthodox

---

1 "The circumstances of the last defense of Constantinople are suggestive, too, for in 1453 the ancient, medieval, and modern worlds seemed briefly to meet." *Encyclopedia Britannica* (EB), 2005

Church today believes, like most Christians should, that Jesus Christ was both human and divine.

If Constantinople had recanted, the West might have prevented the Ottomans from advancing into the Balkans. But this would also have meant the subordination of Greek Orthodoxy. It has been said over and over that the Christian east preferred Turkic to western European imposition because the Ottomans were more tolerant than westerners would ever be. Orthodoxy not only subsisted vigorously inside the Ottoman Empire but it had centuries earlier spread to Russia, which became the largest land empire in history under the sign of the Greek cross.

The history of both the Habsburg and the Ottoman empires is that of their mutual wars. The Habsburg eventually were having the better part but both perished at the end of World War I, in which they fought as allies.

Some empires were extremely ephemeral. Amerindians were building empires in Meso-America and from the Andean plateaux on the foundations of long lines of previous political formations only just before Columbus arrived. They were stone age-empires that could not resist European weaponry.

The Mongol Empire was a burst of contained energy, like a historical supernova. It was born and fragmented in less than two generations. But it was so dazzling that for centuries after Jenghiz Khan died, his lineage was legitimating from Mongolia to Anatolia. The Turkic Timurid Empire was another burst, even briefer than the Mongol Empire. Because Timur claimed descent from Jenghiz, his own line had only derived prestige and it was soon diluted. The Mughals were actually Timurids, hence Turks, but they called themselves Mongols in the style of Timur.

Apart form these categories or groupings of empires, there are also in history what can be called honorific empires. The imperial condition frequently connotes power, bigness, and multi-ethnicity. However, the Japanese, who are very proud of their racial "purity", considered their home islands an empire until the Americans disabused them.

Napoleon constructed a very brief continental European empire. His brother Louis was named king of Holland. He became such an ardent Dutch patriot that Napoleon had him removed from the throne. Louis' son, Louis Napoleon, was barely French—he had been a captain in the Swiss army—when he entered French politics at the fall of the Orléanist monarchy in 1848. In four years he formed a Bonapartist party, he got elected president, abolished the republic and was elected dictator in a plebiscite, and finally crowned himself emperor. France ipso facto became an empire. France had colonial outposts here and there and had already begun the conquest of Algeria. But when Germany was constituted as an empire it didn't have an inch of non-European territory. Both France and Germany were empires from their assessment of their own power. But the biggest empire ever in history was formed by Great Britain, which was only a kingdom.

(3) If nature abhors a vacuum, power cannot but hate weakness

The British Empire, small to vast areas of red spanning the earth on pre-World War II atlases and globes, was a colonialist empire. The red was from the color of British officers' tunics. European colonialist empires were, with the exception of Russia, sea-borne empires. But this was only at the beginning.

The Irish sometimes claim that they were the first overseas colony. Earlier, Norwegians had settled Iceland, Greenland, and Vinland, but Norway was not a cohesive kingdom. The real explosion of overseas imperialism was the doing of the Portuguese prodded by Prince Henry, called the Navigator, although he himself did not navigate much. He had crossed the Straits of Gibraltar and fought in northern Morocco, where he found out about gold from Ghana, then the incipient kingdoms of Akwamu and Ashanti.[2] There were also reports of a Prester John, who ruled a Christian kingdom surrounded by heathen. Some historians trace those reports to Abyssinian monks who had reached Rome, although Ethiopians have always been monophysites and monophysitism is odious to Rome.

Prince Henry launched a project that wove together the search for gold, military aid for Prester John, portolanos or sailing maps, and the caravel, a small sailing ship that mounted cannon. The original quest for gold had various consequences: it begot the intra-coastal African slave trade, antecessor of the Atlantic slave trade. As the Portuguese sailed further and further east, projects to monopolize the spice trades were

2 The kingdom of Akwamu (17th-18th centuries) was formed by Akan-speaking tribes who occupied territory in today's southern Ghana. The rulers of Akwamu were called akwamuhene. They absorbed the coast (Fanti) and in the early 18th century they took Whydah from Dahomey (today's Benin). Like other Sub-Saharan proto states, Akwamu participated in the slave trade, but it also had gold. Ashanti to the north had prospered even more and under pressure from that direction Akwamu disintegrated. Ashanti was famous for its gold mines, which were the initial attraction that Africa held for the Portuguese. Kumasi was the Ashanti capital. Partly to curtail the slave trade, the British initiated the annexation of the Gold Coast in 1821. Ashanti was subjected to three colonialist wars (1824-1827, 1893-1894, and 1895-1896). As Ghana, the Gold Coast became independent in 1960.

engendered and the search for new maritime routes led to the Caribbean Sea and the Antilles.[3]

Columbus broached this route to the Portuguese, who of course knew it was feasible but did not want it undertaken because they couldn't afford to do it themselves and didn't want any one else doing it. Columbus had to gallop off to Spain to avoid spending the rest of his life in gaol. Prester John was never found but at a time when Muslims from Adal were ravaging Ethiopia, Portuguese musketeers from Goa arrived and routed them. As to the technology of maritime exploration, it was soon the common knowledge of Europeans and thus began the great expansion of western civilization.

It is a matter of self-evidence that the individual European colonialist empires were not thrown together for the love of God, not to say of mankind. The profit motive can usually be found in one way or another in most imperialist enterprises, but it has to be nuanced. Ireland was an English royal claim with papal blessing before it was economically brutalized. In the stirrings of the Portuguese colonialist project, gain and religion were inextricable. Spain made a great show of its shock over the heathen cannibals of Mexico, but it proceeded to enslave all Amerindians except where there was no profit to be made.[4] The Dutch made no bones about their commercial intentions. They never undertook a colonialist move that was not calculated to profit investors. The British colonial expansion, though usually conceived in terms of profit and loss, had its shadings, as when it followed upon its own momentum or tracked the wanderings of missionaries in Africa.

The man-on-the-spot theory of imperialism argues that the growth of the European colonialist empires was due to individuals who advanced by their own initiatives the cause of empire. From this view, the Scottish missionary David Livingstone was an imperialist, for it was he whom Henry Morton Stanley tracked down in central Africa. Stanley later claimed the Congo River basin for Leopold II of Belgium (1878-1884), but Livingstone had nothing to do with that. A more illustrative case of man-on-the-spot imperialism was that of Gen. Charles Napier, who annexed Sind (southern Pakistan) to British India without superior authorization (1843). Napier is famous for the "peccavi" (I have sinned) telegram, which he did not write but was attributed to him by the illustrious comic weekly *Punch*.

Often in the debate over colonialist imperialism a plain fact is overlooked, perhaps because it is so plain it seems inadequate to explain

3 John Reader, *Africa: a biography of the continent* (1997), ch. 36
4 Marvin Harris, *Cannibals and kings: the origins of culture* (1977)

so much history. If Europe colonialized most of the world it did so because it could. If nature abhors a vacuum, power cannot but hate weakness. European empires were possible because it was the West that had the means to build them. This does not explain everything but without this understanding nothing else is explicable. Political power was founded on technological progress. It was the balance of forces and the quest for trade monopolies and captive markets that determined the conquest of India and other great colonialist enterprises, but it was through specific technological advantages—crucially naval artillery and the disciplined regiment—that colonialist empires could grow and consolidate.[5]

(4) A democratic republic that was born the size of an empire

If bigness alone defined empire, the USA was an empire at its inception. But there was more than bigness to the new country. The USA was the most populous and the most developed country in the Western Hemisphere. It had a nautical tradition to rival those of the Europeans. During the American War of Independence, American ships raided on the seas around the British islands. The most famous American exploit was the capture of the Serapis by the Bon Homme Richard captained by John Paul Jones. Herman Melville's *Moby Dick* gives the measure of American pride in its whaling fleet.

The USA was the best-organized polity not only in all of America but perhaps in the entire world. And it had a continent for a backyard. In the Barbary wars, waged to protect its commerce and to put an end to tribute payments, the USA demonstrated its naval strength and the extent of its military reach. Few countries in the world then could conduct military campaigns, including land forces, in two continents. The USA did not actually subject any of the Barbary States of northern Africa, and it negotiated as often as it attacked, but in the end it critically weakened piracy, so that the occupation of the Algerian coast by France was like crushing a rotten orange.

---

5 Richard Pipes' summary, in *Russia under the Old Regime* (1974), is brief and to the point: "In order to gain the greatest possible advantages from the new [powder] weapons, soldiers were drilled so that...they advanced unflinching against the enemy alternately firing and loading their guns, until, having reached his lines, they charged with fixed bayonets. Chains of command were established, with heads of each unit responsible for the behavior of their troops on and off the battlefield; unwieldy armies were broken down into brigades, regiments, and battalions; artillery was separated into a distinct arm; special engineering and sapper units were formed to carry out siege operations. The introduction of military uniforms...symbolized the transition from medieval to modern warfare."

The USA was practically impervious to foreign conquest. Instead, it considered annexing Canada, which was the cause of the War of 1812 with Great Britain. The British were heavily engaged against Napoleon at the time, so it couldn't be said that they put all they could into the war, but individual operations against America were sizable and they were all repulsed. Britain was the gainer in that the USA gave up imperial ambitions with respect to Canada, but American self-confidence was so enhanced that in 1823 president James Monroe had the gall to tell Europeans not to meddle in the political affairs of the countries in the Western Hemisphere. This was imperialism in the grand Roman manner: serene authority for maximum effect with a minimum of effort. Washington did not claim one inch of territory outside the Union but it was to be understood that it had the power to interdict every inch of territory within its vast sphere of influence against any interloper. There was a great deal of bluff in this. But the point was that America would not accept any threat to its security.

With the Louisiana Purchase (1803) the USA already had acquired more than half the land west of the Mississippi and south of whatever reasonable frontier was traced between the USA and Canada in their western reaches (eventually fixed along the 49th parallel). Mexico had the rest of that territory, including notably Texas and California. But Mexico was something of a paradox.

(5) A make-believe empire faces a really voracious land-eater

Mexico became independent by default. It was practically autonomous to begin with. Spain named the viceroys and it had a military staff. But the soldieries were Mexicans. It could actually be said that Mexico was a colony only because the local upper classes were loyal to the Spanish crown and that they were loyal Spanish subjects because it was to their advantage. The wealth of the tiny local oligarchies rested on a system of peonage, which embraced the majority of the population. The Creoles did not want this order changed. Amerindians had their own communities with collective ownership of the land. This was the doing of Spain. Collectively, Amerindians were on the margins of colonial society even to having their own languages, customs, and syncretic religious practices.

The first Mexican independentist movements, led separately by the priests Miguel Hidalgo y Costilla and Jose Maria Morelos y Pavon, demanded social reform. They were quashed and their leaders executed by a Mexican army led by Gen. Agustín de Itúrbide. When in 1820 Spain itself adopted constitutional reforms, the Mexicans became apprehensive and decided that they weren't going to have Spanish liberals telling them how to organize their society. Itúrbide declared

Mexico not only independent but also an empire whose main constitutive principle was that nothing should ever change in the social order of things. Now, since the Mexican elite was small and had all the wealth it wanted, to retain which it could not release peons from servitude, and since the Amerindians had been brutalized and marginalized, who was going to settle the lands north of the Rio Grande? The paradox of Mexico was that of an understaffed, under-inhabited, socially skewed, gigantic country.

For a real empire such as the USA, Mexico was biting far more than it could chew. Americans were already more numerous than Mexicans in Texas. Some large Mexican landowners had their peons. Cattle roamed freely in great herds. But the land was comparatively empty. No real empire could resist that temptation. California too was already heavy with American settlers. It was only Mexican from the names the Spaniards had bestowed on the villages and the principal natural features. Mexican California was a land of villages and tiny garrisons. Imperialism, however, was not the American way, so it was said that American democracy was "destined" to embrace the western part of North America to the Pacific Ocean.

The American settlers of Texas were the ones who got the imperialist ball rolling. They declared independence. When the Mexicans tried to scotch it they were defeated.Texas was not immediately accepted into the American Union.But it was considered an American protectorate, so that when Mexican troops crossed the Rio Grande, the USA considered this a casus belli and declared war. There were two theaters of operation in Mexico: the land invasion south to Monterrey and on to the capital and naval operations, which secured Veracruz, from where another prong advanced on Mexico City. Surprisingly the war lasted a couple of months. Mexico was forced to cede California and the entire American southwest.

Americans knew something important about Mexico and it was that it could not hang on to the land it had not adequately settled or garrisoned, but they learned that Mexico itself, the large core of the Old Spanish viceroyalty, was another matter. Trying to conquer it was different from grabbing empty wasteland such as New Mexico and Arizona. It couldn't be done without getting bogged down in an interminable struggle.

The USA already had enough political problems deciding how to admit states to the satisfaction of the representatives of free and of slavery states to be even thinking of annexing Mexico, even if the Mexicans had wanted to join the Union. The Dominican Republic, which at one point did want to be annexed by America, was turned down irrevocably. The lesson about the Mexican heartland was useful in the relations between

America and European powers, so that when France intervened in Mexico and set up an "empire" with a Habsburg prince on the throne, the USA was not unduly alarmed, even though this was out-and-out imperialism and a most gratuitous breach of the Monroe Doctrine.

(6) While the USA meticulously built a maritime empire, Spain hung tenaciously on to parcels of territory

The USA was also hampered by its own Civil War, which severely restricted its ability to intervene externally. After the French left, significantly because the American Civil War had ended, Emperor Maximilian was so bereft of native support that he was soon defeated and stood in front of a firing squad. Maximilian and his Empress, Carlota, had actually been social favorites of the upper crust in Mexico City, but the kindly Emperor was far too progressive for Mexican landowners, who wanted to lay their hands on Amerindian communal lands.

Towards the end of the 19th century, American imperialism had constituted the actual USA, except for some territories still to be admitted to the Union. The Monroe Doctrine was more than ever operative. That's when America began thinking in terms of colonialist imperialism. All of Africa was definitely within the European sphere of influence. The rest of the Americas were already part of the informal American empire. But the Far East lay approximately midway between the USA and Europe.

There is a six-hour difference between Manila and London and a nine-hour difference between Manila and San Francisco. The British Empire was obviously much closer to China and it was British imperialism that had begun opening Chinese ports to foreign commerce, but America was already acknowledged to be in the first rank of the great powers and it was America that had forced an opening to the Japanese Empire, much smaller than China but more compact. China was like a bursting watermelon whereas Japan was like a walnut. In one bold move, Commodore Matthew Perry, one of the naval heroes of the Mexican war, had entered Tokyo harbor and let the shogun know that the modern world wasn't going to go away.[6] But America also had its eyes on China. No self-respecting commercial nation could not but be thinking of the Chinese market.

The American colonialist empire, though on the surface contrived, was acquired as if with a precise blueprint, not one beam not one post missing, not one inch short in any piece. To start discounting the advantage that Europe had over America in distance to the Far East, the

---

6 W.G. Beasley, *The Meiji restoration* (1973).

USA annexed the Hawaiian Islands, whose queen disliked missionaries but could do nothing to get rid of them.[7] Then gunpowder in the hold of the battleship Maine was packed too tightly and a spark set off an explosion when the ship was at anchor in the bay of Havana. This was an accident.

Dreadnoughts were expensive and at the time not that numerous. The USA and Spain had a war of nerves, an early version of the Cold War, going on over Cuba. The Americans wanted the Cuban cane fields. Cuba is a green, fertile island. It grows the sweetest oranges and the creamiest mangoes in the world, not to mention the best tobacco leaves. From way back, Spain had an obsession with land sovereignty as opposed to purely commercial interests. This was in part the result of the American discovery, in part that of its Habsburg inheritance.

(7) The only thing that Spain retained from the Netherlands was flamenco music

Most early sea-borne empires were about anchorages and entrepôts and stone fortresses, either on nearly deserted islands or on the skins of weak or careless native kingdoms. For Spain, empire in the Western Hemisphere meant acquiring a lot of land, basically because the riches it craved were found far inland, in fact, in the most inaccessible and remote part of the empire. Huge lodes of silver, next to mercury deposits, were found in the three-mile high plateau that is today a large part of Bolivian territory. This was almost as if one had to go to the center of the earth to find the ring of power. To get to Alto Peru, where the silver lay, the Spaniards had to traverse a lot of territory from every direction except the east, which was impenetrable jungle or swamp, and they claimed for themselves and the Spanish crown everything they stepped on or could see. Potosi became one of the bigger cities of the world because of the silver.[8]

---

7 Captain Cook visited Hawaii, a Polynesian kingdom, in 1778. American missionaries Christianized it during the 19th century. King Kalakaua granted the United States naval rights to Pearl Harbor (1887), to which queen Liliuokalani (1891-1895) was opposed, and rightly so for she was deposed and Hawaii was annexed outright in 1898.

8 Besides Alto Perú, Bolivia was also known as Chuquisaca and as Charcas, from the changing names of its capital, originally founded as La Plata in 1538. Charcas became of crucial economic importance with the discovery of a silver lode in nearly three-mile-high Potosí (1545), which kept Spain supplied with species for over two centuries at the cost of thousands of enslaved Indian lives. Potosí grew by the hour until it had a population of more than 150,000. La Paz, today Bolivia's capital, was founded in 1548 as ancillary to Potosí.

The other piece of property that conditioned Spanish foreign policy came from king Charles I Habsburg, who was also duke of Flanders and Holy Roman emperor. When he died, Spain possessed what today are Belgium, the Netherlands, and Luxembourg (among other Habsburg European possessions). The Low Countries, the collective name for these ancient provinces, is not contiguous to Spain. Culturally, they were not and never became close to Spain, although the Spanish gypsy tradition was named Flemish or flamenco because of Charles, who probably enjoyed guitar music and castanets.

The Dutch were particularly fractious to Spanish rule. The only thing Spaniards and their Lowland subjects had in common was religion and that too changed when the Dutch adopted Calvinism. The Spanish economic ruin, and its consequent loss of political influence, military power, and territory, came about in part because of the efforts Spain expended to keep the Low Countries in subjection, which meant civil war and wars or hostilities with France and with England over a long period of time; and in the end for nothing, because the United Provinces of the Netherlands became independent and when the last Spanish Habsburg, afflicted with idiocy, died, the Spanish crown was obtained by a Bourbon and Spain forfeited the rest of the Lowlands to the Austrian Habsburg. Some historians argue that the Lowland wars benefited Spain in that they kept religious disunity at bay, but religious wars did not weaken France and most historians see Spain's religious unity as a retarding influence.

(8) Wars of independence inside a war of independence

When Spain's American colonies demanded their independence, Spain was engaged in its own war of independence from Napoleonic France. Most of the colonies simply separated or went autonomous, like Mexico, but in places, especially in Venezuela, the peons, who were cattle-herders and instant guerrilla-fighters, rebelled against the Creole aristocracy and resisted independence.[9] Patriot leaders like Simon Bolivar and Jose Antonio Páez gradually won these horse riders for independence.

When the British-Spanish alliance finally expelled the French from Iberia, Spain barely paused to take its breath before it sent a large army to Venezuela. In normal European conditions, this army would have been decisive on the battlefield, but in Venezuela it was fighting the climate and the topography and fending off hit-and-run tactics and it became so onerous and useless that the same Spanish constitutionalist movement that scared the Mexican oligarchy into independence recalled

9 John Lynch, *The Spanish-American revolutions 1808-1826* (1973).

it and left the field for the patriots to mop up local resistance. Even then, Spain gave up land so reluctantly that it sent expeditions (all failed) to recover Chile, Peru, and Mexico.

After it had lost most of its huge empire, Spain retained Philippines, Cuba, and Puerto Rico. When the USA became independent, Britain adopted the policy of encouraging self-government in Canada and its other colonies of settlement (Australia and New Zealand). Spain never even contemplated loosening colonialist screws. But the contrast shouldn't be exaggerated. Britain did not encourage self-government in India and the colonies that Spain still had were mostly peopled either by non-Europeans or by descendants of mixed couplings. The Spanish and Spanish-descended minorities preferred Spanish absolutism to non-white democracy. The USA was not exactly the champion of racial democracy, but there were some white Cubans agitating for independence.

(9) Roughly one half of the USA was purchased for $51.2 million, which sounds like peanuts not considering that it could have been had for nothing

In the final analysis, America was hankering for a colonialist empire, it had its eyes set on China, and it wanted to lay its hands on the Philippines, which was next door to China, a perfect base for all sorts of operations. Therefore, when the Maine exploded, Spain was unfairly blamed for it and the USA went to war. A common conspiracy theory is that William Randolph Hearst should have been blamed because his *San Francisco Chronicle*, part of a newspaper chain across America, blared the news and practically declared the war on Spain before Congress did. This assertion is based on the time difference between New York and San Francisco, the argument being roughly that San Francisco knew about the Maine a mite earlier than New York.

Be that as it may, the forces for colonialist imperialism were much more powerful than the Hearst newspapers. Theodore Roosevelt was just one among many politicians who was for the war. In American historiographical mythology, President William McKinley, the man who actually presided over the war and decided what to do with the former Spanish colonies, was the only one agonizing over their fate.

The war itself was brief. The Spanish navy was small and obsolete. The American fleet was dazzlingly white, spic and span and supremely efficient (except about storing gunpowder). The battle off Santiago de Cuba was classically depicted as the white American warships firing on the black Spanish ships trying to put out to sea.

A widely accepted version of the land war in the Philippines is that the Spaniards, unwilling to hand authority to the Filipino leader Emilio Aguinaldo, staged a mock-battle with the Americans in Manila and thus justified their surrender to the USA, which paid an indemnity of $20 million to Spain (a sum hardly within the reach of Filipinos).

Aguinaldo declared Philippine independence although it is unclear whether from Spain or from the USA, for this happened after the Americans sank the Spanish ships anchored in Cavite but before Spain capitulated in Manila. It was definitely Americans who ran Aguinaldo to the ground and arrested him. Aguinaldo did not forget and became a Japanese collaborator during World War II. Filipinos did not allow him to be punished after the war and President Diosdado Macapagal in 1962 changed the Filipino day of independence from 4th of July, an absurd American legacy, to 12 June, when Aguinaldo had proclaimed it in Kawit or the old Filipino from which the Spaniards got the name Cavite.

The year following the war, called Spanish-American (although it should more reasonably be American-Spanish), the USA enunciated the "open door" policy for China. America never occupied a treaty port on the Chinese mainland. It didn't have to. It had the Philippines.

At its peak, the American colonialist empire included: the Philippines, Puerto Rico, the Panamá Canal Zone, the American Virgin Islands (there exist also a British Virgin Islands), American Samoa, and Guam. During those years (1916-1924), the USA was simultaneously occupying Haiti, the Dominican Republic, and Nicaragua. Cuba was an autonomous dependency. Alaska and Hawaii were still territories. The Panamá Canal Zone was formed with land ceded by the newly created republic of Panamá for the construction of the canal.[10] In absolute terms, the Virgin Islands, purchased from Denmark for $25,000,000, are the most costly piece of real estate America ever acquired. Outside of this late acquisition, roughly one half of the territory of the American Union

---

10 In 1880, Ferdinand de Lesseps, the French builder of the Suez Canal, obtained a Colombian concession to build an inter-oceanic canal in Panamá. His company went bust (1891), partly through fraud, and in 1892 the French chief engineer Philippe Bunau-Varilla picked up the pieces, with which he interested the American government in the completion of the canal. However, the Colombian senate proved uncooperative. Bunau-Varilla gathered some local opposition, even designed a flag, and on 3 November 1903 Panamá declared its independence from Colombia. The USA, which controlled the isthmus railroad, stranded the Colombian troops sent in response. By the Hay-Bunau-Varilla Treaty the US was ceded forever the use of the land needed for the cutting of the canal.

was purchased for $52.2 million[11], which sounds like peanuts but this is not considering that much of this land could probably have been taken by the USA without paying a penny.

Just as it could be said that monetarily the USA was fair and square in its territorial acquisitions, so it is possible to claim that American imperialism was not exactly like the European colonialist empires or any historical empire. It was very functional. There was no flab in it. America was imperial but in a perfectly understandable way: it did not dole out economic favors; it did not tolerate threats, or even the semblance of threats; and it did not like to lose face. But extra land it did not need or want.

Spain never shed the mania for land sovereignty, perhaps also a reflex from the loss of Gibraltar, which was as if Britain had lost the Isle of Wight. In the late 19th century (before the Spanish-American War), Spain re-constituted the colony of Equatorial Guinea, which it had previously neglected for the good reason that it was worthless then (very wealthy now because of oil). The Western Sahara, which Spain also claimed, was likewise nearly without value (it has phosphate deposits). And when France absorbed Morocco as a dependent kingdom, Spain was offered northern Morocco, a chance it apparently couldn't pass up, although here again it was mostly a source of expenses as Spanish forces had to suppress the pertinacious resistance of Abdel Krim. Later, Spanish Morocco served as a base for the militarist assault on the Spanish republic.

The Scramble for Africa, set off by Berlin's anxiety about not having colonies like France did, was also mostly land grabbing for its own sake. There is not one shred of evidence that what motivated late imperialist colonialism were short-term economic prospects, although long-term is another story, so the debate on the nature of imperialism is really quite unsolvable.[12]

---

11 Territorial payments in dollars were: the Louisiana Purchase in 1803 from France (15,000,000); Florida in 1819 from Spain (5,000,000); Mexican territories in 1848 (15,000,000); from Mexico also the Gadsden purchase, southern Arizona and New Mexico, in 1853 (10,000,000); and Alaska in 1867 from Russia (7,200,000). However, of these sums, American citizens from the prices to France and Spain discounted 3,750,000 and 5,000,000 for claims, respectively. The USA agreed to assume the claims of its citizens against Mexico, which must have been considerable.

12 The Germans built a capital in central Tanzania, Tabora, to grand imperial specifications—today it is a monumental ghost-town—so that they were obviously expecting that in time German South East Africa would be a paying concern. Thomas Pakenham, *The scramble for Africa 1876-1912* (1991).

(10) The Platt amendment was invoked only once and that was because blacks were getting rowdy about Cuban discrimination

One thing for certain is that the USA did not relish colonies for themselves. It let Cuba go with the proviso, known as the Platt amendment, that if the island became disorderly the Americans would be back, and they indeed were, on one occasion because blacks were being rowdy about discrimination. Cuban racial discrimination is a class of its own. It was strong before Castro. Communism has socially empowered blacks, who in Cuba are more educated and play a more level field than in the rest of Latin America. However, the Ku Klux Klan is an affiliate of the National Association for the Advancement of Colored People (NAACP) in comparison with the rabid hatred that some Cuban whites still have for blacks.

The American occupation of the Philippines was at all times understood to be temporary. A term for independence was already set in the 1930s and, except for the luxury car he imported, and Gen. Douglas MacArthur impounded for his own use, Philippine President Manuel Quezon was treated by America as virtually a head of state.

The only country that did not gain an inch of territory among the World War I allies was the USA, whose participation in that conflict decided its outcome. Strange as it sounds, and despite America's rough-and-tough reputation, the USA entered the war partly out of idealism or some such abstraction.

World War II was another story, because between German and Japanese aggressions America did feel threatened. And after the war, the USA did make strategic and territorial acquisitions. Some of these acquisitions didn't have claimants or the makings of statehood. They are all now autonomous. Most important strategically, although territorially insignificant, were the military bases the USA established and still maintains in Germany and Japan. At first these bases were a necessity of the occupation. But they were also to let the USSR know how far it could go without provoking America. The USA also has bases in Italy and other countries, but they are mainly for its warplanes and land forces are negligible.

(11) Churchill's obsession with the Balkans and its deadly consequences

It is only in America that it is debated whether Franklin Roosevelt was a patsy of Stalin. Churchill outlived World War II. He was a veteran anti-communist from before the war. The USA was only grazed by anti-Bolshevik hysteria. Between the wars, its two most famous political executions were those of Niccola Sacco and Bartolomeo Vanzetti, who were anarchists and not communists. It is possible they were guilty of killing two men to steal $15,000. It is certain that their politics doomed them.

Churchill was a great one for realpolitik whereas Roosevelt is accused of naivety. However, Churchill's strategic manias were very costly in human lives in both world wars and Roosevelt had a more commonsensical approach, if only in letting the generals make the crucial decisions. Generals were very obtuse in World War I but in World War II it is usually accepted that they were competent. The difference cannot be just a matter of chance. World War I left little room for movement whereas World War II was a war of movement from beginning to end. It is highly unlikely that shrewd Roosevelt, however chummy he might had been with Stalin in their only two personal encounters (Tehran and Yalta), would have allowed the USSR to ride roughshod over Germany. Roosevelt's sympathy for Stalin is also often contrasted with his antipathy for De Gaulle, but even the French admired but did not always like De Gaulle.

It would be inconceivably callow for any one to think that the USA was not making contingency plans in case the USSR became overly ambitious after the war, as callow as believing that Roosevelt was not aware of such plans. In sum, the American government and President Roosevelt had to know that after World War II the non-communist world in its entirety had to become America's informal empire. The opposite of this view is the invention by senator Joseph McCarthy that the State Department was riddled with communists, actively conspiring in the heart of American democracy to let Stalin take over the world. Even the most complicit fellow traveler could not have wanted the USSR to enslave humanity. Fellow-traveling usually connoted a sense of social equity and certainly not the destruction of democracy. The really surprising thing in the Post-War is how quickly the Soviet bear growled, but this might have had to do with that America was being aggressively anti-communist. So who started the Cold War?

(12) The curiously inverted economic relation between the USSR and Finland

When the map of Post-War Europe was drawn it wasn't quite that different ethnically from what it should have been after World War I. Finland had lost most of Karelia to the USSR, but that was back in 1939-1940 and the Finns had paid the Russians back by helping the Germans blockade Leningrad on the north, which was the reason why the city had to be supplied over frozen lake Ladoga. As the USSR bounced back against Germany, the Soviets put the Finnish border back to where it is now. Most Karelians migrated to Finland and Russians moved in to replace them.

After the war, the Soviets had as good a case for absorbing Finland as they had for the Baltic States—they all had been part of the Tsarist

Empire—but Stalin abstained in respect to Finland. In looking back at the history of the USSR, or as much of it as is more or less publicly known, which is only a fraction of what remains to be known, one often has the impression that the communists were not sure that their economic system was really competitive with capitalism and that they retained it out of inertia or political convenience or because they really did believe that it achieved a better distribution of wealth. Otherwise, that Finland survived to become a capitalist supplier of industrial goods to the USSR makes no sense at all.

Finland's contiguity with Sweden might have had to do with the Soviet decision to recognize Finnish sovereignty and neutrality. Though no match for the USSR, Sweden was formidably armed and with the Soviets on the Gulf of Bothnia it would surely have joined any anti-Soviet, American-sponsored west European alliance. The Finns themselves were nerved to resist the Russians. Occupying Finland could have turned into a nightmare for the USSR.

Still, there was the possibility of satellite status, but even that was discarded for a fully capitalist Finland which industrialized, first, to make reparations payments, and then, to become an exporter of manufactured goods to the USSR. In other words, the USSR chose the role of underdeveloped nation by becoming a provider of raw materials to Finland in exchange for ships, locomotives, turbines, and all sorts of industrial products. For all their bragging about communism, the Soviets had to know that capitalism could turn small Finland into an economic powerhouse with the capacity to supply needs that the USSR could not provide for itself. There was yet another thing that the Soviets knew and it was that the communists by themselves would never win free elections.

(13) The communist who became a Hollywood legend because of his heavy Hungarian accent

Returning to the Post-War map, Poland reverted to the Curzon line, which had originally been drawn during the Paris Peace Conference and was modified when the Poles defeated the Red Army and grabbed chunks of Belarus and Ukraine. This is one of those wars that, like Finnish independence, can perplex historians. It began with the Red cavalry riding to the suburbs of Warsaw and ended with the Red Army in full retreat. Yet to this day some very serious Sovietologists—their specialization is still very much alive and has even subsumed much discredited Kremlinology—insist that the war was the Bolsheviks' way of telling the world that communist Russia was now stabilized.[13]

13 Figes, op.cit., pp.701-702

For good measure, the Poles, also annexed the traditional Lithuanian capital, Vilnius, which is less serious than it seems because Vilnius was mainly a Jewish city. After World War II, Vilnius, by then devoid of its massacred Jewish residents, reverted to Soviet republic Lithuania. The ethnic borders of Latvia and Estonia were also respected. The Soviets took a slice of Romania, presumably in punishment for its participation in the siege of Stalingrad. Perhaps the most politically loaded modification to the map of Europe that the Soviets made had to do with a small piece of territory called Ruthenia.

In the over-all balance of European territorial history, one of the countries that has suffered great diminution is Hungary, perhaps even more than Germany despite the latter's loss of eastern Prussia, Silesia, and most of Pomerania.[14] Other states, specifically the USSR, Czechoslovakia, and Yugoslavia, have disappeared altogether. Hungarians were once spread over northern Serbia, northwestern Romania, and the Carpathian mountains (today mostly in Ukraine). The Hungarian Carpathian is the reason why the famous Hollywood Dracula, Bela Lugosi, once the minister for culture of the communist Bela Kun regime in Hungary, speaks with a heavy Hungarian accent. The numbers are hard to estimate but some time in the past there were more Hungarians outside the borders of modern Hungary than inside it. The threat to the integrity of the Austria-based Habsburg Empire did not come from Slavs but from Hungarians and when the empire was shaken to its foundations by defeat at the hands of Prussia, it was re-organized as the Austro-Hungarian Dual Monarchy.[15]

After World War I, Hungary was as penalized as Austria. Romania took Transylvania. And Czechoslovakia retained the bit of land conventionally called Ruthenia, which is probably another name for Russia but was inhabited by Hungarians. Its main city was Ungvar (now Uzhgorod) and its border with what was then Poland followed the

14 In 1921, Poland took western Ukraine and Belarus from the USSR. After World War II, the USSR reclaimed these territories and compensated Poland with all of Silesia (southeastern Germany) and part of Pomerania (northeastern Germany). Eastern Prussia was divided between Poland and a wedge on the Baltic, which Russia retained. Königsberg, the east Prussian capital and Kant's home, was rebaptized Kaliningrad by the Soviets after Mikhail Ivanovich Kalinin, president (technically chairman of the executive committee) of the USSR (1919-1946). Stalin was a believer in changing the names of places to honor great communists. Tsaritsyn, on the Volga, was renamed Volgograd, then Stalingrad, and then Volgograd again. But the battle will always be known as Stalingrad.

15 Upon its formation in 1867, Austria-Hungary had 37 million inhabitants. The territory of modern Hungary had just over five million but the Hungarian kingdom included part of Poland and Transylvania.

summits of the Carpathians. After World War II, during which Hungary was again on the wrong side, the question of Ruthenia was settled once and for all by attaching it to the Ukraine, which in effect meant that the USSR obtained land frontiers with Hungary and Czechoslovakia.

(14) If any one started pushing in Europe after World War II it was the Soviets

In Potsdam, neither the USA nor Great Britain denied the USSR its claim to political hegemony in Eastern Europe. The latter designation was vague. If Germany was part of Western Europe, then Czechoslovakia had as much or more right to that condition. But Eastern Germany was occupied by the USSR. Czechoslovakia in fact was in a grey area and could tilt either way although militarily it was more exposed to the Soviets.

The Sudeten Germans had been expelled and the Czechoslovak communist movement was strong enough to obtain a plurality of votes. Klement Gottwald, the Soviet's truculent Czech agent, forced his way into government. Jan Masaryk, the Czechoslovak foreign minister, son of Thomas Garrigue Masaryk, the founder of post-World War I Czechoslovakia, was very likely defenestrated by the communists for opposing them. The official version was that he committed suicide.

The Red Army had a corridor to Prague in Ruthenia. The Americans, who were occupying Bavaria, the part of Germany contiguous to Bohemia, did not oppose the communist take over. In one decade Czechoslovakia was betrayed twice by the western powers. Clearly, if any one started pushing in Europe after World War II it was the Soviets in Czechoslovakia. Later, Ruthenia was also used by Soviet tanks against Hungary and to snip the Prague Spring in the bud.

Greece was definitely not supposed to be within the Soviet sphere of influence. The British had exerted themselves to save it from Germany. This was the doing of Winston Churchill, who always had a thing for the Balkans. In World War I, the Gallipoli disaster (1915-1916) was a consequence of Churchill's strategic thinking, which was to knock Turkey out of the war and open a third front against the Central Powers. The idea wasn't bad but the generalship, which mucked about giving the Turks time to fortify the heights, was egregious.

The immense reputation of the German Gen. Erwin Rommel can be attributed indirectly to Churchill. When the Italians began to buckle, Hitler sent armies to steel them in the Greek front and in Libya. Churchill had previously become prime minister. To save Greece, he moved from Egypt the British troops that had the Italians on the run in Libya. He wasn't counting on the aggressiveness of Rommel, who overran the weakened British positions and proceeded to invade Egypt.

The Yugoslavs had economic ties with Germany but their sympathies were with France. The German offensive in the Balkans, which had to subdue the impertinent Yugoslavs before it got to Greece, was stupendously successful. It was completed in less than a month with losses of some 12,000 against over 600,000 casualties and prisoners on the other sides. The British intervention in Greece was useless and, to cap it all, the Germans invaded and secured Crete in the first and only purely airborne invasion in history. The Balkan invasion was the most disproportionate of Hitler's decisive victories. It was also to be his last. When Rommel came up against the reformed British line in Egypt, he found that he couldn't dent it, in part because the British were anticipating his moves through the decoding of the Enigma machine.[16]

Upon Germany's surrender, Greece was in British hands, although not quite the entire country, because Greek communist partisans were strong in the mountains to the north and had the support of Tito's Yugoslavia. Great Britain had been so indebted by war that it couldn't afford to help the Greeks fight the guerrillas if it was to be able to support the value of the pound.

If American informal imperialism were to work against Soviet militarist imperialism, it would have to count with the cooperation of its allies all over the world, especially its western European allies. Great Britain's indebtedness was mostly with America and so the British had every right to tell Washington to prop up Greece because they could not afford to do it themselves.

More than to communist subversion, then, it was to a British challenge that America responded when President Harry S. Truman announced the doctrine that bears his name and that committed the USA to help states embattled by communism anywhere in the world. America's economic assistance proved crucial for Greece, although perhaps even more so was Tito's refusal to knuckle under to Stalin.

(15) As Tito had done his own "liberating", he got away with defying Stalin

Yugoslavia was the only one of the Post-War communist states that was not occupied by the Red Army. The Yugoslav partisans did not actually ever defeat the Germans, but they were entrenched in

16 Stephen Budiansky, *Battle of wits: the complete story of code-breaking in World War II* (2000), pp.255-256.

mountainous Bosnia and Herzegovina and could on occasions mount large offensives. As the Germans withdrew Tito's partisans took over liquidating any local resistance they met. The success of the Yugoslav guerrilla was in a way the cause of Bosnia and Herzegovina's later tribulations. Tito made the province prosperous by establishing Yugoslavia's large military industries there and it was in part the Serbs' refusal to give them up that provoked the multiple conflicts and the carnage after the dissolution of Yugoslavia.

What Stalin ordered in the Soviet European Empire went. The rulers of the satellite states were emissaries of the USSR. Some had been luminaries in the Comintern. The Bulgarian Georgi Dimitrov might have been the only self-confessed communist that escaped the Nazis' clutches and that in Germany itself. Accused of the Reichstag fire that brought Hitler to power, he defended himself so ably that a German court acquitted him and he escaped to the USSR. He marched into Bulgaria with the Red Army.

Walter Ulbricht was head of Soviet propaganda at the battle of Stalingrad. He was the political boss of communist East Germany. Another hero of Stalingrad, Warsaw-born Gen. Konstantin Rokossovsky, one of Stalin's non-coms from the Tsarist army, was the Soviet proconsul in Poland.[17]

If Stalin did not like anybody in the communist parties of any of the Soviet satellites, he had that person liquidated, usually in the company of others. A prominent Czech communist, Artur London, survived one of Stalin's purges to tell of communist police interrogation methods (like prolonged sleep deprivation).[18] However, Stalin's brief did not run to Belgrade. Tito refused to take orders and for a time it was touch and go whether the USSR would invade Yugoslavia. Tito did not join the anti-communist camp but instead invented non-alignment, which was alright by America because, as was to be expected, it never went much beyond rhetoric. Without a crucial logistics base, the Greek communists were left in the lurch.

(16) Containment was the inevitable strategy for a super-power that had world imperialism thrust upon it

Stalin might have used Bulgaria to stir things up in Greece, but Tito's defiance, and the support Yugoslavia got from the West, made him so angry that he became reckless. He went for the divided city of Berlin, whose blockade was tantamount to the open declaration of the Cold

17 Shukman, op.cit.
18 Artur London, *The confession* (1970).

War. By then America was fully committed to a worldwide strategy of containment. The Soviets' attempt to choke Berlin failed. The American response to communist invasion in Korea was as inevitable as dropping the atomic bomb on Japan. Containment, in brief, arose as America's spontaneous and inevitable strategic option.

The alternative would have been aggression and the USA had no need for such a drastic course. It might conceivably have been an option to prevent Soviet domination in Czechoslovakia, but this would have involved nuclear attack and conflict with no foreseeable end. Such a course was conceivable in the sense that Mac Arthur proposed atomic bombing China during the Korean War, a unrealistic possibility that wiser counsel needed to oppose and overrule. When later Mac Arthur tested the political waters as a potential Republican candidate for president, polls showed that he had virtually no support among Americans, who might be a pugnacious lot but who also know, or knew, how to scale down their military audacity.

Containment was the obvious American Cold War strategy because the world was mostly with America. Tito's non-alignment idea had many immediate co-sponsors, but these—Nasser of Egypt, Nehru of India, and Sukarno of Indonesia—were not buying into communism. Marxist ideological absolutism, extreme political tyranny, and especially the negation of property rights did not constitute a doctrinal triad that would sway, not just ruling classes anywhere, but even the masses, even when they toiled and were brutalized by ruling classes. Communism was not a political choice with a "natural" appeal. Peasants might have been exploited in most of the non-communist world but most anywhere they could be as superstitious and benighted as they wished, which went against the grain of Marxism, and they could own with full rights a large work-animal or a shanty, if they could afford them, and even if they couldn't, they could still believe that some time they would be able to. Incredible through it may seem to people in developed nations, shanty-owners in poor countries are considered landlords and in third world cities there usually exists a snappy trade in the sale and rental of shanties, usually without land deeds.

But communism was aggressive. It recruited aggressively. It appealed to political and moral consciences. It subverted when and where it could. That it couldn't subvert India was evidence of how unappealing it was. The only important communist subversive movement in India was formed in Bihar, India's poorest state. Its members are called Naxalites and they are recruited from the casteless or untouchables, so its Marxist affiliation is tinged with specifically cultural features. But communist subversion did not make ruling easy for countries where it could operate. It made for instability. It had to be contained.

Each country could of itself probably do a good job of containing communism. But behind the individual communist movements there was the power, first, of the USSR and then of China. And America was the only capitalist power capable of standing up internationally to empires that did not accept capitalist rules of behavior, such as keeping economic balances, sustaining the value of currencies, etc., because they had little respect for individual human life. Despite Marxist allegations and its own turpitudes, capitalism has always been the mainstay of humanism. And so, notwithstanding the lack of appeal of communism and the tendency of humanity for some kind of social order incompatible with basic Marxist-communist tenets, the USA had to take on the role of sustaining an informal world empire.

(17) Kennan's somewhat dubious maître à penser

The containment strategy, which was the cornerstone of the American imperial opposition to world communism, is often attributed to John Kennan, a senior diplomat and adviser to Dean Acheson, Truman's secretary of state and the closest an American public figure came to looking like a retired British major. Republicans vilified Acheson and Kennan. McCarthyism was Republicanism gone ape. Molotov was closer to democracy than Acheson was to communism. Kennan was too liberal for self-proclaimed warmongers. Republicans wouldn't have done anything differently than Truman and Acheson, but they talked as if they would have for political reasons. But Kennan cannot take the credit for something that came to American foreign policy as leaves to a plant. Containment was the strategy for a super-power that had world imperialism thrust upon it.[19]

Kennan's political maître à penser was the Prussian Iron Chancellor, Otto von Bismarck, and if there ever existed a foreign policy that was characterized by fragility and instability it was the one Bismarck foisted on Germany. Bismarck only seems sensible by contrast with Kaiser

19 Kennan's article on containment appeared in the July 1947 issue of the journal *Foreign Affairs*. In it he argued, essentially, that the Soviets only respected power and, if faced by American resolution, would negotiate. He even envisioned the collapse of the USSR. Malcolm Lowry, the author of the autobiographical novel *under the volcano* (1947), wrote that "grim though the picture seems, it doesn't seem half so hopeless as it did in 1939—or even in 1938. Even if communism were temporarily victorious it doesn't carry with it such a hopeless teleology of tyranny—even if tyrannical in its present phase—as did Nazism. In short anything [that] is a revolution must keep moving or it doesn't revolute; by its very nature it contains within it the seeds of its own destruction, so by 1989, say, everything ought to be hunky dory, all of which certainly doesn't make it any easier to live in 1950."

William II, who made the horrendous blunder of encouraging Austrian imperialism in the Balkans and thus struck the spark for World War I; but Bismarck filled the famous Balkan powder keg itself with his arrogant curtailment of Russian influence in favor of the doomed Ottoman Empire. Russia wanted an independent greater Bulgaria and Germany (and Britain) seemed to prefer many quarrelsome little states, or what used to be called Balkanization.[20] After much bloodshed and barbarity, full Balkanization has finally prevailed in our times, under the aegis of the EU, hopefully in stable and peaceful circumstances.

It was Bismarck's knack for cool deception that provoked France into a war for which it was not prepared whereas Prussia was. Bismarck was seeking ways to have Bavaria accept Prussia's embrace. The occasion to do this presented itself when the Spanish military toppled Queen Isabella II. Gen. Juan Prim y Prats had the not-so-brilliant idea of offering the vacant Spanish throne to a prince of the Prussian Hohenzollern dynasty. When Napoleon III found out about the Spanish Hohenzollern initiative he went gunning for the Prussians, who had actually turned down the Spanish offer, and they gave him re-assurances. However, Napoleon was taking too seriously France's imperial status and his ambassador to Berlin was a tad too imperious in a personal remonstrance to Kaiser William I. Bismarck, who had oiled the Prussian war machinery well, saw a terrific opening for real imperialism in the heart of Europe. He doctored the conversation between the French ambassador and his king and he leaked it to the press. The French saw in this an unforgivable breach of international etiquette and declared

20 In 1876, Serbia tried to take on the Ottomans and was defeated provoking the intervention of Russia and the rout of the Turks. By the treaty of San Stefano (1878), Russia acquired lands in the Caucasus; The Porte recognized Serbia, Romania and Montenegro as independent states; Romania acquired Dobruja; Bulgaria was created, comprising Macedonia; and Greece was ceded Epirus. Great Britain and Austria-Hungary resented the increase of Russian influence in the Balkans and, through cumulative international pressure, achieved the convocation of the Congress of Berlin (1878), hosted by chancellor Otto von Bismarck, in which the terms of San Stefano were modified. In the arrangement that emerged, the recognition of the independence of the Balkan states was kept, as well as the aggrandizement of Greece (excluding Epirus), but Bulgaria was divided into two autonomous provinces (Bulgaria proper and eastern Rumelia) over which the Ottomans maintained formal rights. Macedsonia and Epirus (including southern Albania) were left under Ottoman sovereignty. Russia retained its Caucasian acquisitions and its possession of Bessarabia was recognized. Austria-Hungary was given the administration of Bosnia and Herzegovina, much to the annoyance of the Serbs, and Great Britain was allowed to occupy Cyprus. The Russians were aggrieved and this eventually resulted in their alliance with France against Germany and Austria-Hungary (1894).

war, but the Prussians, under Gen. Helmuth von Moltke, barely gave them time to mobilize before they were marching on Paris (1871).

Victory resulted in German reunification, but Bismarck overreached when he annexed part of Lorraine and all of Alsace, which had been fully incorporated by France since the mid-18th century. Thus Bismarck's Reich was born with a neighbor on the west that was its sworn enemy and later made its neighbor on the east, Russia, its unforgiving antagonist. Germany was welded to the Austro-Hungarian Empire. France and Russia formed an alliance which Great Britain later loosely joined. Bismarck's vaunted realpolitik, described in admiring terms by Kennan, created the conditions that led to World War I and even determined the two sides in that conflict.

If containment was meant to foil the USSR and prevent a world confrontation, Kennan was inspired by the most disastrous example in history of how not to attain lasting peace. But containment was not Kennan's doing: it was America's inevitable reaction to communist aggression. One thing for which Kennan does merit recognition is that, unlike Bismarck, he was never an advocate of the use of war as a strategic expedient. Containment in itself ruled out the very idea of aggrandizement. But containment had as a corollary the theory of falling dominoes, which made guns nearly unavoidable.

(18) It did not look good that America had allies and the USSR satellites

American informal imperialism, precisely because it was not the T-rex type of imperialism that the USSR preferred, relied on regional alliances. NATO was the first of these alliances, the most indispensable, best structured, and longest lasting in the Post-War. The rock-solid bilateral USA-UK alliance might have a longer history. But possibly NATO has been the most successful multinational alliance in history. As Finland's independence was the USSR's unspoken tribute to capitalism, so the Warsaw Pact was Soviet imperialism's recognition of the efficiency of American imperialism. Unlike what it might seem, Warsaw was not, like East Germany in respect to Federal Germany, an immediate response to NATO but a belated realization that it did not look good that the USA had allies in Europe whereas the USSR had satellites.

NATO was supposed to be the prototype for other regional alliances that America either joined or sponsored. Containment was such a consensual American response that its greatest exponent was the Republican John Foster Dulles, secretary of state during most of Eisenhower's two presidential terms. Dulles was also the begetter of another foreign-policy truism that when first uttered sounded terribly risky. This was brinkmanship, which in essence meant that America was disposed to go the distance (massive retaliation) to contain the USSR but that it would try to keep well short of nuclear war. Brinkmanship was the forerunner of MAD (mutually assured destruction).

Dulles was famous as a traveling secretary of state, not surprising in that before he had been named ambassador at large by Truman, in which capacity he negotiated the peace treaty with Japan. This was important because Japan had renounced war and America was given military bases in perpetuity on Japanese territory. In his travels Dulles tried to replicate NATO all over the world. But this was a hard act to accomplish because NATO was such a real, well-oiled war machine that you were not likely to build anything like it anywhere else. NATO had a unified command structure and only France under Charles de Gaulle contested America's right to preside it.

(19) Dulles' inoperative regional alliances

In Latin America the USA had a ready-made alliance, which was the Rio Treaty. But the Rio Treaty was about external military aggression and it didn't do an informal empire much good, so the Organization of American States (OAS) was founded to deal with states that would have strayed from the straight and narrow path of American hegemony. Latin American leftists were so aware of the ultimate purpose of the OAS that when it was constituted at the Pan American Conference in Bogotá, Colombia, in 1948, they staged some of the most savage riots ever seen in a Latin American capital. The occasion for them was provided by the assassination of Jorge Eliecer Gaitán, a popular politician though not a communist. Fidel Castro was among the rabble-rousers in Bogotá.

When Guatemala tried to go its own way, the OAS condemned it as a spoilsport and the CIA gave it a good whacking. Later the OAS couldn't do much about Cuba but Cuba couldn't do much against loyal members of the OAS either. When Cuba really got out of line by accepting Soviet missiles, American informal imperialism bared its teeth, as it did when the Dominican Republic was drifting leftwards.

With the rise of communist China, South East Asia seemed to be at risk. In the past, when China was a real empire, that region was known as Nanyang and was considered tributary to Chinese dynasties. Philippines, for example, which is said to have Spanish (weak) and American (strong) cultural influences, was subject to Chinese ethnic penetration centuries before a European ship hove in sight.

Dulles prodded friendly governments into establishing SEATO (South East Asia Treaty Organization). The members of SEATO were Australia,

France, New Zealand, Pakistan, Philippines, Thailand, the United Kingdom, and the USA. Pakistan's presence in it, as we saw, was schizoid. The country then consisted of western Pakistan (west of India) and eastern Pakistan (inside the east of India) and its two sides didn't get along. France, which had already opted out of Indo-China, had no business being in SEATO. Australia and New Zealand weren't involved, and did not want to be involved, in South East Asian affairs. They were also, especially New Zealand, very far away, although the SEATO treaty had a sort of rider about the Pacific Ocean that made New Zealand's participation less irrelevant. SEATO's legacy was the American commitment to Vietnam, which was also the reason why SEATO eventually disintegrated.

In the Near and Middle East Israel was already a firm American ally, but it hadn't yet the military power, including nuclear bombs, that it has today. So Dulles sponsored the Baghdad Pact, which comprised Turkey, Iraq, Iran, and Pakistan. Pakistan's simultaneous presence in two American-backed alliances is proof positive that Islam was not militantly anti-American and that the phenomenon of Islamic (as distinct from Arabic) anti-Americanism is of recent origin. Considering its problems as a unified nation, Pakistan was over committed. Also, despite the superficial modeling after NATO, the Baghdad Pact, like SEATO, did not have a unified command.

A few years after the Baghdad Pact was signed, the Iraqi monarchy was overthrown and its king, Faisal, a Hashemite cousin of Hussein of Jordan, was killed. Iraq went radical but not communist. It had been a reluctant party to an alliance backed by the USA, Israel's main ally, and most Iraqis considered Israel as evil incarnate. Hussein, a true survivor, had good reasons not to join the Baghdad Pact.

Self-evidently, "Baghdad Pact" was now a misnomer. The alliance was renamed the Central Treaty Organization (CENTO) and was headquartered in Ankara, capital of Turkey, which was a member of NATO, so CENTO was not a Turkish priority. Dulles' dream of having a chain of alliances from Turkey to New Zealand was definitely not an easy goal. CENTO was not operative. Turks and Persians were not about cede anything to each other, much less military rankings, which Europeans had no problems with vis à vis America. Pakistan split into Pakistan proper and Bangladesh. CENTO hobbled on until Iran went theocratic.

(20) Dominoes did not normally fall, and when they did, they fell the wrong way

One of the fundamentals of the Baghdad Pact and especially of SEATO was the domino theory, which consisted in the reasoning that if you allow communists to gain power in one country they are sure to do so in the next one geographically and so on until the American informal empire was undermined and the world had turned completely Russian red. It is not clear how the theory arose. Some trace it to the Truman doctrine, but this makes no sense if only because of the fact that of Greece's four land neighbors three were already communist and the other one was Turkey, which was not likely to accept Soviet overlordship at any time. The takeover in Czechoslovakia was not accompanied by any further communist territorial gains in Europe. The Korean War was naked aggression and it was contained. Communists could no more have annexed South Korea by other means than they could really deify Kim Il Sung.

After de-colonization, there were "socialist" states springing up here and there all over the third world. When they called on the USSR, they were heard and provided with weapons and some aid. But this was as threatening to America as bilharzia or the tsetse fly. Besides these countries did not even follow a domino pattern, just the opposite. When Somalia went "socialist" it tried to take the Ogaden from Ethiopia. When Ethiopia then went "socialist" the USSR changed sides and, through the Cubans, helped the Ethiopians kick the Somalis out of the Ogaden. Hardly falling dominoes!

This flip-flop, incidentally, provides a good measure of how irrelevant were ideological considerations in the "Marxist" alliances that the USSR made in the third world. In the probing light of historical analysis, Marxism and third world, once so seemingly chummy, were merely concomitant phenomena through their connection to the over-all Cold War.

The only potentially "domino country" that really got total, unconditional Soviet support was Cuba and that was because it was next to the USA and Castro did seem to spout Marxism-Leninism as if he were an expert, which he wasn't. Also, Latin Americans were taken with Castro and there was a chance among them of a sequence of falling dominoes. But Castro got where he did by feigning and when communists and fellow travelers in Venezuela tried imitating his revolution they put on such a sorry show that even Castro had to dismiss them as bunglers. They acted like burglars telling the beat cop which house they were going to break into that night. Arnaldo Ochoa, the dashing Cuban general who reported to Castro on Venezuelan would-be guerrillas, was later executed on charges of drug smuggling.

Angola and Mozambique went "socialist" at the same time, but they were both former Portuguese colonies and were physically separated by Zambia and Zimbabwe. In this case it was as if a falling domino did not make its neighbor tumble but a domino two-pieces away. The disintegration of the Baghdad Pact, first with the defection of Iraq and then with the overthrow of the Shah, produced nothing like falling dominoes: whereas Iraq became secular and socialist, Iran turned to fundamentalism.

Why didn't domino theory work in general? Ruling and middle classes all over the world identified with America, which offers an adaptable economic pattern or paradigm. Economic liberalism is easily accepted, because it is a conservative doctrine that respects property rights. Aside from this basic appeal, it is more often parroted than actually applied. Bureaucracies have always opposed it. On the whole bureaucracies are not loved. Even its partisans fear American imperialism because it represents efficiency, and bureaucracies, behind which privileges usually lurks, are inefficient. In the third world it is common to blame America for this or that. But in fact the third world is its own worst enemy. However, despite deficient governance, what the sociologist Gunnar Myrdal called the "soft state"—brutal making lathi-charges but lenient at collecting taxes from the rich—was perfectly capable of disarming internal communist subversion.[21]

(21) Unfortunately for the USA, Indo-China seemed to fit Domino Theory to a T

There was one area, which domino theory seemed to fit to a T and that was Indo-China. It is often said that the Vietminh was a purely nationalist movement but that is inaccurate: Ho Chi Minh and his military commander, Vo Nguyen Gap, led a nationalist and communist movement. There is no truth in the charge that it was American opposition that made communists out of the Vietnamese nationalists. Even if the French had told them to keep Vietnam, Ho and Gap still would have established a communist regime. There is no reason to believe that they would have become capitalists over night if the French first or the Americans later had sat down and reasoned with them and even offered them economic aid.[22]

Nationalists in the rest of South East Asia were not communists. But Vietnamese nationalists were, particularly because they had imbibed their ideas from France. Frenchmen are no more communistic than other Europeans but in France communism had always had the sort of mass following it did not have in Britain or in the Netherlands. There were also significant differences between Indo-China and other European colonies.

The Dutch perpetrated some atrocities in trying to reconstitute the Dutch East Indies after World War II, but they had only put the entire

21 Gunnar Myrdal, *Asian Drama* (1968).
22 Stanley Karnow, *Vietnam: a history* (1991), ch. 3

colony together as late as the early 20th century. It took them in all nearly 400 years to do so. They knew that it would prove uselessly expensive to try to bring it under their rule again.

The British were committed to granting independence to their large Asian colonies. The only reason they delayed the complete independence of Malaya was because Malays themselves wanted them to take care of a communist insurgency, which the British did with admirable dexterity. The insurgents were mostly disaffected Chinese peasants in the interior of the Malay Peninsula. The Japanese occupation was particularly harsh on the Chinese in Malaya. But communists had little internal support and no external sources of weapons. The British isolated them and in the process invented the "strategic hamlet", a fenced in, self-defensive unit that kept guerrillas at bay at night.

(22) The French couldn't have challenged the Vietnamese communists in a worst place than Dien Bien Phu

The French, for some reason, perhaps a loser-complex from World War II, were intent on retaining Indo-China. Despite France's economic travails, they were not counting their francs. They knew that Vietnamese nationalists were communists, so they had no difficulties in convincing America that it should help them in their fight to re-establish colonialist rule for the sake of anti-communism. This proposition was more complex than it might seem on the surface.

Indo-China was not one but three different countries: Cambodia, Laos, and Vietnam. The name Indo-China itself was a somewhat pedantic French invention. In the remote past Indian influence had pervaded the region, the Angkor Wat temple in Cambodia being perhaps its most splendid, though not an early, manifestation. Northern Vietnam had always had Chinese cultural influence. India and China thus formed Indo-China. But the Vietnamese never accepted Chinese political hegemony and their linguistic roots were Austro-Asiatic, which made them remote relatives of the Cambodians (although no self-respecting Cambodian will admit this). The Laotians were Tai-speakers. The Cambodians, who in the past followed Hinduism, had long ago forgotten Sanskrit and adopted Buddhism. In simple terms, there was no Indo-China. Nevertheless, military victory in Vietnam, which was by far the most important of the three countries, the one that had most suffered under Japanese occupation, would have had repercussion in Laos and in Cambodia.

Vietnam has a large border with China. It has a very extensive border with Laos, which also bordered on China. These borders were quite porous because they were mostly mountainous and covered by thick tropical forests. If ever there were odds stacked against colonialism, it was in Indo-China against the French. It wasn't too hard for the French to retake Vietnamese cities, which they did brutally, but they could not make their rule stick in rural areas, especially deep in the back country, close to China. Outside of Vietnam, France thought it had things more or less under control by granting a kind of supervised independence to Laos and Cambodia. The situation in these two countries was extremely fragile.

In Vietnam, the tide of war began to turn against the French after the communists came to power in China, but only gradually. The decisive defeat on the French was self-inflicted. The high command in Vietnam decided to lure the communist guerrillas into a pitched battle in a makeshift military base in the valley of Dien Bien Phu. The theory was that parachuted artillery and an airport to keep the base supplied would suffice to rout the enemy. The Vietnamese communists were not only nationalists but also disciplined and well-armed (precisely because they were communists). Giap stealthily surrounded the Dien Bien Phu garrison with more men and guns than the French had and then started closing in. At the time there were two related processes in full operation: one political in France, the other military in Asia.

(23) The USA went into Vietnam because of a politician who tried to make the French drink milk

The French were tired of the Vietnam war and the socialist economist Pierre Mendès-France, a former Free French aviator, became prime minister with the solemn undertaking that he would end it in one month. While the Dien Bien Phu Garrison was being constricted, he convoked a conference in Geneva and by agreeing to divide Vietnam along the 17th parallel he got all the parties to agree to a truce.

In the south there was a pro-Western government headed by Ngo Dinh Diem, a Catholic in a country overwhelmingly Buddhist. In the north, Ho Chi Minh and his atheistic nationalists-communists took over. It was agreed that elections to reunify the country were to be held in 1956. Cambodia was under the multi-talented, saxophone-playing king Norodom Sihanouk. In Laos things were not so clear. The Vietnamese communists supported the Pathet Lao. But prince Suphanouvong, who was a cousin of the neutralist prime minister prince Souvanna Phouma, led this guerrilla movement. There was an unsteady balancing act between the capital Vientiane and the peasant-based Pathet Lao, but for the West it was not necessarily as lost a cause as Hanoi.

Mendès-France was like a brilliant comet in the international firmament, but he had certain handicaps. He was a milk-drinker—or said he was and ostentatiously drank milk during parliamentary debates—and he wanted other Frenchmen to do likewise, which was overdoing it. France's contemporary history demonstrates that high national indexes of alcoholic consumption are not incompatible with economic progress and technological prowess. Finland is another example. But Mendès-France's really crippling political handicap at the time was his sincere anti-colonialism and France was not then ready to give up Algeria. It would take a de Gaulle to make Frenchman swallow that bitter pill, with wine.

(24) Domino Theory turns containment into military imperialism

The most disappointed party by the Geneva settlement for Vietnam was the USA. By the time the French left the country, Americans were already involved with Diem. The French might have induced them to look towards Vietnam, but it was containment, or rather a misconception of containment, that did them in.

Devised against communist imperialism, containment turned America from informal imperialism to active imperialism through the agency of domino theory. The start of America's long and painful trek in the heart of the Vietnamese darkness originated in a deceptively simple reasoning. When the time came for national elections in Vietnam, President Diem refused to celebrate them with the historically impeccable argument that communists always rigged them. In hindsight, this was a no-win situation. If you held elections, the communists would make sure that every northern Vietnamese voted for uncle Ho. But if you did not hold them, as indeed happened, then a war was on that the communist had a good chance of winning, as they eventually did. It needn't have been that way.

American intervention ideally was meant to contain tyranny and promote democracy. In reality, containment could be misconstrued as American arrogance. Once the USA became actively involved in Vietnam, what the Vietnamese in general saw was interference. Poor to start with, South Vietnamese did not observe any difference in their economic situation through the American presence, but what they did notice were soldiers of another race and from another land virtually taking over their country. And as to freedom and democracy, apart from meaning very little to Vietnamese peasants, they were scarce commodities even in the cities. Ultimately, the culprit was the fateful and unsubtle idea of the falling dominoes.

Domino theory was like obsessive containment. Diem's refusal to hold elections was the signal for North Vietnam to put into effect plans it had been contemplating from long before: a nationalist political front, guerrilla-formation in the south, and military supplies and infiltration from the north along the Ho Chi Minh trail which threaded the jungles that straddled Vietnam, Laos, and Cambodia. Since North Vietnam was communist, it seemed as if South Vietnam could also be made communist; and if Vietnam was united as one communist country, the rest of Indo-China was as good as gone. Thailand would then be the next domino to fall.

(25) The ugly American

Domino theory was distilled for the American public in a best-selling novel, adapted as a 1963 film titled *The Ugly American.* The movie was set in a hypothetical neighbor of Vietnam. At the time, the USA was not yet irretrievably committed to the Vietnamese civil war. The real country used for the filming was Thailand. Hollywood was trying to make a real-life political statement.

Films as a rule do not make fashions but follow and re-inforce them. *The Birth of a Nation* (1915), one of the most politically horrendous movies ever made, was part of the same racialist trend that made the Ku Klux Klan briefly the main political force in Indiana. *One Flew Over the Cuckoo's Nest* (1975) extolled the closing of psychiatric wards. All movies are inherently unlikely, but this one was particularly far-fetched, with the aggravating circumstance that it was also socially irresponsible.

The Ugly American tried to make the point that the USA had to take a less self-righteous approach towards manifestations of social protest or inconformity in third world countries, which was alright as far as that went. The film was also spot on about the seriousness of the communist strategy in Vietnam. But it got its signals crossed in its overarching arguments. It conceded that the "Thais" knew their country better than "ugly", fanatically anti-communist American functionaries who confused reformers with troublemakers. Then it portrayed communist subversion as nearly unstoppable. And it made the from-the-blue-beyond suggestion that only an enlightened American public, a concept it presented as an oxymoron, could actually prevent the spread of communism! This entailed that the domino theory was self-perpetuating—from its premises it couldn't be stopped from coming true in reality—and that the USA had an unlimited number of Vietnams in its future.

However, it was conceivable, even back then, that capitalist, autocratic, incompetent South Vietnam could have staved off the communists if adequately supplied and left to fend for itself. The results of the Vietnam War—the whole country under communism, the humiliation of America, the boat people (Chinese refugees fleeing communism), etc.—were a terrible misapplication of the doctrine of containment wedded to domino theory.

(26) Doubtful of potential allies, the USA plumped for coups and massive bombings

Aside from the bitter Vietnam entanglement, the American informal world empire was generally in good health, which is not to say that people under capitalism the world over were doing square dances. USA foreign policy was usually successful in furthering American interests with a minimum of military exertions, which makes the Vietnam intervention all the more anomalous and hard to understand.

Historians tend to divide on whether Kennedy would or would not have gone to the lengths that President Lyndon Johnson went in Vietnam. Those who argue that Kennedy would have withdrawn are on shaky counterfactual ground. The growing American military presence in Vietnam came in large dollops. But the diplomatic, political, and intelligence infrastructure for the successive increases in contingents was in place when the first 10,000 "advisers" went in; and from this figure to one hundred thousand there is but a quantitative leap whereas between zero fighting men and 10,000 there was a qualitative difference.

In Vietnam, perhaps because of its proximity to China, the USA lost the steady hand and good wrist it showed when Eisenhower told the UK, France, and Israel to evacuate the Suez Canal and the Sinai, even though Egypt was already a military client of the USSR. In Suez, America acted as an imperial arbiter. The Soviet imperial counterpart to Suez was Hungary, where America did nothing to prevent Soviet strong-arm imperialism.

America responded when Lebanon asked for help, but left as soon as the political crisis passed. Lebanon had Israel to the south and Syria on its other borders. Syria might have been unpredictable at the time, but there was little fear that it might go beyond "socialism", which in the third world can mean totally anything except out-and-out communism. Syrian politics, which are thoroughly Western if undemocratic, is another reason against the controversial thesis of insurmountable cultural incompatibilities between Islamic countries and the West.[23] From a wide historical perspective, Syria is strongly anti-American to the extent that it is anti-Israel.

In Vietnam there was fear for the Cambodian and Laotian dominoes. Insofar as Cambodia and Laos were a priori considered "dominoes" that had to be propped up, the theory seemed indeed to be self-

---

23 The author of the thesis is Samuel Huntington, whose perceptiveness can be gauged by another one of his ideas: that Hispanics can only become truly "American" if they dream in English.

validating, for it was American actions that were making worst-case scenarios possible. Sihanouk and Souvanna Phouma might not have seemed trustworthy—the first was too Frenchified, the other too complaisant—but they were better than the solutions that the USA chose: military coups and massive bombings.

(27) Efficient, discreet bilateral alliances

Ironically, while the Vietnam War was going on, by which time Dulles' alliances were inoperative, the USA was grasping the usefulness of solid, discreet, and efficient regional and bilateral alliances which did not require an American military presence. Because of the Cold War, South Africa was not yet the pariah state it later became and so it was useful for keeping Angola and Mozambique in disarray, although bloody chaos was more like what it achieved. Arguably, it was the end of the Cold War that finally made Apartheid unsustainable, so it could even be imagined that it was unobtrusive American support that kept racist South Africa going despite the world's opprobrium. Moral sensibilities during the rough patches of the Cold War tended to get callous.

Israel and Iran were American pillars in the Middle East. Iran turned out to be a miscalculation but American strategists did not have a crystal ball and had Khomeini wanted an interview with Kissinger he wouldn't have gotten past the first telephone operator.

Just as it was a film that demonstrated the futility of domino theory, so it was another film that caught the essence of the American predicament in Vietnam even if to do so it had to pay the price of kowtowing to extreme cultural prejudices. Coppola's *Apocalypse Now* was ballyhooed for its whimsical and cynical exoticism (although it was filmed in the unexotic Philippines), but its main argument was quite valid: in Vietnam the USA got mired in a situation it did not comprehend and did not know how to deal with. What makes the movie thesis unacceptable is that the enemy is presented as the heartless Asiatic whose habitat and whose despotism and cruelty drove the idealistic American to insanity and worse excesses.

(28) The American informal world empire was never in better shape than when it threw in the towel in Vietnam

American idealism was always a relative quantity. But it was real. Nixon was an exceptional statesman because he wasn't an idealist. He understood that containment did not require Vietnam wars.

China had undergone the Cultural Revolution, which was like a person applying to himself the death by a thousand cuts. China had the bomb but it did not have the delivery means. Such a crude state was less to be feared than to be courted as an antagonist to the fearsome USSR. So Nixon and Kissinger initiated the process for normalizing relations.

When Egypt and Israel were at war in 1973 and the USSR cut to the chase and told the Israelis to go no further or else, Kissinger went the limit in brinkmanship and ordered a nuclear alert. This sounds more threatening than it was because there were winks and nods in the form of the previously agreed SALT and the ABM treaty.

More than anything else, "massive retaliation", "brinkmanship", "mutually assured destruction" (MAD), and "flexible response" were catchwords for possible strategies in the age of bipolar nuclear confrontation. They also expressed what were essentially shared human motivations . MAD was an inescapable reasoning about nuclear arsenals. "Flexible response" was a formula used by Kissinger. It expressed what the USA had been doing since the end of World War II. It is often used as a contrast to Dulles' "massive retaliation", but it was Kissinger who put American forces in a state of readiness for "massive retaliation" and Dulles' alliances were in essence "flexible responses". Both in the USA and in the USSR, the Cold War was permeated by rhetoric.

At any rate, the American informal world empire was never stronger than when America threw in the towel in Vietnam and realized that Cambodia and Laos too were lost. It was stronger because the USA had not lost its military force yet it had shown (1) that it tolerated extreme dissent within itself and (2) that it was capable of rational restraint, and America was imperial precisely because it was so politically seductive. It was an empire that sat so lightly that only fanatical communists could feel it as burdensome.

Carter made American imperialism not only informal but also benign. This might have encouraged the Soviets to march into Afghanistan with nary a trace of a possible domino effect. Although no one was suspecting it then, that's when the real domino theory began to operate and before long the dominoes would start tumbling backwards, not against but in favor of America. The USA by then had reverted to pure containment.

There was no containing the scowling, ill-mannered Khomeini and the American empire got another buffeting in Iran. That's when Islamic extremism began turning against America. As it was already anti-Israel, its two targets, the USA and Israel, became indistinguishable.

(29) The American unipolar world was a result of the 1990s consensus

Despite his loss of face before his own countrymen, Carter did not in any way diminish the American world position. But his stance was definitely not imperial. Americans felt they were being pushed around, which is something that really riles them, and Reagan instead was saying out loud that he wanted to push back. Carter didn't stand a chance. But Reagan's chest thumping was accompanied by a pout.

Reagan was like a heavyweight taunting his opponent and crying foul at the same time. He wanted to keep the world empire but fence America out from it. He received the Liberian dictator Samuel Doe and called him Moe, as if he didn't really give a damn to whom he was talking. Why invite him in the first place? The astonishing thing is that for Reagan, the proponent of "fortress America" through the SDI, the American informal world empire became less important precisely when it reached the peak of its efficacy.

Reagan's greatest achievement, the end of the Cold War, was not really his doing but Gorbachev's. Americans got the wrong impression. When the Soviet Empire collapsed and the world became unipolar what Americans retained was a sense of victory, the belief that America was invincible and infallible, not that, as happened to be the case, what had occurred was the downfall of a very imperfect system. The USSR had not been defeated. It was coming apart. Reagan had no more done this than Stalin. In fact, it might have been the doing of Lenin. But as Soviet power eroded, the entire world had to admit that the USA was the foremost nation on earth. It wasn't even a question of an informal world empire anymore. The category of empire was valid and necessary when America had to face a real empire. But with the end of the Soviet empire, there was no longer a need to sustain an empire to confront another empire.

China was also an empire. But it didn't even have the power of the USSR, so hardly a rival to the USA. President George H.W. Bush understood that America was unchallengeable. He also knew that to retain this eminence America had to act prudently. This world peace that was now shaping up could easily turn into bedlam. Consensus was the objective to seek. International aggression would not be tolerated. Neither would gross infringements of human rights go unresisted. Americans generally might not have trusted the UN, but the USA accepted the principle of collective action. The UN was not the only international organization through which unipolarity could work. There was also NATO and the EU, which was powerful and big enough for Washington to consider it an equal partner in the quest for world peace. The go-it-alone Reaganite streak was no longer policy. Bush laid the cornerstone of the 1990s consensus with the Gulf War. The unipolar world over which America presided was an expression of this consensus.

5

The Crisis Brewing

If Gorbachev's dissolution of the Soviet Empire can be considered to be the starting point for the time when the world seemed to be on a roll, then it is also fair to say that world crisis started brewing when Gorbachev, who was vacationing with his wife Raisa in the Crimea, was held hostage by hardline communist plotters from 19 to 21 August 1991. These are conjunctural markers for a series of events that were going in the world but that weren't necessarily inter-related.

Saddam Hussein's wars involved America originally on the basis of an unlikely scenario (a domino effect if Iran defeated Iraq), but they had no connection with events in the USSR. And in Israel the confrontation with the Palestinians was home-grown, even if it heated up because the USA tended to turn a blind eye on whatever Israel did.[1] In the normal course of things, the USSR would have been extremely antagonistic towards Israel, but if it disengaged from its European empire because it did not have the means to maintain it, then it was obviously in no condition to make its power felt in the Middle East.

The USSR still was one of the two super-powers and whatever it did had to have worldwide repercussions. The Tiananmen democratic

---

1 Perhaps the most astounding instance of American cosseting of Israel, if true, occurred when Israeli warplanes attacked the American intelligence-gathering ship Liberty off Sinai during the Arab-Israeli 1967 war (the Six Days war) causing the death of 34 American sailors. This attack is usually believed to have been an accident, but the writer James Bamford, in *Body of Secrets* (2001), claims that it was deliberate. The Johnson administration and Congress made light of the incident. Israel paid the victims' families some reparation.

movement might not have taken place if democracy hadn't been on the rise in the USSR. That China contained it to follow its own Chinese road to reform offered the alternative of remaining "communist" and still benefiting from capitalist economic growth.

The processes that led to the present multipolar world situation could then be related, indirectly related, or not related at all among them. But in general if the late 1980s and early 1990s were hopeful years because the Cold War ended and the USSR was converting warily to democracy, the rest of the 1990-decade were the years when all hell broke loose, especially in Russia. Therefore, it is not entirely inaccurate or excessively superficial to claim that the first signal that conditions were not just for smooth sailing flared when the communists wrested power from Gorbachev for a few days, sufficient time for political courage as well as political opportunism to have a red-letter day. In the USSR, concretely, the carefully calculated heading towards a processual, humane transition to capitalism was blown away like torn sails in a strong gale.

(1) What the USSR was getting were not leaders but members of cliques

The pro-communist coup can be traced to the ambiguous relation between Gorbachev and the CPUS. Gorbachev was still its leader but he had been responsible for its de-officialization, so fellow party hierarchs could not be blamed for being hostile or at least extremely suspicious. The strange thing is that they had not acted before and the explanation could be that Gorbachev still stood head and shoulders above the others and he still exercised a soothing influence on their sour moods.

These men were genuinely the product of a collective leadership structure of power. Under Stalin, either he let others know his will or he let them have their cautious say and then made the final irreversible decision. After Stalin, there was disorientation. Beria could not bear the fuzziness, so he tried to dissipate it by assuming dictatorial power. The others cut short his ambitions. Thus was born collective leadership.

Khrushchev was not a dictator in the Stalin sense and when the collective leadership so deemed he was removed. Brezhnev had the supreme post of secretary general for sixteen years, but he did not cast too strong a shadow on the other presidium members. Suslov for one, as we saw, was like the eminence grise of the regime. By the time that Gorbachev rose to leadership, CPSU leaders were used to the arrangement whereby one of them stood up for all the others. But Gorbachev, unlike his predecessors, had unorthodox ideas of his own.

By then the center of power was no longer the presidium of the CPSU. The party itself was neither constitutionally nor in practice setting the rules for the USSR. The plotters were indecisive and cautious to a fault—probably indicative of why Gorbachev was still officially accepted as their superior—and they struck too late. The crisis of the Soviet system was not only economic: it was also, perhaps above all, a political crisis in the higher realms of power. The means by which the USSR chose its leaders were extremely deficient. What the country was getting were not leaders of masses but members of cliques.

(2) Yazov's hands were shaking so badly that it was hard to take the conspirators seriously

According to a common theory, Vladimir Kryuchkov, the head of the KGB, organized the conspiracy but the spokesman for the conspirators was not Kryuchkov but Dmitri Yazov. Gorbachev's vice-president, Yanayev, was with the coup, as was a majority of the party presidium. It was a conspiracy to restore things as they had been before Gorbachev began re-arranging them, but communism was then beyond salvation. Incredible as it might sound, it had taken less than the six years that Gorbachev had been in power for Soviet society to acquire a stake in the order (or more accurately disorder) of things that was replacing a system installed nearly three quarters of a century before. Also, and crucially, another exceptional product of the Soviet system, Yeltsin, was around.

Almost everything about the USSR, and specifically Russia, during the Gorbachev years sounds as if it had been taken from a ciphered text that had been garbled and written back to front, somewhat like Churchill's depiction of Russia as a riddle wrapped in a mystery inside an enigma. It was as inexplicable as how the most stifling social system in history had turned itself into a superpower. How had Gorbachev been possible? Why did the Communist Party accept being trussed up like a pig and taken to slaughter? And how did communists have the unerring flair to discover in Yeltsin the man who would finally stick it to them?

In a normal world, Yeltsin would have seemed the least likely candidate for the role of democrat and founder of capitalist Russia. Politically, he had been born in and was nurtured by the CPSU, which he seemed to obey without squirming. His personal authoritarianism was more compatible with communism than with anything resembling democratic constitutionality. Yet, over all, his actions from the moment he was summoned from Sverdlovsk to Moscow leave no doubt that he had sincerely changed, either by degrees or suddenly (like St. Paul, another authoritarian), from apparatchik to unyielding enemy of communism.

When he learned of the coup against Gorbachev, Yeltsin gathered military support, which the plotters assumed would be completely on their side, and stood on a tank in front of the modernistic Moscow high-rise called the White House, where the Russian Supreme Soviet sat, and defied the communist conspiracy in the name of constitutional legitimacy. Despite his personal grudges, he also demanded that Gorbachev be released and restored to the presidency of the USSR. Yeltsin by then very likely had few illusions about the viability of the USSR but the absolute priority at the moment was to restore the process that Gorbachev had initiated, even if Yeltsin's ultimate intention was to derail it.

The plotters had multiple links to instruments of power. They counted on the support of the Soviet bureaucracy and possibly every Soviet diplomat abroad knew about the coming coup. They certainly were aware of it in Havana, where high diplomatic functionaries assumed a sly but unmistakably smug look when Gorbachev and Soviet reformism were mentioned. The Americans, who warned Gorbachev, very likely learned of the plot from diplomatic sources.

What the plotters lacked was leadership and especially self-confidence. When he announced over television that Gorbachev had been overthrown, Yazov's hands were shaking so badly that it was hard to take the conspirators seriously. Outside of the USSR, people were much more apprehensive. With Soviet precedents in mind, it was feared that Gorbachev might have been liquidated.

Yeltsin rallied opposition to the coup and had the plotters arrested to general cheering, in Moscow at least. The CPSU was legally dissolved, although the plotters were released not long afterwards.

(3) Gorbachev's speeches were like trying to stop a bulldozer on auto

Gorbachev was re-instated as president of the USSR. On the surface, it was like recovering a guideline that had been momentarily lost in a storm. But this superficial impression was wrong. Gorbachev had been winged. He had undermined his own communist legitimacy and his former communist buddies had undermined his legitimacy period. Gorbachev himself was not unaware that he had been made to look bad. When Yanaev came back to him as if nothing had happened, Gorbachev asked him if he was trying to "hang noodles from his ears", the earthy Russian expression for taking a person for a fool.

Aside from the mailed fist, the CPSU was what kept the USSR together, so Gorbachev was now reduced to his powers of persuasion alone, and with these it was impossible to block the trends that were in what seemed like gravity-pulled motion. He might as well have tried to stop a bulldozer on auto with speeches. The trends could only have been braked from within and, aside from Gorbachev and the people who betrayed him, no one important or influential seemed to want to save the USSR. Perhaps a majority of Russians would have preferred to keep the USSR alive, but at the time what mattered above all was eliminating communist dictatorship. First things came first. But without communism there was a real second possibility: the fall of communist power and the disbandment of the USSR were all one.

To save the USSR there was also the alternative of Russian military might. But even to achieve his goal of saving the USSR in another form, Gorbachev would probably not have unleashed Soviet armed forces on its neighbors, even if it still had been in his power to command them. The Lithuanian experience had been bitter and Gorbachev himself was conscious of the damage it had done to his prestige.

Besides, the effective president of Russia was Yeltsin, and, as he had already accomplished the task of saving the Russian Supreme Soviet, the source of his power, he was not keen on voilence for the sake of Gorbachev's political ambitions. It could also be said that, after some mutilations, and a leak here and there, the USSR was basically Russia and the armed forces of the USSR were mainly Russian. Yeltsin and other leaders of Soviet republics concurred publicly with Gorbachev when he argued that to sacrifice the Soviet federation was unthinkable, but, as they say, actions speak louder than words, and in retrospect for these men it was not only quite feasible to do without the USSR but it was what they wanted to do.

(4) While Yeltsin read polls, Gorbachev was losing touch with reality

After the August putsch, the rest of the USSR, in the wake of the separatist Baltic republics, started to disintegrate. Uzbekistan opted for independence just eight days after Gorbachev was released. The secession process became irreversible when Yeltsin's Russia recognized the independence of the Baltic republics. Despite these discouraging signs, Gorbachev persisted in his talk of a reformed and reborn USSR. Though not alienated, Gorbachev was not entirely in touch with reality either. Unlike the imperturbable Yeltsin, whom crises transformed into a giant, Gorbachev was a hands-on man increasingly now pre-occupied by theoretical and constitutional issues, and these had but a slender connection to events.

If the dissolution of the USSR was what Gorbachev most dreaded, what he probably could not even consider seriously was that the Ukraine would separate from Russia. The Ukraine was part of the Russian heartland. Christian Russia was founded in Kiev, in the Ukraine. After Mongol power in Russia waned, Ukrainian history was mostly about its gradual absorption by Russia against the pretensions of Poles and Turks, both of whom the Ukrainians detested. Much of the Soviet central bureaucracy and of its diplomatic service was Ukrainian. The inhabitants of Eastern Ukraine (the industrialized Donetsk basin) and Crimea were mostly Russians.

Yeltsin had seen polls that showed Ukrainians inclining by a large majority to independence, so large that it had to include even ethnic Russians. Gorbachev, who later for a long time refused to accept his own unpopularity in Russia, wouldn't have believed them. Yeltsin did not have Gorbachev's obsession with federation. He would later pay a steep price for his habitual nonchalance, so steep indeed that it almost cost him the presidency of Russia.

(5) Stalin's idea of "federation" was to enter guns blazing into any republic that showed signs of wanting to be un-federated

The terms "union", "federation", and "federated" have specific meanings in the context of the USSR. "Union" is the least specific and it is the same as "united", as in "United States": constituted by partially sovereign but not independent states. A Soviet "federation", unlike the "Confederate States of America", was a union divided into political entities or parts each inhabited by "nationalities", people of the same ethnic stock who usually spoke the same non-Russian language. The Confederacy was just a replica of the United States but with an economy based on the "peculiar institution" of black slavery. "Federation" and "federated" were inalienable Soviet inheritances from Tsarist Russian imperialism.

During the early part of the Russian Revolution, Stalin was commissar for nationalities. Though Georgian by birth and upbringing, he was unmistakably what is known as a Great Russian chauvinist. One of the reasons why Lenin, stretching the meaning of politeness to the point of limerick, called him "impolite" was that Stalin's idea of "federation" was to enter guns blazing into any republic that showed signs of wanting to be un-federated. Stalin did it in the Ukraine, which is when Lenin showed his disapproval. Since the memory of nations is long, this incident was possibly one of the reasons why now Ukrainians wanted to separate from Russia. Stalin did it again in Georgia, where he himself was born, prompted by another communist Georgian "federalizer", Sergo Ordzhonikidze, whom Stalin later drove to suicide.[2]

The "federated" parts of Soviet Russia were themselves "autonomous" but far from sovereign, not even in the limited sense in which American states are sovereign. The USSR was a super-federation of "Soviet republics", which in theory were the equal in sovereignty to Russia. In

2 Figes, op.cit., p. 715; Simon Sebag Montefiore, *Stalin: the court of the red tsar* (2003), ch. 18.

practice, "republics" were only privileged in having their own communist parties, which were entirely subservient to the PCUS. Russia itself was officially the Federated Russian Soviet Socialist Republic because it contained many nationalities.

Peoples usually do not occupy lands according to agreed settlement schemes or deliberate, commonsensical partitions of territory, which is the reason why the autonomous republics of the USSR and of the Russian Federation today have very irregular shapes whereas in the USA state borders were often defined by surveyors and there is not one American state (except Hawaii) that does not have a part of its limits looking as if it had been drawn with a straight-edge.[3] Try searching for a straight line in the political map of Europe and see what you come up with.

During the frequent Soviet political re-organizations of the Russian Empire, mostly before World War II, there were federations, analogously like federated Russia, such as the Turkistan Autonomous Soviet Socialist Republic, including the present territories of Tajikistan, Turkmenistan, and Uzbekistan. It was from this federation that the Uzbek Soviet Socialist Republic, including Tajikistan, was formed. Finally, Uzbekistan and Tajikistan were made separate Soviet socialist republics. These different republics, and Kyrgyzstan, had in common that they were Muslim. Tajiks were Indo-Iranian and the others were Turks.

On the other side of the Caspian Sea, the Soviets created the Transcaucasian Soviet Federated Socialist Republic with Armenia, Azerbaijan, and Georgia. This federation was also dissolved into separate Soviet socialist republics. "Soviet" and "socialist" denoted a higher political status without the "autonomous" qualifier, which always implied belonging to a federation, hence not very autonomous. Roughly, these jurisdictional subtleties were respected after the USSR was dissolved: Russia became a federated republic and the former Soviet socialist republics became just republics.

(6) There was a reason why Chechnya never became a full-ranking "Soviet republic"

On Georgia's northeastern frontier, lies tiny Chechnya, known in the USSR as the Chechen-Ingush Autonomous Soviet Socialist Republic

3 Uzbekistan has perhaps the most tortuous borders of any country in the world. They are the result of the Soviet policy of nationalities carried to absurd extremes. An arm of Uzbekistan sticks over mountains far into Kyrgyzstan and extends over more than half the valley of Ferghana, whose non-mountainous entrance is part of Tajikistan. As there is no history of enmity between Kirghiz, Tajiks, and Uzbeks—the khanate of Kokand (ca1710-1876) ruled indistinctly over all or portions of all three peoples—this was bending over backwards to accommodate non-existent ethnic claims.

(now it is the Checheno-Ingush Republic). Though in principle a nationality like those which were constituted as independent republics, the Chechens, who are Muslims and speak a Caucasian language of the same family as Georgian, had the will but not the historical past and the tradition of sovereignty that would have justified the full rank of Soviet socialist republic. By contrast with Chechnya, Armenia and Georgia had long national histories of their own. Azerbaijan had not usually been an independent kingdom but it was from Tabriz, the Azeri capital, that the Mongols ruled Persia and the Middle East.

Chechens had a reputation as fighters the equal of the Cossacks, but the Cossacks spoke Ukrainian and were good Orthodox Christians. Given their head, Chechens could have spelt trouble. When the Soviet republics were going for independence one after another in the wake of the foiled August coup, the Chechens threw Soviet jurisdictional niceties to the wind and went and declared the independence of Chechnya.

However tyrannical the USSR, it had its moments of political lucidity. One of them was not unduly empowering Chechens. On the other hand, the opposite, that Chechen ferocity was Soviet-bred, can also be argued, for Chechen independence was the work of the freakish Dzhokhar Dudayev, a Soviet general serving in Estonia who was made dictator of Chechnya by thugs and promptly converted the country into a court of miracles, a place where the illegal was legal and the arbitrary consensual.

One of the ironies about the Chechnya wars to come was that Western journalists knew the kind of smugglers' and thieves' dens that Chechnya became and yet they persisted in characterizing Chechens as unbeatable warriors and heroic patriots. Another important point is that if Yeltsin later suffered recurrent Chechnya nightmares, it was because he did everything he could to deserve them.

(7) After dissolving the USSR, post-prandial celebrations went to Yeltsin's head

Yeltsin and the leaders of the other Soviet republics, especially Ukraine and Belarus, were growing weary of Gorbachev's virtual soliloquies about a new democratic, USSR-like federation. After his rescue from the clutches of the KGB through Yeltsin's intervention, it was obvious that Gorbachev was a lame duck, just as the USSR itself was pure formalism, a shadow that Russia still cast.

For one reason or another, Yeltsin did not challenge Gorbachev and ask him to step down. Perhaps it was that, as he had opposed an illegal communist power-grab, unseating Gorbachev against his will would have seemed like a reversion to communist political practice. It could also have been judged unconstitutional and no one then knew the depth of Gorbachev's lack off popular support. Whatever the case, there was another way to achieve exactly the same thing and that was to make Gorbachev irrelevant, like having an eloquent atheist address a Baptist convention, or simply by leaving him without an audience altogether.

In the first week of December 1991, absent Gorbachev, who astonishingly appeared to have suspected nothing, Yeltsin met with Leonid Kravchuk of the Ukraine and with Stanislav Shushkevich of Belarus in Minsk, the capital of Belarus. The three presidents agreed to dissolve the USSR. During post-prandial celebrations, Yeltsin got so drunk he had to be carried to his bed. It wasn't his best moment, but Yeltsin had the gift of bounciness and during his period as president of Russia he showed that, at critical times, he didn't give a damn for anything but the central issue and that to achieve legitimate political ends he was capable of controlling his tendency to drink excessively and even of facing up to illnesses that, in the circumstances, would have done in a lesser man.[4]

On 8 December the presidential trio unveiled the Commonwealth of Independent States (CIS), their version of the new voluntary "federation" that was to take the place of the defunct USSR. Ukraine voted by over 90% for independence. On 21 December, to close the cycle of the downfall of the USSR and the birth of the CIS, all the former Soviet republics except those on the Baltic and Georgia signed on to the CIS in Alma Ata, the former capital of Kazakhstan.[5] Georgia did not do so because its principal politician and future president, Eduard Sheverdnaze, had been until recently the foreign minister of the USSR and one of the protagonists of Gorbachevism.

As successor state to the mighty USSR, the CIS did not quite fit the bill, but the armed forces of Russia are still officially those of the CIS. Technically, CIS and not Russian forces defended the border of Tajikistan against infiltration from Afghanistan, in effect a shield for Uzbekistan and Kyrgizstan. CIS forces were also in view when they manned the borders of Turkmenistan and Uzbekistan with Afghanistan during the American-led and Russian-supported War on Afghanistan.

4 Yeltsin's public drunkenness had two signal moments: in Germany during a G7 meeting when he took the baton from the conductor to lead a military band and in a stopover in Shannon where the highest Irish dignitaries were gathered to receive him and he apparently was too drunk to deplane.

5 In 1996, the capital was officially transferred from Alma Ata (plum garden) to Akhmola (white tomb), which was renamed Astana. Alma Ata is just north of Kyrgyzstan.

(8) In the balance of history, Hitler was far more influential than his enemies

On 25 December 1991, without a state to govern, Mikhail Gorbachev resigned to the presidency of the USSR. He was a man of only sixty years. Arguably, he did more than any man in the 20th century to change the world. Franklin Roosevelt and Winston Churchill had done splendidly what was expected of them. The "splendid" qualifier here is what counts, for, with or without Churchill or Roosevelt, Britain and America would have opposed the Axis, and with America's resources, the Allies, under any military command, would have defeated the Axis. This is admittedly counterfactual, which is dubious historical reasoning, but it is only used as a stay for the historical thesis that history is made up of processes and that it is determined neither by the lack-of-a-nail nor by the heroes of the moment.[6]

Roosevelt did not end America's Great Depression. The war did. And Neville Chamberlain, the appeaser, is today judged to have been as good a fighter as Churchill, for even as he appeased he was vigorously promoting British re-armament. When the campaign in Egypt was going badly, Churchill, who had weakened British defenses there to succor Greece, replaced Gen. Claude Auchinleck with Gen. Bernard Montgomery, about whom almost every historian agrees that he never fought a battle he did not know for sure he could win.[7] Truman, who succeeded Roosevelt, was considered a mediocrity: a failed haberdasher who entered politics through a back door; yet he had the atomic bombs dropped on Japan and he made America a mighty fortress against world-wide communist expansion. Lenin created the USSR but Stalin carried his mentor's political methods to extremes. The USSR was crucial in the defeat of Hitlerism, a task that it had not chosen.

In the balance of history, Hitler was more influential on history than his enemies. Without Hitler there might not have been an Israel. The revulsion at his crimes made the world less susceptible to messianic

---

6 For want of a nail, a shoe was lost.
For want of a shoe, a horse was lost.
For want of a horse, a rider was lost.
For want of a rider, a battle was lost.
For want of a battle, a war was lost.
For want of a war, a kingdom was lost.
All for the lack of a horseshoe nail!

7 Exception must be made of his atempt to capture the bridge at Arnhen, in Holland (September 1944), which failed miserably. Max Hastings, *Armageddon: the battle for Germany 1944-1945* (2004), ch.2

despotism and to the politics of hate. Of all historical ironies, perhaps the greatest one is that history's most reviled figure may be the one that provoked the greatest "sanitation" of history. Yet Hitler for all his evil singularities was himself the product of a revanchist milieu. His first notorious public appearance, during the failed Munich beer-hall putsch, was beside Marshal Erich Ludendorff, the fight-to-the-last-drop-of-blood commander of German armies at the end of World War I.

(9) For all his pains, the best that Gorbachev got was grudging recognition mixed with scorn

In an oblique way, Gorbachev was a result of Hitlerism. Stalinism in practice was little better than Nazism. In theory, the USSR stood for everything that was execrated in Nazi Germany. Unlike the rest of the great political figures of the 20th century, Gorbachev did not face an external enemy easy to recognize and circumscribe. He believed in some of the ideas that his political adversaries also held and for those practices that he wanted to change in Soviet society, as we saw, he had to feign that he believed in the system in its entirety. Gorbachev's situation did resemble Nixon's, whose certified anti-communism permitted him to break down official anti-communist barriers in the American government. But Gorbachev's task was far more difficult, for it involved going against the grain of a heavy, intolerant, and suspicious system.

For his pains, Gorbachev obtained neither personal gain nor gratitude in his country, and in the West, a sort of grudging recognition mixed with scorn, such as the journalist David Remnick evinced reporting that when the USSR was dissolved Gorbachev asked: "And what about me?" Gorbachev did not dissolve the USSR. His rival Yeltsin did. Gorbachev democratized Russia and he liquidated the Cold War. He did not complete the process of democratization because he was not given the opportunity to do so and his plans were for a much more equitable and orderly process than the one that got underway after him. Under Gorbachev, the USSR was weakened militarily, but this process was going on before, and the USSR did not lose the Cold War completely under Gorbachev but only after Gorbachev was sabotaged by the communists.

With all its faults, the USSR had a steadying influence in the world that a still wobbly Russia cannot exert. If the downfall of the USSR enters the picture of the world as it is today, it is not because of what Gorbachev did but because of what he could not do. So basically the worst criticism that can be levelled at him is that he was not up to the gargantuan task of successfully transforming the crumbling USSR.

(10) Charismatic under the Soviet regime, in a democracy Gorbachev gave people the blahs

Another of the Russian riddles is why Gorbachev is so despised by his own countrymen. During the early Yeltsin years he was made a figure of derision and satire. For some reason, rock bands were particularly vicious in their mockery, which, if one believes Remnick, went beyond words to the cruel prank of bilking Gorbachev's mother of her house in the Stavropol region. They also associated him with Stalinist economics. Apparently, Gorbachev was blamed for all the ills of Russia without getting the recognition for his accomplishments, mainly that without Gorbachev Russians would not now have the right to vote freely, to travel, and to enrich themselves. When presidential elections later came up in Russia, despite the surveys that showed he hadn't a ghost of a chance, Gorbachev ran anyway and got less than one percent of the total vote. Such a massive rejection, incomprehensible to an external observer, must have been unthinkable for Gorbachev himself.

The reasons usually attributed to Russians for Gorbachev's electoral defeat do not stand up to scrutiny. In general, they have to do with the decay of Soviet might, as if it hadn't been decaying before Gorbachev came to power or as if he had deliberately set about reducing the USSR to the status of a second-rate power or even down to a condition of economic underdevelopment. Yet Russian voters ratified Yeltsin, who was more responsible for Russian economic and political chaos than Gorbachev ever was. In sum, Russians yearned for the good old communist-imperial days even as they enjoyed their liberties and they blamed Gorbachev for liquidating the past without crediting him with having inaugurated a new Russia and having tried to manage change so that Russians would not have to be nostalgic about the USSR's standing in the world.

In the end, it could just be a matter of personal appeal: Gorbachev was charismatic under the Soviet regime, especially among his communist colleagues, but in a democracy he gives people the blahs. Yeltsin instead, who had all the vices of a Russian autocrat, but also enough patriotism to know when he was doing more harm than good, and to act accordingly, had the charisma that Gorbachev lacked. Gorbachev's detainment in the Crimea by communists that until then he had trusted probably convinced the vast majority of Russians that he was not the man to steer their country on the roaring seas of the new politics. It may be that Russians are still not comfortable unless they feel they have a strong man at the helm. But it is also not likely that they will give up their flawed democracy without a fight.

(11) The demise of the USSR was probably a boost for world destabilization

The downfall of Soviet communism was on the whole a good thing. It was politically beneficial for Russians and for the world. It made definitive the end of the Cold War and the triumph of America, the land of the free, the paradigm of economic prosperity. But there is the other side of the coin.

Even before it had ended, the Cold War was in a steady state because the USA and the USSR knew enough not to get reckless with their nuclear arsenals. Still, the rivalry was there with the possibility of destabilization. Reagan's antagonistic attitude and his threat of undermining the MAD equilibrium with the SDI were evidence either that the balance of world forces was very delicate or that the world had attained such a degree of stability that nuclear war was out of the question.

Reagan's America used its power with swagger and seemed willing to go the distance against the USSR. This was alright because the USSR, by then, was fooling no one about being the Marxist paradise, the paladin of peace, or a real economic rival of America. But it was not alright if Reagan's "evil empire" was a valid representation of the USSR, for evil knows no bounds and if America really had come up with a workable SDI there was no reason to believe that the USSR would not have struck.

Two things are more likely: one, Reagan did not really mean what he said about Soviet evilhood and what he and his advisors wanted was to put the USSR under the greatest possible strains; two, the USSR far from being an evil empire was conscious of its responsibilities as a nuclear super-power that would not let the worse come to worst in the confrontation with America. Gorbachev cannot be explained except as a product of a form however attenuated of responsible government. It is conceivable that no Soviet leader would have let himself be provoked into a nuclear misstep by Reagan's taunting.

In the balance of history, the existence of the USSR was not a menace to peace but a force for peace. With Gorbachev it became even more so, because Gorbachevism stood, not only for glasnost and perestroika, but also for relations with America not on the basis of reciprocal fear but of cooperation. Admitting that Gorbachev himself was probably never altogether clear about his precise goals, if anything like Gorbachev's agenda had been allowed to follow its course, the USA and a democratic USSR could have cooperated in managing the crises that beset the world after Gorbachev was set aside and the USSR was dismantled.

Yugoslavia might just possibly not have come apart without the Soviet example. America certainly could have benefited by having a Soviet counterpoise to Pakistan in Afghanistan. Conceivably, an arrangement like this could have prevented 9/11 from happening. This is not to say that Gorbachev the individual could have saved the world a lot of grief, but it is to make the admittedly risky claim that the absence of the USSR from the world in general and from crisis-prone regions in particular has contributed to the instabilities that are the traits of the world situation today. A transformed USSR would have carried much more weight in the Middle East and the Far East than Russia, its wobbly successor, does.

(12) The "Russian devolution"

With Gorbachev's fall, there began one of the most traumatic periods in the history of Russia. Yeltsin was the outstanding and indisputable leader of the country. In the light of the economic policies he adopted, it is undeniable that he had extirpated from his belief-system any residue of communism. He still had a political strain from his communist past, which emerged in the run up to the presidential election in 1996, but, as we shall see, he did not allow it to flourish. At any rate, the crucial events during Yeltsin's tenure after Gorbachev's resignation were economic in nature. Fading to background, politics let the "economic revolution"—in a New York Times article it was called the "Russian devolution"—take its course.[8]

By profession, Yeltsin was a construction foreman. Like peasant Khrushchev, he looked the part. Unlike Khrushchev, he had only a rudimentary knowledge of economics. Gorbachev might not have been an economic expert either, but he knew that, starting from a communist base, economic change is better slow than swift. China is proving Gorbachev at least partially right and if it ever truly democratizes it will wholly vindicate Gorbachev's approach.

The contemporary history of Russia is still barely known, much less understood.[9] Russia is so huge and diverse and skewed in so many

8 John Lloyd, "The Russian devolution", NYT (August 16, 1999). The information in this article is used in the text as an important source on Russian privatization.

9 Taubman, op.cit., pp. xii-xiii, has this to say on the accessibility of original official sources in Russia: "With the fall of the USSR, long-closed Soviet archives finally opened, erratically and not necessarily permanently, but at least for a while. The Presidential Archive (formerly the Politburo Archive), which contains particularly sensitive material on Soviet leaders, and the KGB archives remain closed to all but a favoured few, but key party depositories became accessible, not only in Moscow but throughout the former Soviet Union."

different ways that it is impossible to generalize about all of Russia. It is even impossible to generalize by denying all generalizations about Russia. Many patterns emerged as the country was transformed economically: from the huge capitalist wave that swept Moscow and other cities, to the many variations on the privatization program as it applied to the different cities, provinces, and regions, to the autonomous nooks and crannies where communist habits skulked like vices from the past.

Either tipped by Russian insiders or by foreigners who had some access backstage, Western observers took fixes on facets of the economic process: how banks were still granting unsecured loans to industries; how inefficient producers, in the absence of liquidity, bartered inventories among each other; how corruption had become a normal part of doing business; how rivalries or debt-collections or turf-competitions were settled by violent means; how, in general, the communist economy was disassembled without the adoption of saving capitalist graces, including, in the understanding of many of those observers, letting foreign managers run the Russian show the way it should be. Russia was supposed to become a model of a smoothly functioning capitalist economy overnight and since it couldn't achieve this water-into-wine miracle any journalist could write as if he knew exactly what it was that was wrong with such a backward, corrupt, violent, and incompetent country.

(13) Russians were quite good at what Americans had only learned to do ten years before

It is often said that Russia had an option between a gradual and a speedy way of going about change. The gradual way, presumably Gorbachev's, although he isn't usually credited, consisted in legislating capitalism into existence with solid time-tested capitalist institutions brought in and put in place, thus subjecting the new system to oversights and reasonable restraints. The speedy or fast-track way, called "shock treatment", was to privatize massively, to let market forces determine who survived and who succumbed, and along the way to improvise the legal and institutional framework for Russian capitalism. That there existed this option is purely speculative. There is only one possible way in history. Background or antecedent conditions determine what that way is.

The background conditions in Russia were certainly not for gradualism. Before it became official, privatization was already under way, and privatization, according to the probably accurate general view, consisted in stripping and selling assets to make quick millions, just as quickly stashed away outside of Russia. This is what junk bonds were all about in America in the 1980s: raising capital to buy large diversified corporations and break them up to sell its profitable parts at huge profits letting the rest rust or sink. In other words, Russians were quite good at what Americans had discovered only a decade earlier. That in Russia such opportunities to get rich quick would be ignored or rejected was not in the nature of human affairs.

Those profiting from these operations were not rich foreigners and not ordinary Russians either, but Russians who under the Soviet system were inscribed in the nomenklatura (the party-privileged class). They were the insiders who managed Soviet enterprises, to do which they had to belong to the CPSU. Their condition as insiders did not come about after the USSR dissolved but had been attained long before, so it can be said that under communism, even of the extremely conservative Brezhnevian sort, capitalism was already in a healthy, fetal stage. When privatization became official, its practical mechanisms were already known down to the subtlest details. Also, the process showed how under any system, whether capitalist, communist, mixed, or whatever, whether in a village or an empire, talent in one-way or another always outs.

Yeltsin's economic inner circle was partial to fast-track privatization and its members were always putting under the president's nose specialists who favored that approach. The more prominent figures in the circle were Gennady Burbulis, Yegor Gaidar, and Anatoly Chubais. Burbulis was an all-purpose advisor. Gaidar was acting prime minister. Chubais headed a ministry for privatization.

(14) Privatization was like keeping the silver and not giving the family a penny

It doesn't take a profound knowledge of economics to know what privatization consists in. If I have in my possession on trust a family heirloom, I can privatize it by paying my relatives something or I can simply keep it if nobody asks about it or if they all die. Alternatively, I can sell the family silver to a third party and either give my relatives their share or keep the money. I can take the silver and melt it into ingots and put them in a bank or I can pay myself a tour of the world with them. In all cases, I have privatized.

In the case of the Russian economy, it helped, for legitimacy and for the adoption of standard capitalist practices, to have the sanction of foreign experts and institutions. Some professorial economists had made a career of privatization schemes. It was these who invented the phrase "shock treatment" and who told Russians how to privatize above aboard instead of just grabbing what you could lay your hands on.

One of these foreign advisers, the one who got the most publicity, was Jeffrey Sachs, who before going to Russia had privatized for the non-communist Polish government. Organized privatization rather than the grab-as-grab-can variety took the form of auctions in which in theory ordinary citizens bade with scrip for installed capital. This was like giving the inheritors shares in the heirloom. From the results of important auctions, it was observed that, before the bidding commenced, deals had been struck by which those who had already made bundles ended up with the ownership of the industrial plants or whatever it was that was being put on the block. This was in theory like paying the heirs for the heirloom.

The Agency for International Development (AID), an American organization for channeling economic assistance to under-developed countries, pitched into the Russian privatization process with $300 million, some of which reputedly ended up in the pockets of economists charged with administering it. The International Monetary Fund (IMF) and the World Bank were also involved.

The biggest plum in the privatization process was the immense monopolistic Gazprom, the company that owns most of Russia's natural gas industry. With a payroll that ran to over 350,000 persons, it was Russia's biggest company. In Gorbachev's time Viktor Chernomyrdin ran it. Gazprom was undersold so scandalously that even Sachs declared that it should be re-nationalized. It is conceivably the biggest scam in history, but it has remained private and has made millionaires of many Russians that were in on the quickie de-statisation of Russia's economy.

In all, it is estimated that from 1993 to 1999 capital flight from Russia lies somewhere between 200 and 500 billion dollars, a vague but appalling estimate even at its lower end, for much of that money was made by individuals and groups of individuals despoiling the Russian economy practically under the eyes of a government which should have prevented it and of a public who could do nothing about it but stare. Admittedly, too, given the dates for the estimate above, part of those transferences, perhaps most of them, were made by what had become legitimate ex-communist businessmen and not just the dismantlers of state enterprises for a fast buck and a quick get away.

(15) The new Croesuses could even afford their own small armies

In 1993, Gaidar, by then himself a millionaire, as was Chubais, handed executive power to Chernomyrdin. Russia had spawned a congeries of multi-billionaires, two of whom, Boris Berezovsky, automobile magnate, and André Gusinsky, a former theater director who made enough money to nurture aspirations of becoming the number one media baron in Russia, were the most visible. But there were many others making a rich display of their wealth, such as the Russian drugs-firm owner seen in a *New York Times* photograph in the process of purchasing in his Moscow office a bottle of claret with a $40,000 price tag.

There has never been in history such a fantastic proliferation of nouveaux riches in such a short term and of such a magnitude of opulence. During the 1980s, America had made wealth-flaunting not only respectable but even a sign of good taste, a development which would have floored Molière, or even the rich themselves before the vulgar but undeniably prestigious celebrations for Reagan's first inaugural. Thus, exhibitionist rich Russians, even those in the Mafia, were well within internationally admired social norms.

As the process for the re-arrangement of the social order, with a consequent rise in criminality, had gone on unabated from Gorbachev to Yeltsin, some of the new Croesuses, notoriously Gusinsky, had their own platoons of armed-to-the-teeth bodyguards. Russia had become the sort of place in which money was unflinchingly and unashamedly power, a living society that in America existed only in the caricatural form of a film such as Coppola's *Godfather II*.

All of this obviously had to trouble ordinary Russians profoundly. It wasn't that some Russians were getting very rich and most weren't. After all, Russians, especially in the larger cities, were now free to do many things that before were forbidden, among which was making a better living for themselves without having the secret police on their backs. Since Russians knew the basics of privatization as well any one else, what shock therapy introduced were such things as a price spiral through the removal of controls and subsidies and the reduction of spending in the "social net" because of the need to balance budgets. Free convertibility was implicit in privatization itself, for what would be the point of stripping and selling if what you had left were heaps of rubles, which had to be made productive in more strip-and-sell schemes?

Privatized firms handed less money to the government than state-run enterprises, so fiscal receipts went on falling making budgetary discipline even more painful. The most troubling consequence of this was that while a few benefited hugely from privatization and shock therapy, many Russians were having a hard time adjusting to the new order of things. Some, particularly the elderly and others that depended on government transfers, were hurting acutely. In the countryside people were more affected than city-dwellers, who had more water in which to swim.

(16) A choleric Chechen and Yeltsin's handpicked VP try to make an end-run

As Russia had become a democracy even before it became a showcase of capitalist inequality, politics might have offered a way to get at the rascals. There were a few stumbling blocks here also. No major elections were scheduled for the immediate future. A non-binding referendum, which means Yeltsin could have ignored it if it went against him, gave him a majority. Another stumbling block to effective political action was that Russia had no political parties!

The history of Western Europe and its American offshoots is almost unimaginable without the existence of political parties. In the 18th century, England had Tories and Whigs, whose roots went back to 17th century dynastic changes. The names were reciprocal insults. They originated in pro-Stuart (Tories, or Irish bandits) and pro-Hanoverian (Whigs, or Scottish raiders) sympathies, but there existed between the two bands sufficient substantive social differences to make them the cores of the great 19th century Conservative and Liberal political parties.[10] Because of where representatives sat in the National Convention, the French Revolution was the source of the right-left political classification of parties, which of course also made possible centrism.[11]

The Supreme Soviet had emanated from elections held in December 1988 and at that time, although there had been some multiple-candidate elections for people's deputies, there existed only the CPSU. After the CPSU was disenfranchised, many parties had been founded, various mainly as purely personal political instruments. The most important were: Russia's Choice and Democratic Russia, created for the specific purpose of supporting Yeltsin; the Liberal Democratic Party, an empty formula that the eccentric and once much-feared Vladimir Zhirinovsky used to give some kind of respectability to his public antics; the re-founded Communist Party of Russia, headed by Genady Zyuganov; and smaller

10 It was during the reign of Charles Ii Stuart (1660-1685) that parliamentary and party politics began to take form with the pro-Stuart but especially pro-Anglican Tories on one side and the less exclusionary Whigs on the other. The issues were how far to tolerate dissenters from Anglicanism and to exclude non-Anglicans from public positions including Parliament. If only because he preferred toleration for Catholicism, Charles was in favor of non-exclusion. That Tories could reconcile their support for Charles with their extreme Anglicanism is only explicable from Charles' ability to dissemble.

11 The French Revolution was hardly what could be called "socialist" and the National Assembly passed a law disallowing workmen's unions. Party politics had begun, along general lines, with moderates, called Girondins (because many were from Bordeaux), on one side, and radical Jacobins (because of the name of a convent) and the even more radical Cordeliers (cobblers) on the other. "Radicalism" in this context was chiefly defined by the degree of anti-monarchical sentiment. Robespierre became an idol of radical leftists. It was he and his followers who gave a political connotation to "left", because that's the side where they sat in relation to the head of the National Convention, which was elected in 1792 to supplant the Legislative Assembly, elected in 1791, to succeed the National Assembly (1789).

groups such as Civic Union, Yabloko, the National Salvation Front, and the Movement for Democratic Political Reform. Except for the communists, these parties, even those for Yeltsin, did not have national organizations.

Most of the members of Russia's parliament followed the dictates either of their conscience or their convenience. The sense of accountability to a constituency just wasn't there. But you would have had to be deaf and blind not to sense Russian discontents and the Supreme Soviet during 1993 became vociferous in its opposition to Yeltsin and to everything that emerging capitalist Russia stood for.

There arose a confrontation between the executive and the legislative branches in which the latter demanded a return to the past and Yeltsin not only was not prepared to budge but also assumed the role of defender of the new Russia whatever its shortcomings. The ringleaders in the Supreme Soviet were Ruslan Khasbulatov, a choleric Chechen, and Aleksandr Rutskoi, Yeltsin's handpicked vice-president and former general.

(17) Yeltsin comes out like a fighting bear and puts the weirdos in their place

As the conflict spiraled, enlightened public opinion in Moscow realized that the parliament really did intend to legislate Russia into a communist-fascist Dark Age and that only the bulky, boozy Yeltsin could prevent that from happening. Through a patently unconstitutional decree, the Russian president on 21 September 1993 dissolved parliament. Rutskoi and Khasbulatov defied Yeltsin's ban and organized a resistance movement in the White House.

The conflict could have been solved quickly through the use of military force, but neither side had at first the power to command its intervention. Parliament was legally in the right in refusing to disband, as a constitutional court confirmed, but Yeltsin was the lawfully elected Russian president and if he was deposed the armed forces would be assuming a heavy responsibility that could degenerate into a social tornado with divisions ranged against one another.

However constitutional, the Supreme Soviet was not seen as a viable political option, not anyway at the stage at which Russian society had arrived in the process of shedding communism. The defiant deputies were not even wholly communistic but had a heavy admixture of socially aberrant tendencies such as fascism, extreme nationalism, and anti-Semitism. Neither as communists, fascists or as whatever else they stood for could they be considered a fair reflection of Russian public opinion.

Physically, the Supreme Soviet, or the quorum of deputies that sustained its constitutionality, was in the disadvantageous position of being contained within the White House. The deputies were the besieged and Yeltsin was the besieger. But the siege was not entirely constricting. The deputies chose to be inside the parliament building because if they left it, they had no place to go but home. After ordering that the police put all possible pressure on them short of an attack, Yeltsin took a detached, unworried attitude to the situation, until some deputies left their redoubt and tried to occupy a television center known as Ostankino that transmitted nation-wide.

Things were beginning to get out of hand when Yeltsin came out like a furious bear, as he had done during the coup against Gorbachev. He swung the minister of defense, Gen. Pavel Grachev, to his side and tanks arrived and surrounded the White House. After firing some rounds at the central floors of the building, where flames and smoke poured out of windows charring the walls around them, an attack followed that left fourteen dead. Soldiers occupied the White House and the last defenders of parliament dispersed. As had happened to the conspirators in the August 1991 coup, the parliamentary ringleaders were arrested, held prisoner for a time, and then released. There was a difference in that Gorbachev had been illegally detained and this time it was Yeltsin who acted outside of the law. Grachev's support was to be at the origin of Yeltsin's greatest mistake, a worse blunder than Gorbachev's consent for KGB intervention in Vilnius. Things would get much worse for Yeltsin before they got better.

(18) Russian voters gave a plurality to a near lunatic

One thing emerged clearly from the taking of the White House. It was obvious that Russians did not relish the thought of bringing back communist despotism. Many who were struggling to keep afloat probably reasoned that their chances of improving were better under a system which permitted individual enterprise than under one that illegalized it. Wasn't the history of Russia before and during communism that of the state encroaching without restraint on the private lives of its citizens? The modernizing Peter the Great had converted the Russian Orthodox Church into an instrument of the monarchy through the Holy Synod, which enjoined priests to break the secret of the confessional if the security of the state was at risk.[12] Lenin had wiped out the few gains for due process that were made under the last Romanovs. When he met the psychologist Ivan Pavlov, Lenin practically asked him to device means to train people the way he had done with dogs.[13] Under Stalin

12 Pipes, op.cit., pp.239-243.
13 Figes, op.cit., pp.732-734.

of course there was no real legality, at least in the political sphere. Collective leadership was an improvement, but it was potentially Stalinist. And under Yeltsin Russians were not willing to risk a reversion to Stalinism.

After Yeltsin's coup, Russia was endowed with a new constitution in which the power of the president was considerably enhanced. Before, any minister who served as spokesman for the president, such as Gaidar or Chernomyrdin, was considered the equivalent of a prime minister. Now, the post of prime minister was officially created, although it continued to be entirely responsive to the president, who could dissolve the Duma (the re-adopted traditional Russian name for legislature) and call for new elections if it failed to ratify the president's choice after three tries.

Moscow had come too close to a legal reversion to communism for Russian voters' tastes, but capitalist Russia and its flagrant abuses were still so distasteful that in December the electorate gave a plurality to Zhirinovsky, as repulsive a politician as a democracy could throw up. Zhirinovsky was what in America would be called a "plain speaker", but he was also extremely politically incorrect—among other things, he was an anti-Semite with a Jewish father—so he raised many hackles by assuming fascist stances, using ethnic slurs, and turning violent when challenged. Just as Gorbachev was admired more outside Russia than in his country, so Zhirinovsky was taken more seriously by American journalists than by Russian politicians.

Yeltsin's economic policies went on unchanged and social conditions in Russia tended to deteriorate rather than improve. Gusinsky was building up his conglomerate of media, in which facts were crudely reported, though not in a manner that would discredit the free and easy ways through which he himself had made his huge fortune. Yeltsin unwittingly provided him with the opportunity to become the Russian champion of freedom of information.

(19) Chechnya was like a stomach ulcer, tiny but constantly painful

Russia had been too preoccupied with one thing and another, especially the crises stepping on the heels of each other—August 1991 and its sequels, shock therapy all through 1992, and Yeltsin's own coup in 1993—for the central government to do much more than to try to keep the Russian Federation in line with its policies, or for that matter, its lack of policies, which is often what laissez faire is about; and Russia was also, among the other singular things it became in that time, the greatest historical exemplar of the abuses to which laissez faire lends itself. The first communist state in history, the greatest historical refutation of all the basics of capitalism, had become in only a couple of years the embodiment of the worst excesses of capitalism.

In the midst of these concerns, the unacceptable situation in Chechnya had been neglected, although not entirely forgotten. Chechnya was like a stomach ulcer, tiny but constantly painful.[14] Since in Chechnya itself everything went, Chechens became visible members of Russian mafias. So here was a situation in which a province of a country had declared its independence unilaterally and still had the gall practically to encourage its own citizens to engage in unlawful activities within the country it officially wanted to have nothing to do with.

From reports about Dudayev, the former general and self-proclaimed president of Chechnya, he was probably partly insane—not a good reference for the Soviet higher-officers class—so any possibility of a negotiated settlement was out of the question. Yeltsin was already under pressure from Grachev and people in his entourage to do something about Chechnya. Separatism was in vogue and much of the information about Russia that the Western press printed was about this or that local de facto dictator, or about cities that were still living in a twilight zone between communism and capitalism, or of entire provinces and regions trying to ignore the changes that Russia had undergone.

In October 1994, the ruble took a big dive, which was not really that significant in Russia itself, most of whose citizens were not making currency transactions on a daily basis, but which showed that the Russian economy was doing badly. Not only had social conditions been deteriorating, but also the chances that they would improve through economic growth were being visibly diminished. It was at that juncture that Yeltsin gave Grachev the green light to take Chechnya by force. Russian military capability, already discredited in Afghanistan, had been declining as the entire country went downhill. Even so, the Russian high command believed that it would subdue Chechnya practically by marching in.

Chechnya is about the size of New Jersey with some 1.4 million inhabitants, more than half of whom lived in the capital Grozny. The Russians sent in 40,000 soldiers, but the Chechens had spent the previous years setting a gigantic ambuscade and the fighting was hard, much more so than the Russians expected. The Western press instead of sticking to the facts went on about how one Chechen was worth ten Russians. Gusinsky's television network, which by then covered all of Russia, made

14 The image is Napoleonic and refers to Spain, where, despite its occupation, French arms experienced their first ominous defeat at Bailen (1808). It was in Spain also that guerrilla warfare started and it was defeat in Spain that first adumbrated Napoleon's abdication.

a name for itself with reporting that was as unsparing as that of the American media in Vietnam. In exasperation, the Russians did a blitz in Grozny and caused the greatest destruction and loss of life that any city had experienced after World War II, to no useful purpose for the Chechens went on resisting without let up and the two sides got bogged down in a small but awful war that had no end in sight, even after Dudayev's cell phone was tracked down by the Russians and he was killed by a well-aimed missile.[15]

(20) The worst capitalist excesses were coming true in the land which first espoused Marxism

Even as the war in Chechnya ground on, the insatiable Russian billionaires were engaged in bigger and better deals, most of them at the expense of the complaisant state that Yeltsin headed. One of the magnates, Vladimir Potanin, a typical commie insider who turned the Soviet Vneshtorbank into the privately owned (and better sounding) Uneximbank, invented the ultimate racket, which was to lend the state money that probably came from underpaying taxes in exchange for shares in lucrative state companies. This was the equivalent of the rich using money stolen from the poor to make themselves richer at the further expense of the poor. It was the most apocalyptic Marxist prediction coming true in the country that had first espoused and then repudiated Marxism. Communism had been terrible but not quite that economically inequitable. This was in 1995 and parliamentary elections were set for December.

On polling day, the voters ignored lingering scruples about the Soviet past and gave a strong plurality to Zyuganov and the Communist Party. This was not aberrant voting to needle the powerful, as in the case of the vote for Zhirinovsky, but a real protest vote. Since there were to be presidential elections in 1996, it might have been construed as the ram with which the communists were going to break down the huge Kremlin portals and recover what had been theirs.

One of the winners in the parliamentary elections was another plain speaker, Gen. Aleksandr Lebed, but not a violent clown like Zhirinovsky or a mad dog like Dudayev. He had become famous in a situation, which would not have induced much trust in his ability to achieve what he later did.

---

15 Grozny is one in a list of cities that have been ravaged by war after World War II. The list includes: Sarajevo, Kabul, Mogadishu, Hama, Freetown, Monrovia, Brazzaville, and various provincial capitals of the Democratic Republic of Congo.

The Moldavian Soviet Socialist Republic, peopled historically by speakers of Romanian, declared its independence during the time when most of the other Soviet republics were doing the same, but the circumstances were somewhat special. Moldova, the country that emerged from the Soviet womb, was very small and it was half Russian. The Dniester River divides Moldova and most Russians live on its left or eastern bank. Lebed, who commanded the regional Soviet land forces, was ordered to butt out of Moldova. Instead he occupied eastern Moldova and set up a Russian administration for the region—a statelet within a statelet, as *The Economist* put it—that has become known as Transdniestra.[16]

After retiring from the army, Lebed participated in the 1995 parliamentary elections with his own personal party, the Congress of Russian Communities. Yeltsin, whose sense of opportunity no modern politician can match, co-opted Lebed and, of all people, gave him a free hand to end the interminable conflict in Chechnya. Lebed accomplished his task with a truce extricating the battered Russian forces. Having achieved this, Lebed, who had his own presidential ambitions, left the Kremlin to campaign for himself.

(21) The Kremlin and the robber-barons

In opinion polls before the presidential election, Zyuganov was leading Yeltsin by large margins. The American financier George Soros, who took a great interest in the Russian process, was prognosticating a communist victory. This had already happened in former Soviet satellites. It had even happened in Catholic Poland, a pioneer in the conversion from communism to capitalism. Yeltsin was his unflappable self. But he was surrounded by advisors, in particular his bodyguard and intimate friend, former Gen. Aleksandr Korzakhov, who insisted that he do a coup d'état and make himself dictator, discarding Russia's rudimentary democracy with the antithetical justification that a communist victory would mean the end of democracy in Russia, which was not necessarily true if one went by the orderly changes of government through elections in ex-communist countries.

16 Romania reached its greatest extension after the World War I, when it embraced Valachia, Transylvania, northern Dobruja, and Moldavia as far as the Dniester River. It sided with Germany in the Second World War and in 1947 the USSR annexed Moldavia as far as the Prut River and eastern Bukovina. The Moldavian Soviet Socialist Republic was created with eastern Moldavia (Bessarabia) and eastern Bukovina. Southern Bessarabia was annexed to the Ukraine. Upon the dissolution of the USSR in 1991, the Moldavian Soviet Socialist Republic declared its independence as Moldova (4.5 million inhabitants). Bukovina is northern Moldavia.

Yeltsin's temperament was authoritarian, but he was also committed to democracy, much more so than Gorbachev had ever been, for it had been by democratic means that Yeltsin had survived politically when his fellow communist hierarchs had practically thrown him in the gutter. Besides, the biggest of the big magnates, Berezovsky and Gusinsly, also had Yeltsin's ear, and these men, although they had enough money salted away to live a thousand times over in the lap of luxury, did not want to be shut out from the power games they had been playing so lucratively and so notoriously in the past few years.

Berezovsky and Gusinsky were no friends of each other, but together they convinced Yeltsin that, through the use of the state's media and by pooling their own private communication resources—Berezovsky like Gusinsky also controlled some media—if Yeltsin played his political cards well, including the invaluable one of being the incumbent, he could win, whatever people were muttering about him at that moment. And Yeltsin for the third time in five years went down into the political arena.

With high-saturation TV coverage working for him and the privatizer Chubais managing his campaign, he pulled a sensational hattrick by winning the presidency and sinking the high hopes the communists were entertaining in the democratic process they aped or spurned when they held power. There were three incorrigibles at work here: the magnates' lust for wealth and for their share of power, Yeltsin's willingness to indulge them and his determination to keep Russia on its shambling gait towards some kind of stability, and the Russian electorate's penchant for ultimately preferring the devil they knew.

Yeltsin, who suffered a heart attack during the campaign but managed to keep calm enough to survive it (and have bypass surgery later), was destined for a still greater moment, perhaps historically the most ennobling of all, in his astonishing career. For now, his presidential victory sealed the alliance between the Kremlin and the capitalist lords of Russia, particularly Berezovsky, who was awarded an oil company and became a political force through his influence in the Kremlin.

(22) The long pedigree of ethnic cleansing

When the despotic, totalitarian USSR broke up it turned out to have been harboring similar inequalities and disparities to those that had arisen over the centuries through uneven international economic development under capitalism. A similar experience as Russia's awaited the federation of Yugoslavia, but here it was like putting a torch to a hold full of explosives.

An attempt by the Serbs to co-opt the Yugoslav presidency led to the secession of Slovenia and Croatia, followed by Macedonia. The latter had been an ancient Greek kingdom, not in the Greek heartland but Greek enough for Athens to claim that the use of the name Macedonia for an independent mainly Slavic country was like a sort of copyright infringement. The misunderstanding was finally solved sensibly: the Greeks gave ground, although they got Macedonia to prefix its name with "ex-Yugoslav republic of Macedonia". Serbia and Montenegro formed a new Yugoslav federation.

According to often quoted census figures for Bosnia and Herzegovina, 44% of the population was Muslim, 31% Serb, and 17% Croat. Since Serb and Croat are identical and Muslims speak the same language, these ethnic definitions were a matter of choice by Bosnian respondents, and this meant that Bosnia and Herzegovina as such had no loyalties, apart perhaps from those of Muslims.

When Bosnia and Herzegovina attempted to secede from the Yugoslav federation, the Bosnian Serbs refused and Serbia supported them. There followed civil war and "ethnic cleansing" (the displacement of a people by another in a territory shared by both). The latter practice had ancient credentials.

The Hebrews, for instance, did something of the sort to the Philistines in their midst, who admittedly before had also treated the Hebrews like intruders. The Babylonians later did some ethnic cleansing in Israel, mainly of the more recalcitrant Jews. The Byzantines were so prejudiced against Slavs that emperor Basil II went down in history with the sobriquet of Bulgaroktonos or slayer of Bulgars, which he did systematically in the Balkans.

Contrary to widespread belief in the West, the Ottomans did not try to expel or exterminate peoples that fell under their rule, but when Christians began to drive the Turks back they often literally pushed them towards a core Balkan Turkish area around Istanbul. After the Ottomans lost most of their former Balkan lands, they consolidated a homeland in Anatolia, including many Kurds and Armenians. The Kurds are Sunni Muslims and they had no problem with Ottoman rule, but Armenians were Christians and when the Russians threatened Anatolia during World War I, the Armenians applauded. This was the occasion for ethnic cleansing of such ruthlessness that it is often called the Armenian holocaust.

Perhaps the vastest attempt at ethnic cleansing was carried out by Europeans in the Americas against native Amerindians. As Europeans did not like physical work in the tropical heat they brought in Africans to replace Amerindians. As long as blacks were chattels, they were in their proper place, but once emancipated they became an encumbrance. By then it was too late to do ethnic cleansing.

In the Balkans, the Ottoman Empire left pockets of Islam in Albania, in Kosovo, and in Bosnia and Herzegovina. The Catholic Croats and the Muslim Bosnians lost no love on each other, but as they were being put upon by the Orthodox Serbs, they became allies of convenience when the country as a whole voted for independence. They agreed on a Bosnian government to which the Serbs, who had taken Bosnian territory disproportionate to their numbers, were ferociously opposed. In operation Deliberate Force, NATO intervened with air strikes that made the Serbs back down. On the ground, UN troops were positioned in safe zones. The air offensive allowed the Croats to recover territories occupied by Serbs in Croatia itself. Bosnian Croat forces also overran Serb-controlled areas in northern Bosnia.

With Serb defenses crumbling, all parties signed accords in Dayton, Ohio, in which Bosnia and Herzegovina was divided into a federation including Muslims and Croats (51% of the territory) and a less federated Serb republic. The Bosnian Serb leaders, Ratko Mladic and Radovan Karadzic, were declared international outlaws. Bosnia and Herzegovina was headed a collective presidency and propped up by an UN-backed NATO force of over 50,000 troops. Rather than tending towards integration, Bosnia and Herzegovina seems to be drifting towards greater ethnic separatism and elections in 2000 gave support to Serbian and Croatian nationalists.

(23) In conservative America, Clinton was like a man walking on egg shells

In the 1990s, Americans elected Democrat Bill Clinton twice. But they did not do it out of liberalism and Clinton had to do a lot of trimming to keep up with an electorate who, among other signs of extreme conservatism, refused restrictions on the individual ownership of weapons, rejected Medicaid reform, and espoused the lex talionis with Semitic passion. Some Americans might have been forced to accept the principles of racial equality, but, by Jiminy, no one was going to deprive them of the right to execute black murderers, even if there are grounds for assuming the possibility of infinitely many miscarriages of justice, and even in the light of evidence that through the disproportionate application of the death penalty basically the lives of whites are given more value than those of blacks.[16]

16 "Since 1976, blacks have been six to seven times more likely to be murdered than whites, with the result that blacks and whites are the victims of murder in about equal numbers. Yet 80% of the more than 840 people put to death in the USA since 1976 were convicted of crimes involving white victims, compared to the 13% who were convicted of killing blacks." Amnesty International, as quoted by Bob Herbert in "Bring Down the Curtain on the Death Penalty", IHT, 25-5-2003. The American disposition to capital punishment is so strong that as recently as 11 March 2003, a federal appeals court ruled that an insane person on death row could be taken off medication and executed, despite a 1986 Supreme Court decision prohibiting the execution of the insane as, in the words of justice Thurgood Marshall, "savage and inhuman". Subsequently, the Supreme Court voided the lower court's decision.

187 The Crisis Brewing

During the Clinton years, the United States was plagued by worldwide terrorist attacks: attempt to blast the foundations of the WTC in New York; attacks on American targets: military buildings in Riyadh and in the eastern city of Dhahran (the Khobar Towers, near King Abdul Aziz Air Force Base), both in Saudi Arabia; embassy bombings in Kenya and Tanzania; sea-borne attack on the USS Cole in Aden harbor.

Islamic fighters in Afghanistan against atheistic communism were called mujahidin. The latter is an Arab word meaning those who fight jihad. One of these mujahidin was Osama bin Laden, a very rich man from Saudi Arabia. He had inherited millions from the fortune that his Yemeni father had made in the construction business. Bin Laden put his money where his loyalties were and contributed financially to the Afghan struggle. Apparently, he did not appreciate the American backing for the Afghan resistance movement.

When he returned home, he found to his horror that the USA was stationing troops in the "land of the two holy sites" (Mecca and Medina), where it was an Islamic duty, enjoined by Muhammad himself, to repel the presence of infidels, not to speak of infidel soldiers. In the normal course of events (before the discovery of oil), Arabia would have been as likely to be attacked by foreigners as by thunderstorms. Yet the worst assault on Islam committed by the Crusaders, much more so than the carnage they provoked in Jerusalem—al Quds, or the Holy, for Muslims—was when French knight Reynald of Châtillon tried to invade the Red Sea coast of Arabia, for which he paid with his life when he was captured by Saladin in the battle of Hattin.

American troops were stationed in Saudi Arabia during the Gulf war. It was this conflict that exacerbated Osama bin Laden's hatred, also stoked by the fate of Palestinians under Israeli domination. Bin Laden became so strident in his denunciations that he was stripped of his citizenship and forced out of his country and into exile. He chose Sudan, where Hassan Turabi, a Muslim ideologue and an eloquent orator, was very influential.

Turabi was a man after Osama bin Laden's heart. However, Sudan had its eyebrows singed when the Americans attacked it with cruise missiles on suspicion of supporting Islamic terrorism. It turned out that the specific target of American ire, a factory outside Khartoum where supposedly chemical weapons were being manufactured, was really just a regular drugs firm, as its owners said. The Islamic Sudanese government, which already was embattled in Sudan's rebellious southern region, where Islam is not the predominant religion, decided to avoid further complications and asked Osama bin Laden to decamp. By then the

Taliban were in power in Afghanistan and when bin Laden asked for asylum, he was received with open arms.

It was a fateful decision. Bin Laden was bankrolling an organization called al Qaida, a probable suspect in the terrorist attacks against America, and it was from extremely backward Afghanistan that he began planning the destruction of the twin towers of the WTC, in other words, finishing the job which other Islamic terrorists had previously failed at. Through a Cold-War turnabout, America had made possible the Afghan platform that later was used for the greatest external attack it had ever experienced.

(24) NATO forces the Serbs to back down in Kosovo

There were still large patches of clear skies even as the thunderclouds soared and storms gathered. The blue horizons that were perceived with the fall of communist despotism and the deterrence of Iraqi aggression were once again being clouded with potential anvil heads. Liberal economic reforms were gaining ground in China when Deng Xiaopin died and was succeeded by Jiang Zemin, party secretary general, whose theory that the communist party represented not only workers but the wider interests of society (read the new capitalist class) was adopted as official Chinese policy. Subsequently, guarantees for the private sector were incorporated into the Chinese constitution.

Serbian president Slobodan Milosevic, the same who had fomented the civil war in Bosnia and Herzegovina, had previously deprived the provinces of Kosovo and Vojvodina of all autonomous powers. Serbs consider Kosovo as their original homeland, but through time Albanians, who are Muslims, had peopled it. There is a substantial Hungarian minority in Vojvodina (northern Serbia). Despite warnings by NATO to abstain from applying ethnic cleansing in Kosovo, Milosevic proceeded to do so. One million Kosovars fled to Albania and Macedonia.

For the first time since it was created to counter Soviet-Stalinist military pressure in Europe, NATO acted as a unitary force led by the USA and after nearly two months of bombing, mostly of Serbia, forced the Serbian troops out of Kosovo. Kosovar refugees returned to their homes and in turn began persecuting the local Serbs that hadn't left. A multinational force called KFOR runs Kosovo, which is not likely to become an effective province of Serbia in the foreseeable future, although there is no concrete talk of its independence either.[17]

17 Serbs have hardly given up on recovering Kosovo. As it is Javier Solana, the Spanish EU "foreign minister", who has been responsible for political arrangements in Kosovo, they joke that the province should be given independence as "Solania".

Milosevic was defeated at the polls by Vojislav Kostunica. A special international tribunal for genocide and violations of human rights indicted him. Not much later, he was handed over by Yugoslavia to the tribunal sitting in The Hague. Earlier, Montenegro had proposed that Yugoslavia be converted into a very loose confederation. After the downfall of Milosevic, Yugoslavia appeared to be hanging together, but in 2003 the federal parliament voted to scrap the name Yugoslavia and renamed the country Serbia and Montenegro.

(25) For being a moderate socialist, Lassalle was called a "Jewish nigger" by Marx

It was leftist Castro who introduced mass political executions into Latin American politics. But the right was an adept learner. But for a period of authoritarian rule under Carlos Ibañez del Campo before World War II, Chile was a functioning, mainly conservative democracy. It was also different from most of Latin America in having a more advanced economy, which however was still dependent, like those of other developing countries, on one basic export and foreign-currency earner. In Chile's case it was copper. Because of the world depression, the country had rough going during the 1930s. Chile had a Radical Party, which in a Latin or French-influenced context usually means middle-class. It was through the Radicals that socialists and communists started filtering into power.

Socialists and communists were implacable enemies since the times of the Socialist Internationals.[18] In these congresses of delegates of workers' organizations, Marxists went in one direction and other socialists in another: the former were truly "radical" and the latter were gradualists, not unwilling to accept concessions to workers from conservative rulers, such as the social legislation introduced by Bismarck in Germany. Ferdinand de Lassalle was one of the socialist leaders who was willing to recognize the merits of these measures, for which Karl Marx called him a "Jewish nigger".[19]

Lenin was the prototype of the intransigent Marxist and Karl Kautsky and Eduard Bernstein were "revisionists", as contemptible to Marxists as

18 The International Workingman's Association, better known as the First International (1864-1876), was founded in London with the enthusiastic support of Karl Marx. It disintegrated because of international polemics between Marx and the anarchist Mikhail Bakunin. The Second International (1889-1914) also known as the Socialist International was founded in Paris. Its headquarters were later established in Brussels. It dissolved when member parties supported their respective states at the start of World War I.

19 Wheatcroft, op.cit., p.30

Marxists were to respectable politicians. After the Russian revolution, the Soviet Comintern reviled socialist revisionists. Or it did until Hitler began ranting against Bolsheviks and Stalin then sought alliances with socialists known as popular fronts.

In Post-War Europe, with Stalin gorged on victory, communists and socialists were again at loggerheads. It was a socialist mayor, Willy Brandt, who opposed Soviet bluster over Berlin in 1958. But in far away Chile, socialists and communists were like the thumb and the index. The Chilean Radicals were in power during most of World War II and in the immediate Post-War.

Despite or because of greater American investments and a growing urban population, the conservatives came back to power with the election of the former dictator Ibañez del Campo. They retained the presidency with Jorge Alessandri Rodriguez. Economic prosperity was very inequitably shared. Thus, the stage was set for a confrontation between the Christian Democrats and the re-invigorated socialists and communists.

The Christian Democrat Eduardo Frei won a landslide majority. He tried to better social conditions by fractioning landed estates and partial nationalization of the copper mines, although it was not clear exactly how these measures were going to help the poor. Land reform might have, but it required costly investments in infrastructure, which were undertaken only very slowly. What happened was that a very leftist coalition called Unidad Popular won a plurality and carried the socialist Salvador Allende to the Presidency. This was the first time in history that a genuinely revolutionary government, in the sense of openly Marxist, gained power through the ballot box and without external pressure.

The performance of the economy under the Popular Unity government is a matter of debate, but nationalizations did not increase productivity and external capital flows stopped. The Nixon administration allowed the CIA to conspire in the open against Allende. The middle classes turned against the government and the usually reactionary military staged a textbook coup d'état organized by the minister of war, Gen. Augusto Pinochet, about whom Allende had no suspicions. The conspiracy embraced all branches of the armed forces. When the plotters acted, Allende was isolated in La Moneda, the presidential palace. Resistance there was shattered when a Chilean pilot dropped a bomb with such precision that it went through a window and harmed nothing outside of its target. At first Allende's widow accepted the plotters version that her husband had killed himself, but later evidence emerged that such had not been the case. Allende was killed resisting in his office.

Pinochet promptly restored full capitalism and began a national manhunt against any one even suspected of leftist sympathies. Tens of thousands of Chileans (and many foreign nationals) went to prison; thousands were tortured, assassinated, and disposed of secretly. These crimes have been thoroughly investigated and documented although they have not been punished. The Argentine military observed how Pinochet put his country under a military boot and they initiated their own "dirty war", which produced a high estimate of 30,000 "desaparecidos" (disappeared ones).

As in Spain under Franco, the Pinochet regime brought complete social and political stability to Chile. Like Spaniards before them, Chileans had nothing more engaging to do than to better themselves economically, which they went about quite nicely, in the rural areas on the basis of some previous social reforms. Under internal and external pressure, Pinochet allowed a plebiscite in which Chileans voted against him.

Through fiscal discipline and economic enterprise, which attracted foreign investment, the economy was flourishing when Pinochet allowed free elections with the proviso that he remains head of the armed forces for eight more years. The official candidate lost to the Christian Democrat Patricio Aylwin Azócar.

With Chile a fully functioning democracy, Pinochet travelled to Great Britain and got the surprise of his life when he was arrested for an extradition trial on charges of violating the human rights of some Spanish citizens brought before an English tribunal by the Spanish judge Baltasar Garzón. Pinochet was detained and held under house arrest while the case moved through British courts. He was released for health reasons, which was a cover for Britain to extricate itself from a difficult situation, although the precedent of charging former heads of state for crimes committed under their rule was securely established.

(26) Yeltsin's last astonishing political somersault

While crisis was brewing, the most encouraging process of all occurred where one would have least expected, in equally unforeseeable circumstances, and that was in Robber-Baron-ridden Russia. That privatization and democratic elections had not done the trick of turning the Russian economy around was shown with the devaluation crisis of August 1998, when the ruble lost 40% of its value.

Not in good health, Yeltsin was sincerely trying to find a replacement and during two years he went through four prime ministers. Chernomyrdin had been around as Yeltsin's prime minister or its equivalent since 1993. He got the sack in March 1998 and was replaced by Sergei Kiriyenko, who was blamed for the currency crisis. Chubais was also sent packing, although, as he left to run a huge energy company, hardly empty-handed. When Yeltsin tried to re-appoint Chernomyrdin, the Duma reared up. Whatever his faults, Yeltsin knew when not to press a point. This time he gave in. After caretaking for a few months, Yevgeny Primakov substituted Chernomyrdin.

Although Berezovsky still had the run of Kremlin hallways, Yeltsin appeared to be searching for a real manager for Russia and not just a wax doll of the magnates. Dissatisfied with Primakov's performance, he named Sergei Stepashin, a young and earnest bureaucrat, whose influence from the start was no match for Berezovsky's. Before the year was out, without previous notice, Yeltsin thanked Stepashin and fired the dumbfounded young man. In his place he put the also young and also serious-looking Vladimir Putin.

There were important differences between the two. Stepashin had one facial expression but Putin had frequent flashes of ironical humour. He once said that if the anti-Gorbachev coup had succeeded he might have ended up using his own car as a taxi in order to survive, which sounds both plausible and unlikely. In Moscow, anyone driving an automobile, including cops on duty, work as part-time taxi drivers. But Putin wouldn't have been at that job for long.

Another difference with Stepashin was that Putin seemed to be sharper. He had spent fifteen years as intelligence officer in the KGB. Afterwards, Putin had occupied visible academic and political posts in St. Petersburg that would not have endeared him to the communists. In 1996, he moved to the Kremlin as administrator. He was close to Chubais, but particularly he came to the attention of Yeltsin himself, who finally, through God knows what "intuitive" shortcut, decided that Putin was the man not only for prime minister but also to succeed him.

Thus Yeltsin closed his presidency on another astounding note. From the moment he put Putin forward, to the world like a rabbit out of a magic hat, to the presidential transition on 31 December 1999, there was an interval of about four months. But the most surprising of all turns of event is that Putin, who in 2000 was elected president in his own right, exerted such a firm leadership that the Russian economy began to grow again.

American observers have accused Putin of authoritarianism because his government has instituted legal proceedings against Gusinsky, in effect impounding his TV network, but this could also be interpreted as ridding the state of undue business influence and putting an end to the wild phase of Russian capitalism. Boris Berezovsky also fell afoul of

Putin and his extradition was being sought in a London court on fraud charges. In 2004, the king of Russian post-Soviet billionaires, Mikhail Khodorkovsky, the owner of Yukos, the biggest Russian oil company, was accused and jailed for tax-evasion and fraud, which does give some grounds for the suspicion that the Russian government is being selective in its prosecutions. As we shall see, there's more than meets the eye in the Yukos case.

One potential source of disruptions for Putin's Russia is still Chechnya. The Chechens attempted attacking Dagestan and were suspected of terrorism in Russia itself. It was a grievous error of judgment, because the Russians had been spoiling for a rematch and they invaded Chechnya again, although, as time would tell, not with the entirely favorable results they expected because of better preparations than in the previous war.

(27) So little was made of Iraq's aggressive capability that the man in charge of special weapons programs wasn't even interrogated by USA agents

Russia might have been recuperating after a decade of topsy-turvy, but in other parts of the world the sound of thunder was beginning to be heard loudly. Not content with having escaped personally unscathed from the Gulf War, Saddam Hussein began constricting Iraq even harder during the 1990s, although, as the country was de facto partitioned, he might have been trying with his usual mailed-fist methods to prevent Iraq from coming entirely apart. He did not flinch at making public his murderous methods, which he applied to his own sons-in-law when, after fleeing to Jordan, they were enticed back and promptly executed.

One of Saddam's sons in law, Gen. Hussein Kamel, had been in charge of the special weapons program in Iraq. He was never taken up by the USA as a possible source of information on a potential enemy, so little was then made of Iraq's aggressive capability.

In the aftermath of Iraq's utter defeat in the Gulf War or First Iraqi war, Hussein was hardly appreciative of President Bush's statesmanship in not going after him and instead declaring peace once Kuwait was liberated. Bush's claimed that he had g no truck with idealisms, but he actually sounded like the idealistic Carter when he spoke of a "new world order". This was noble but ingenuous of him, for history is on the qui vive to quash any deliberate manifestation of excessive optimism.

The last time for such talk was in the 1970s when, flush with petro-dollars, some very rich but very backward countries were drumming up something called "new international economic order". This was basically the legion of the poor asking members of the Organization of Oil Exporting Countries (OPEC) for handouts.

OPEC was the creation of J.A. Perez Alfonzo, an insomniac, health-obsessed Venezuelan politician, and of the Saudis. It became one of the most successful oil cartels in history, although, if truth be said, it was based on a pattern set by the "Seven Sisters", the cartel of multinational oil companies that existed long before World War II. The difference was that OPEC involved sovereign states. However, Perez Alfonzo himself once admitted that multinationals knew so many accounting tricks that the governments of oil-producing countries couldn't even dream of beating them at their game.

The Yom Kippur War and the ensuing oil embargo emboldened OPEC countries to nationalize their oil industries. Oil-rich Arab countries were courted like deities and many soft-loans were arranged, although the Saudis still let London handle their private finances. After OPEC's salad days were over, and they lasted into the early 1980s, the Arabs' munificence had not changed the third world one whit. Venezuela, as we shall see, went into free fall. Perez Alfonzo, who saw disaster looming, died prematurely of cancer despite extremely healthy living.

After the Gulf War, Saddam Hussein had to accept a considerable mutilation of Iraqi sovereignty. The UN was empowered to keep the dictator in check in case he began to act up again. UN control was loose, although it was strict in the matter of the legal sale of Iraqi oil. It was an open secret that Iraq was making surreptitious oil deals but the UN was not empowered to look into these, much less try to prevent them.
Never one to let pass an opportunity to act like a bully, Hussein ordered UN arms inspectors out when they tried to inspect his main presidential palace. He wasn't counting on the son of George H.W. Bush being elected president of the USA. But Iraq wasn't the only place in the Middle East where the conditions for world crisis were building up.

(28) A fanatic slays Rabin and Israel elects a brilliant commando leader

Israeli Prime Minister Yitzhak Rabin, who had put on hold Israeli settlements in the West Bank, was assassinated by an Israeli fanatic whose mentor was an ultra-nationalist Orthodox rabbi who held a supposedly *Bible*-based theory about the legality of killing a "pursuer". The elimination of Rabin was the crucial signal for the emergence of Israeli extremisms claiming that Arafat was still the same old terrorist and that it wasn't possible to negotiate in good faith with Palestinians. The consequences of this infamous criminal act have been given democratic sanction four times over by the Israeli electorate.

Rabin had prestige along almost the full spectrum of Israeli politics. Having used muscle to crush the First Intifada, he was above suspicion of softness on Palestinians. He was a Sabra, the first Israeli prime minister born in Israel. Given the byzantinism of Israeli politics, in which short-term political gains are paramount, no stronger leader could be hoped for. With Rabin dead, the enemies of a peaceful solution to the Palestinian issue, which even under Rabin was not a sure thing, had the right of way. The fundamental moral flaw of Israel's anti-Palestinian policies is that they originated in an atrocious deed with which no decent human being, Jewish or non-Jewish, could be in agreement.

Rabin was succeeded by Peres, who called for elections in which he expected to get support for the continuation of a peace policy. From the start, there were many unsettled issues. Some, like the status of Hebron and the Palestinians' right of return, got the most headlines, but in fact these were minor issues and the major development was that antagonism between Israelis and Palestinians was generally on the rise. Hamas was responsible terrorist attacks on Israel. Jewish fanatics, some of them followers of Meir Kahane from Brooklyn, NY, hit back with reprisals, the most sensational being a single gunman's slaughter of Muslims in a mosque celebrating the end of Ramadan. Israelis saw Arafat's policy of trying to co-opt Hamas as temporizing with terrorism. After Arafat's death, ex-president Jimmy Carter wrote, "Hamas rejected my efforts to have them accept Arafat as their political leader, and they continue to act independently".

The charge that Arafat was not as tough on Palestinian terrorists as Israeli security expected him to be is probably true. But Arafat had two constraints: one, the lesser of the two, was that he had built his reputation on pugnacity and, although internationally he could not afford to be seen as pugnacious, to Palestinians, especially Gazans, he could not entirely disown the "martyrs" for the Palestinian cause; and the other constraint was that Israel never actually ceded to the PA more than nominal control of what was in effect a truncated Palestine. Israel ceded the PA the cauldron of discontent that was Gaza, which even Israel under Sharon's ruthless policies was not able to tame, but denied it the real core of Palestine, which was the West Bank.

In the elections, Israeli voters backed Binyamin Netanyahu, who said that he was not going to respect the Oslo deal. He was as good as his word. Israel should by then have expanded the PA's area of police control, but it offered only meager concessions such as ceding 9% of the West Bank, which Arafat rejected only to be told by Netanyahu that there would be no more concessions. The Israeli PM cancelled Rabin's freeze on settlements and authorized thousands of permits for new Israeli housing in the West Bank. Netanyahu was not just flouting the pact with the Palestinians: he was also antagonizing Arab and Muslim opinion the world over. This was one conflict that did not admit areal containment, as was the case of the Balkans. But Arafat had little power on the ground and all he could do was threaten to declare unilaterally the independence of Palestine, which caused some international alarm but which Israelis saw through as just bluffing.

His coalition coming apart from political jockeying and minor corruption charges, Netanyahu resigned and Israel went to the polls again. The Labor Party candidate was ex-general Ehud Barak, a distinguished soldier but particularly well known as the leader of a commando unit called Sayeret Macal. Barak directed the rescue of hostages in a plane hijacked by Japanese terrorists at Lod airport, in Tel Aviv. But the most spectacular commando action the group carried out was so far from Israel, in such challenging conditions, that it left the world utterly astonished.

(29) Others didn't but Israelis knew whom they were dealing with in Uganda

In 1976, Uganda was under the dictatorial rule of Idi Amin, a former British army non-com who had an international reputation as not squeamish about shedding blood or torturing. He was in some ways the proto-type of the third world radical: not much in the way of coherent ideas but always ready to pull the beard of former colonialists. When pro-Palestine terrorists (including Germans of the Baader-Meinhof gang) hijacked an Air France flight out of Israel en route to Paris with 258 passengers, they already had made a deal with Amin and forced the plane to land at the airport in Entebbe, the main one in Uganda.

The non-Jewish passengers—except the plane captain who chose to remain a hostage—were released and the hijackers kept 105 Jews captive. This was a real catch. The bargaining possibilities were limitless. Why, the terrorists and Amin, who kept up the pretense that he was only being helpful, could squeeze even the national treasury from Israel. There was one hitch. The Israelis knew their third world and to them Amin was, besides his other unendearing qualities, a total incompetent.

Israel mounted a raid with a battalion and four C-130 Hercules long-range military transport planes—three with soldiers and the fourth for the hostages—and they pulled off the neat hattrick of: (1) rescuing the hostages with only two casualties, (2) liquidating the seven hijackers (four had acted in the plane and three were waiting at the airport) and as many Ugandan soldiers as opposed them, and (3) destroying the Ugandan air force's some eight MIGs. The Israelis suffered one military loss, the leader of the rescue party, Lt. Col. Yonatan Netanyahu, brother of the politician. With this sole deed, Israel gained more admiration all over the world than it had in all its war victories. The planner of the Israeli raid was again Barak.

The former general was elected prime minister. Barak and Peres were both members of the Labor Party and it was hoped that, after some bargaining, the Oslo Accords would proceed. President Clinton arranged for Barak and Arafat to meet at Camp David in the hope of seeing results like those obtained by Carter hovering over Begin and Sadat. Clinton did all he could to nudge the two sides towards each other, but there was a monumental confusion in the signals that were being transmitted. Barak represented a nation for which just his presence at Camp David for talks with Arafat was giving in to terrorism. In general, the sides did not come prepared to make reciprocal concessions.[20] In Israel, Barak was specifically accused of having been too generous with Arafat because he consented to the principle of the formation of a "Palestinian state" whereas the Oslo Accords only mentioned "the Palestinian side" and the PA, which had emerged from them, was considered a provisional arrangement rather than anything resembling an independent nation.

(30) Sharon does his best to offend Palestinians and makes a big splash with the Israeli electorate

Despite having taken a hard line with Arafat, Barak was in political trouble in Israel and he was forced to call for elections. The Israeli electorate was very fragmented. Neither Labor nor Likud were able to muster majorities on their own. Israeli politics had become extremely labyrinthine, sometimes-fanatical religious parties having the power of decision with only a few representatives in the Knesset. There was substantial Russian-Jewish emigration to Israel and the newcomers tended to extreme conservatism, if not outright intolerance, in Israel's relations with Palestinians.

As political campaigning for new elections was going on, Sharon, the Likud party candidate, visited the Al Aqsa mosque under heavy armed escort. This ancient building, constructed over the foundation of Solomon's temple in the area known to Jews as Temple Mount, is one of the holiest places in Islam. On its walls are inscribed quotations from the *Koran* dating from a time when it had only recently been compiled. For Palestinians it was a symbol of their national aspirations. Sharon's purely political gambit provoked the start of the Second Intifada.

The initial Israeli response was exactly what it had been during the First Intifada: extreme force, which had then produced estimated ratios of anywhere between 25 and 7 Palestinians dead for every Israeli killed. This time in a week there were already 60 dead Palestinians and around 1,500 wounded for hardly a handful of Israeli casualties. Israeli troops used "rubber bullets", which have a steel core and can kill as easily as other ammo. An unexpected reaction was that Israeli Arabs, who during the First Intifada kept to themselves, this time rioted in Jaffa and other places.

20 Deborah Sontag, "Quest for Mideast peace: how and why it failed", NYT, July 26, 2001.

The conflict was at first of low intensity. Then a large majority elected Sharon. All hopes of peace evaporated. It didn't contribute to a solution of the problem that Jewish settlements numbered 125 in the West Bank and ten in Gaza. Israel had started building a system of fences and walls to protect them, to isolate Palestinians from Israel, and even to encircle Jerusalem. Suicide bombings were adopted by the Palestinians as a terrorist tactic and soon became commonplace.

(31) At the start of the millennium, ominous rumbles announced the coming storm

One millennium had ended and another began, but the roll that had started barely over ten years before had lost momentum. The sky was pregnant with clouds ready to burst. On the cheery side were the Chinese process towards economic liberalism, the downfall of Milosevic, the arrest of Pinochet however symbolical, and the rise of Putin. If China succeeded, and there was no reason to think the contrary, the world economy faced a future of steady prosperity. If Putin did, and on this there were doubtful notes, Russia would regain its balance and start counting again as a force for world stability. Iraq had expelled the UN arms inspectors. But then these had found nothing to justify their presence, which did not mean that Saddam Hussein had changed his tyrannical stripes.

The Russians thought that they had Chechnya under control the second time around. They were not counting on Chechen obstinacy. In 2002, 41 Chechen terrorists captured a theatre in Moscow and held 763 persons hostage. Russia's security forces pumped a strong anesthesic into the building. In the assault that followed the unconscious Chechen terrorists were liquidated, but also 129 hostages died, mostly from the consequences of inhaling the gas. In March 2003, Chechens, anxious for peace, approved by an uncontestable majority (96%) of a majority (79%) of eligible voters a constitution giving Chechnya autonomy as part of Russia. Before and after, however, there had been Chechen terrorist bombings. In July 2003, two women suiciders carried Chechen terrorism to a rock show on the outskirts of Moscow causing seventeen deaths. There was also ample evidence that resistance in Chechnya itself continued.

Worst of all was the failure at Camp David. Israelis and Palestinians would pay for this with thousands of unnecessary deaths. But the thunderstorm struck where no one expected, in the metropolitan heart of America at a time when a recently elected president was bragging that he could protect his country from the worst that could imaginably happen to it, which was precisely what did happen.

6

The Coming of World Crisis

In November 2000, the election for the presidency of the United States was a contest between Republican George W. Bush, son of former President George H.W. Bush, and Democrat Al Gore, vice-president under Bill Clinton. The national vote count narrowly favored Gore—demographics actually made it the largest vote ever cast for any presidential candidate—but the Electoral College hung on the balance of the votes in the state of Florida. In the American system, this discrepancy is possible because states, which have a number of electoral votes proportional to their population, are enjoined to cast all their electoral votes for the direct-vote winner however slim the margin.

Gore conceded before the Florida count was over and then changed his mind when it seemed as if he could still win in that state. A recount by the voting machines, which given the slight difference in votes (1,784) was virtually mandatory, still gave Bush the lead though by a smaller margin. Gore then went to the Florida Supreme Court arguing that the electoral machines were not reliably counting the votes ("undervotes") and that manual recounts should be undertaken in some counties. The cause of the problem was that, unless the ballot is punctured neatly, the partially attached so-called shad may or not be counted as a vote by the machine. The Supreme Court went Gore one better and ordered that tabulations be carried out by the electoral authorities in all Florida counties.

Bush's legal team went into action in the federal Supreme Court to countermand the Florida decision. And here the justices had the final word. Arguing from equal protection under the law, the court as a whole and not by majority decision stated that all votes should be counted equally and that there should exist no discrimination between voters. As there were no guidelines or criteria to determine by manual recount which ballots, apart from those clearly punctured, should be accepted as valid and which should be disregarded, it was impossible to do a tabulation in all of Florida that did not offer its citizens' right to vote equal protection. Consequently, in essence, the machines had the last word and Bush was the winner. Gore conceded a second time.

(1) Bush was buckling up against the wrong "devil"

There has never been in history such a deliberate attempt to duplicate a historical episode as there was in Bush's script-like imitation of Ronald Reagan. It is also perhaps the most telling demonstration of Marx's dictum that history only repeats itself as farce. When Reagan was around, the world was still bipolar. The USA-USSR confrontation was still there. Reagan inveighed against the "evil empire". For Reagan "evil" meant "enemy". Otherwise, his future collaboration with Gorbachev could be interpreted as a pact with the Devil

Bush the younger was not facing the threat of an "evil empire", itself an ethical trope. He denounced an "axis of evil" that wasn't even an "axis" but a triangle. The "axis of evil", in which two Muslim countries were included, was a concoction. The tendency to bandy about the epithet "evil" is peculiarly American. It went counter to Arabic and Muslim perceptionS of Israel as the real "evil". The Iranians had actually outdone the Americans by calling the USA "satan". (They couldn't very well call it "devil", a word whose Indo-Iranian cognate means "god".) So, basically in 2001, you had two "devils" glaring at each other: the USA-Israel alliance against anti-Israel and anti-American Muslims. But Bush was hitching up his trousers and buckling up his gun belt against the wrong "devils".

Although the American Congress had already re-activated the SDI, Bush put the full weight of the presidency behind it, something his own father had withheld. A priori the second Bush's act could not work. The USSR, the so-called evil empire, did not exist any more, and the "axis of evil" was not remotely comparable to it in military power, even if the three countries which formed it had been welded physically and all their resources pooled.

The three members of the "axis of evil"—Iran, Iraq, and North Korea, also called "rogue states"—did not even have very much in common. North Korea, where the deified Kim Il Sung had died and had been replaced by his son Kim Jong Il, was still an unreconstructed, cynical Stalinist regime. Iraq was an irrational, quintessential dictatorship.

But Iran was neither: it was a democracy struggling to emerge from under the suffocating cloaks of the ayatollahs.

(2) Khomeini's funeral was like a necrophiliac orgy

Khomeini died in 1989. His funeral was like a necrophiliac orgy in which the pale, naked corpse of the stout old cleric was torn from its shroud and manhandled by the frenzied crowd. He was succeeded by other conservative ayatollahs but in 1997 an open-minded ayatollah, Mohammad Khatami, was elected president, and re-elected in 2001. The Iranian Majlis or parliament was also in the hands of reformers. But the Islamic Republic of Iran was constituted as a real theocracy, engendered by the only theocratic revolution in modern history, and the power of Islamic fundamentalists and conservatives remains decisive. In addition to the "civil government", there is a Council of Experts, which is headed by a cleric considered the spiritual leader of Iran.

What Khatami and his liberal supporters aspired to achieve was to temper the extremism of the theocratic heirs of Khomeini. Though seemingly incongruous, a comparison of Iran to the USSR, where the party ruled and the government obeyed is not amiss. In Iran the Islamic conservatives are the "party" and Khatami can be described as the head of the state "anti-party" group. This sort of opposition never worked in the USSR, but Khatami is an ayatollah, which means he is not entirely outside the party.

A crucial point is that, however uphill the struggle of Iranian reformers and moderates, a political equivalence between Iran and Iraq was absurd. Despite both being neighboring Islamic countries, their linguistic and historical backgrounds are quite distinct. What they did have in common was their opposition to Israel and the fact of having awakened Bush's undiscriminating moral reproof.

As to the SDI, it could have seemed justified against a rival nuclear super-power like the USSR, but against "rogue states", with primitive delivery means and scant nuclear capability, to invoke the old Reaganite "star wars" sounded like a joke, a dark one as it turned out. So the obvious question seems to be: why did Bush choose these particular countries as the objects of his ire? Why not Afghanistan, where it was known that Osama bin Laden was living? Or Libya or Syria, both militantly anti-Israel and both hardcore dictatorships?

Iraq could have been chosen to close the chapter that George H.W. Bush had started and not finished. It could have been the influence of Vice-president Dick Cheney and of secretary of defense Donald Rumsfeld, both advisors to the elder Bush. Rumsfeld in particular might have wanted to undo the mistake he made in giving Saddam Hussein more respect than he deserved and contributing to Iraq's annexation of Kuwait. The choice of Iran might have been to get even for the sequestration of American embassy personnel back in 1979. And North Korea was probably a smoke screen so that it would not seem as if Bush was picking only on Islamic countries. Nuclear capability cannot have been what these states had in common, because that particular technology was beyond the reach of Iraq under the constant aerial surveillance of the USA and the UK and the budgetary constraints imposed by the UN.

Since the early times of Bush's administration coincided with the heating up of the Second Intifada in Israeli-occupied Palestinian lands, the impression that the Israeli tail was again wagging the American dog, and more violently than ever, was irresistible. Even Clinton, whose affinities with the Jewish lobby were well-known, had never been as willingly instrumental as George W. Bush now appeared to be.

(3) Bush the younger dissimulated his angers with an unctuous, easy-going smile

The world had been unipolar since Yeltsin and his ex-Soviet colleagues of Ukraine and Belarus had disbanded the USSR. That had been in George H.W. Bush's time and the USA had responded in a constructive, helpful manner that did credit to the greatest country on earth. This did not mean that America was going to sit back and let crackpot dictators do as they chose. It meant ideally that America was going to exercise its world hegemony through consultation with other states and in as moderate a manner as possible. By way of contrast, the second Bush made his entrance bandying moral epithets and dictating America's terms to the rest of the world. Russia came around to his views or it didn't. The USA couldn't care less. Russia was being treated like a nonentity, a palpable error, as Russia is a historical acrobat.

Part of Bush's message was "terrorists beware!" which at that time could be read as "Palestinians behave!" His father had stood up to the Jewish lobby and told Israel that there were limits to America's support. Bush the younger was pulling out all stops. Whereas the father gave the impression of being fair and unbiased, the son did not hesitate to let his prejudices and his angers hang out, dissimulated by his unctuous, easy-going style. George H.W. Bush had addressed crucial issues but George W. Bush did not seem focused despite the emphatic manner. Had he been, he would have (1) included Afghanistan in the gang of evil-doing nations and (2) tried to mediate between Israelis and Palestinians. Gesturing and posing are no substitutes for statesmanship.

The young Bush had a terrible attitude problem, and America was being made to seem like a cranky and intolerant super-state, not exactly what a unipolar world called for.[1]

There is one important point on which father and son agreed, but only approximately. The third part of young George W. Bush's trifecta are his tax-cutting propensities, which represent a vigorous renewal of the supply-side economics Reagan favored and Bush senior up to a point considered dubious. Bush senior did believe in some tax cuts for the people who made a lot of money in stocks, but he did not accept the doctrine of quick massive income-tax fixes for millionaires. Bush the younger on the other hand did not have, and apparently still does not have, reservations about huge tax cuts for the very rich. On this point he might even be out-Reigning Reagan.[2]

(4) September 11, 2001

During the early months of Bush's administration, America seemed to be on its way, in intention if not in reality, to complete, isolated invulnerability against all enemies real or potential. The anti-ballistics shield was Bush's guarantee to the American people that their way of life would be secure forever. The strong emphasis on this commitment might have arisen in part to compensate for Bush's feeble electoral showing. Since the president had a weak mandate, what better political strategy than to act as if he had a huge mandate? After all, there wouldn't be presidential election for four years and until then Bush was the sole and unchallengeable president of the USA. This was an error, which, with lack of focus, already made two.

Bush, then, was an unfocused president who was acting as if he were a Franklin Delano Roosevelt or a Ronald Reagan. The policies he was proposing for America were in some ways the most radical the country had ever before been offered. Bush appeared willing to break the world nuclear equilibrium for the sake of a theoretically total protection against what were essentially very minor threats. It was as if Reagan had responded to Gorbachev's peace overtures by ordering the USSR to destroy its nuclear arsenal. Bush's attitude in the privileged position he got to by the skin of his teeth was what the Ancient Greeks called hubris.

---

1 This is not meant to imply that Bush senior might not have agreed with Bush junior, but if this was the case then Bush senior must have done a turnabout after he left office. As it was possible that he lost to Clinton because he did not go along 100% with the Jewish lobby and because he did not carry the Gulf War to a hawkish conclusion, it is conceivable that he might have made a personal re-assessment of his statesmanship, but there is no evidence that he has done any such thing.

2 Steven R. Weisman, op.cit.,pp. 364-365.

On 11 September 2001, Islamic terrorists hijacked four airliners: American Airlines flight 11, out of Boston to Los Angeles, with 81 passengers and 11 crew; United Airlines flight 175, also Boston to Los Angeles, with 46 passengers and nine crew; American Airlines flight 77, out of Washington to Los Angeles, with 58 passengers and six crew; and United Airlines flight 93, out of Newark to San Francisco, with 38 passengers and seven crew. The planes out of Boston were flown against the twin towers of New York City's WTC: flight 11 against the north tower and flight 175 against the south tower. The steel structure of some floors melted from the intense heat causing the buildings to collapse. Flight 77 nose-dived against one side of the Pentagon causing 189 deaths. Flight 93, with 45 persons on board, crashed over Somerset County, near Pittsburg. Its hijackers were resisted in their attempt to aim the plane at another target. As of March 2005, the estimated number of victims was 2,996.

This was the greatest shock America had ever experienced and the most spectacular terrorist act in history. The authors of the outrage, led by Mohammed Atta, were young, well-educated Muslim fanatics, who had learned to pilot in simulators in the United States itself and had commandeered the planes through the use of muscle power and carton cutters. For the first time in history the Federal Aviation Administration ordered that the skies over the USA be cleared of all civilian aircraft. They remained shut down for a week while drastic measures were taken to prevent other possible insidious attacks.

(5) Social terrorism can always be subjected to historical examination

American and British intelligence quickly tracked the attack to Osama bin Laden and al Qaeda.[3] What was not clear was why America was being targeted? Why not Israel, the obvious target for Arab terrorism? Israel is a tiny country always under a tight lid. At the height of airplane hijackings, El Al had created a security system so efficacious that no matter how hard they tried Palestinian terrorists could not break through it. However, the same or similar means as had served to destroy the twin towers might have been used to crash a plane, say, in the center of Tel Aviv. Bin Laden and al Qaeda had deliberately chosen the specific 9/11 targets rather than the immediate object of Arab extremist fury.

One simple explanation was that Osama bin Laden hated America with the same fierce intensity as Khomeini. This is what in the USA is

3 "Britain's Bill of Particulars: 'Planned and carried out atrocities'", NYT, October 5, 2001.

often, if not as a rule, assumed without further elaboration. After all, what reason had Osama bin Laden to emit a fatwa declaring Americans fair targets for Muslims all over the world?[4] It had to be hatred pure and simple, just as 9/11 was terrorism without ifs or buts and any attitude towards terrorism beyond condemnation, final and absolute, was unacceptable. The idea that there could be something called state terror meant nothing whatsoever. There was only one sort of terrorism and that was what America had just experienced.

There were clues which if followed could provide not justification but some explanatory grounds for bin Laden's hatred. Many Irish-Americans might not have openly approved of Irish terrorism against British rule in Northern Ireland, even as they understood how it had come about.[5]

(6) T.E. Lawrence might have contributed to Osama bin Laden's fanaticism

Virulent anti-Americanism had not been anything but incidental to any Islamic political agenda until the Iranian theocratic revolution. Before Khomeini transformed Iran into a breeding ground of fanaticism, Islamic fanatical fundamentalism had its ideal home in Saudi Arabia. All other Arab countries outside the Arabian Peninsula, with the exception of

4 Fatwa is a decree emitted by Islamic ulema or scholars. The most famous contemporary fatwa was the result of Khomeini's indignation at Salman Rushdie's novel, *The Satanic verses* (1988), which portrayed a less than perfect Muhammad. It decreed Rushdie's assassination on sight by any Muslim. Apparently, Osama bin Laden himself authored the fatwa against Americans which said in part that "the killing of Americans and their civilian and military allies is a religious duty for each and every Muslim, to be carried out in whichever country they are until Al Aksa mosque has been liberated from their grasp and until their armies have left Muslim lands."

5 Perhaps the most famous case of a Britain-bating, Irish-American was Joseph Kennedy, father of President John F. Kennedy. Joseph Kennedy was so influential with President F.D. Roosevelt that he got himself named ambassador in London, where he served from 1937 to 1940. His reports on Britain's ability to resist Germany were pessimistic and urged American non-intervention, advice which Roosevelt disregarded. His son, President John Kennedy, wrote a university thesis titled *Why England slept*, which wasn't entirely Statistically, the Troubles in Ulster had produced more victims than 9/11. Lynchings and related killings of blacks in America also accounted for more deaths than 9/11. And could any sane person in America deny that the persecution of blacks was a form of terrorism? Stalinism was monstrous in too many ways to count but it imbrued the USSR, a constituted state where social order generally prevailed. And did Stalinism not represent a form of terror different from the terrorism involved in 9/11? However, horrendous its results, terrorism can always be subjected to historical examination.

Sudan, which is only half-Arab, had secularist, nationalist governments. Some of them were also socialistic in the sense of placing static restrictions on economic freedoms. Yemen is exceptional in Arabia in that it was once divided into a socialist, even "Marxist", south and east, and a traditionalist northwest. Although Yemen has remained a republic, its political schizophrenia was finally cured through the eventual preponderance of traditionalism.

The fundamentalist roots of Saudi Arabia lay in Wahhabism, a religious movement that had a political symbiosis with the Saudi clan since the late-18th century. Wahhabism, which is still strong in Saudi Arabia, and had a determinant influence on Osama bin Laden, is purely domestic. It considers itself the guardian of Islam's holiest sites. Wahhabism was not made for export, and since its inception Saudi Arabia has not shown any marked hostility to Western countries. American companies developed Saudi Arabia's oil wealth. The Saudis were willingly won over to friendly relations with the USA, especially as their rivals, the Hashemites, had been under British tutelage. The triumph of the Saudis and of Wahhabism in Saudi Arabia was in part due to the Hashemite friendship with the British, and especially with the British agent T.E. Lawrence, which was hard to reconcile with the Hashemite status as hereditary rulers of Mecca. The integration of Saudi Arabia was accomplished occurred when the Saudis ejected the Hashemites from the latter's Meccan heritage.[6]

---

6 The Islamic fundamentalist Muhammad ibn Abdul al Wahhab (1703-1787) founded a politico-religious movement. In 1726, the Saudi dynasty ruled in Ad Diriyah (west of Riyadh, in the Nejd, or central Arabia). Wahhabism and the Saudis became closely associated. Towards the end of the century, the Saudis were dominant in central, eastern, and southern Arabia. The Ottoman Empire included the Hejaz. The Saudis briefly occupied Mecca but Muhammad Ali of Egypt, nominal vassal of the Ottomans, repossessed the Hejaz and Ad Diriyah was destroyed in 1818. The Saudis, under Turki (1823-1834), captured Riyadh, which became their seat of power, but they accepted the nominal suzerainty of the Ottomans. Faysal or Faisal, son of Turki, expanded the Saudi rule towards Yemen and in the east to Kuwait, where the British contained him. Saudi succession struggles and interventions by the Ottomans, allowed the Rashids of Hail (North West of Riyadh) to become the rivals of the Saudis and to capture Riyadh (1887). In 1902, the young prince Abd al Aziz ibn Abd al Rahman al Saud (also Abd al Aziz ibn Saud) wrested Riyadh from the Rashids in a daring surprise operation. Better known as Ibn Saud, he defeated the Rashids and the Ottomans in 1904. Ibn Saud obtained virtual recognition from the Ottomans. He stayed out of World War I while T.E. Lawrence for the Allies gained the Hashemite Hussein ibn Ali, sharif of Mecca. From 1919 to 1924, Ibn Saud defeated Ibn Ali. The British compensated the Hashemites with dependent thrones in Transjordan and in Iraq.

Khomeini vented enough spleen on the USA to mark it as a plausible target of Muslim fundamentalists. Some political analysts accounted for this rage as a consequence of American backing for the regime of Shah Rehza Pahlavi. But this was not likely more than a contributory influence.

America is frequently not beloved in Latin America, where it has condoned and sometimes encouraged extreme political tyranny. But aside from Marxist fanatics, who frequently have psychological stones to grind, there does not exist a massive hate-America movement in Latin America, certainly nothing on the scale that it seems to be acquiring in the Middle East. Despite its hegemonic or informally imperialistic relation with its southern neighbors, the USA inspires more of a love-hate attitude than unmitigated loathing. Contrary to leftist mythology, the poor of Latin America see in the USA the embodiment of El Dorado. Anti-Americanism is more frequent in the middle classes, which were also the bulwark of anti-communism in Latin America.

Elsewhere, America has backed Korean and Thai dictators, to cite two Asian cases, and it is not universally detested in South Korea or in Thailand. One could go on and on in this vein, the point being that the current Islamic fundamentalist hatred of America goes deeper than any set of specific political circumstances, such as those that obtained in Iran, would warrant.

(7) Whereas Arab anti-Israel attitudes are nearly universal and invariant, Arab anti-American attitudes have shadings and variations

But Islamic fundamentalism is not the only area in which to search for the sources of the sort of radical anti-Americanism that produced 9/11 and that today seems to be prevailing in Muslim countries, not excluding Turkey, one of the closest allies of the USA during the Cold War. Arab anti-Americanism is nothing new, although it is not evenly spread out, so that whereas Arab anti-Israel attitudes are nearly universal and invariant, Arab anti-American attitudes have shadings and variations. Egypt, the largest Arab nation, is, after Israel, the largest recipient of American aid. Jordan might have had its flutters because of its fraught situation as a moderate Arab neighbor of Israel, but its relations with America have generally been cordial, at worst standoffish as during the Gulf War.

Despite instances of reciprocal distrusts, Saudi Arabia is still as firm an ally of the USA as Germany or Japan, even more so because, if in all three countries the American military presence is considered indispensable to their defense, in the case of Saudi Arabia it is there by choice and not by imposition. Osama bin Laden has justified his hatred for the USA because of its military bases in Saudi Arabia. Yet there is no proof of an al Qaida terrorist attack on a specific Saudi Arabian target as opposed to American or foreign targets in Saudi Arabia.

Even though it was America that backed Egypt against the British-French-Israeli coalition in the Suez Crisis, Nasser preferred Soviet military aid to working with and through the USA, a policy that his successor, Anwar el Sadat, reversed. Syria was another important Arab client of the USSR.

In the 1980s, Libya became the worst enemy the USA had in the world. President Reagan had Libya bombed because of a terrorist attack that targeted American military personnel in Germany. One of the bombs intended for Qadaffi killed one of his daughters. Libyan agents were suspected in the terrorist destruction of a PAA flight over Lockerbie, Scotland, which killed in all 270 persons. This has been interpreted as Qadaffi's revenge for his daughter's death. Under heavy international pressure, Libya handed over the suspects to a Scots tribunal sitting in The Hague. One of them was convicted. The anti-terrorist Libyan precedent set by Reagan was surely a crucial inspiration for George W. Bush's war on terror. What is remarkable is not that the American military should have silenced the guns of an enemy, but that the rumble of enemy guns, and the occasional hit, should be such a persistent motif in America's relations with the Arab world today.

One obvious source for Arab anti-Americanism is Israel, probably not in itself since the PLO already has recognized Israel's legitimacy, but in Israel's unyielding attitude towards Palestinian demands. Opposition to Israel on this issue, in one form or another, is practically unanimous among Muslim states. Even Turkey, which in the past has cooperated with Israel, is trying to keep its distance. There might be the odd Muslim-majority state which is less emphatic on this point, but Muslims generally react negatively to Israel. Since the USA is the principal ally of Israel, Muslim antipathies naturally ricochet against America. Thus, it is not hegemonic American foreign policy as such, which is the case in Latin America, but specifically American policy towards Israel, combined with some cultural antagonisms, that constitute the deep and intricate roots of Muslim and Arab anti-Americanism.

(8) If one must choose an incubation period for 9/11, the Arab use of oil as an economic weapon is a likely candidate

As president, Clinton was a likeable figure, full of good intentions if somewhat weak in the flesh. He tried to carry on with Bush's vision of a new more equitable world and no one looked more pleased than he did when Arafat and Rabin shook hands in the White House lawn denoting their commitment to the Oslo accords. But if his presidency was characterized in the domestic front by vacillation and poll watching, it could hardly have been expected to prevent the tragic course that political events in Israel later were following.

Clinton lost the opportunity, especially during the mourning over Rabin's assassination, to let Israel know that the USA would be most displeased if the Oslo Accords were flouted. When Egypt and Syria attacked Israel in 1973, Egypt wanted to recover the Sinai and Syria the Golan Heights. Part of the justification for war was the Palestinian issue. The Egyptian military momentum was not inexhaustible and before its reserves subsided the advance stopped along a line east of Suez. Soviet and American pressures were instrumental in braking the Israeli military counter-offensive. But perhaps equally influential in bringing about a truce and an Israeli withdrawal was that all Arab oil-exporting states—and at the time they controlled a larger proportion of the world's supply of oil than they do today—declared a boycott producing the oil crisis of 1973-1974. Countries like Iran and Venezuela did not participate in the boycott but, together with the multinational oil companies, they profited hugely as oil prices for the first time went not only from single digits to double digits but well over the $20 mark for the barrel.[7]

The oil crisis was a watershed in the sense that, also for the first time, all Arab states, and not just those in the "frontline", showed in a palpable way, and not just with verbal stances, their unanimous hostility to Israel. If one must choose an incubation period for 9/11, the Arab use of oil as an economic weapon is a likely candidate, for it demonstrated openly the intense Arab hatred of Israel and implicitly the unanimous Arab condemnation of American support for Israel. 9/11 was a terrorist act and Arab governments rejected it. But this does not lessen its implication as an Arab blow against what Arabs generally see as the main prop of Israel.

After the 1973 war, Egyptian president Sadat applied a land-for-peace strategy, to do which he had to remove Egypt from the anti-Israel "frontline". By the time Sadat went to Jerusalem and proposed peace, Egypt had renounced its role as the main Arab antagonist of Israel. Syria could have followed Egypt's strategy, but it chose to maintain its tough stance. Syrian territorial losses to Israel were not as

7 Based on the purchasing power of the dollar in the year 2000, oil prices reached historical highs at the start of the Iraq-Iran war (1980), when they reached a value of $70 per barrel. By the same measurement, they had been at over $40 in 1974, but went down to between around $20 and $30 from 1985 to 1996. In 1997, they dipped to $12 and were back up to around $22 in 2000. "Oil and war: seeking stability, at any price", IHT, 26 October 2002.

large as Egypt's, but just as Israeli forces were closer to Damascus than they were to Cairo, so the Golan Heights represented a greater menace to Israel than the Sinai ever could. Still, Syria could not fill Egypt's shoes as the leader of Arab opposition to Israel. Vocally it assumed the Palestinian cause, but it did not possess Egypt's massiveness and in Lebanon it showed that it had strategic concerns that were not coincident with Palestinian goals.

The 1973 War had demonstrated that, whatever the circumstances, the USA would never remain indifferent to Israel's fortunes. The Palestinians' plight after Egypt's defection was worse than it had ever been before, especially as the only limit on Israeli intervention in Lebanon was the number of casualties that Israel was willing to take. There was nothing to prevent Israel from intensifying its policy of dotting Palestinian lands with innumerable Jewish settlements. It was then that Qadaffi decided to take on the USA. International terrorism, which was what Libya supported, becomes vulnerable to counter-terrorist measures when it offers a visible target. Libya was that target and it was soon put out of commission.

(9) Was Saddam Hussein trying to pull a fast one on the USA by going after the ayatollahs?

When the un-upstageable Khomeini died, there was a need for a new figure to lead the anti-American, anti-Israel international opposition. Saddam Hussein was made for the part, but there was the problem that Iraq and the USA had a tacit understanding forged during the Iraq-Iran war. Did Hussein really believe that he could maintain his credit with Americans if he invaded and annexed Kuwait? Or did he proceed to do so even in the knowledge that the USA would be opposed? Hussein cannot or should not have been surprised by the condemnation of his attack on Kuwait. No amount of diplomatic equivocation could have induced the belief that Iraq's move would not receive the international reprobation it got. If it is difficult to fathom the motivations of a democratically elected head of state such as George W. Bush, the mind of a despot like Hussein is opaque to external analysis. But like terrorism, he had to have reasons.

Hussein was unpredictable almost but not quite to the point of incoherence. His war on Iran seemed irrational from afar. There were some historical grounds for it in the past rivalry with Iran for control of Shatt al Arab. But was this sufficient justification for such a costly and eventually fruitless war? Was Hussein trying to pull a fast one on the USA by taking on the America-hating Iranian theocracy?

Given Iran's militant Shiism, Hussein had grounds for believing that his Sunni Arab neighbors were using Iraq as a shield. Also, in attacking Iran he would be isolating his own Shiites from the influence of the ayatollahs. America would certainly not object to seeing the Iranian clerics humbled. But in making war on Iran, Hussein chose the bloodiest and least efficacious means of achieving his ends. To control the Iranian oilfields without conquering the rest of Iran was impossible. To attack Iran in order to repress Iraq's restless Shia population was certainly a circuitous way of going about it. Lastly, to attack Iran in order to enlist America in Iraq's war against Israel was absurd, but then Iraq making war on Iran was in itself also absurd, so one cannot exclude the absurd in dealing with Hussein.

(10) Pan-Arabism, for which the Palestinian cause is paramount, was much closer to Baath than it ever was to Nasser's Egyptian nationalism

It is possible that Hussein might have thought that international opposition to his annexation of Kuwait would not go beyond words and resolutions and, in the very worst of all scenarios, that Iraq would be subjected to embargos such as those decreed against Rhodesia and South Africa. These for him would have been like rain drops on a slicker. Hussein was a dictator but his rule did not make odious distinctions such as those between whites and kaffirs. He had the Kurds to deal with but Kurds were not anything like an organized opposition, nor did they, like blacks in South Africa, have entire neighboring countries as bases for refuge or arms supplies. If Kurds rebelled in Iraq they would not get a helping hand in Iran (under normal circumstances), in Syria, and least of all in Turkey, where they were carrying on guerrilla and terrorist warfare. Before 9/11 made the USA the greatest foe of social or anti-state terrorism in history, Hussein himself could have been considered an inclement persecutor of terrorism, even if only in Iraq. What most bolstered Hussein's expectation about literally getting away with Kuwait was that he counted with considerable international support.

Most Arabs are inured to dictatorships. A distinction between the Iraqi and the Kuwaiti autocracies would have seemed pointless in the Arab world. Unlike non-Arab Islamic countries, where the tendency to democracy is noticeable if erratic (Indonesia, Malaysia, Pakistan), Arab democracies are virtually non-existent. Yemen celebrates elections and some Arabic Gulf states have been making cautious moves towards democracy. This is not to exclude "democratic practices"—as different from electoral democracy—which are gaining ground in formerly autocratic countries, such as Morocco and Jordan. Tunisia and Algeria are still basically one-party states. Egypt has an institutional dictatorship. Syria is outright dictatorial. Saudi Arabia is still an absolute monarchy. Sudan, which is only half-Arabic, celebrates elections under precarious conditions.

Hussein believed not entirely without foundation that by acting aggressively he could become the Arabs' paladin. He wasn't a fundamentalist, but fundamentalism and Arabism are not the same thing. The Iranian Shiites tried to make fundamentalism quintessentially Muslim. But Iranians and Arabs are linguistically and culturally dissimilar. Hussein was Arabic and Iraq has both Sunni and Shia populations, with Shias in the majority but not quite as disproportionately as in Iran. Hussein belonged to the inter-Arabic, non-religious Baath party. It was as a Baathist that he had become dictator. He had the makings of a new Nasser, the first and the greatest of the Post-War charismatic Arab leaders. Pan-Arabism, for which the Palestinian cause is paramount, was much closer to Baath than it ever was to Nasser's Egyptian nationalism. Little wonder then that Hussein could have thought that his Kuwait gambit could succeed.

(11) When Iraq invaded Kuwait, it was doing it in part for Palestinians

In addition, there existed in all this another important political influence: half of Kuwait's population was Palestinian and like Palestinians all over the Middle East the Palestinian community in Kuwait had no political rights. The Palestinian diaspora was not as mobile as the Jewish diaspora. When Jews were ejected from Judaea by Roman emperor Hadrian, they dispersed in the multi-ethnic Roman Empire. After that, Jews moved about in a world in which political frontiers were changeable—except in the core of China, where not many Jews settled—and would remain relatively fluid for centuries and only gradually become powerful barriers to the movements of peoples. The Jewish Pale of settlement was made possible because of the permeability of national frontiers. The much shorter Palestinian diaspora had nowhere to go but to the Arab states surrounding Israel. One of Israel's arguments against Arabs is that they did not assimilate their fellow Palestinian Arabs into their societies, which is as if you despoiled some one of his home and blamed the neighbors for not taking him in. The argument has so many holes it is totally worthless and now seldom invoked.

Not all Palestinians stayed in refugee camps. Those who could emigrate, perhaps as many as remained in the camps, usually did so to the oil-rich countries of the Arabian Peninsula (Saudi Arabia, Kuwait, the United Arab Emirates, Oman,. Qatar, and Bahrain). Many Palestinians had good educational backgrounds. For most, it was the ticket out of the misery of the refugee camps. The nations that accepted them could put them to good use but only under very stringent rules of residence. Thus, for Palestinians in general anything or any one who would break down national frontiers in the Middle East was good. Hussein was about the best thing that had come along for them in a long time. Americans tend to blame Arafat for supporting Hussein and the Iraqi annexation of Kuwait. Most Israelis, it goes without saying, just consider that one more reason to despise him. But under objective historical scrutiny, Arafat had little choice but to do so if he wanted to retain his credibility with Palestinians.

When Iraq invaded Kuwait and later resisted instead of retreating in the face of impossibly superior forces it was partly acting in the name of Palestinians, which might mean that if Iraq had gotten away with its annexation of Kuwait, sooner or llater there would have been another confrontation between Arabs and Israel. Bush's determination to stop Hussein was not only for deterring aggression but also to spare Israel from a military threat such as Egypt constituted in the past. Iraq's assault on Kuwait can be interpreted as another phase in the Arabs' long war against Israel.[8] Seen in this light, it was also the first time that America had physically and massively intervened in defense of Israel, which could mean that Iraq was seen as the greatest threat that Israel had ever faced.

Hussein's stint as pan-Arabic and specifically Palestinian vindicator was as brief as the actual fighting in the Gulf War. His aggression was rolled back by a large coalition led by the USA, integrated mainly by American troops, but sanctioned by the UN and including significant Arab contributions and contingents. Saudi Arabia was an essential base of operations, but even Syria pitched in with a combat unit. So fascinating for Palestinians, Hussein's charisma definitely did not seduce other Arab leaders. It did not endear him to anyone that his bid for power in Kuwait failed so catastrophically. Nasser at least did not surrender Egyptian

8 The concept of "long war" is particularly, though not exclusively, Islamic. Jihad is theoretically interminable. It took nearly a century to break the power of the Crusader States. Timur's long reign was one of incessant warfare. The years of war of the Ottoman Empire were probably as many as the years of peace. The Mughals of India were never at peace. By contrast, the two longest European wars were the Hundred Years War, and this was really two wars with a long uneasy truce, and the Thirty Years War, which is remembered as war at its most savage. However, Spain's reconquista or its long war against Islam lasted from the 8th to the end of the 15th century. It must be added that it was not always a war of Christians against Muslims and Spain's epic hero, Ruy Diaz de Bivar, hired himself to Muslim kings and the name by which he is best known, El Cid, is of Arabic origin. Jihad is an obsolete concept, as out of place in our times as the Taliban regime. But the Israeli-Palestinian issue can justifiably be described as a permanent "state of hostilities", although it would be inaccurate to say that it is strictly so because of Islamic militancy.

sovereignty with the loss of Egyptian territory. Hussein not only had to accept the mutilation of Iraq but he also had to give up some basic prerogatives of statehood, such as arming itself and carrying on trade without external fetters.

Even if after the Gulf War Hussein still retained some prestige among Arabs, at the very least as the man who tried, every one could see that he no longer had the power to threaten, and that is the minimum that is required of an international leader. At that point in time, precisely when the world seemed to be on a roll, the Arab world did not have any outstanding international personality that could speak authoritatively in its name. Besides, even Arabs could wonder whether there was the need for one.

By abstaining from destroying Iraq altogether, Bush showed that he respected Arab sensibilities. His opposition to Israeli encroachment on the occupied territories was another positive sign. That Bush was a Republican, in many respects the prototype of a conservative, and that he was coinciding with the aspirations of Palestinians, whom many if not most Americans consider troublemakers, was another one of those convergences of opposites that characterize some signal moments in contemporary history. Unfortunately, the Bush approach did not prosper.

(12) If terrorism could not cow Israel, what chance did it have against the most powerful state in the world?

Enter now Osama bin Laden, not with the daredevil somersaulting with which Saddam Hussein had made his presence known on the world stage (as at the start of a Red Army Chorus Cossack skit), but in a sidewise, sly, murmurous way, almost, one could think, as if he, like Ronald Reagan before, were a believer in the soft-talk-big-stick American foreign-policy routine. Arab strategy against Israel had started with overt military confrontation, which had veered to terrorism, and then reverted to war. In all phases of this epochal confrontation, the Palestinian cause had been rebuffed and Israel, with unconditional American support, had emerged each time not only the winner but stronger than before.

The first one to perceive this was Arafat, who could be accused of many things but not of lack of political nous. The UN had already recognized the PLO as the legitimate representative of the Palestinian people. As the UN was not about to give the PLO any military sustenance, its gesture of recognition was predicated on the possibility of Israeli-Palestinian talks. Arafat reciprocated by an unconditional recognition of Israel.

To Israelis, as to Americans, this might have been no concession at all in that to persist in trying to ignore Israel would be folly. Egypt neutralized, Libya bombed, and Syria a loud but feeble champion, the last military straw Palestinians grasped was Iraq, and it had been another illusion. The PLO itself was powerless. And the sundry guerrillas operating out of south Lebanon were only pinpricks on Israel's toughened hide. Arafat might have had little choice but to negotiate with Israel. Nevertheless, his decision was not devoid of merit or of value, not least because he had to overcome the opposition of the intransigents within the PLO. The Second Intifada can be traced directly to the total Israeli disesteem of the value of Arafat's recognition.

Al Qaida might have been founded shortly after the conclusion of the Iraq-Iran war. Its deadly activation with bin Laden's financial means followed the defeat of Iraq after its Kuwait adventure. Open warfare against Israel had failed. International terrorism against Israel had not worked. Through its excesses, it recoiled on the perpetrators and gained sympathy and admiration for Israel. State-sponsored terrorism of the Libyan sort was vulnerable to effective countermeasures. With all roads blocked, the PLO had chosen the path of conciliation. Al Qaida thought it had found the effective alternative strategy, which was back to terrorism, not mainly against Israel, but against America.

Now, this would seem to be counterintuitive, for if terrorism could not cow Israel, what chance did it have against the most powerful state in the world? The seemingly impossible contrary is what bin Laden set out to prove. He also believed that his chances improved if he broadened the scope of terrorism. Instead of Palestinians against Israelis, he would make it Muslims against America. But could Muslims be goaded into such a dangerous confrontation? The average Muslim was not a potential recruit. Islamic fundamentalists who still revered the memory of Khomeini would have been ideal recruits but they were Iranian Shiites and they could rub Sunni the wrong way.

There was also an incipient Muslims versus Christians struggle but it fed on the discontents of Muslims in European countries and it was, first, specific to each nation, and, second, one that could be dealt with on a case-by-case basis. Hardly the stuff for an apocalyptic international terrorist campaign! But there were Sunni fundamentalists a-plenty in Arab countries and especially in Saudi Arabia and Pakistan. Al Qaida was, from the start, a Pan-Islamic organization. Bin Laden's second in command within al Qaida is still the Egyptian Ayman Zawahiri.

(13) During the Oslo process, risible Israeli offers were counterpoised by their immediate retraction

When Osama bin Laden and al Qaida were attacking opportunistic American targets, the Palestinians were looking for a negotiated solution.

The year that Netanyahu was elected prime minister of Israel can be said to mark the preliminary breakdown of realistic negotiations between Palestinians and Israelis. In effect, Israel voted against the Oslo Accords. It was the closest to a plebiscite on whether Israelis wanted peace or even to make some concessions to Palestinians.

Arafat or the PLO had not given grounds for an Israeli rejection of their aspirations to a Palestinian state. The mainstream PLO was not then engaged in terrorism. Its willingness to negotiate was as pronounced as the Israeli rejection of negotiations. Basically, when Palestinians thought that they were within sight of a political arrangement that they could live which did not imply doubts on the legitimacy of Israel, Israelis jerked away from Oslo, from committing themselves to a Palestinian state and even from negotiations that could result in anything resembling one.

That Palestinians had transformed themselves politically was not of course gratuitous but the result of Israel's dogged resistance to Palestinian and pro-Palestinian pressures. But there was in this no reason to doubt the sincerity of the Palestinian offer. It would be difficult to imagine a situation more conducive to open dealing than one in which survival is at stake, and the survival of Arafat, of the PLO, and of the possibility of a Palestinian state were then indeed at stake. After decades during which it was claimed by Israelis and Americans that Israel represented negotiation and the Palestinians conflict, it was now going the other way: Palestinians wanted negotiations and Israelis were adamantly and, what was even more discouraging, democratically, opposed to negotiations.

Not all Palestinians were disposed to negotiate with Israel and there exists the Israeli argument that Arafat and the PLO were giving surreptitious, and not so surreptitious, support to Palestinian terrorism. The most damning piece of evidence, if some Israeli figures are accurate, is that Palestinian terror attacks against Israelis increased significantly between the signing of the Oslo accords in September 1993 and 1999. In 1994, 1995, and 1996, 73, 52, and 87 attacks, respectively, are reported, which compares with an average of seventeen yearly attacks from 1967 to 1992. The West Bank was annexed by Israel in 1967 and the policy of Israeli settlements began to be applied systematically during the 1970s. The First Intifada is conventionally bracketed between 1987 and 1993. Most of the attacks reported in 1993 occurred before the Oslo interim agreement. The escalation of Palestinian attacks began not in 1993 but in 1988. It cannot be said that Oslo marked the onset of intense hostilities, but at most that it did not put an end to Palestinian terrorism. The rise in attacks after the Oslo accords—in point fact really noticeable after the assassination of Rabin—is part of a pattern of growing Palestinian hostility to Israel and, if the increase in the number of attacks is to be related to the existence of the PA, then a significant drop in attacks in 1997 should in principle also be attributed to the PA.[9]

Palestinians, or at least the Palestinians that Arafat represented, were willing to negotiate because they had no alternative. This says nothing particularly good of Arafat's sincerity, but one thing is what you intend or wish and another is what you can achieve, and in life the latter is usually what you have to accept. But whatever Arafat really wanted, whether he was an unrepentant terrorist still aiming at wiping out Israel, a common Israeli view, or whether he was really intent on negotiating a peace, what he was getting was what Israel decided to give and Israeli offers during the Oslo process were risibly small and every one was counterpoised by their almost immediate retrieval. Before shutting down the Oslo process, Netanyahu offered 9% of the West Bank. The PA asked for 13%. Israel's rejection of this modest demand angered Palestinians. This is when Arafat started talking of unilateral independence. Israel then offered to redeploy its troops in the West Bank and hand over 195 square miles of territory, an offer that was cancelled virtually the following day.

Even Barak, the last Palestinian hope for a negotiated peace (as opposed to the precarious peace that Sharon's has imposed by force), only offered the PA 7% of the West Bank. He also consented to the free flow of traffic between Gaza and the West Bank along controlled roads. But he also authorized more settlements than Netanyahu had and when the PA asked for another 5% of the West Bank it was turned down flat. By then the Oslo process in a strict sense, which should have culminated with Palestinian statehood in 1999, had run out and what Israel finally offered the PA were two thirds of the West Bank in which instead of Israeli pockets there were Palestinian areas almost entirely surrounded by Israeli settlements.[10] Negotiations had broken down. As the Israelis were bartering something that they really possessed (land) for something that Arafat could not guarantee (the end of terrorism), it would appear as if the negotiators were the Palestinians and the Israelis, with their impossible demands on Arafat and the PA, the opponents of negotiations.

(14) Bibi was a loudmouth but Sharon was Sharon

In November 2000, al Qaida organized the attack on the American warship Cole in the harbor of Aden. The Second Intifada began around

9 See www.eretzyisroel.org/~jkatz/oslo.html
10 See www.palestinehistory.com

the same time. Early in 2001 Israel was going to vote again and the issue, aside from political subtleties, was again war or peace. The Second Intifada was of course a sort of war, but what sort of war could it be that pits mobs against an army?

Sharon crushed Barak in the Israeli elections. There exists the plausible view that Barak had some blame for the failure of the Camp David negotiations.[11] Barak had not modified his antagonistic attitude to Arafat and the PLO. Netanyahu was a loudmouth intransigent with the earnest manner of an American college debater. On American television Larry King called him "Bibi" and treated him as if he could have been your friendly next-door neighbor. But Sharon was another proposition altogether. This man was tough in a way that Bibi could never be. He was a veteran of the Israeli war of independence. He had been responsible for reprisal attacks on Arabs. He was as good a politician as he was a brave soldier. Sharon was the greatest promoter of the invasive Israeli policy of settlements in lands that sensibly should have been left to the Palestinians.

Considered by many the greatest modern Israeli soldier, one of the most successful strategists and tacticians of our times, Moshe Dayan had been willing to let Palestinians alone. He also once admitted that there was not an inch of Israel that had not been Arab at one time.[12] This statement is ambiguous enough to make Dayan's thinking on the Palestinian issue murky. But he, like Sharon later, had been minister of agriculture and it did not occur to him take land from the Palestinians and give it to Jews, which all it did was make worse an already bad relationship. Sharon had been the author of Israel's strategy to strike at the PLO in their Lebanese bases. He had looked the other way when Christian gunmen killed Palestinians in the refugee camps. Sharon's election was like opening the gates of Janus.

(15) The Jewish soldiers at Masada were essentially suicidal fighters

Palestinian police were involved in the fighting during the Second Intifada. But a police that existed at the sufferance of Israel, which essentially expected it to function as an anti-terrorist arm of Israeli police, was as powerless as ululating Palestinian crowds. Suicide bombers were almost an inevitable tactical choice for Palestinian terrorists.

---

11 Alan Sipress, "Behind Mideast talks Clinton fury at Barak", IHT, July 19, 2001; Deborah Sontag, "Quest for Mideast peace: how and why it failed", NYT, July 26, 2001, has a more balanced view of the Arafat-Barak talks, but she blames Sharon and his visit to Temple Mount for causing the end of the talks.

12 Geoffrey Wheatcroft, op.cit., p.345

The origins of this sort of terrorism have been debated. As in the more conventional forms of terrorism, in which the perpetrators do not intend to immolate themselves, suicide tactics can historically be attributed equally to states or to rebels or outlaws. The most famous 20th century wave of suicide attacks was the Japanese Kamikaze during the final year of the Pacific Ocean war. These were not social terrorists but soldiers trained to fly under religious oath to kill themselves by wreaking as much destruction as they could on the enemy. The Kamikaze could not prevent the momentum of the American advance, but they inflicted heavy losses on ships and men.

There were suicide fighters long before the Japanese formed their self-immolating squadrons. Leonidas at the Thermopylae resisted the Persians to death. The Spartan hoplites, which numbered only 400, could not have contained the huge Persian host. They in effect committed suicide to delay the invasion of the Greek heartland. Leonidas is the heroic western prototype of the suicide fighter.

Jews had their own suicide fighters: the Zealots at Masada who killed themselves rather than be crucified by the Romans. In Muslim lands, resistance to conquerors almost certainly had fatal consequences. Mongol persistence and destructiveness were legendary. The defenders of cities against Mongols were sure to be slaughtered. If they survived in the ruins, Mongol detachments were left behind lurking to finish them off.

There existed suicidal war rituals in India and in Indonesia. In Rajasthan when a Rajput fortress was doomed its defenders often opted for gaujar, in which fighting men went out for a final stand as their women immolated themselves and their children. In Bali, when Dutch cannon and rifles were besieging the nobility of Denpasar, they chose to mount a puputan or charge with swords and krises: death rather than surrender. The cases of certain death in modern European wars are legion.

In our times, the Tamil Tigers of Sri Lanka made their suicide attacks notorious. Women volunteers were especially fearsome. It was a Tamil woman who blew Rajiv Gandhi up. But the Tamils, however great their devotion to suicide tactics, cannot claim primacy over Arabs. The great terrorist attacks in Beirut that resulted in the deaths of hundreds of marines and dozens of French soldiers was the work of suicide bombers and it anteceded the Tamil use of human self-detonating bombs. Terrorism and suicide bombers in particular, have been described as the weapons of last resort of the downtrodden everywhere. Israelis and Americans may dislike the idea that suicidal terrorism can be a weapon of self-defense or of self-assertion but the evidence that such is the case is too voluminous to ignore.

Once in power in Israel, Sharon let loose the Israeli armed forces on the Palestinian police and on all manifestations of open Palestinian defiance. Among other things, Israeli army tractors tore up the runway that had been such a seductive symbol of statehood when the PA was constituted. Suicide bombings against Israel were either being planned or being carried out at the same time that Muslim fanatics were receiving flight-simulator pilot training. When the WTC towers were downed no one mentioned the Palestinian issue or the Second Intifada or Israeli repression. But no one with even an elementary sense of history could avoid making the deduction that Osama bin Laden and al Qaida had finally succeeded in making America hurt because the open sore of Israeli-Palestinian relations was suppurating more than ever before.[13] The connection is still not usually made but events subsequent to the Second Iraqi war have served to reinforce it.

(16) Pakistan is the only modern state created solely for religious reasons

Once it became evident that Osama bin Laden was behind 9/11, partly because he bragged about it, America demanded Afghanistan to turn him over. The Taliban refused. 9/11 was such a shock not only for America but also for the world that the USA did not have to exert itself to form a coalition and to obtain support from some key states. Russia has in Chechnya a terrorist problem of its own, quite as bad as anything that Al Qaida can do to America. American media still currently insist that the Chechen problem is different from the Al Qaeda threat to the USA because it is the doing of Russia itself. Such distinctions are lost on Russians, who obviously consider that America is not for nothing in its strained relations with Arabs.

As a rule, America does not recognize that Israel uses terror as a weapon of reprisal. That is not how much of the world, and not just Arabs or Muslims see it. It is not the USA that is persecuting Palestinians, but America would find it hard to deny that its support for Israel is, if

13 Various quotations attributed to Osama bin Laden in "Britain's Bill of Particulars" make it obvious that al Qaida's terrorism is directed at much at Israel as at America: "The people of Islam have suffered from aggression, iniquity and injustice imposed by the Zionist-Crusader alliance and their collaborators...My Muslim brothers, your brothers in Palestinian and in the land of the two Holy Places [i.e. Saudi Arabia] are calling upon your help and asking you to take part in fighting against the enemy—the Americans and the Israelis."

not unlimited, of such magnitude and of such a degree of commitment as to be inaccessible to arguments even of practical political convenience.

This policy is not solely the making of the executive branch of government. Contrary to what usually obtains on controversial issues in most countries, the American Congress is not a moderating but an extremist influence on American policy towards Israel. Israel chose Jerusalem as its capital and insists that foreign embassies should be based in Jerusalem. But Jerusalem was a divided city until 1967 and it is still disputed by Jews and Arabs. It is Congress, particularly the House of Representatives, that has been insisting for years that the USA move its embassy from its Tel Aviv site to Jerusalem, and it is the executive branch that has resisted doing so.

It was Pakistan that had made the fundamentalist Taliban regime possible in the first place, so in an oblique way it had some responsibility for 9/11. Pakistan itself was a religious creation, a theocracy in principle if not in practice. All modern Islamic countries were created out of territories with Muslim populations or in which Muslims were politically dominant. Their territorial demarcations were not dependent on religious considerations. Pakistan is the only modern state actually created for religious and only religious reasons. Israel too was created with Judaism in mind, but most Jews are not that observant and they affiliate to Judaism in ways that are not necessarily religious. Also, there were political reasons for the formation of Israel that were not religious in character. Hitler persecuted Jews not for their religion but because of their "race". Without the Muslim population of the Indian subcontinent, where Hindus are a large majority, Pakistan would have had no raison d'être.

Pakistan's foreign policy was based to some extent on terrorism. It was Pakistan that served as a conduit for arms for Afghan resistance to Russian occupation and in that conflict terrorism was a feature common to both sides. Whether it had history on its side, as it claimed, or whether it simply was too vulnerable to the influence of Muslim extremists, Pakistan sponsored terrorism in Kashmir, at the very least in that it tolerated Kashmiri terrorists, and in the extreme case, in that its soldiers trained, armed, and infiltrated terrorists into Kashmir. So when America launched its war on terror, it had to ask a country that had little compunction about terrorism to join it.

Normally, Pakistan would have demurred, but the images of 9/11 had had their impact. Never the possessor of a flourishing economy, Pakistan had reason to fear diplomatic isolation. With the end of the Cold War, its only ally of consideration was China, and China too was thinking of joining the war on terror, in words if not physically, because of problems with its discontented Uigur minority. Therefore, when the USA offered Pakistan economic incentives, its president, the pragmatic Gen. Pervez Musharraf, decided that Pakistan too had to take part in the anti-terrorist movement.

(17) A most peculiar war that turned out to be a bargain

In view of the alliance that the USA had spatchcocked, the War on Afghanistan had the makings of a very peculiar war. Here was a powerful state making war in the name of anti-terrorism, but not properly speaking against another state but against a man and an organization that were being protected by a state. States are the usual historical instruments of terror and there was no instance of a state going to war against terror per se as against going to war to destroy another state's terrorism.

The Austrians declared war on Serbia because the Serbs would not allow Austrians to flush out anti-Austrian terrorists in Serbian territory. But Austria couldn't have cared less if Serbia terrorized Ottomans or Bulgarians as much as it wanted. And to make its war on terror, the USA sought or insisted on the support of a state, like Russia, which, from an American perspective, had acted in an openly terrorizing manner against Chechens, and in the case of Pakistan actually had a foreign policy that on the ground promoted terrorism and had done so in the case of Afghanistan with American backing.

These circumstances did not make the war on Afghanistan less justified than it was but as a "war on terror" it sounded somewhat misnamed. Ultimately, what made the contrived alliance possible was that, with or without it, America was going to attack Afghanistan, and for some it was advantageous to join it and for others it was very difficult to abstain from doing so. At that stage, whatever name was given to what America was waging, War on Afghanistan or "war on terror", it had unrestricted international support. But it wasn't clear to what extent America wanted to make war on terror a worldwide war.

The War on Afghanistan was a brilliant example of "flexible response": invading by land and air, bombing all strategic points in the country, financing native fighting forces. Resistance to the Taliban had been kept alive in Afghanistan by the so-called Northern Alliance, in the region next to Uzbekistan. Arab suicide bombers posing as journalists assassinated its leader, Ahmed Shah Massoud. Mohammed Fahin succeeded him. After the War on Afghanistan got on its way, CIA agents showed up with literally bundles of cash to re-supply the guerrillas and to buy the adhesion of scattered fighting groups that were not active against the Taliban. CIA operatives and their local allies prepared the way for the landings of troops and acted as spotters for targets of American bombing raids. The Taliban-occupied city of Mazar-i-Sharif, in the middle of Northern Alliance territory, was captured.

In all the CIA spent $70 million dollars to invigorate the Afghan resistance. When given this figure, Bush is supposed to have said: "That's one bargain".[14] The initial American invasion force consisted of 110 CIA men and 316 Special Forces. Very quickly, the Taliban regime caved in. It was after all the feckless fundamentalist front that it had seemed when it first came on the scene. Without its Pakistani base, the only resistance American forces encountered came from fanatical foreign fighters.

American forces, which made strategic drops (in Kandahar particularly), later concentrated on flushing out fight-to-the-death Taliban and al Qaida resistance in northeastern Afghanistan and along the frontier with Pakistan. The areas where Al Qaeda presumably was holing out were blasted and scrutinized foot by foot. According to official American reports, hundreds of terrorists were arrested. Suspected al Qaida members, some 680 of them, were captured and detained in Guantánamo Bay, America's military base in eastern Cuba, so that they could be held without appeals inside the American legal system. But no trace of Osama bin Laden was found.

Whether the arch-terrorist that America wanted to get its hands on had survived or died (perhaps inside a carpet-bombed cave) was impossible to say for sure. It was not likely that, like Hitler, he might have committed suicide, although al Qaida, being an international organization that requires of its agents a renunciation of the will to live for the glories of paradise, it is not unthinkable that bin Laden might have considered that avoiding capture by Americans, even through suicide, could have the same impact as that of a Palestine suicide bomber. In fact, bin Laden was very much alive as subsequent tapes showed conclusively.

Despite the harvest of terrorist suspects taken in Afghanistan, plus the others that have been captured outside Afghanistan, the War on Afghanistan itself as a "war on terror" cannot have been entirely satisfactory for Americans. Ironically, it might have been more fulfilling if Afghanistan had put up a stronger resistance. The harder you struggle for something the more valuable its possession. Afghanistan was a very soft target and part of getting even is making the other side kneel

---

14 "CIA's deep pockets helped overcome the Taliban", based on Bob Woodward's *Bush at war*, IHT, November 19, 2002

gradually and humiliatingly by the application of excruciating force. Afghanistan barely resisted. Except for snipers here and there, the Taliban regime collapsed before the USA really had a chance to repay it for its hospitable attitude towards USA-hating terrorists. A war on terror, whatever finally that was, could not have been won in such undemanding circumstances. And after nearly two years, despite tough detainment conditions and practices tantamount to torture, the USA has not yet produced a single indictment against its crop of presumed terrorists, which means that the War on Afghanistan in the end had only netted small fry. For president Bush there was no "closure" for 9/11 in the War on Afghanistan. There were other good reasons for why there was no closure.

(18) As long as there is the fear of death, there will be those who will want to exploit it

Closure is nonsense. There is never closure. There is only forgetting or remembering without undue pain. Time is the only possible means of closure. But for many Americans impatient with abstractions, time is too abstract by half. Where is time? Can you touch time? And isn't "time" somewhat like taking the fifth? Another reason, the strongest of all, for why war on terror could not bring closure as a result of the victory in Afghanistan was that you cannot win a war on terror. You cannot even wage war on terror. Terror ultimately is the fear of death. And as long as there is the fear of death there will be those who will want to exploit it. Nevertheless, since the media blared daily "war on terror", it took on the appearance of the real McCoy and criticism was either complicity with terrorism or bunk.

You can turn "war on terror" into War on Afghanistan. After the horror of 9/11, that war was more than justified. The Taliban regime might have brought some stability to Afghanistan. But it wasn't much good for anything else. Its refusal to surrender Osama bin Laden was a crucial mistake. On the basis of pure religious fantasy, it defied the greatest power on earth. Also, it took the side of social terrorism. Like Libya, Afghanistan became a fair target. And beyond the country, there was the man the Americans wanted. So it wasn't a case, as in Libya, of dropping some bombs and killing some people. The USA wanted the self-confessed perpetrator of 9/11. What's more it wasn't just the USA as a country: it was president Bush as a person, as the president of the USA, whose plan to isolate America from attacks by "rogue states" had been made a travesty, who had a stake in the War on Afghanistan.

Despite Bush having been hoist by his own petard, the world understood that America had a rightful grievance and support for the War on Afghanistan was practically universal. Who needed a regime that, because of disputable interpretations of religious texts, bragged of destroying cultural treasures? As far as the world was concerned, the Taliban were discrediting the majestic Muslim cry of "Allah akhbar".

9/11 unleashed an unlikely war. The Israeli-Palestinian conflict was quite concrete. It consisted in Israel dictating terms on Palestinians and imposing Israeli settlements in their lands. The Iraq-Iran war and the Gulf war were also concrete, well-defined events, as had been Vietnam and Afghanistan. There were no doubts in any of these conflicts of who was fighting whom and where, although admittedly in Vietnam the enemies of the Americans were often indistinguishable from ordinary civilians. But what Bush declared after 9/11 was called "war on terror" and the media accepted the expression as if it referred to something real, which it didn't.

American desire for revenge after 9/11 is understandable. But there are limits. One limit is that you cannot turn revenge into "war on terror". Another limit is that wars as such have limits and war on terror is open-ended. War is war and there are enemies in a war. If you declare war on terror, you are simply picking enemies of your choosing. You can make any war a "war on terror".

But where exactly was "terror"? How was a "war on terror" fought? Could it ever be won? What would signal victory? And the great unthinkable, could it actually be lost? Well, "war on terror" was in practical terms what Bush and his people identified as "terror". "Terror" was terrorism, which, as we have argued, in certain circumstances is understandable, even justified. Afghanistan was terror/terrorism; because it hosted Osama bin Laden and al Qaida. Bin Laden had been inciting Muslims to kill Americans and al Qaida was the perpetrator of 9/11. Al Qaida was an international system for recruiting willing agents of terrorism and channeling flows of funds for terrorist acts. But terror was much more than Afghanistan.

(19) A Taliban-free Afghanistan was a plus but not that much of a heart-warmer

There were other causes for American discontent. Some were less important than others. The world situation after the American victory was not that cheery. And especially the feeling was still there that 9/11 had not been avenged. There were grandiose plans to replace the WTC towers but it was hard to come up with satisfactory substitutes. Some of the projects looked as if inspired by the toon-world, high-rise whims of Shanghai. Economic imperatives required that the lost office space be replaced, but New York would never be the same without the lost towers, the monumental landmark that, after its construction, no movie ever filmed in the city could fail to include.

A Taliban-free Afghanistan was a plus, but not that much of a heart-warmer. Besides, post-Taliban Afghanistan was not that impressive an achievement. In Kabul, a central government headed by President Hamid Karzai was installed, but its brief was limited by over-all warlord prevalence in Herat, Jalalabad, Mazar-i-Sharif (ethnic Uzbek territory), Kandahar, and Kunduz. After various terrorist attacks, Karzai sought the protection of bodyguards from the substantial American military presence in the country, a task that was later assigned to I-don't-care-who-you-are security companies.

The evidence that even in post-war Afghanistan terrorism had not been eradicated was available to Bush and to American hawks on terror. It did not induce doubts about the feasibility of war on terror but seemed to harden their resolve, as if Don Quixote after being mauled by a windmill had mounted Rocinante and attacked another one. For sure, American forces had not been mauled in any way but the windmills were there, their sails turning and turning.

7

The Fleas in America's Ears

The USA had not fought the War on Afghanistan primarily to make that country democratic however much Americans—or the half of Americans who bother to exercise their democratic right to vote—cherished democracy. What's more, on balance, the real winner from the War on Afghanistan might just have been Russia, which used it to put some muscle in the CIS. Other winners were a pair of "stans", Tajikistan and Uzbekistan, and the "stans"—from the Persian word for country—are more often a source of hilarity than of concern or interest for most Americans. The fall of the Taliban and the reining in of aggressive Islamic fundamentalism benefited Tajikistan, where Russia acted as a shield. The stabilization of Tajikistan should have a reverse domino effect: instead of other Central Asian countries falling to waves of fanatics, they swivel and drive the fanatics back. Uzbekistan should feel safer now that it is not in the path of Islamic guerrillas. But what the USA wanted above all was to get its hands on Osama bin Laden, to give him a fair trial, and to put him on a lethal-injection gurney. Unfortunately, there was no bin Laden. Afghanistan, in short, was a most disappointing victory, although, as things have turned out, if its primary purpose was not attained the secondary one, the establishment of democracy there, now seems at the very least plausible.

There was also the worrisome precedent that America had waged a war of what can only be described as vengeance with more than a touch of personal grudge on the part of President Bush. The very existence of Osama bin Laden was an affront to the American president whose rash promise of making Americans invulnerable to foreign attack had not made him a laughingstock only because of the tragic gravity of 9/11 and because you don't laugh publicly at a super-state with impunity.

That Bush had made such a fool of himself was fuzzed by the tragedy that befell upon his foolishness.

There was another flea in America's ear. Even before the war on terror, there existed signs of world malaise. The signs were economic and political. Globalization had been a tremendous American victory. It was part and parcel of the good times that seemed to be dawning on mankind after 1989. But globalization had started taking a drubbing.

(1) Globalization takes a pratfall in Argentina

Globalization was founded on the belief that worldwide capitalist prosperity was feasible. One of the doctrinal achievements of the 1990s was that globalization, which in the normal course of things in many places would have been called capitalist imperialism, was generally accepted as a form of arbitrage for the rational channeling of world financial flows. In theory, there was no conflict between national aspirations and the interests of international capital. Competitiveness was the key to economic growth and the best way to make it happen was through free trade.

Argentina was one of the success stories of globalization. It was an economic winner with politically rosy cheeks. Before Castro, Perón was the symbol of the Latin American refusal to accept American hegemony. Like Castro after him, Perón embodied a rejection of the spirit of the Monroe Doctrine, the presumptuous American imperial proclamation implying that the Western Hemisphere was out of bounds for European powers because it was inside the political sphere of the USA. For a long time, and for many reasons, some obscure gut anti-Americanism being undoubtedly one of them, Argentines by a large majority were simply Peronists. But even Argentines realized that Peronism as a political philosophy left much to be desired, the main deficiency being that Perón himself was not easy to classify. Arguments could be elaborated placing him anywhere from fascism to leftist nationalism to syndicalism (the idea that workers' unions were the instruments for social justice). A communist he wasn't and he couldn't be said to be a laissez faire capitalist either. Therefore, Peronists came up with the name "justicialismo", which doesn't mean a thing but which derives from "justice", so Peronists could go on being Peronists under a vague but high-sounding label.

The Justicialists, then, came to power in Argentina with Carlos Menem, an Arab-descended Peronist who had been a competent provincial governor. Once in power, Menem forgot whatever it was that Peronism had been about and went all out for liberal capitalism and globalization. He got himself an economist who subscribed to the theory that the way to stop inflation in Argentina forever was to tie the peso to the dollar. This was about as globalized as you could become. How more integrated to the capitalist world economy could a country get than by adopting the American currency while still issuing its own currency? The plan worked wonders. Menem radiated self-confidence and elegance. The only discordant note was his pesky Peronist wife who insisted on calling him a womanizer and a traitor to Perón. As Perón had been a notorious womanizer, Menem's wife, also Arab-descended, was in an equivocal position.

Argentina would soon be on shaky grounds. Menem was elected president in 1989. He served two terms during which inflation was controlled, the doing of economics minister Domingo Cavallo. Argentina was living a period of great prosperity. The opposition candidate Fernando de la Rua won in 1999 and formed a cabinet laden with economists. He tried to solve the growing financial crisis by cutting back on pensions, among other measures, and street protests forced him to resign in 2001. In 2002, the economy foundered (lay offs shot up and government spending dried up) producing social dislocations and extreme political instability. The trouble with the peso-dollar peg was that it let Argentines, who are bon vivants by vocation, spend their money on goods they should have been exporting, and it also made capital flight so easy that any imbalance could set off a stampede, like the snap of a twig and insomniac cattle on the Chisholm trail.

Argentina's economic collapse was relative—by 2004 the Argentine economy was buoyant again—but it sent shivers all over the world. Maybe globalization was not what it had been made out to be. Mexico, for example, where globalization was good news and foreign investors poured money into assembly plants of all sorts, began to see that as productivity and wages increased the same investors left because they could maximize profits in China. This was closer to the Marxist notion of productivity, which was about worker exploitation, than to capitalist productivity, under which salary gains for workers are usually permanent.

Another problem with globalization was that Mexican farmers were unable to compete with highly subsidized, industry-like American "mega farms".[1] Even Brazilians, who had some of these, couldn't do it. The Soviets had tried mega farms in the form of kolkhozes and sovhozes and failed, principally because they eliminated the profit motive. Even more crippling was that mega farms are mechanized and Soviet mega

1 Thomas Black, "Mexico falls victim to its success as jobs move to low-wage China", IHT, October 31, 2002; Tina Rosenberg, "Why Mexico's small corn farmers go hungry", NYT, 3 March 2003

farms were conceived as labor-intensive little rural cities. So much for agricultural productivity under central planning. The big flaw with globalization was that capitalist productivity worked where capital was home grown and if it wasn't it was global and not likely to strike roots in any specific country.

(2) "Growth is good"?

Globalization was having problems not only for reasons intrinsic to globalization itself but to problems that important nations were experiencing. Germany was really the place where the world had begun its brief roll. The fall of the Berlin wall was arguably the true symbol of the new world order that George H.W. Bush later proclaimed. However, ten years after the two Germanys had been politically united, the disparities between them persisted, not as great as between capitalist Federal Germany and communist "Democratic Germany", but quite impossible to dissimulate either. The process of unification had cost a fortune. It is possibly the reason why Germany today is recession-prone and has chronic double-digit unemployment, unthinkable in the thick of the "German miracle". But worse, the results of that huge expense have not resulted in a fully integrated German economy. This is palpable in the way national production is shared.

On a state-by-state average basis, eastern Germany has only the equivalent of 58% of the GDP of western Germany. The richest German Lander (states), Hamburg and Hessen, are both in western Germany while the five less affluent are in eastern German Lander. West Berlin, which during the separate existence of the two Germanys was probably the richest part of western Germany, is today, because of East Berlin, below the median for all German Lander. All the unemployment rates for East German Lander are above 17%. The lowest at 17.3% is in Brandenburg, perhaps as an overspill effect from Berlin, and that is more than the highest figure for a West German Land (Bremen with 16.8% unemployment rate). But Bremen's per capita GDP is 19% higher than Brandenburg's. Even within the same country, where capital flows have no nationalist constraints, the financial essence of "globalization" did not seem to be a quick equalizer, if it equalizes at all.[2]

In its 27 May 2000 issue *The Economist* published, "Growth is good", an article based on the work of two World Bank economists. The question was: does globalization make the poor poorer? And the answer given was that, according to the statistics, globalization favored the poor as much as it did the rich. Since it assumed that globalization

2 "Survey of Germany", *The Economist*, 6 February 1999

was good for national growth, the implication was that the poor were getting less poor wherever globalization reached. The argument certainly was inapplicable to Argentina, at least for a time. And in practical terms it demonstrated very little on the economic inequality between nations. As the criteria for globalization are not uniform, all the authors had to do to prove their point was to use available statistics on per capita income growth in developing countries and attribute them to globalization.

(3) "Third world" was just an euphemism for backwardness

The goodness of globalization had its best representatives in Asia and crisis struck Asia in the late 1990s, after which economies slowed down or declined to near stagnation. The Philippines was saddled with an irresistible urge to pro-create—75% of its population is less than 16 years old, hence economically unproductive—but Japan, which with Germany was the other "miraculous" Post-War state, had the same problem in reverse: whereas in the Philippines the productive part of the population is burdened with the expense of child-rearing, in Japan the workforce has to sustain an aging population that did not contribute enough to its own retirement fund when it was active. With falling demand, Japan's economy was in recession and the banking system was rotten with non-performing loans.

In the first quarter of 2003, the South Korean stock market had the worst performance in Asia. Even tiny, but hyper-prosperous Singapore, was hurting from the economic ills that affected the formerly booming economies of South East Asia. During 2004, most of these economic trends were reversed, but it was generally agreed that it was not due to globalization but to "regionalization" in the form of the Chinese economic locomotive pulling forward the neighboring economies.

Despite early promises of world prosperity, globalization was far from fulfilling expectations. "Third world" had always been an euphemism for "poor world". It was the deceptive name many poor countries chose for themselves. Another euphemism, the most respectable and widely used one, was "developing countries", now superseded by "nations in transition".

The origins of "third world" are obscure. They can be traced to before World War II, always meaning a sensible third position between two squabbling extremes. In the Post-War, poor countries wanted quick growth. Many believed that their poverty was due to "capitalist exploitation". Also, they did not want to line up behind their former colonialist masters, but they did not want to become Soviet satellites either, so they chose non-alignment and this was made to order for a middle economic category, neither capitalist nor communist, which was "third world". In practical terms, third world had the worst of both worlds. It was more capitalist than communist in its inequalities and it was more communist than capitalist in its dictatorial or bureaucratic flouting of individual liberties and in its propensity to waste money on unneeded, boondoglish economic projects.

During the 1970s and 1980s, mainly by being un-third-worldly, some economies in Asia began to grow at rates that justified hopes of overcoming underdevelopment, which was the not-so-diplomatic word for which "developing countries" substituted. The most successful were the economies of South Korea and Taiwan. These two, with the city-states of Hong Kong and Singapore, were called the "four Asian tigers". The other fast developing states were Indonesia, Malaysia, and Thailand, all in the tropics. It was these Tiger cubs that were hardest hit by economic crisis. Brazil is an economic giant also mostly equatorial and tropical. But Brazil has the problem of racialism, which, unlike the USA, it does not admit, and so it has done nothing special, like educational or bureaucratic quotas, to incorporate blacks into its social and economic mainstreams.

By the end of the millennium, despite the consensus that globalization was, as president Bill Clinton put it, "the best engine we know of to lift living standards", the third world was still there. Developing countries just went on developing, like the joke that Brazilians tell of themselves about Brazil being the country of the future and, by Golly!, we will always be the country of the future. There was a growing consensus that globalization standards were not untouchable. Malaysia had weathered the Asian crisis by imposing currency controls, the biggest no-no among orthodox globalizers, and when Argentina emerged from its seemingly catastrophic depression it was realized that it had done it by telling creditors to get in line (another no-no) and by working harder on its export economy. The example of Argentina is now currently cited as a symbol of the vulnerabilities of globalization and its main paladin, the International Monetary Fund (IMF).

(4) Most economists are wrong most of the time but when most economists agree they must be on to something right

Ironically, globalization was getting its worst drubbing in America, the country where the ideology behind it originated and where it should have felt most at home. On March 10, 2000, NASDAQ peaked at 5048.62 after doubling from previous August 1999. Eleven days later (March 21) the American economy was declared to be in recession. In such a complex economy to blame a single circumstance might seem an over-simplification, but the closeness in time of the two events surely meant that one thing had to do with the other.

233 The Fleas in America's Ears

NASDAQ (National Association of Securities Dealers Automated Quotations) is the capital market where financing was obtained for high-risk, computation-related companies. In the world of computation the Internet was the cynosure for research and development. And the Internet did indeed seem like a magical medium. Inside it you could have in an instant all the latest information on anything that was going on in the world. If you wanted to buy and sell stock you could do it through the Internet without paying the high commission charges of brokerage houses. From the Internet you could extract the information you needed to make your own investment choices. Readers had in the Internet the ideal bookshop, one you didn't have to walk to and which you could search through without having to walk in circles or ask questions from illiterate or moody employees. Every important company in the world had its own website. And if you needed reminding that you could be requiring one thing or another, the Internet had the advertising potential to let you know. So a great deal of money was poured into internet-related companies to make the Internet and its services more varied and efficient. However, with all its power to dazzle and enthrall, the Internet like all else had points of diminishing returns, one of which was reached shortly after George W. Bush was sworn in.

Capital flows to where it can make itself again, but one, capital flows do not in themselves carry a guarantee of profit, and, two, if capital flows get hung up somewhere they are going to be missing elsewhere. Globalization is not a miraculous, loaves-and-fishes process. It is still the best way for growing economies to obtain know-how and acquire competitive skills, but it has its worldwide cycles. Bush had the bad luck to get the tail end of a cycle. But Bush's response to the cycle was not re-assuring. For one thing he showed a definitely un-globalist penchant for protectionism, as well as turning thumbs down on anything that the rest of the world advocated. Among the international protocols not subscribed to by the USA were those on the Law of the Sea, the Kyoto global-warming accord, and the international tribunal for crimes against humanity. Perhaps these causes were seen in the USA as standard UN blather. Americans generally would probably rank the UN as rather an institution they can do without (often they are openly hostile to it). But the USA lost nothing by joining the choruses and it showed a mean, self-important obstinacy by deliberately singing out of tune.[3]

---

3 The United Nations on the Law of the Sea has been in force since 1994 and was ratified by 157 states not including the USA. The International Criminal Court came into being in 2002 and the Kyoto Protocol became operative in 2005.

Bush also favored tax cuts for the very rich as a means to get the economy moving again quickly. Most economists are wrong most of the time but when most economists agree they must be on to something undeniably right. And most economists were against Bush's let's-stop-soaking-the-rich approach, especially where the evidence was not that the rich were being soaked but that highly paid CEOs were soaking investors.

This dismaying part of the economic picture went beyond "emerging information sciences" to some very big and complex corporations that were toying with the numbers. In the biggest of all corporate scandals--but one among many that hit the summits of the American corporate world like bursts of lightning--that of Enron, a company that played on futures with energy sources, the book-keeping was done in such a way as to seem that Enron was making huge profits. But there was no cash to show for them. Futures are a form of financial speculation about whether prices will go up or down. If you go short, you expect prices to go down; if you go long, you expect them to go up. Futures are considered extremely risky even for investors with big pockets. When outflows are not replenished, somebody is sooner or later out of pocket, so basically what Enron had created was an ultra-sophisticated Ponzi scheme. In a Ponzi scheme, money is obtained under false pretenses and partially recycled to encourage "investors". Through Enron's fabricated profit-making deals investors were putting money into nothing. However, Enron did have ultimate ownership of assets that are being recovered to pay creditors. Shareholders, as every one knows, are the last in the collecting line.[4]

(5) Development economics

Under the circumstances, to try to reverse an overdue downturn in the business cycle by encouraging greed and protectionism did not seem to be the most admirable of moves and President Bush was not getting the backing to push through his risky economic program. The American economy was "officially" out of the recession by December 2000. But the financial markets were sluggish and employment was not picking up. According to the National Bureau of Economic Research, the American economy had dipped into recession again in March 2001 and emerged from it in December of the same year.

There was also a subtle political malaise lurking here and there. It had to do with the very essence of democracy, a sine qua non condition

4 Kurt Eichenwald, "Enron's accounting binge chronicled", IHT, March 7, 2003. In his book *The New Industrial State* (1967), John K. Galbraith argued that corporative management is independent of ownership, but what he did not foresee is to what extent CEOs can be unresponsive even to the interests of firms.

to gauge the global state of human affairs. To speak of a crisis of democracy would be going too far. But to question the infallible efficacy of democracy is well within the rules of democracy itself.

The handful of Asian economies that either had made the breakthrough or were on the breakthrough path to development had done so mostly in undemocratic circumstances. South Korea became a democracy in 1987. The first fully democratic presidential election in Taiwan was held in 1996. Thailand had only become democratic in 1997 and this is much too recent to say that it is over recurrent military rule. Indonesia was under the strongman rule of Gen. Suharto from 1965 to 1999. It is a huge country beset by instabilities of all sorts.[5] In Singapore, the authoritarian rule of Lee Kuan Yew antedated the country's independence in 1965. It lasted formally until 1990, but the press quotes to this day what Lee says as if it were official policy.

Of all the really developing countries of Asia, only India, Malaysia, and Sri Lanka have had elections since their inceptions, yet even in Malaysia authoritarianism was the rule and prime minister Mohammed bin Mahathir was in unchallengeable power from 1981 to 2004. The fact is that, if globalization was the key to economic progress, democracy did not seem to be part of the package. And if one went by the experience of the impeccably democratic South American state of Venezuela, democracy was an utter failure at economic development.

In the Post-War, to counter the appeal of communism in poor countries the set of prescriptions adopted and propagated as unofficial policy, mainly but not exclusively by the USA, was known as development economics. This was in effect a doctrine with aspirations to theoretical status. It went against the grain of conventional economics, yet it tried to

---

5 Under Suharto, nepotism and corruption became so blatant that the Indonesians forced him out of power in 1999. He was succeeded by Vice-president B.J. Habibie, followed in 2000 by a weak government led by Abdurrahman Wahid, a nearly blind Muslim scholar. After prolonged rebellion and waves of repression, East Timor became independent in 2002. Sukarno's daughter, the taciturn Megawati Sukarnoputri, was elected president by the Indonesian parliament. In October 2002, Bali was the object of a totally unprovoked, though not entirely unforeseeable, terrorist attack that left over 200 dead. According to intelligence reports emanating in Singapore (January 2003), Indonesian Muslim terrorists constitute a distinct threat capable of acting independently of al Qaida. Indonesian police estimate at 5,000 the number of Islamic extremists in the country. Notwithstanding the Bali bombings and the general restiveness after the fall of Suharto, the general trend in Indonesia has been towards political stability and economic growth. In 2004, ex-general Susilo Bambang Yudhoyono defeated Megawati in a clean election for the presidency.

use its jargon and methodologies. Whereas capitalist, free-market economics were always imagining what was called a Pareto equilibrium, a situation in which total information obtained and economic flows, including labor, moved about unimpeded, development economics proposed all sorts of barriers and distortions for the economies of poor countries.

Free trade and the international division of labor were out of the question. Tariff walls to protect nascent industries were to be built. Subsidies and incentives, where possible, should be applied freely to stimulate investment and job creation. There had to be planning to remember what exactly all these measures were about. But, as development economics was in essence a set of contrivances to create strong market economies, planning was not compulsory but indicative. This basically meant that third world countries got into the habit of quoting figures in the plans rather than real-world statistics and so they ended up in cloud cuckoo land. But this was not at first clear, in part because development economics had a brilliant genealogy.

One could go seeking for its ancestry very far in time if one wanted, but the soundest precedent was mercantilism, which advocated national self-sufficiency and gold hoarding through protectionism. But mercantilism was cutting-edge doctrine at the time Europe was practically on the threshold of industrialization and development economics was very derivative. In the 19th century, the case of protectionism was famously made by the German-American economist Friedrick List, who also advocated the Zollverein or the customs union of all the German states before German unification in 1871. It could be argued that basically List was for economic nationalism, not at all unlike what mercantilism was about.

All things considered, development economics embodied the sort of spontaneous arrangements and manipulations that governments tended to adopt, if they could, when they were at an economic disadvantage with respect to other nations. There were some pre-World War II theorists of development economics. They came up with concepts like "economies of scale" and "externalities" and had the Balkans in mind. These were meant to justify large-scale industrialization schemes even when the economics didn't click.[6]

Just to keep things in perspective, Argentina, which in the Post-War adopted the development-economics model, before the war was considered among the ten richest countries in the world through the export of beef and wheat, hardly requiring special economic nostrums. It could even be argued that Argentina actually "underdeveloped" because of its intense desire for "balanced-growth" industrialization.

6 C. Ramirez-Faria, *The origins of economic inequality between nations* (1991).

The policies associated with development economics had not been shown to be very successful in the past. Heavy protectionism was unarguably a powerful cause of the Great World Depression of the 1930s. But in the Post-War there were many economists working on development-economics premises, because the industrialized countries were a mostly struggling handful, the rest of the world was generally dirt-poor, and with the end of the colonialist empires, communism could have rich pickings among the myriad states, often really pseudo-states, that were being, or about to be, created.

(6) The sad case of the democratic showcase for the Alliance for Progress

Venezuela was definitely a notch or two above dire poverty, mainly because it had a lot of oil. The state's coffers were brimming over and there was a trickle-down, bureaucratic effect. It wasn't trickle-down from wealth-formation but from large fiscal income, which means that most of the money was being recycled and not re-invested.

Venezuela's first great bureaucratic expansion occurred during a brief democratic phase between 1945 and 1948, after which it continued but under a very pro-USA, intolerant, though hardly brutal, military regime. In January 1958, street riots undermined military discipline and the then dictator, Marcos Pérez Jiménez, fled the country with dollar-stuffed valises. During a demagogic transition to democracy, a subsidy for the poor was pegged at above going wages in rural Venezuela, which meant unemployed peasants who built shanties with astonishing rapidity inundated the cities.

It was at this time of social ferment that Vice-president Nixon visited the country. Security was so lax that mobs in Caracas surrounded Nixon's car, rocked it back and forth, broke the windows, and spat at the vice-president and his wife. The USA was about to intervene when the Venezuelan government managed to get the situation in hand. It is another plus for Nixon that, after going through that hellish experience (in situ he was especially indignant at the treatment his wife got), he could write in the safety of his own country that American foreign policy towards the Venezuelan dictatorship had been misguided.

When Kennedy defeated Nixon, he took his rival's conclusion to heart and created the Peace Corps, aimed at all poor countries in the world—America at its idealist best—and, specifically for Latin America, he announced the Alliance for Progress, which adopted development-economics lock, stock, and barrel. Since Venezuela had been at least partly the stage for America's awakening to the shortcomings of its policy towards Latin America and since also it was a democracy and had government funds to spare, it was only to be expected that it should have become something of a showcase for the Alliance for Progress.

(7) Democracy was definitely not a sure-fire formula for economic development

Venezuela remained faithful to the electoral system, but that's about all it retained from the days when it was the model for state-guided capitalist development and the cornerstone of America's commitment to democracy in Latin America. Venezuela participated in the great OPEC oil-price bonanzas of the 1970s and early 1980s. As one of the loudest voices for the heralded "new international economic order", Venezuela was led by the hyper-kinetic but not very brilliant Carlos Andres Perez. Its economy was "booming". To fight unemployment, Perez decreed that there shouldn't be an unattended toilet or elevator in the land. (The first high rises in Venezuela were constructed in the 1950s and the country had not even known hand-activated elevators.)

In the early 1980s, despite another boost in oil prices, Venezuela's currency, the Bolivar, began an incredible descent from 4.3 to the dollar to the near 2,500 to the dollar at which it is traded today in the black market. Thinking of undoing his previous mistakes, Perez was re-elected in 1983. He decreed the immediate end of price controls and subsidies, starting with public transportation, which in the third world stirs discontent more than any other issue, except food increases. There were riots in Caracas and before the first year of his second presidency was out Perez was the most detested man in Venezuela and he ended up in jail accused of corruption. His main advisor in the botched attempt to reform the Venezuelan economy, Moises Naim, got himself a job as an editor in Washington.

After nine consecutive fully open and honest presidential elections, Venezuela in PPP terms is today at least as poor as it was at the end of the military dictatorship in 1958, and the electoral system itself was used by the current president to overturn the constitution the country had for nearly forty years and to get himself re-elected, one year after his first election, for a period of six years with the chance of re-election at the end of his current term. The author of these institutional commotions, former paratrooper Hugo Chavez Frias, had tried to overthrow the government elected in 1988. The president legally elected in 1993 pardoned him. It is estimated that under Chavez, who came to power advocating a revolution for the poor, Venezuela's per capita GDP had a year-on-year deterioration of something in the order of 5%, until the recent spectacular oil spiral set a bottom to the downslide and Venezuela's growth today is one of the highest in the world, no doubt in part due to Chavez' real concern for the people's welfare. So much for oil-wealth, development-economics, and democracy as the sure-fire formula for prosperity in developing countries!

However singular the set of circumstances surrounding the spectacular Venezuelan economic crash, the economic failure of democracy is not unique. Despite the period of dictatorial rule by president Ferdinand Marcos, who did not begin as a dictator but won two consecutive elections, the Philippines has a longer record of democratic politics than its South East Asian neighbors, Malaysia excepted, but the Philippines is among the poorer countries in the region, not as bad as Cambodia, Laos, or Myanmar, but lagging in growth even in comparison with Vietnam, which has retained many features from its communist past.

The most striking contrast of all is between democratic India and un-democratic China. China might at one time under Mao Zedong have qualified as the world's poorest country, certainly poorer than India. After some 25 years of economic reform, but without free elections as in India, China has surpassed India in economic performance and there's no limit to its growth in sight, whereas India, which adopted the development-economics model with even more enthusiasm than Venezuela, had heavy going for decades. After 1991, India too chose to rid itself of useless, stifling economic controls and obstructions and its perspectives for the future at present rival those of China.

(8) A brief exercise in psephology

But it isn't only in the developing world that democracy is open to criticism. Even in its American citadel it seems to work in contrary ways. Low voter participation is one of the traditional characteristics of American elections.[7] It is worse in congressional elections than in presidential ones. The rate of voter abstention has not seemed in the past to have distorting effect on political practice: despite low voter turnouts no one doubts that the results of elections reflect general American opinion.

From 1940 to 2000, the average percentage of voters from the voting age population was around 53. For the elections from 1940 to 1968, the percentage is higher (an average of 59%), but it dropped on average over 6 points when the electoral franchise was made mandatory from the age of 18 by the 26th Amendment to the Constitution. The six highest turnouts in American presidential elections were (winner first): (1) Kennedy-Nixon 1960, (2) Clinton-Bush-Perot 1992, (3) Johnson-Goldwater 1964, (4) Nixon-McGovern 1972, (5) Eisenhower-

7 www.fce.gov

Stevenson 1952, and (6) Nixon-Humphrey 1968. The five lowest turnouts were: (1) Truman-Dewey 1948, (2) Clinton-Dole-Perot 1996, (3) Roosevelt-Dewey 1944, (4) Bush-Dukakis 1988, and (5) Bush-Gore 2000. Corrected for the 26th Amendment factor, the vote in 1948, the lowest for the period, was 44.7%.

Some of these results seem to have easy explanations: McGovern was too much of a radical for America to accept passively; Eisenhower was a brilliant soldier and he was running as a Republican after five consecutive terms of office for Democrats; Dewey never generated much excitement and Truman benefited from being the incumbent (no reasons here to rush to vote); neither Dole nor Perot enthused voters; Roosevelt was a shoo-in; Bush the elder, Dukakis, Bush the younger, and Gore were also unexciting. Kennedy and Johnson rode the crest of the wave of liberalism in America. Some results are frankly contradictory. Humphrey lost because he did not disavow Johnson's war in Vietnam, but Nixon beat a genuine peacenik like McGovern.

In the period covered, there were six landslide votes: (1) Roosevelt over Dewey, (2) Eisenhower over Stevenson, (3) Johnson over Goldwater, (4) Nixon over McGovern, (5) Reagan over Carter (1980), and (6) Reagan over Mondale (1984). Of these overwhelming victories (the large margins are usually reflected in the electoral votes), only (2) and (4) occurred with high voter turnouts. In the other landslides, the turnout was close to average, hence low. This could mean that America's turn to conservatism was not as massive as it might appear, but Clinton won twice when the basically conservative Perot took support away from the Republicans. On the other hand, had Gore not had Ralph Nader nibbling at his liberal base, he might have made an easy meal of Bush the younger.

Summarizing this brief exercise in psephology, in no presidential election in the last 63 years have more than 62.8% of legally enfranchised Americans voted for president. Out of twelve elections, the adjusted results have been 55% or less of the electoral age population. Certain elections can be considered to have marked watersheds or to have manifested significant general changes in public-opinion orientation: the end of the Democrat domination of the presidency in 1952, the liberal surge that allowed Kennedy to become president despite his Catholicism (1960), the conservative turn represented by Ronald Reagan (1980). Only in the case of Reagan was the turnout somewhat below the six highest turnouts for the period, but only barely, so basically it can be said that he had a solid mandate for change, as did Eisenhower. Kennedy did not markedly campaign on change. Eisenhower had done little to alter the Post-War political consensus, itself a Rooseveltian heritage. The only major issue that seemed to divide Americans then, apart from the

Southern attachment to extreme racial discrimination, was who could get tougher on communists. The scion of a very wealthy Catholic family, Kennedy could stare down any charge of softness on communism.

(9) As compensation for having entered the White House to less than universal hurrahs, Bush began his term like a hurricane named Ronald

In the sixteen presidential elections covered in this survey, there was only one in which the direct or popular-vote majority did not tally with the electoral-vote majority and that was in 2000, when Al Gore obtained more votes than George W. Bush. In addition, the turnout for that election was 50.7%, well below the average for the previous seventeen elections covering a span to 2000 of sixty years. In other words, if ever a president had been elected during that lapse of time with the least semblance of a mandate it was this Bush. His father won indisputably but did not pretend to go beyond the Reagan program, except on abortion, on which issue he veered to extreme conservatism. Clinton never had a mandate and he acted accordingly. Yet his electoral victories were clear-cut.

Paradoxically, perhaps as a sort of compensation for having entered the White House to less than universal hurrahs, Bush began his term like a hurricane named Ronald. The only historical grounds that could have justified Bush's extreme conservative activism was the assumption that the USA was still very inclined to that view, as had been the case in the past with the landslide that put Reagan in the White House. But that had taken place eighteen years earlier and there was then no conclusive electoral indication that America was still wedded to Reaganism.

Bush went all out for a program for which he had not obtained unequivocal popular support. A more sensible person in his position would have chosen, as Clinton had, to play it by ear. There were no compelling reasons to believe that his let's-give-the-rich-a-break philosophy was what American voters were thinking about when they gave him the slimmest of electoral-vote majorities and did not even give him a popular-vote endorsement. Bush was formally within the democratic rules of the political game. He espoused a policies version of the Jacksonian "to the victor belongs the spoil" attitude. But he was going against the grain of democracy, which is supposed to reflect public opinion and not interpret it as one wants to.

The terrorist attack on 9/11 and Bush's forceful reaction to it changed the political coordinates over night. In face of that tragedy, it is difficult to imagine any other reaction than the grieving yet defiant one that Bush assumed. But it was Bush who had the chance to assume it and this made him what he had not been before: the near-unanimous choice of Americans as the living symbol and the spokesman of their country for the rest of the world. The American victory in Afghanistan, where Bush showed resolution, further shored up his growing stature. The irony was that Bush became a hero-president because he began his term by shooting off his mouth and by being completely wrong about America's potential, or need, for the sort of invulnerability he was after. He became the man who could do no wrong because he showed how completely wrong he could be. It was as if the naked emperor first elicited laughter because of his gullibility and then admiration for his splendid physique.

Bush duly got the mandate he did not have before in the congressional elections of 2002, when he pulled the trick of increasing his party's vote in a midterm election. Republicans controlled both houses of Congress. The voter turnout was also the lowest in history, as if Americans on the whole had reservations about Bush but feared that voting against his party would be unpatriotic. Democratic politics in America showed more than ever that they were reactive rather than reflective.

To some extent democracy has always been a game of smoke and mirrors, as the elder Bush once described political skullduggery, but there was always a strong link between what the public wanted and what the public got. With Bush the younger one got the impression that the public did not know what it wanted and that the president was leading the country in one direction or another through sheer chutzpah and American disorientation. Government of the people, by the people, for the people might no longer be exactly what the words said. Or at least America might have gone astray momentarily from those ideals.

(10) First-past-the-post and proportional representation

There was another democracy giving a distorted image of an ideal democratic process. There are two basic ways of counting electoral results: first-past-the-post and proportional representation. First-past-the-post is the British and American way. From Britain it spread to all the former dependencies of the British Empire. It is a solid system in that it makes the elected representative of a constituency inescapably responsible for his voting record. Every time there is an election the representative or the parliamentarian has to go back to his electors and convince them that he, as an individual mainly (although party performance also affects public perception), deserves to be re-elected. In the first-by-the-post system you would have to be in a land of utter ignoramuses to get away with malfeasance in office.

As not all voters are created equal, the first-past-the-post system is vulnerable to special pleading by campaign contributors. It has also against it that through gerrymandering, or the redrawing of congressional districts or constituencies, it can be made to distort over-all electoral results, so that, in theory, it becomes likely that representation will not reflect public opinion. In America, it is the electoral-college system, which carries the first-past-the-post principle to unconscionable extremes that has allowed politicians on four occasions to reach the presidency with a minority of votes.[8] In Britain, the Conservative or Laborite bent of regional electorates causes the disregard of many millions of votes.

The usual way that first-past-the-post anomalies are corrected is through proportional representation, by which places in parliaments are allotted according to party election results. This sort of system, though seemingly fair, makes representatives more accountable to the parties that choose them than to the electorates, who vote for the party rather than for the candidate. Under proportional representation, in principle, even in a land of acute political observers, you could get away with murder and be re-elected if a party was willing to back you.

The trend in the world's democracies, except where first-past-the-post is entrenched, is for a combination in which first-past-the-post is the basic system but minority votes in every constituency are totted up and assigned proportionally to parties which fulfill a minimum-requirement of popular support. In Venezuela, perhaps the world's worst performing true democracy, proportional representation in practice divided the country into party chiefdoms. There indeed it was the case that, whatever else you did as long as you did the party's bidding, you were assured of re-election. It was the essence of clientelism.

(11) "Ethnicity" thrives in a state where it shouldn't exist at all

There is another potentially big flaw in proportional representation and that is where the electorate is fissured in many different ways, such as happens in Israel. One would imagine that a state that was formed for a people that could claim affiliation to one religion and descent from one ancient tribe would tend towards social homogeneity, but that is not the way things have turned out in Israel, partly because of the Diaspora, partly because Jews can be Jews without actually being religious Jews.

To start with, "ethnicity" in Israel was always important. Here again you could ask: what "ethnicity" since Jews claim they are a people and

8 In three other elections, besides that of 2000, Americans voted in greater number for the loser than for the president-elect: in 1824, John Quincy Adams won over Andrew Jackson with electoral votes; in 1876, Rutherford B. Hayes over Samuel J. Tilden; and in 1888, Benjamin Harrison over Grover Cleveland.

they share a religion that informs all aspects of life? Well, there existed three "ethnic" trends: the Azkenasim, or the Jews of central and eastern Europe, speakers of Yiddish (a German dialect); the Sephardim, the Jews of the Mediterranean, speakers mainly of mainly Spanish; and the Sabra, or Jews native to Palestine, who learned to speak Hebrew. With the adoption of Hebrew and the passing of various generations, the Sabras are no longer a recognizable ethnic identity. The separation between Azkenasim and Sephardim still exists.

Jews are also divided religiously. Some are agnostics or atheists, some are reformists or modernists, and some are Orthodox or fundamentalists. Within the Orthodox, there are various groups, animated by charismatic religious figures or followers of certain special traditions. There was even an ultra-Orthodox sect that was against the existence of the state of Israel. These Orthodox Jewish sects are agreed only on their hatred of Jews who do not observe the Sabbath strictly, which happens to be the case of the majority of Israelis.

But the complexity does not stop there. During the 1970s and the 1980s, some Russian Jews began agitating to be allowed to emigrate from the USSR on the grounds that they were a persecuted minority. The degree of persecution of Jews in Russia is a debatable issue. They were certainly persecuted in The Pale before World War I. In the last few years of Stalin, there were signs of official support for anti-Semitism. But despite the millions of Jews that immigrated from the Pale mostly to America and even with the great Jewish migration from the USSR to Israel, due to natural reproduction there are probably still more Jews or descendants of Jews in Russia than those that emigrated.

The Jews that emigrated from the USSR to Israel also alleged that, after all, there was a Jewish state they could go to so they could not be considered state-less refugees. Perhaps many ended up in America as refugees. But most probably did settle in Israel, and they were so numerous that they represent a considerable political force with its own party or parties. These fissures in Israeli society were not at first very compulsive and there were three main political trends: the Labor Party, which was the strongest force at the creation of Israel; Likud, which was the "conservative" opposition to Labor; and Orthodox Jews, who have always been around, always as a tiny, fragmented political minority.

(12) In Israel, there was a consensus on the one issue that should have been foremost in electoral debate

Politics in Israel, as elsewhere, is about power, but in Israel it often seems to be about sharing power and about nothing else. At first there was no challenging Labor. But Labor had a laid-back attitude towards Palestinians, as exemplified by Dayan, and the Likud anti-Palestinian view gradually gained ground. Begin, the first Likud prime minister and a former terrorist, was also the man who signed the peace with Egypt. This, and the death of his wife, depressed him so much that he left politics and soon died. Begin's electoral success opened the sluice gates and anti-Palestinian militancy became so much a part of the Israeli political scene that Labor was partially sucked in.

With the relative prevalence of anti-Palestinian attitudes, resulting in a consensus of sorts on the one issue that should have been a crucial theme of debate, Israeli politics became almost exclusively about maneuvering for political advantages. The Israeli electoral system had been made meticulously proportional—the requirements for official recognition of parties are minimal, among other things—because, despite Israel's secularist Zionist roots, Judaic Orthodoxy has always been considered to have a special place in Israeli society, partly out of respect for tradition, partly because of the stridency of Orthodox Jews themselves. As Orthodox Jews were numerically insignificant, it was necessary to lower requirements for representation in the Knesset. Conversely, which is another minus for Israeli democracy, Israeli Arabs have a quota of representatives that does not correspond to the fifth of the population of Israel that they constitute.

This mania for proportionality, combined with the general tendency in Israeli society away from accommodation with Palestinians, has resulted in that the Palestinian problem is, by some accounts, no longer an electoral issue, which is as if you were certifying as extremely healthy a person with obvious symptoms of some deforming disease. Israeli politics contain an element of extreme radicalism that may not be a true reflection of Israeli public opinion. In Israel, proportional representation, which is usually invoked as a corrective for electoral unfairness, has been skewed towards virulent and unrepresentative extremism.[9]

If democracy has not contributed significantly to economic growth in developing countries, if it was used to impose a political agenda that voters did not approve in America, and if it is a means of obstructing peaceful solutions to the Palestinian issue, then there are grounds for claiming that democracy is going at present through what appears to be a crisis. This is not to say that democracy is a failure or that there is an infallible substitute for democracy. Democracy is still the best means not only for governance but especially to mend the ways of democracy itself. But as long as democracy impedes rather than encourages world

9 Shlomo Ben Ami, "The peace process is irrelevant", IHT, January 21, 2003.

peace, there will be grounds for arguing that democracy is not quite what it is stacked up to be. Such being the case, the Chinese way to development, in which, outside of communist party elections, democracy is mostly about democratic-sounding noises, could seem like a respectable option. And Russia's penchant for authoritarianism will also have a sound historical justification. If there is indeed a crisis of democracy, therefore, it is not because of democracy per se, but because of things that democracies are not getting right.

(13) The USA was in a black mood and Bush was still fighting mad

The War on Afghanistan properly speaking was a very brief affair. The hunt for Osama bin Laden and for terrorists all over the world is still going on. But as America's international enemy number one had escaped it, closure was not there, nor was it to be had either in the meticulous search in New York's Fresh Kills landfill for scraps of skin and bits of fingernails. There was definitively something macabre about searching for pieces of dead Americans and for corpses in Afghan caves. Little comfort could be derived either in the thought of suspected terrorists being kept in concentration-camp conditions in Guantánamo.[10] This might have been the least they deserved, but it wasn't the outright torturing that the offended sometimes wish to see their enemies undergo, although this is what it was made to seem at first, and as reports and enquiries have been piling up it has become plain that Guantanamo was in fact converted into "torture central". But at the time, the USA was in a black mood and Bush was still fighting mad. There was also to consider that the president was now a highly acclaimed leader instead of the dubious winner of the 2000 elections. Bush did not want to lose the momentum his presidency now had. Like the world from 1989 to 1991, he was on a roll. But unlike the world, there was a way to keep his roll going.

Israel was being beset by terrorists, no matter that it was being attacked by suicide bombers and that this should have given any sensible person reason to pause and wonder whether these suicidal young people might not have a good cause to sacrifice their lives. From the American perspective, conditioned by 9/11, in which suicidal terrorism was carried to an apocalyptic extreme, they were simply terrorists. The war on terror was still going in Israel.

There is little doubt that most Americans really believe that you can wage a war to extirpate social terrorism. This is not unlike the tragically misleading concept of a "war to end all wars", whose culmination was

10 Carlotta Gall with Neil A. Lewis, "Freed Guantanamo captives tell of suicidal despair", IHT, January 18, 2003

World War II and the Holocaust. It was believed that after such carnage as occurred in World War I no one ever again would want to make war. In our times, the passionate search for closure was not about to submit to rational analysis or to historical quibbling. Afghanistan had not been a catharsis. More revenge was needed. War on terror had to be taken very seriously. New lessons had to be taught.

(14) Lynch the bastards and apologize later

No one questioned America's right to attack Afghanistan. The Taliban were no one's heroes. To be sure, there were means other than war to neutralize terrorist threats to the USA, but war was definitely one hell of a spectacular way to do it. Bush had stoked the fiery war mood America was in and he wanted to keep the fire going. He also had the target to hand. In fact, he had already singled it out, long before 9/11. Combined with the likely Israeli repression of the Second Intifada, it was like a one-two combination that would leave terrorists reeling everywhere. The USA was going to declare war on Saddam Hussein and conclude what it had started and had not finished back in 1991. The commonsensical view was that Bush the elder had refrained from doing so because of the foreseeable complications of occupying Iraq. Another view was that it had been sheer idiocy.

Although the issue has not been raised much, Bush the younger's choice of a target after Afghanistan did put his father's either statesmanship or intelligence in question, but that was not a problem next to what now seemed like a certain win. Historians could debate about the details at their leisure as time went by. Judgments would be passed and rights and wrongs apportioned. Bush called his critics "revisionists". Revisionists during the Cold War were authors who faulted America's unyielding anti-Soviet policies. Revisionism was also one of America's open society's traditional ways: roughly put, lynch the bastards and apologize later.

Bush had plunged into his presidential duties with bravado, not to say braggadocio. He included Iraq in his axis of evil. During the Gulf War, Iraq had flung Scuds at Saudi Arabia and at Israel. Saddam Hussein the Iraqi dictator had gotten away literally with murder. And later he had the audacity to kick out the UN arms inspectors, as if he had gained any merits towards international respectability. Now, war on Iraq was to be made in the name of anti-terrorism. It was part of America's war on terror. There were a few problems with the American case against Iraq before and after 9/11 and Afghanistan.

(15) Iraq was a terrorist state but the terrorism it practiced was against its own people

There was the matter of the accusation that Hussein was manufacturing WMD, including maybe even nuclear weapons. This was as unlikely as that Iraq could put a man on the moon. Perhaps the UN had acquiesced too easily in letting its personnel be ordered out of Iraq, but, although there were some loud dissenting voices, most of the inspectors truly believed that Iraq did not then pose a military threat to anybody. True, four years had elapsed since Iraq had been let off the hook, time enough for a determined state to produce and store significant amounts of poison gas or toxic germs, but the probability that Iraq had a secret and dangerous weapons program was risible under the stringent surveillance conditions under which the country was kept.

The other problem was that, yes, Iraq was a terrorist state but in the general sense that the use of terror is a state practice. In essence, Iraq was as terrorizing to Iraqis as Israel was to Palestinians. Saddam Hussein was undoubtedly a terror to his political enemies and to people in Iraq who did not bend to his will. Hussein had terrorized internal opposition to inexistence. But Iraq was not a terrorist menace outside of its frontiers. It was not giving support to social terrorism against Israel. It wouldn't even have dreamed of doing so. Iraq didn't want war with any one and least of all with America, and it knew that any suspicion that it was aiding and abetting Palestinian terrorism would have brought America's wrath on its head.

Iraq had not sent volunteers to Afghanistan. Under Hussein, if truth be told, Iraq was the least fundamentalist of Muslim states. The USA tried to link Saddam Hussein to al Qaida, but it could not dig up even the minimal evidence that would have persuaded the most sympathetic observer. So here again the USA didn't have anything resembling a court case against Iraq.

So finally why Iraq? Why not Iran, which militarily was much stronger than Iraq and did not conceal that it financed the Hizbollah and Israel has called Hizbollah a terrorist organization time and again? Why not North Korea who was a real menace as it had shown when it send a Taepondong rocket zinging above Honshu and who could have plunged the Korean peninsula into a flurry of fiery tornadoes?

To some extent, these questions are self-answering. Bush wanted victory. And he wanted victory fast. He did not want a long, bloody war and a long, bloody resistance or occupation. If you give Bush the benefit of the doubt, he really wanted to wage a war on terror, but if you don't, and it doesn't take much to get really skeptical on that point, he had to know that he was not really carrying on his war on terror by attacking Iraq. What he was doing was setting up a dummy target, keeping Americans in a high dudgeon, and probably making political calculations. If there were political motivations, they would have been about his re-election, also perhaps about being the American president who brought peace to the Middle East by solving the issue of Palestinian statehood. Basically, then, the answer to "why Iraq" is that Iraq was the softest and easiest of the targets that Bush could choose and still win another round in the war on terror.

(16) Sharon and Arafat hated each others' guts but Sharon had 3,800 tanks and Arafat did not

In Israel, the Second Intifada was on a larger scale than the first one, particularly as there already was in place the PA headed by Arafat. But there was no question of a lightly armed constabulary facing down an army, which counted with 3,800 tanks and 2,000 war aircraft. Israel needed to deploy only a tiny fraction of its arsenal to crush whatever armed resistance the Palestinians could put up.

There was one way that Palestinians could dent Israeli military supremacy. That was to inflict losses on Israeli military and civilians in sufficient numbers to make Israel's occupation of Palestinian territories painful enough to induce negotiations and concessions. The only way to achieve that was through the use of suicide bombers. The basis for the success of this tactic is, to put it simply, that Arabs and many Jews are physically much alike and once inside Israel suicide-bombers can pass unnoticed and choose targets of opportunity, especially markets, bus stops, pedestrian streets, and so on. Suicide attacks during 2001 caused 81 Israeli dead, but this was only a prelude to the massive campaign that was to occur in 2002.

It is conceivable that Palestinian radicals might have considered that 9/11 was as much an attack on Israel as it was on America, in which case they could have hoped for a slackening of Israeli repression, perhaps even an opening for a negotiated return to the Oslo Accords. But America's war on terror, which Israel supported unreservedly, demonstrated that, if anything, 9/11 probably would lead to a hardening of the Israeli stance. After all, if the USA regularly echoedIsraeli exhortations to Palestinians to disarm and to refrain from terrorism, it wasn't to be expected that, after suffering the devastation of 9/11, it would adopt a softer attitude towards Palestinian terrorists.

Sharon's government was neither interested in reviving the Oslo Accords, nor in modifying the settlements policy, nor in sitting down to negotiate with Arafat and the PA, which every day that passed seemed to fade further into unreality. Rabin and Barak might have been willing to meet with Arafat, but there was no way in heaven or earth that Sharon could be made to sit down as an equal with his arch-enemy, a dislike that Arafat fully reciprocated, except that for him just getting Sharon to talk to him would have been a kind of triumph.

This was one of those reversals of roles that make history so fascinating and so perilous for absolutes and for inflexibilities. In the days when Israel, facing the implacable hostility of its Arab neighbors, seemed to be almost eagerly seeking contacts with them, an Arab diplomat once accepted to appear on the same American TV program as his Israeli counterpart, on condition that they would be separated by a solid screen preventing them from seeing one other. Israel won points on this occasion by simply being sensible. During the first half of 2002, when Arafat was doing his utmost to get even a phone call from Sharon, he was being cold shouldered as implacably as the artificial barriers that Arabs used to put up against Israelis.

(17) Overcrowding was one reason why Palestinians could arm themselves with bombs

Israel was never actually on the defensive during the Second Intifada. It was going to suffer losses but it was always also taking its own initiatives. As between Gaza and the West Bank, the former seemed the least difficult to secure for it was flat land and its inhabitants were confined between straightedge borders and the Mediterranean Sea. Nevertheless, it was in Gaza that Palestinians forced the Israeli army to engage in pitched battles and even managed on a few occasions to destroy heavy Israeli Merhava tanks. These lumbering machines are the ones that appear in countless photographs of Palestinians, often only children, standing before them or on their sides, attacking them with stones, in a defiant attitude that in a single protester in 1998 in Tiananmen Square "thrilled" the world, but which Palestinians repeated so often that it appeared only to elicit ho-hums.

It was also Gaza that Israeli armed helicopters patrolled day and night, using their machine guns whenever there were signs of suspicious Palestinian displacements. The poverty of the Palestinian military arsenal is demonstrated in that whereas Intifada fighters disabled a few Israeli tanks, there are few if any records of Israeli choppers being downed, and there is no more vulnerable instrument of war than a helicopter. Palestinians did not even have crude SAMs or rocket launchers that could have easily brought down these aircraft, especially at the very low levels at which they operated.

Israel had probably secured Gaza by February 2002. But bomb factories can be concealed almost anywhere, especially in overcrowded areas, and if Palestinians had one thing it was overcrowding. The high point of the campaign of suicide bombings occurred during March, when an estimated 80 Israelis were killed. It was then that the Israeli government opted for a full-scale invasion of the West Bank including the encirclement of Arafat's headquarters, located in a large, solid building from British colonial days in the city of Ramallah. Despite the offensive, the suiciders continued during April and May and the Israelis were forced to intensify their offensive in the West Bank and to carry on the work they had undertaken of fencing Gaza in, at least in its northern limit, which is not far from Tel Aviv, and partly along its eastern limit.

While this conflict was going on in Israel/Palestine, President Bush publicly identified Iraq as the next "logical" target of war on terror. He might have expected an international surge of support. The USA had practically fought the war against the Taliban regime by itself, with only the significant on-ground support of Afghan allies. The British played a certain role. But it was an USA show and there was international recognition that Americans, after 9/11, had every right to act as they had.

Against Iraq, except for Great Britain and Australia, the American initiative encountered from reticence to strong opposition. The obvious reason for this was that there existed the possibility of pressuring Iraq to any extreme by means short of war. This was what became known as the negotiated or diplomatic option. It was even surprising that America should have found immediately two such unconditional allies, and it is the positions assumed by the British and the Australian governments, and not the generally skepticism, that merit some analysis.

(18) The USA was big enough to be isolationist but too powerful to remain isolationist

In the case of Great Britain, there was the "special relationship". Between America and Britain there existed a close, unshakable alliance. If ever a state was born in the womb of another it was the United States in the United Kingdom. The American War of Independence was almost like an uprising of a part of Britain against authority in London. There was something that made all the difference, which was that colonials did not have any representation in parliament. The British argued back that it cost enough to defend the colonies at the exclusive expense of the metropolis or imperial center without its inhabitants also wanting to have a say in their foreign policy.

Whether American representation in parliament would have made any difference to the colonies' aspirations to self-rule, is debatable. One can easily imagine American MPs shrugging their shoulders over British concerns about events on the continent. The obvious solution for colonies of settlement, and the one that Great Britain, the sagest colonialist power in history, adopted, was dependent self-rule, but self-rule was a step towards independence, and at the time of George III that was not in the manual. When Britain accepted that colonies of settlement could safely be granted self-rule, it was too late for America, which was already a power capable of taking on the United Kingdom itself, as it did in the War of 1812.

This was the last confrontation between the USA and its former colonialist metropolis. There were some border incidents, and Americans tended to be hawkish about Canada, but all subsequent differences were resolved amicably. During the American Civil War, London was placed in a dilemma. At the time, the manufacture of cotton goods was still important to the British economy—although it wasn't the industry par excellence that it had been during the British Industrial Revolution—so that British foreign policy might have hesitated between the United States, an industrial competitor given to high tariffs, and the Confederate States of America, a natural British market and a source of cheap raw cotton. The weight of historical circumstances makes it unlikely that Britain was really inclined to recognize a slaver state whose fortunes in war had to decline before superior power. When the USA defeated the Confederates at Antietam, Maryland, containing decisively the strongest southern thrust northwards up to that time, the decision against recognition of the Confederacy was virtually made for the British.

America was big enough to be isolationist, but it was too powerful to remain isolationist. Industry and commerce pushed it towards internationalism, especially in the Orient, which was too strong a magnet for the USA to resist. There was also the lure of imperialism.

The vestiges of the Holy Roman Empire were compacted by Prussia into Germany. By the definition of empire as rule by a state over different nationalities, Germany, which was peopled almost wholly by German-speaking Germans—the Alsatians were Germans by ancestry whose main language was French—was not an empire, but it called itself a Reich, a word which can mean empire, and as such it was interpreted. The second German Reich, the first having been the Holy Roman Empire founded by Otto I in 962, decided that it too, like Britain, France, and even a minor power such as Portugal, needed a colonialist overseas empire. It started creating one with African coastal garrisons here and there and in 1884 Bismarck, the Junker chancellor who had engineered the Reich, convened a conference in Berlin which gave international sanction to a large German colonial empire in Africa and Oceania, and not incidentally also to the Congo Free State, the huge personal fief that Henry Morton Stanley had created for Leopold II, king of the Belgians, out of the dark heart of equatorial Africa.[11]

The inhumane exploitation of the Congo made it relatively profitable, but the German colonial empire was completely profitless. It existed for prestige. Towards the end of the 19th century the USA too got a hankering for a colonial empire and it proceeded to get one. A great phrase maker, Rudyard Kipling considered that colonialism was not a Western imposition but a duty that Europeans fulfilled out of altruism, which he called "the white man's burden". America took its empire mainly from Spain and thus did not even have the excuse of being an addition to the "white man's burden". But it did not generate frictions with any other colonialist powers, and especially not with Britain, with which America was on excellent terms.

(19) America broke Germany's choke hold on Britain

In entering World War I the USA was heeding as much Britain's as France's plight. "Lafayette, we are here!" was the motto that characterized the presence of American troops on the continent of Europe as repayment for France's aid to the American colonies during the war of independence. There are two curious historical circumstances here.

Arguably, the greatest achievement of the American intervention in World War I was not on the land front, although this was important, but in the defeat of the German submarine blockade of Great Britain. So basically, what the Yanks did was to give succor to a one-time ally and crucial aid to a former enemy. On the other hand, as America was significantly settled by German immigrants, and only by few Frenchmen, president Woodrow Wilson's decision to enter the war on the Allied side was made easier in terms of domestic politics by presenting it as support for France on principle and not on account of an ethnic affiliation with Britain. But in the final analysis, it was in America's interest that Great Britain, a fellow English-speaking state, should prevail in Europe to prevent an aggressive continental power such as Germany from becoming hegemonic, perhaps even too big for its breeches, which was exactly what occurred in World War II.

In the latter conflict, there was no doubt whatever why America entered the war. France had fallen to Germany, which bragged of Festung Europa (the European fortress). The first Fortress Europe was

11 John Reader, op.cit., pp. 527-531

Napoleon's continental system, which had failed because the French could not get Portugal and Russia to cooperate. World War II was a repetition of that experience along very general lines. But before Hitler launched Operation Barbarossa, or his war against humanity disguised as a war against Stalin and communism, America and Britain were already tacit allies and in August 1941 they became fast allies through the Atlantic Charter, which contains the germs of many features of today's world (including the United Nations) and which specifically can be said to inaugurate the special relationship.

When Japan attacked Hawaii, World War II also became America's war.[12] The USA was committed in two theaters: in the Pacific and Asia and in Europe. Britain had been mauled in Asia, but Australia stepped in to contain Japan in New Guinea. America made no secret that it could not concentrate fully on Europe before it had turned the situation around in the Pacific. Therefore, until the Normandy invasion transferred the bulk of American soldiers in the Atlantic theater to the European continent, Britain, and England in particular, was America's home away from home.

After the war, Britain was America's fortress in Europe against the USSR, even though American troops were mainly based in Germany. War at the time was quickly becoming intercontinental, but Britain was still conceptually America's last line of defense in Europe, the only ally, except for Australia, and maybe Israel, on which it knew that through thick or thin it could count. These considerations were probably more theoretical than practical, but they were motivating nonetheless and, as every one who has an inkling of collective reactions knows, expectations are as important as facts.

(20) How Australia displaced Argentina as central to American foreign policy

The American-Australian special relationship is part of another but equally crucial cycle for both sides. Up until World War II, Argentina was more important to America than Australia, which, despite the distance, was in the economic sphere of Britain. Argentina was also an important destination of British capital investment. The tariff wars during the Great Depression hurt Australia more than they did Great Britain. Australia's main export was wool and the economy was severely affected even to showing negative net migratory flows, particularly galling for a country which had approved immigration laws designed to discriminate against

12 Because the USA entered the war after it was already a global affair, some British historians prefer to call it the 1939-1945 War.

non-whites and which in the post-World War I Conference of Paris had resolutely opposed a Japanese declaration for racial equality. Once World War II became America's war, Australia became one of America's indispensable allies.

Australia's army had been depleted by the surrender of Singapore. There was no question of Australia, with its very low population, mounting an offensive by itself against the Japanese war empire. But Australia was used as America's main military base in the Far East, the way Britain was America's base in Europe. In this condition, Australia also became the recipient of large American investments. Argentina, which anyway shilly-shallied about the Axis, was relegated to a marginal site in America's world view.[13] By force of circumstances, and not by any imperialist design, Australia was detached from Britain's Sterling zone and attached to America by strong financial links. Australia's economy not only recovered from its pre-war prostration but also started prospering as it never had before. Australia took off and has never stopped flying.[14] Argentina became extremely nationalistic and had to fall back on development economics for lack of financial flows from Britain or America.

When it came to the international campaign for war on Iraq, America could count on these two special relationships. But there were additional specific circumstances, which encouraged Britain and Australia to join in. Prime Minister John Howard represented a prickly Australian nationalist mood. Recently, in a terrorist attack on a disco on the Indonesian island of Bali, a majority of the victims, and there were more than 200, had been Australians. Howard reacted with extreme anger and even made threatening noises, quite obviously completely

13 In 1943, the military installed a government in which Col. Juan Domingo Perón, leader of a clique of officers, had considerable influence. Perón built for himself a political base among the labor unions. Argentina remained neutral during World War II until 1945, just in time to be a founding member of the United Nations. As minister of war, Perón approved the declaration of war on Germany, although Perón has been accused of harboring Nazis after the war and one of the main executors of the Holocaust, Adolf Eichmann, settled in Argentina and was run down and captured by Mosad, the Israeli intelligence agency (1960).

14 Australia entered World War II with Great Britain (1939) and Australian troops participated in the African campaign and in the battle of El Alamein (1942). But once Japan attacked Pearl Harbor and extended its empire to New Guinea, Australia, where Gen. Douglas MacArthur had set up headquarters during the fall of the Philippines, became America's principal ally in the Pacific theatre and concentrated on fighting the Japanese, whose principal land enemy until the end of 1942 were the Australian forces in New Guinea. War brought rapid industrialization and prosperity.

hollow, that raised blisters in Indonesia, where the response was immediate and scornful.

The Indonesian police got on the case quite efficiently and in a brief period of time had arrested the authors of the attack and indicted the possible minds behind the plot, which was part of a world-wide Muslim terrorist campaign.[15] Even then, the Australian press sounded indignant that the head of the Indonesian national police appeared in public chortling with the culprit instead of beating him to a pulp, which would of course have incensed Australian human rights groups. Australia had, therefore, good reasons to join a war on terror, even one that did not immediately concern it and that was more than mildly bullying, as hundreds of thousands of marchers in Sydney and other Australian cities believed.

(21) All Blair had to do was ask himself: what would Margaret have done?

As to British primer minister Tony Blair, his immediate and enthusiastic support for President Bush has another set of historical coordinates. The winter of 1978-1979 was so miserable for the British because of strikes and other labor disruptions that they elected the ultra-conservative and strongly anti-union Margaret Thatcher with a swingeing majority. The conservatives hung on to power until 1997, a total of eighteen years, and the longest for continued government by one party in Post-War Britain. For a time it seemed as if there was nothing Labor could do to get the Conservative bulldog to release the bone of 10 Downing Street. Neil Kinnock started reforming Labor by distancing it from union extremism, represented by Arthur Scargill, who led a long, bitter, and unavailing coal miners' strike. Pre-election polls on the eve of one national election showed Kinnock ahead, only for parliament to end up again in Conservative hands and Thatcher queen among pols.

Thatcher's tenure was finally cut not by Labor but by John Major, one of the strangest characters in contemporary British politics, a man

15 The Bali bombing (October 2002), whose authors and accomplices the Indonesian police caught, was believed to be the work of the fundamentalist Jemaah Islamiyah, headed by Abu Bakar Bashir. It was reported that Jemaah Ismailiya had training camps in the Philippines. In 2003, Imam Samudra was condemned to die for masterminding the attack. The actual perpetrator, Ali Imron, who showed remorse, got life. During the course of the investigation, Indonesian police and courts had caught, tried, and sentenced 27 people connected to the terrorist attack. No evidence implicating Bashir himself was found. Nevertheless, Bashir, who was completing a short term in jail for a minor offense, was re-arrested. Bashir was tried again in 2005 and he was exonerated of the charge that he had any direct connection with the Bali atrocity.

with so mild a public presence it was almost inconceivable in one who challenged and forced the "Iron Lady" to step down, in addition a politician without an university education or a public school background. In other words, basically a prole who had done well in the anti-prole party. He only cornered Thatcher in a Conservative Party national conference because the prime minister held to such extremely anti-European views that her fellow party members began to perceive her as a liability and to think that conservatism could not only survive but win again without her, which is exactly what happened.

It must also be mentioned that Thatcher's downfall was in no small part due to her passionate espousal of the poll tax, by which municipal levies were to be made per head in households rather than by the value of the property. This meant that the brunt of the tax fell on poorer households, which usually have many members. Little old ladies on pensions and with homes of their own were all for it, even if they detested Thatcher's guts.

In national elections, Major ran on a moralistic, family-values platform and won a term as prime minister for himself. As he was not really defending a political program but a heap of vague truisms, it was probably Conservative inertia that empowered him. During the campaign and after, Major, a married man, was carrying on a very secret affair with Edwina Currie, the conservative mayor of Westminster, as controversial as Margaret Thatcher but not quite the national figure the other one was, more a strictly London phenomenon.

Labor finally understood that it was time for a u-turn. In the process the man who ended up at the party's pinnacle was Tony Blair, whom caricaturists depicted as all toothy smile and youthful vim and enthusiasm. He also had a slight squint that actually gave him a friendly look. But what decided the issue was that Blair simply espoused the Thatcher program, with but one exception: the National Health Service (NHS), which for the British comes after holiness and cleanliness, and which Thatcher actually had the gall to think of dismantling. The Laborite government of prime minister Clement Attlee had established the NHS. Fully in the Labor tradition, Blair was for keeping it. The NHS, incidentally, is free medical service which varies depending on area economic levels: staid, by-appointment-only surgeries, as generally in Wimbledon, to seedy, first-come-first-served, and don't-complain-too-much surgeries, as usually in Battersea.

Blair won by the biggest landslide in British history, which also probably means that the British had had it with the Conservatives' long permanence in power. When Bush called on Blair to join America's war on terror aimed at Iraq, Blair, who probably had to have an understanding of the vacuity of the phrase, did what political expertise suggested. He asked himself: what would Margaret have done? And the answer was clear as daylight. When the Argentine invaded the Falklands, Britain mounted a successful naval counteroffensive which would have been much more difficult without the American help it got. Thatcher could no more have said no to an American foreign policy initiative than she could stop looking the way she did. Blair said yes forthrightly.

(22) Being so close to Africa, Spaniards were unsure about their Europeanism

There was another staunch American ally from the beginning and that was the conservative Spanish government of Prime Minister Jose Maria Aznar. Spain was blackballed by the UN and by its democratic west European neighbors until the death of its dictator Francisco Franco, who gained power with the aid of Hitler and Mussolini. Franco's rule was harsh but not fascistic in the sense in which Hitler and Mussolini tried to make Germans and Italians docile to their respective parties. Franco had ties with the Falangist Party of Jose Antonio Primo de Rivera.[16] Falangism, from the Greek Phalanx, is only vaguely fascistic and Franco, apart from naming a main thoroughfare in every Spanish city after Primo de Rivera (usually "avenue or street Jose Antonio"), was not really keen on political parties of any sort and he let Falangism fall of its own weight.

The USA was never really unfriendly to Franco. But it couldn't very well be seen arm-in-arm with a former ally of Hitler and of Mussolini. Consequently, Spain had a hard time during the Post-War. When Franco died, Spain soon became a constitutional monarchy, although not before a mad-dog colonel of the Franco school took over Cortes with a platoon and spangled its ceiling with machine-gun bullets. Ironically, this breach of military discipline, which King Juan Carlos instantaneously reproved, did more than a million speeches to cement Spanish democracy and the monarchy. Spain was already emerging from its economic backwardness to full development status. Spain's political isolation was completely ended when she joined NATO and its economic achievements were rewarded with membership in the EU.

Because of their politically unstable 19th century and because of the problems they had during the 20th century—specially the 1936-

16 The name Falangism survived among a sector of Lebanese Christians. Some historians ascribe this to the Lebanese politician Pierre Gemayel's visit to Berlin during the 1936 Olympics and the admiration it instilled in him. Falangism did not have the extremely nationalist connotations of fascism or Nazism.

1939 Civil War—Spaniards had a collective complex about not being fully Europeans or about being part Africans. This last was in the metaphorical sense of foreignness, any part of Africa, and Spain is physically closer to Africa than any other European country, being of course culturally distinct from Europe.[17] For Spain joining NATO and the EU was essentially like being told: yes, fellows, you too are Europeans.

Since then, Spaniards have tried to live up to their Europeanness in as many ways as possible, perhaps most visibly in the person of Javier Solana, the virtual foreign minister of the EU. Solana speaks perfect if accented English, which always evokes wows of admiration from his own countrymen, the most monolingual people in Europe, after maybe the British. Felipe Gonzalez, the socialist prime minister who put Spain in the map of Europe, took his Europeanness casually. But his successor, Aznar, had the more awed attitude. Therefore, he was a cinch for eager compliance when Bush asked him to join the coalition against Iraq. However, Spaniards have by now gotten quite used to being Europeans and Aznar's alliance with America for war on Iraq was not appreciated by a majority of his countrymen, who might have thought that Aznar was overdoing the Spanish wanting-to-be-loved stance in the world.

---

17 There was also the historical fact that Spain had once been a mainly Islamic country known as Al Andalus. Islam had swept northern Africa during the 7th century. In 711, Arab-Berber forces under Tariq ibn Ziyad crossed from Morocco to Spain and in the equivalent of an early Medieval blitzkrieg destroyed the Visigothic Kingdom and drove its Christian rulers to the ramparts of Asturias and to the foothills of the Pyrenees. Representatives of the Damascus-based Umayyad caliphate ruled Muslim Spain. The Umayyads were overthrown and mostly killed by the Abbasids in 750. Abdul al Rahman, a survivor Umayyad, managed to reach Córdoba where he founded an emirate independent of the Abbasid Caliphate. Abdul al Rahman III in 929 proclaimed the caliphate of Córdoba. Under Christian pressure from Barcelona and from the kingdom of Navárre. The Córdoba caliphate broke up in 1031. Its disintegration engendered the Taifa Kingdoms. In 1035 Navarre broke up into Aragon, Castile, and Navarre. A Berber dynasty from southern Morocco, the Almoravids invaded Al Andalus and defeated a Christian army in 1086. The Almohads overthrew the Almoravids in 1150. By then Aragón was a flourishing kingdom and Castile was an aggressive state at the head of the Reconquista, the general name for the long war in which the Muslims were expelled from Iberia. Muslim domains were gradually reduced to the southern part of the Iberian Peninsula from Valencia to Lisbon. In 1212 Alfonso VIII of Castile defeated the Almohads in the decisive battle of Navas de Tolosa. Córdoba was lost in 1236. In 1238, Rodrigo Diaz de Vivar seized Valencia. With the conquest of Granada from Boabdil in 1492, Muslim Spain was ended.

(23) Germany must be a part of America's wars whether it likes it or not

Outside of Australia, Great Britain, and Spain, and of a string of other less vocal states, Bush's war was not getting much appreciation. China, which had abstained in the Security Council on the approval of even the Gulf war, was certainly not going to be in favor of a Second Iraqi war, and from the start it was known that it would use its veto power against it. Russia, which had fully supported the War on Afghanistan, was realistic enough to understand that war on Iraq wasn't going to get it extra points on the Chechen front, which only Russians and Chechens could roll up. Another veto could be expected from there. Basically, Putin and the Chinese didn't see the need for a war if the Iraqi problem could be resolved by diplomatic means.

This was the position adopted by President Jacques Chirac of France, supported generally by Europeans. It was also the one that was espoused by the great majority of countries. It could easily be seen that Bush's accusations were groundless, not that Saddam Hussein had many admirers anywhere, not even in the Arab world; and many people believed, as did some American servicemen at the start of the Second Iraqi War, that Bush the younger might have been trying to get even for his father, to finish his father's war, so to speak, although there is no indication that Bush senior considered such avenging necessary. France practically became the world spokesman for the anti-war, for-diplomacy stance, because it is not only a permanent member of the Security Council but also because it is a cornerstone of the EU, within which France and Germany were of one mind.

Behind the opposition of Germany, there is the unmentionable circumstance, in addition to the reasons it shared with France, that fifty-eight years after the end of World War II, it is still a partially occupied country. German autobahn used to have speed limits for tanks. The largest American foreign military bases are in Germany. They lodge troops in the tens of thousands and planes in the hundreds. In any war that America fought Germany would necessarily be involved.

Now, this was perfectly acceptable for Germans when the Russians deployed their SS-20 missiles. The USA was a necessary ally of Germany. The SS-20s along with the American Pershings were removed during the Gorbachev years. The communist menace to Germany was practically ended when the USSR allowed the two Germanys to merge. Under a strict strategic and foreign-relations rationale, there is no essential justification for maintaining American bases in Germany. Yet Germany is still apron-tied to America in case of warfare by America.

Warfare by Germany is almost inconceivable. Probably most Germans have no objections to the large American presence in their country despite the peace treaty between the two countries. But any sovereign state must feel constraints when it is obliged to be a forcible host to foreign soldiers on its soil. Apart from the principled opposition to the war on Iraq, then, Chancellor Gerhard Schroeder might also have been sending a subtle message to Washington that it might be time to re-negotiate the American military presence in his country. In September 2003, Schroeder discreetly proposed a permanent seat for Germany in the Security Council, another signal that it wanted to be shot of its former pariah state condition.

That Germany's message might have been implicit, however subtly, in the events leading to the actual war against Iraq, is suggested by the case of Japan, which is similar to Germany's. Unlike Schroeder, Japan's prime minister Junichiro Koizumi backed America to the hilt, although a few decibels less noisily than Aznar, and there was unconfirmed talk of America shutting down its controversial bases on the island of Okinawa, whose inhabitants suffered from last-ditch Japanese resistance in 1945 and probably felt then as victimized as non-Japanese by Japanese militarism.

(24) "Suiciders" make a gruesome difference

Sadly, the only way to measure success or failure in a war of attrition such as that between Israelis and Palestinians, especially one in which the people on one of the sides is visible and accessible to the enemy's firepower but cannot be accused of participating collectively in the struggle, is to do body counts. The significant loss of territory that Palestinians had been suffering since the time Sharon became minister of agriculture under Begin was one of the causes of the Intifadas but it wasn't part of the battlefield. It was just an imposition by Israelis on Palestinians to which the latter could have replied only if they had an army.

But the Intifadas were very peculiar wars, the likes of which had never perhaps been seen in history. Armies were not facing each other. But these weren't wars of resistance either, such as the maquis and the partisans during World War II. The Intifadas were as if Nazis were fighting uprisings in border zones of Germany where the resistance could strike at German civilians. Had the Nazis been involved they probably would have done various things: they could have shot so many hostages for each Israeli killed, civilian or military, or they could have rounded up Palestinians and put them in concentration camps, alternatively walling special areas and locking Palestinians inside them. The walling was in part already being done in Gaza. Elsewhere it was

Israelis who were walling themselves in against Palestinians. As to the execution of hostages, Israeli indiscriminate fire on Gaza or the West Bank in reprisal for Palestinian attacks became its virtual equivalent.

There were important historical differences. World War II had left its macabre heritage of mass slaughters. Jews collectively had been one of its victims. During the Intifadas, Israel was not fighting an enemy army, so its survival was not at stake. Israel would have brought the world upon its head, even American righteousness, if it used Nazi tactics openly. Thus, between September 2000 and March 2001 it was possible to have a ratio of five Palestinians killed to one Israeli, which was less lopsided than the counts at the end of the basically stone-throwing First Intifada when there were nearly seven Palestinians dead for each Israeli life lost. But that was before the suicide-bombers campaign, to which Israel responded by tightening its previous security measures, particularly increasing the pressure on Arafat without actually trying to kill him, which they of course could have.

The suiciders' offensive slackened but did not end and by June 2001 Israel had to strike against the West Bank again. Again Israeli reprisals had results. In August the conflict was experiencing a pause and it was possible, on the basis of information from the Red Crescent (the Muslim Red Cross), the Israeli government, and human rights organizations, to come up with the startling balance that there were between 1400 and 1705 Palestinian dead to between 566 and 610 Israeli dead (the latter mainly due to Palestinian suicide-bombers), or a ratio somewhere in the order of three to one.[18] The discrepancy in the Israeli body count is intriguing in that Judaic laws are very strict about recovering every bit of human remains, which casts some doubt on the reliability of these statistics.

The results in deaths to either side were due to Palestinian desperation over their military powerlessness and to relative Israeli restraint. But desperation is a no-alternative situation and restraint is an alternative. Israel could have, in sum, stepped up the price any time it wanted. Palestinian suicide bombings could not be planned with the precision of Israeli military operations, so for some days or even weeks it would seem as if they had been controlled only to have another big one or a whole rash of them. By September there had been two Israeli incursions in the West Bank and the noose on Arafat had been tightened twice. There was some deterrence effect, but the Intifada was not over when Bush got the support he really needed for the war on Iraq.

---

18 Molly Moore and John Ward Anderson, "Suicide bombers shift the military balance in the Mideast", IHT, August 19, 2002

(25) Donald and Colin had a bad cop-good cop routine going

During the second half of 2002, the highest American officials involved in a possible war with Iraq were busy making their case to potential allies and to critics, not only abroad but also at home, because support in Congress was not unanimous. The position of the USA was not exactly unambiguous. In order to persuade China, for example, Americans had to meet the Chinese demand that in the western province of Xinjiang, where Turkic Uigurs had been the majority in the past but were being swamped by Han Chinese, the Uigur opposition to Chinese rule was terroristic because of the occasional detonation. The USA conceded the point, even though the American attitude to Chinese rule in Tibet has been extremely critical. So how one could read this?

The Chinese government, which terrorized Tibetans, was itself being terrorized by the Uigurs, whose cultural and political rights were being trampled by the Chinese? Who, in the balance, were the real terrorists, the Chinese communist juggernaut or the more or less feeble resistance of a people who represented much less than one percent of the entire population of China?[19] If state terrorism was the norm in Tibet, what name did the Israeli repression of Palestinians deserve? And if Uigurs were terrorists, was China justified in attacking them with its army, the way the Israelis did to Palestinians? Whether mentioned publicly or not, the American campaign for war on Iraq had around its neck the albatross of the Palestinian issue. The Chinese got what they wanted but they did not back down on their position on Iraq.

---

19 The Uigurs were a Turkic nation leading a nomadic life in Junggar and Mongolia during the 6th century CE. In 603, the Uigurs rebelled against their overlords, the Tujue, the first historical Turks, with whom they remained at odds until in 741 they decisively defeated them in Mongolia. The Uigur capital was Karabalgasun, on the Orkhon river valley. Around 840, another Turkic people, the Kirghiz, invaded Mongolia from Siberia and overwhelmed the Uigurs, who retreated to the Tarim basin. Despite being the most culturally advanced of the many Turkic peoples at that time, the Uigurs did not manage to create a unified state, although the Tarim after their occupation became known as Uiguria and is still referred to as Chinese Turkestan (modern Xinjiang). The former Sogdiana, known to the Arabs as Murannawarh, was Turkicized and Islamic and the Uigurs too became Muslims (10th-12th centuries). With the final defeat of the Tibetan Xixia (modern Ningxia in China) by the Mongols (1226), Uiguria became part of the Mongol Empire. When the Mongol Chaghataite khanate gradually dissolved (16th century), Uiguria became a mosaic of Muslim theocracies. The Oirats or Western Mongols invaded Uiguria and as far as Tibet in the 17th century. The history of the Tarim Basin after that is mostly of Chinese encroachment until the Qing definitely established Chinese authority over the region (1759). Through emigration the ethnic Chinese or Han have become a majority in Xinjiang.

Secretary of defense Donald Rumsfeld, not a loveable public personality, was the hatchet man on France. He not only spoke openly of the French beyond the limits of politeness, but also appeared to have such a grudge that, even after Bush declared the war ended, rumors against France, especially that it had been a secret ally of Saddam Hussein, were being attributed to the Pentagon. It appeared as if had Rumsfeld had his way, the USA would have gone to war against Iraq before it did. There were no real grounds for thinking that the younger Bush wanted to "avenge" his father. But Rumsfeld's sense of urgency was so marked that it really did seem as if he were trying to compensate for his previous role as the man who brought America and Iraq together.

None of this spoke highly of America's leadership in the unipolar world. Both support for Saddam Hussein, the known dictator and unscrupulous killer of Kurds and Shiites, and intense detestation for the same dictator, seemed to be opportunistic and reactive, not what you would expect of a steady hand at the helm of the global ship. Statesmanship it wasn't. Colin Powell was put in charge of that department. There were only unconfirmed reports that he tried to restrain Rumsfeld, so basically what these two characters had going was an international bad cop-good cop routine. If there was ever any equivocation about the possibility of war on Iraq, it was purely speculative, for president Bush was palpably and unwaveringly for it.

Colin Powell might have been the instigator of going to the UN for international support. But he seemed to expect from this no more than the effect that reading the warning on cigarette packs would have on a hardened smoker. Taking the American case to the Security Council could hardly be considered a seriously threatening end run by Powell against a solid scrimmage line of war-mongering behemoths. In retirement, Powell has admitted that he considers a "blot" on his record the false statements he had to make at the UN about Iraqi WMD, for which he faults the intelligence he was being fed.

Bush and his top men had decided on war and no one, not France, not China, not Russia, and least of all the UN, would change that; but it was still better to go through the paces of trying to obtain a surrender from Saddam Hussein, as likely to happen as that Bush would have a change of heart. Besides, it was on the understanding that the USA would first go to the UN for support that the White House and the Congress, particularly the Senate, where Democrats had a slim majority, agreed on the conditions for war as well as on restrictions on the American use of force. That was the ground on which the debate was to proceed. This was happening in September and October 2002.

(26) Bush gets the go for war

The war on Iraq was part of the war on terror. The War on Afghanistan was the first episode in this struggle of world-historical dimensions. War on Iraq was to be the second episode. Bush's axis of evil had not included Afghanistan, but it did include Iran and especially North Korea. You could sooner expect a South Pole meltdown than a North Korean gesture of reasonableness. In the American view of things, Iraq for sure had WMD, even though even the USA had to admit that they weren't in view, which, on the other hand, was just what one would expect from deceitful Iraqis. But North Korea did have a nuclear plant in a place called Yongbyon (northwestern Korea) and it also had missiles. The Korean communist government had built Yongbyon in full sight of the world in 1994. It was intended as an uranium-using energy generator. But its residue was plutonium, the raw material for nuclear bombs.

According to Kim Young San, president of South Korea from 1993 to 1998, President Clinton was ready for a pre-emptive strike at Yongbyon when Kim talked him out of it with the not negligible argument that North Korea could retaliate against South Korea by firing at Seoul missiles and artillery it had concealed in mountain emplacements. Clinton desisted. At the time, North Korea was already experiencing food-production difficulties and famines were to be expected. In exchange for mothballing Yongbyon, it was offered aid in the form of fuel and food supplies.

When the USA was claiming in the UN what a great threat Iraq was, North Korea, as if on cue, bragged about how it had not discontinued its nuclear program. If Bush was incensed over Iraq, the North Korean admission should have provoked conniptions. But it didn't. Aid to North Korea was curtailed and a few months later some long-range bombers were sent to Guam. North Korea responded by backing out of the nuclear non-proliferation treaty. In realistic terms, the whole idea of axis of evil was turned on its ahead with America making ready to go to war against an unlikely possessor of nuclear weapons, Iraq, while another member of the axis of evil, North Korea, was admitting publicly that it could very well possess nuclear weapons in the near future, if it didn't already have them.[19] Was this really a war on terror, whatever that was? Or was it a "war against evil", another poser? Or was it just a war against a dictator for whom Bush had it in regardless of the consequences?

19 Don Kirk, "North Korea says publicly it needs a 'nuclear deterrence'", IHT, June 10, 2003.

(27) As soon as it got the fig-leaf resolution for a possible war on Iraq, the USA tried to change the rules of the game in the Security Council

Expressing a minority viewpoint, Maureen Dowd wrote on 13 March 2003: "It still confuses Americans that in a world of slime balls, the US is about to bomb one that didn't attack on 9/11." But on Iraq a clear majority of the minority of Americans who vote in congressional elections apparently was in step with Bush's weaving on international issues. When elections were held in November 2002, the party of the presidential incumbent increased its representation in both houses of Congress. The crucial issue was war or peace. American voters demonstrated that they were definitely for war and not confused at all as Dowd said. They weren't taking any chances that Democrats would become a hindrance to Bush's war on terror.

With this endorsement in hand, Powell went back to the UN for a resolution for war. The opponents to war as the only alternative had not changed their minds, adding more fuel to the American distrust of the UN, and the USA was forced to compromise. The compromise was called Security Council Resolution 1441. It called for a collective declaration of war on Iraq, as in the Gulf War, if it did not comply with arms inspections to determine how founded were America's suspicions that it possessed WMD. The inspectors had to present a report not later than 17 March 2003.

This was the doing of Powell the good cop. But a good cop is a cop all the same and as soon as he got the fig-leave resolution for possible war, Powell began toying with the rules of the game. The USA started acting on the assumption that to carry a resolution in the Security Council only a simple majority was required. It also assumed that 17 March was not a deadline for a report on whether war did or did not proceed, but a deadline for war period. It seemed as if America and her ally Britain were not going to war right away because basically they were not yet ready to do so and not because they really wanted or cared for UN approval.

But in the air the war had already started. The USA and the UK began war against Iraq (operation Southern Focus) in June 2002, according to an assessment of Gen. Michael Moseley, the chief allied air war commander during the Second Iraqi war. In his statements in July 2003, Gen. Moseley said that 606 bombs had been dropped on 391 selected targets. In all, about 1,800 aircraft conducted 21,736 sorties against southern Iraq. Secretary of defense Rumsfeld approved all these attacks, which were justified as aiming to disable illegal anti-aircraft defenses. By the time the actual war started, Iraq had virtually no means of self-defense.[20]

(28) The good cop makes the UN increasingly irrelevant

Powell's implicit, one-sided modification of the decision-making procedure in the Security Council took guts. It broke with not just a tradition at the UN but with a fundamental rule of the organization. Close to the end of World War II at San Francisco, it was agreed that the UN would not be saddled with the inability under which the League of Nations labored of not having the power to act militarily. The charter of the UN accepted the principle that the new organization could wage war to contain war and that it could recruit soldiers from its members to enforce peace. But it was never a question of leaving this decision to the universally representative General Assembly, because this forum contained too many small powers, some with no power at all, that could vote for the soldiers of the big powers to fight for them.

Such an arrangement was unworkable and would soon have torn the organization apart. It also might have been foreseen then that the UN would shortly be inundated by independent ex-colonies with primitive political cultures. Therefore, it was decided to have a small body, the Security Council, entrusted with the decision on the military operations that the UN could carry out.

The Security Council would be composed of five permanent members, the five great powers at the end of the war, upon whose unanimous decision the UN could or could not act. The USSR would not have accepted anything less than unanimity. In the League of Nations unanimity was required at the assembly and in the UN unanimity was required of only five states, still a hurdle but not a barrier. Unanimity meant that any of the five permanent members had in effect the right of veto on decisions by the Security Council. Three of the five permanent members were self-evidently entitled to seats in the Security Council: the UK, the USSR, and the USA as the victors in the war. China was a victor because the others were but China was the largest nation in the world and so it was also included.

France was not a victor at all, but by recruiting here and there all over the world, the Free French led by Gen. Charles de Gaulle consisted of 300,000 troops, a minuscule force compared to the big Allies, but still a sizable army. Also, everyone knew that France freed from trammels to its sovereignty could emulate the other powers. France, for instance, had

20 Michael R. Gordon, "U.S. started attacking Iraqi air defenses in mid-2002", IHT, 7 July 2003

the potential to develop atomic bombs in short order and you did not want to have a nuclear power outside the Security Council. So France too went in as a permanent member. Finally, to placate the rest of the world and as not to make the UN seem like a club of five, it was also decided that the Security Council would include ten non-permanent member states to be rotated every two-years on an approximately regional basis. These ten additional members did not have the right of veto.

The UN worked because of the Security Council. Stalin would have tried to choke it at birth if it hadn't been for the veto. America would not have joined either without the veto. Before the Gulf War, the Korean War was the greatest conflict the UN had participated in. It was an anti-communist move and the resolution for war was rushed through at a time the Soviet representative was boycotting the Security Council because it had not ceded the Chinese seat, held by Taiwan, to the Maoist government in Beijing. Thus the USSR did not have a chance to exercise its veto power.

When it came to the Second Iraqi war the USA was willing to forego sacrosanct veto power for a simple majority in the Security Council. This was a one-side abrogation of the spirit and the letter of UN law. It went against the grain and made America seem reckless and bullying in the unipolar role it had in the world. But even America's attempt to bust the UN charter would be of any avail.

(29) A frowning Powell said that Iraq had dangerous drones and the Iraqis dutifully carted out a cardboard-and-glue caricature with two engines the size of grass whackers

With the approval of Resolution 1441, the UN gathered a team of arms inspectors, headed by the Swede Hans Blix, whose credentials must have been satisfactory to the USA or he wouldn't even have gotten the job, and Iraq was told to open its doors to full inspection or bear with the consequences. Iraq was so aware of what would ensue if it refused to comply that it accepted all UN terms without even trying to amend them or raising objections of any kind. When the inspectors arrived, they went wherever whenever they wanted, even catching Iraqi soldiers by surprise with only minor delays in opening gates, even to Hussein's presidential palace, which had been the cause of the Iraqi termination of the first inspection campaign. The indications were that Iraq was cooperating fully with every demand of the arms inspectors. In addition to giving access to premises, it handed over a list of 500 Iraqi scientists who could have been involved in weapons production. It also turned over an inventory of its arsenal.

Back in the UN, American diplomacy was urgently trying to put together a majority of the Security Council members. Every report of Iraqi cooperation with the inspectors was scoffed at by American diplomats, often by Bush himself, as just another form of deception, which was as if the police had a suspect incriminating himself and they kept saying he was lying. Another transparent maneuver was that American functionaries and spokesmen were assuming, as if the rest of mankind should also have assumed it, that an UN declaration of non-compliance by Iraq was inevitable. But that simply was not the case. And it wasn't, because Blix and his team declared that, although they were far from having finished their job, they had not found evidence of a threatening Iraqi weapons program.

The long and the short of it was that the USA had already decided on war, with Blair tagging along, and the UN resolution and the stipulated inspection were all part, as far as the USA was concerned, of a mime routine. The farcical side of the affair was made evident—although there was no public guffawing—when a frowning Powell said that Iraq had dangerous drones and the Iraqis dutifully carted out a cardboard and glue caricature with two engines the size of Grass Whackers. The great "aha!" were some Iraqi rockets barely outside permitted range, which the Iraqis began to bulldoze in January 2003?

(30) Rumsfeld was decidedly not only the bad cop but also the obtuse cop

Despite its best efforts, the USA wasn't getting anywhere near a majority in the Security Council. Pakistan, a mainstay in the Afghan war, said it wasn't convinced by the American case. Bulgaria, which had recently been accepted as a candidate for membership in NATO, and could therefore have scored points with the USA, also demurred. The unkindest cut of all was given by Turkey, on whom the USA was relying as a base for operations in northern Iraq.

Turkey's request to be given a date of accession to the EU had been answered with a mumbled "sometime in the future". The USA was a strong backer of the Europeanization of Turkey. The moderate Islamist government of Turkey was bent on demonstrating that despite cultural differences it deserved to enter the EU. So the Turkish government had every interest in keeping on the good side of America, and America was trying to make sure of that by offering Turkey billions of dollars in economic aid. The hitch was that Turks almost unanimously condemned the war on Iraq, and the Turkish parliament, which reflected that opinion, voted not only against joining the anti-Iraq coalition but as well against even allowing American forces the use of Turkey's airspace. When

Rumsfeld was told about this he shot back: "They did what?" Rumsfeld was decidedly not only the bad but also the obtuse cop. Powell did not seem quite that obtuse, so the routine was not really good-cop-bad-cop but dumb-cop-smart-cop.

In America, the only forthright opposition to the war by a major politician came from the last of the Kennedy dynasts, Senator Edward Kennedy, who said that the war was wrong and that it wasn't the way to fight terrorism.[21] Over time, whereas Edward once was the family's black sheep and the other two Kennedys were the knights in shining armor, albeit priapic, Edward has become one of the most respected politicians in the country's contemporary history, a liberal without demurrals and a man who often stands alone strictly on principle.

Something tragic happened that normally should have given pause to wonder whether America was getting everything right, but which probably strengthened the collective support for war: the shuttle Columbia burned up as it returned from space on 2 February. The current scenario for this accident is that a tile of insulating foam from the shuttle's front fuselage had come off during take off and struck back making a tiny puncture on the leading edge of the left wing through which plasma or white-hot atmospheric gas went in on re-entry leaching the foil inside and causing the destruction of the shuttle and the death of its nine occupants.

Columbia's demise makes the shuttle the unsafest mode of transportation in history: two flights missing out of less than 120, with 14 dead in all.[22] Although in national tragedies such as this one there is understandable hesitation about finger pointing, many suspected that the causes were under funding for NASA and overconfidence in NASA itself about flight risks. That the shuttles are unsafe can be observed in footages of launchings in which the heat-resistant tiles fly off like a mis-shuffled pack of cards.

(31) Bush's obsession with Iraq was like a bull ignoring a bevy of red capes to charge a dying matador

The USA went on maneuvering on the assumption that a majority of the Security Council was still feasible for a resolution of war against Iraq regardless of the inspectors' report. Blix let it be known that his team would probably not have concluded its work before 17 March, but that it was still trying to find the weapons that Bush and company

21 "Kennedy says Bush wants wrong war at wrong time", IHT, January 23, 2003.

22 "Space shuttle mission chronology", at www-pao.ksc.nasa.gov/chron. There have been a total of 21 deaths in space accidents.

insisted Hussein had. The USA persisted in that 17 March was the date not for another debate on Iraq's culpability but the deadline for Iraq to give up, which concretely involved Saddam Hussein's resignation and the peaceful occupation of Iraq by USA-UK forces.

The pretence of war against WMD was again shown up when the North Koreans launched a shore-to-ship missile practically before the echo of another one of Powell's denunciations had died down. The USA versus Iraq confrontation was like a bullfight in which a bull is shown a bevy of provocative red capes and the animal refuses to take notice and charges instead the gored matador bleeding on the ground.

The South Korean government was giving the American cause lip service—there too majority opinion was overwhelmingly against war—but it was still for negotiations with its boorish northern brother. Was Kim Jong IL trying to get Saddam Hussein off the hook? Or was he just being his normal ornery self? Whatever it was, Bush was playing the anti-terrorist, anti-evil hero but he certainly wasn't keeping to the obvious priorities of his axis-of-evil doctrine, which made one think that maybe he was just playing the hero for the olé-ing home crowd.

It was late in the day for changes of plans anyway. France announced that it would also veto an UN declaration of war on Iraq. Coming from a long time Cold War ally, this was much more grievous than the threatened Chinese and Russian vetoes. It provoked great American indignation and it ignited in Congress the controversy that resulted in the renaming of French fries as "freedom fries". For some reason, despite the German opposition to the anti-Iraqi campaign, there was no such anger about frankfurters or hamburgers.

(32) There was a hint of hysteria in Bush's claim that Hussein was a threat to American suburbanites

On 11 March, UN Secretary General Kofi Annan, who got his job through decisive American support (because of decisive American rejection of the previous secretary general, the Egyptian Boutros Boutros-Ghali), declared that war on Iraq without an UN resolution would be a contravention of the UN charter. The Americans ignored Annan as if he was some harebrained expert on aliens. They accused Blix of underplaying the Iraqi threat. Theoretically, that made him an accomplice of Hussein.

The invasion forces were in a state of readiness and it was inconceivable that the USA would back down. The situation was reminiscent of the Prussian Gen. Helmuth von Moltke's situation when he ordered German mobilization for World War I and admitted he would have preferred going to war even if the chance of peace came up because of the complexity of drawing up new mobilization plans.

The last act of the drama leading to war was Bush saying, with a hysterical edge in his voice, that Iraq was a direct threat to America's streets. He followed that up with the flat statement that the USA was going to war against Iraq come hell or high water, which made the 17 March deadline totally meaningless. In fact, it made the UN superfluous.

In Britain, Blair survived a rebellion in Labor ranks. You could discern reminiscences of Margaret Thatcher in the unanimous backing he got from Conservatives. Blair knew that the Iraqi threat was bunko. He laid stress on Hussein as a despicable tyrant, which raised the issue of all the other "slime balls" mentioned by Dowd. But Blair endeavored to demonstrate that Hussein was in a class of his own, which wasn't a very convincing argument either but it made Blair look humanitarian, better than Bush at least. When he and Bush held a news conference together and were asked who the other allies in the coalition were, Bush's answer was in essence: "I don't have time for this. Ask my secretary for a list". Blair tried to be somewhat more condescending.

The 17 March deadline for whatever came and went and war had not been declared. As a final "peace gesture" Bush gave Hussein another chance to leave Iraq. Hussein told him to stick it and on 19 March the attack order was given. The Americans had the good idea of taking Hussein out and they sent out Stealth bombers with MOABs (huge 900 kgs. bombs) and Tomahawk cruise missiles against a site in south Baghdad where Hussein and his sons Uday and Qusay were supposedly staying. The target was hit. American and British forces rapidly moved from Kuwait into Iraq.

When the Second Iraqi War started the real war on terrorism had been going on in other ways and in other places. Also, there had been no respite in the Israeli-Palestinian struggle. Despite the seeming finality of the War on Afghanistan, mainly due to lack of press coverage, which went to wherever the American government shifted its focus, the country was hardly pacified. From the end of 2001 to early 2003, there had been twelve major offensives against Taliban and presumably al Qaida recalcitrants. These operations usually involved some 800 to 1,000 American soldiers and anti-terror operatives. In response, Kabul was being regularly hit by scattered rocket attacks.

In this continuing low-level struggle, the death toll on the American side was around fifty and growing. In February 2003, American and Afghan soldiers launched Operation Anaconda, which was in response to attacks in southern Afghanistan. Two USA soldiers were reported killed in March. These figures are in themselves not very impressive, but one must put them in a historical context, which includes the American evacuation of Somalia.

The most significant blow against al Qaida was the capture by Pakistani police of Khalid Shaikh Mohammad, reportedly a member of the highest leadership echelon, possibly even one of the planners of 9/11. As he was caught without resistance in his home in Peshawar it is possible that he was a burnt-out case. The betting was that, if anything, despite the commitment of the Pakistani government to America's war on terror, the resistance to the American presence in Afghanistan and perhaps even the survival of Osama bin Laden himself were possible because of grass-roots Pakistani connivance. In early May 2003, Walid Ba'Attash, like bin Laden a Saudi of Yemeni parentage, also considered a high al Qaida operative, was captured by Pakistani security forces in Karachi.

(33) Israel deliberately and unequivocally chooses a hard line against Palestinians

At the time that Bush got the mandate he wanted from the American electorate for the Iraqi phase of the war on terror, there was a recrudescence of Palestinian terrorist attacks. The Al Aqsa Martyrs' Brigade and Hamas claimed most of the suicide bombings. The American press was punctilious in pointing out that Al Aqsa was a branch of Arafat's Fatah organization, even though, one, Arafat was no longer primarily head of Fatah but president of the PA, and two, whatever his official position, the Israeli chokehold on his Ramallah quarters meant that he was hardly in a position to command anything, least of all a suicide-bent terrorist. An Israeli count of suicide attacks showed that Hamas mostly perpetrated them.

The Israeli reaction to this wave of Palestinian attacks was implacable. The body-count strategy came fully into play and during November and December 2002. For nineteen dead Israelis there were 32 Palestinians killed. Gaza was converted from a pro forma to an effective concentration camp, so much so that Palestinians who were suspected of terrorist sympathies and extended families of known terrorists were "exiled" to Gaza after their homes in the West Bank had been demolished. During early 2003, while the Palestinians scored a large terrorist suicide attack that left 23 dead, Israeli troops killed 36 Palestinians.

The numbers still seemed much less lopsided than those of the First Intifada, but the truth was that Israel had the offensive. Israeli soldiers struck at will anywhere they wanted in Palestinian territories. Israeli commanders chose their targets, not haphazardly as the Palestinians forcibly had to, but according to plans, and these now called for liquidating the clandestine leadership of the terrorist groups. America looked on and occasionally told the Israelis to go easy, but both Sharon and Netanyahu rejected half-hearted American peace plans. Arafat made calls on Palestinians to stop targeting civilians, which Israelis described as hypocritical since the rationale of the confrontation dictated that Arafat had to be directing the attacks on Israel.

Unable to keep together a coalition that included Labor, Sharon dissolved the Knesset and called for elections. The Labor Party chose Amram Mitzna as its candidate for primer minister. Mayor of Haifa and a former general, Mitzna was favorable to negotiations with the Palestinians and the end of settlements. In February 2003, Labor suffered a total electoral rout and Sharon's Likud gained seats. Although there wasn't an outright endorsement of Sharon, mainly because of the finicky proportionality of electoral representation, this was the third time—the fourth if we count Barak's victory—that Israel had deliberately and unequivocally chosen a hardline against Palestinians.

With two electoral triumphs under his belt, Sharon made perfectly clear, and it was tacitly accepted by American authorities, that he would not negotiate with Arafat under any circumstances. As Israel had in effect roped in the Palestinians, these had little choice but to follow Israeli dictates, and so it was that the PA, or whatever was left of it, created the post of prime minister, in theory independent of Arafat's presidency. The Second Intifada was not over. Terrorism, as could be seen in Afghanistan, has a habit of recurring. But between walls and reprisals and its other tactical advantages, Israel had near-control of the situation. This was in effect the way things stood on the day the Second Iraqi War started.

(34) The Second Iraqi war left little room for war's manic-depressive syndrome

Wars impose a sort of manic-depressive syndrome on observers. During the Gulf war it was Saddam Hussein who said the "mother of all battles". He coined a phrase that was in vogue for a time in America. Despite the self-evident technological disparity, some believed that Iraq could actually hold back an invader that bombed the country at will, equipped its soldiers with night-vision goggles, and had tanks that fired heat-seeking missiles. Reality soon set in and those that had been hoping for an Iraqi surprise felt at least a tinge of depression, even if rationally they had no cause to. After all, it was Hussein who had started the war, it was he that got himself and his people in difficulties, it was he who was ultimately responsible for the heaps of corpses rotting under the desert sun, but it was President Bush who had sheathed the sword.

The persistent brutality of the Hussein clan became glaring after the Gulf war was over, when it was too late to re-kindle hostilities. When the Iraqis attacked the Kurds during the war, the order to use gas was imparted by a cousin of Saddam Hussein, Gen. Ali Hassan al Majeed or Majid, who thus earned for himself the sobriquet of "Chemical Ali". At the end of the war, the Kurds again rebelled. A spare-no-one campaign in the north, called Anfal and led by Majid, killed at least 100,000 Kurds, by Majid's own admission, according to Arab sources. To Majid, whose military command was in Basra, is also attributed the repression of Shiites in southern Iraq.

Besides, and any objective observer had this clear back in 1991, if Saddam Hussein was a dictator who could gas Kurds in the thousands, well, Turkey was not exactly being conciliatory with its own much more numerous Kurds, with greater grievances than Iraqi Kurds. The Turks' excuse was that Kurds were really Turks who happened to speak a language totally unrelated to Turkish. At least the Iraqis didn't make such inherently absurd claims. Their reason was that they weren't going to let Kurds tear their country apart. But was it their country? The Kurds certianly wanted no part of it. Unfortunately, the Kurdish case for independence was weak both in Turkey and in Iraq: they had never been a sovereign people and were as wont to fight each other as to fight Turks and Arabs. During the Gulf War, that on some issues Iraq had a case made some people first irrationally hopeful then irrationally despondent.

On the Second Iraqi war two things were certain: one, Saddam Hussein was an obdurate and incorrigible tyrant; two, if Iraq seemed to have a glimmer of a chance in the Gulf war, solely on account of Hussein's bragging, it had none whatsoever the second time around. It was the anti-Iraq coalition this time that was doing the bragging about bringing down Hussein in no time flat, mainly because of expectations about Iraqis rising up against the tyrant, and it was the Iraqi government that was being modest about its chances of survival.

In all, the "official" war lasted 23 days. If it had been Nazi Germany attacking, it would have been over in a week. The American-British coalition took its time about its operations, probably in part to avoid causing undue civilian casualties. But observers who were enthusiastic for the war went into a fit of depression and even talked of a "morass" when coalition troops were not inside Baghdad within two days. The military were genuinely surprised that they were being resisted not only by the Iraqi army but also by fedayin militia. This could mean that there was popular support for Saddam Hussein and the Baath party. It left no doubt that the invaders were unwanted.

(35) Iraq "butchered" soldiers and American bombs killed only enemy troops except for the odd ally who got in the way

There is no reason to believe that the invasion did not go according to plan. The oilfields in southern Iraq, a number one objective, were immediately secured. The Iraqis had not set the wells ablaze as they had in the Kuwaiti oilfields during the Gulf War. Saddam Hussein appeared on Iraqi TV on 24 March. Within six days, the Americans had secured bridges over the Euphrates river, which the Iraqis had not destroyed either. In the north, the greatest fear was a sub-war between Turks and Kurds, but Turkey acted with restraint and the Americans parachuted a brigade near Arbil, mainly to support or oversee the Kurdish militias.

By 6 April, Baghdad was encircled. The following day the British occupied Basra. The battle for Baghdad lasted about five days. According to rumors, Saddam Hussein was last seen alive in the sector of northern Baghdad known as Adhamiya, a Baathist redoubt. By 10 April, American losses were officially 101 killed and 390 wounded. Iraqi losses were impossible to estimate, because basically no one was counting. The war was virtually over when Mosul, the largest city in northern Iraq, fell without a fight on 11 April, as did Tikrit two days later, where resistance was expected because it was Hussein's birthplace and the base for a unit of Republican Guards.

Baghdad was in a lawless state. American forces, presumably, were spread out securing the rest of the oil fields and responding to fire wherever it erupted. The Baghdad Museum was sacked and, for unknown reasons, the national library was burned to cinders, although valuable manuscripts had been stored elsewhere by the Baathist regime. American coverage of the war was of the sort in which Iraq "butchered" soldiers, which was false as the soldiers in question were found safe and sound, and American bombs killed only enemy troops, which was not true at all, for there were British casualties from "friendly" American fire. President Bush declared the Second Iraqi war officially over on 1 May 2003. In fact, it had hardly commenced.

The balance of the war till then was as brief as its duration. Iraq was wiped out as a country. Its economy was mauled. Much of the population was living in precarious conditions, far worse than before the war. Neil Mac Gregor, director of the British museum, declared that the looting of Iraqi museums was the worst calamity to befall any national art collection since World War II. There was an American civilian administration whose head, L. Paul Bremer 3rd, blamed Iraq's straits on the UN. The reasoning behind this seemed to be that the Security Council had not immediately lifted the sanctions on Iraq, but the USA had as much to do with this as any other country. The Iraqis were now "officially" free. Officially, in fact, everything was hunky-dory. UN sanctions were removed on 21 May.

An important result of the war was that president Bush did appear to have achieved closure for 9/11. He was exultant. It was arranged that, duly suited and helmeted, he land in a slowish warplane on a carrier that, according to David Barry's relative exaggeration, was docked in San Diego. To say that the Second Iraqi war had farcical elements would not be overdoing it. The farce included the hardly comic implication that Bush was already on campaign for re-election in 2004. Part of the over-all spectacle was that, according to polls, Tony Blair had a higher popularity rating than Bush among Americans.

(36) The specter of nuclear was out of its purgatory

Bush's satisfaction had an interesting and ironical consequence: the original, purely America SDI was quietly buried. On 24 May, a presidential "directive" stated that the anti-missile shield had really been conceived to forestall extortion from "rogue states" with long-range missiles and that it should consist in a cooperative effort between America and its allies. One glaring reason for shelving SDI was that occupying Iraq would be costing $3.9 billion per month during the first nine months. Budget deficits, due to tax cuts, were estimated at one trillion dollars over five years. The state of the American economy was also engendering deficits. State and local governments had surpluses until 2000, after which they began having significant deficits, according to statistics of the government Bureau of Economic Analysis.[23]

The most visible reference of the presidential directive was to North Korea, which possessed such weapons and on 18 April had reiterated that it was busy working to produce nuclear bombs. Also worrying was that the American military had traded SDI for the development of low-yield or tactical nuclear weapons, plans for which had been on hold for years but which now were to be re-activated for their possible use against such threats as were posed, presumably, by North Korea and Iran. The specter of nuclear war was out of its purgatory again.

President Mohammad Khatami of Iran, the moderate on whose shoulders the hope for anti-fundamentalist reforms in Iran rested, had perforce to respond to America's aggressive stance. On 15 May, he expressed his country's support for Hizbollah, Israel's Shia bête noire in

23 David Firestone and Thom Shanker, "Rise in U.S. costs in Iraq surprises Democrats", IHT, July 12, 2003; Edmund L. Andrews, "Budget forecast puts deficit at $1 trillion", IHT, March 27, 2003.

South Lebanon, also blacklisted by the USA. On 8 June, the UN International Atomic Energy Agency (IAEA) confirmed reports by the Iranian opposition that Iran was constructing new nuclear facilities on 8 June. Instead of taming the "rogue states", Bush had made the other two more dangerous, and one at least, North Korea, madder and more defiant. So much for war on Iraq as a step forward in the war on terror!

(37) The case of the missing WMD

The USA had attacked Iraq for two crucial reasons at least: one, to eliminate the threat that Iraq posed as a terrorist state with WMD; two, to overthrow Saddam Hussein and confer on Iraqis the gift of democracy. Democracy for Iraq was still far out at sea. There were in Iraq at war's end what in the American south after the Civil War were called carpetbaggers, but their political chances were not clear.

As would have been expected, there were reports such as: "Graves yields Saddam's victims", "Saddam kept up bloodbath until three weeks before the war", "Families comb Iraqi killing fields", and so on. By this logic, the USA should have been faulted for not taking over in Sierra Leone or Liberia, or for not having invaded Chile and Argentina during their respective "dirty wars". In those countries too, many skulls were dug out and photographed. Why, carrying things to an extreme, that there had not been a nuclear attack on the USSR while America still could do it with impunity, was also morally indefensible. The hoard of skulls would have reached the tip of the Empire State Building.

As dictators go, historically speaking, Saddam Hussein was relatively run of the mill. There is every indication that the Iraqi dictator knew he was doomed. Iraqi military resistance was like a weak reflex. There was talk of corruption. But Hussein's "loot" was supposedly recovered intact in Iraq and in the Baath party headquarters $656 million were reportedly found (out of which four American soldiers were caught commandeering some $900,000).[24] Despite the odium that Hussein provoked, it was remotely possible that he actually promoted in his primitive and violent way the progressive program of Baathism.

The other objectives of the Second Iraqi War were the WMD and the USA military began scouring for them as soon as the war hostilities were over. For days on end there was silence. Probably most every body knew that the war on Iraq was not really about improbable WMD. But questions had to be asked. The world could not be treated to the spectacle of gratuitous American aggression and still be expected to wave American flags.

---

24 Timothy L. O'Brien, "U.S. recovers $950 million in assets stolen from Iraq", NYT, 15 May 2003

A top Iraqi scientist, who surrendered, Amir Saadi, declared that Iraq had no WMD. The Americans countered with an anonymous Iraqi scientist—he feared unexplained reprisals—who could testify that Iraq had destroyed its WMD, from which category by now nuclear weapons had been expunged as too unbelievable while retaining chemical and biological weapons. The anonymous scientist explained that the finest American toothcomb wouldn't have been able to find even traces of the Iraqi weapons. He also obligingly denounced an Iraq-al Qaida connivance. Not long after, the al Qaida leaders captured by the Pakistanis separately declared that Osama bin Laden wouldn't have deigned to make an alliance with Saddam Hussein. Nissar Hindawi, who said he had been active in it in the 1980s and intermittently in the 1990s, gave the closest to some evidence that Iraq had an anthrax program.

The simple fact was that the invaders had not found WMD in Iraq. Weeks after the USA victory, President Bush was saying that he still felt "in his heart" that the Iraqis' WMD would be found. It shows something about media objectivity that he was quoted with a straight face. Bush's final word was that it would take a "long time" to find the WMD. Then Rumsfeld came out with a routine satirized by the Washington Post cartoonist Toles. "Rumsfeld: Maybe the Iraqis disposed of their WMD just before they were caught with them. Or maybe they had a system to create them just in time for when they'd be needed. One reporter to another: Where does he get ideas like these? Reporter to Rumsfeld: What happened to the assertion that Iraq already had WMD? Rumsfeld: We disposed of that just before we were caught with it. Reporter: And these new theories? Rumsfeld: We created them just-in-time for when they were needed."

It became so obvious that there was no excuse for the Second Iraqi war that pre-war Pentagon reports on WMD were said to be fabricated. Their author denied this. Blix however said that all the information he got from American sources on the location of WMD was wrong. The fact practically leaped at you, from the beginning to the end of the war, that there was no excuse for it because there simply was no Iraqi WMD. And Bush and Rumsfeld and the rest of the inner circle, including Powell, knew this to be the case.

Of the false claims made for waging war, only one became the subject of strong controversy and that was Bush's assertion that Iraq had been trying to purchase uranium in Africa. The reason for the headlines was that the "tip" had come from Blair and Blair was under fire because a government expert on WMD had committed suicide after being identified as a source of a commentary on the BBC that the British government was "sexing up" reports on Iraq's WMD capability.[25]

(38) If America had been willing to destroy Iraq, what could Palestinians expect?

While Bush feted his allies in his ranch in Crawford, Texas, and wore a look of supreme self-confidence, terrorism reared up again. In Riyadh, nine suicide bombers struck killing dozens. That almost a third of the dead were the terrorists could mean than terrorism was in a circle consuming itself. But could one be certain? Was the end of Saddam Hussein and the occupation of Iraq really a victory in the war on terror? A crucial litmus test was the Israeli-Palestinian conflict.

One of the unmentionable links of 9/11 was with the situation of the Palestinian people. Nobody mentioned it at the time. No one really wanted to complicate matters. There was a clear target for the USA and the Intifada at that time was definitely a side issue. The War on Afghanistan as war on terror left a gap of closure. It also did not save enough American face. And finally it also did nothing about the festering sore of the Palestinian issue. America did not have to tackle that problem directly. Israel sufficed for that. But the problem seemed not to be going away.

Another of the reasons for the Second Iraqi war was for America to get involved actively in the Israeli-Palestinian conflict. This could be done because it would show Israel that it was willing to destroy Iraq, its most militant enemy in the Arab world, and it would show Palestinians the uselessness of resisting a pax Americana in the region. Once the latter was achieved, one of the causes of 9/11 and of future terrorist attacks on the USA would be eliminated. Perhaps, Bush and Powell might have reasoned, if we do impose a solution in the Near East, a solution acceptable to Israelis and Palestinians, we shall end the Arab and Muslim animosities that are making the world such a rocky place, especially for the USA. The long but indirect linkage between 9/11 and the Israeli-Palestinian conflict was brought into the open with the project called "roadmap", which was being tentatively proposed here and there, now and again, even before the Second Iraqi war.

(39) Sharon made it clear that he did not want Powell to even shake hands with Arafat

The roadmap proposal was a considerable come down from previous Israeli-Palestinian land-for-peace negotiations. This was the essence of the

---

25 "Blix decries coalition's intelligence on Iraq arms", IHT, June 7, 2003; David E. Sanger, "A shifting spotlight on uranium", IHT, July 16, 2003

Egyptian-Israeli peace: Egypt got the Sinai back and it agreed not to make war on Israel again. Of Camp David 2000-2001 it was said that Barak had made some offers on the West Bank and East Jerusalem. The Powell roadmap did include the stipulation that Israel dismantle the settlements in the West Bank that it had built after Sharon became PM in 2001. But more importantly, it contemplated a Palestinian state, to which was Sharon was averse, in exchange for which Arafat would be marginalized.

The Arafat issue was strictly personal. The president of the PA accepted the roadmap. Israeli leaders, who, like Rabin and Barak, had shaken hands with Arafat, had done so and immediately wiped them with handkerchiefs. The memories of the times when Arafat was an out-and-out terrorist were indelible. The times that Sharon had been a terrorist should also have been indelible but Israel had power and the PA did not. Sharon made it clear that he not only did not want to shake Arafat's hands, but that he did not want Powell to do so either. Bush and Powell accepted Sharon's "scruples".

The roadmap was officially delivered to both parties on 1 May, the day Bush declared the Second Iraqi war over. The same day Israeli soldiers killed twelve Palestinians in Gaza. The Second Intifada had been nearly smothered before the Iraqi war, but it wasn't quite dead. Such Israeli reprisals meant that the terror alarms were still very much switched on. Powell was urging Palestinian "authorities" to disarm the militants. The reiteration of this theme was disingenuous. How could Powell not know that Palestinian terrorist organizations were acting independently of the PA? The Israelis pretended that they did not believe any such thing. But Israelis could hardly be accepted as reliable sources on the matter. If Powell accepted Israeli claims, he had to be acting in bad faith. And so obviously had to be Bush.

On 25 May, Sharon accepted the roadmap and got his cabinet to approve it. It really didn't commit Israel too much. On 8 June, a suicider in Gaza killed four Israelis. Hamas, the Al Aqsa Martyrs Brigade, and the Islamic Jihad jointly accepted responsibility for the attack and vowed to crawl all over the roadmap.[26] The USA remained committed to mediate in the Israeli-Palestinian conflict. Israel had made minimal concessions. Given the inequalities in forces, this was only realistically to be expected. But how long would Israel wait before striking back hard

26 "A rebuff by Hamas may stall peace plan", IHT, June 7, 2003. Tom DeLay, the majority leader of the House of Representatives, couldn't "imagine in the very near future that a Palestinian state could ever happen". He described such a state as "a state of terrorists, a sovereign state of terrorists". IHT, July 26, 2003. DeLay was later indicted on suspicion of political fund-raising irregularities.

if Palestinian intransigents were not reined in? Here was another situation in which Bush's war on terror could be stalled.

The USA had won two conventional wars. But now it had to keep the lid on two conquered but difficult countries. It was detested generally in Arab and Muslim nations. Perhaps never in its history, not even during the Vietnam blood-letting, had its situation been more fraught. And to cap it all, the USA was no longer the leader of the pack, not morally or politically anyway. The unipolar world was in crisis and it was not likely that it could be reconstituted again. The younger Bush had squandered in an orgy of international bullying the authority that his father had gained for America. To make matters immeasurably worse, the occupation of Iraq soon turned into a prolongation of the Second Iraqi war.

(40) The immediate global consequences of the Second Iraqi war

What had snapped from the unipolar hopes to the multipolar reality? The western alliance, which stood through thick and thin during the Cold War, was stricken. France might not have been the team player in NATO that America would have preferred, but France could be relied on in times of crisis. It never defied NATO and only demanded the right to have its own independent but cooperative command. For Germany, which not only has American bases on its soil but also had depended on them for its survival if the Cold War had turned hot, to be out of step with the USA is a dramatic turn of events indeed. It is not that Germany has not had its discrepancies with American strategy. Under Chancellor Willy Brandt, it sought to have an independent policy towards East Germany, sabotaged by the East Germans by placing a spy in Brandt's inner circle. Germany was never comfortable as a base for INF, but it knew it had to accept them if only for the sake of Cold War tit-for-tat. France and Germany now have refused to follow a course that president Bush declared to be basic to America's defense. That Bush's argument about Iraq's offensive capabilities was preposterous makes this historical fracture all the more difficult to mend in that it eliminates unconditionally, a tacit Cold War principle, from the NATO equation.

France and Germany formed a continental European opposition to the USA over Iraq. The USA appealed without any attempt at dissimulation to the new central European members of NATO. This does not mean that NATO is now broken beyond repair. But it does mean that the more than half-century old, USA-organized alliance, which was nearly monolithic during the Cold War is no longer rock-solid in the very real sense that its members will examine their options very carefully before committing to any initiative proposed by the USA, unless of course it is one that fits all of their interests.

If radical electoral turnabouts do not dictate otherwise, France and Germany will probably remain as a moderating conservative force within NATO. Despite its expansion and American prodding to modernize individual armies, NATO is probably stagnating. What exactly is its role? If it is related to Europe, the EU already contains the embryos for a common foreign policy and for its own rapid-deployment force. Its first peacekeeping task is being carried out in Macedonia, where there are ethnic tensions between Albanians and Slavs. If it is taken out of a European context, NATO has no reasons for being there. If it exists to prevent Russia from ever again becoming a dangerous and aggressive super-power, then NATO would be reverting to obsolete Cold War patterns, conceivable only in the sense that history can be capacious and quirky. As of now, there are only abstract and unlikely grounds for such a far-fetched scenario. In the final analysis, with or without NATO, Russia is still a super-power and its destructive potential, given that during the Cold War it was large enough to annihilate the USA many times over, is probably only relatively diminished.

France and Germany are especially close within the EU. Because of previous French insistence, Germany, with over 20 million more inhabitants, was on a voting parity with France, which has now quietly renounced this privilege. In 2003, France and Germany revived the obscure and relatively lightweight Elysée Treaty as a symbol of their friendship. The treaty contemplated cultural links and the twinning of cities. But the gesture, which came before the Second Iraqi War, was intended to signify the definitive French-German historical harmonization. Before these events, especially in de Gaulle and post-de Gaulle France, it could be argued that the USA was a bridge between France and Germany. No such a bridging is needed anymore. What's more, in siding with France against the American war on Iraq, Germany was ever so tactfully reminding the USA that in using its military bases in Germany it was coercing German sovereignty.

The break in NATO ranks, coming after the Cold War, is not that consequential and the alliance is not in danger of coming apart. But there is now in NATO a hint of uncoordination and obsolescence that was not there before. Even the special relationship between the USA and Great Britain is under strains. Prime Minister Tony Blair faced adverse opinion polls and a rebellion inside the ranks of the Labor Party. It is not likely that Blair will climb on another limb at the behest of President Bush, who still has North Korea and Iran to deal with. There are limits to how far you will indulge a misguided friend.

(41) What Russia and China have gained in international prestige, the UN has lost in authority

As Russia and China were also opposed to the war, not only did the war on Iraq alienate some of America's crucial, formerly unconditional, anti-communist allies, but it turned the clock back by antagonizing former enemies with whom the USA had been burying strategic hatchets. Relations between Russia and the USA appear to have emerged safe and sound from the Second Iraqi War. But it was Putin who said in the middle of the war that it constituted the greatest crisis the world had experienced since the end of the Cold War. After the war was over, there was no point in flogging a dead horse. When Putin met Bush he did not change his frequent sly, ironical look. Facial expressions are of course anecdotal and subjective. But the West does not fully trust Putin. The Russian government has continued hedging freedom of expression. Unlike China, Russia is of the West, but it is not entirely in the West. One of Yeltsin's strokes of genius was how he crashed the G7 club. With Putin it is now officially the G8. Russia also maintains a liaison with NATO. But Russia has served warning that it is not willing to be patronized by America. Where could the Russian bear growl again?

There are certain noteworthy particularities in the new international balance of power. It will be very difficult for the USA to convince others that there is always good on its side and evil always on the other, which it just about managed to do during the Cold War. The impression of unipolarity was a result of victory in the Cold War. But this victory, though ultimately America's, could not have been achieved without Western Europe.

Moscow, which had been impotent to dam the rising Western tide in Eastern Europe, has reasons to feel that it is no longer at a disadvantage. So often the target of American criticism for its undemocratic ways, China has added to its economic potential and to its military might—so closely entwined to its ambitions in space exploration that it is almost peaceable—the credit of having opposed military aggression.

Last but not least, there is the UN. The Gulf War or First Iraqi war was an US-led UN affair. In the Security Council, the authorization to make war was unanimous (China abstaining). The bulk of the fighting men and the armament that retaliated against Iraq was American, but the war was also indisputably multi-national. The only fully committed supporters Iraq had were the Palestinians, who would clutch at any straw if it helped their cause. Jordan was not an ally but it had to strike a balance because it lies between Iraq and Israel. Though bombarded with questions, which he fielded like a Socrates, king Hussein was not unduly punished for his neutralist stance, precisely because of Jordan's straddling position and its moderating influence in the Middle East.

The war was waged to reverse aggression. Once Kuwait was liberated the USA command halted the advance, well short of Baghdad. This was in keeping with the "new world order" Bush senior had in mind. It was the cornerstone for such a visionary project. Of course, the elder Bush was not faced by the 9/11 outrage, so it is hard to estimate whether he would not have followed the same policies as his son in similar circumstances. But George W. Bush seems so reckless that it is not difficult to imagine basic differences between him and his statesman-like father in any situation.[27]

The Second Iraqi war was a completely different affair from the Gulf War. A vote in the General Assembly would have rejected it by a whopping majority. But this would only have reflected the opinion of states. What counted was the vote in the Security Council, for it is there that collective military responses can be decided. During the Cold War, the Security Council was dominated entirely by its five permanent members. This was one of the inevitabilities of the bipolar world. After the Cold War, veto power, though still part of the rules, has fallen into disuse and it is no longer a metaphor for the struggle between communism and democracy. American diplomatic maneuvers for the principle that decisions in the Security Council should be taken by simple majorities regardless of veto power appeared to trend towards democratization of procedure and a leveling of the field for strong and weak states. But when it was seen that even a simple majority in a body of fifteen members was unattainable, American diplomacy chucked this approach.

In the absence of wide international support, it was obvious that what the Bush administration wanted at the UN was a semblance of international approval by whatever means. America's withholding of UN funding and its barely dissimulated role as decision-maker in the UN (precisely because it can withhold funding) has demeaned the international organization in recent years. The disregard of standard procedure in the Security Council, even of the Security Council itself, on an issue, which the USA initially qualified as of international concern, constitutes a further debasing of the UN. It shows that the USA respects the UN only to the extent that the latter is pliant to America's policies. A further demonstration of the American contempt for the UN came about during the tsunami disaster in December 2004 when, rather than channel its assistance to the affected countries through the UN,

27 Thomas L. Friedman, "The apparent heir", NYT, 31 October 2004

the USA chose to operate through what was called "a separate aid coalition", a development that France and Germany deplored.[28]

The damage could be worse. Since America is the most powerful state in the world and it has shown that it has no fundamental commitment to the UN charter, the international organization has emerged from the Second Iraqi War as virtually inoperative on major international conflicts. Even during the stormiest periods of the Cold War, the USSR, who had reasons to distrust the UN, did not question its value, even if only because it wanted to gain third world adepts, which generally saw the UN as a crucial forum. The Second Iraqi war has left the UN diminished. It may not have been reduced to the impotence of its luckless predecessor, the League of Nations, but the least that could be said of the UN was that it exerted a constant steadying influence and the most that can be said now is that it might in the future recover from its recent manhandling.

28 Brian Knowlton, "Tran-Atlantic flap reaches tsunami aid", IHT, 6 January 2005.

8

The Iraqi Insurrection and the Re-election of George W Bush

The most ironic result of the Second Iraqi war is that it was not a victory at all and Bush's exultation was not only premature but as foolish as the brashness that characterized his first months in the presidency. Despite the early evidence that Iraqis were not overjoyed at being invaded—as of the end of May 2003, there were 150,000 American soldiers in Iraq, one third of them in Baghdad—the military command in Iraq was already making plans to evacuate the Marines by the end of August, as if it was an established fact that the American occupation was acceptable to Iraqis. One could ask how smart is American intelligence? Or alternatively, was there a limit to American self-deception?

The first to bear the brunt of Iraqi post-war resistance were the British who suffered small but premonitory fatal casualties in Basra. There were unexpected ambushes against American troops and these began rounding up Iraqi civilians indiscriminately, as in time it became known they had done to Afghans.

The turning point from self-assurance to the realization that Iraq was not going to be an easy ride came as early as July when there occurred generalized outbursts of violence and the casualty list started to grow significantly. These were unmistakable indications that the occupation would not be about quelling isolated pro-Hussein spams but a much larger manifestation of resistance, one that would quickly be recognized as a national insurrection. The rejection of the foreign presence in the country even targeted the UN, whose headquarters in Baghdad were blown away claiming the life of the head of mission,

Sergio Vieira de Mello. Annan placed the blame on the lack of security for which the US was responsible.

(1) Social terrorism becomes a national insurrection

The occupation authorities were intent on demonstrating that the Second Iraqi war was waged to re-build Iraq as a democracy. A parallel governing council was formed with representatives of the communities that, in the American view, constituted "Iraq": Shiites, Sunni, and Kurdish, a gross misperception that discounted Iraqi nationalism as such. The Kurds were the only ones who had no quarrel with the invasion of the country and in the months to come Kurdistan would remain the only part of Iraq where violence was not part of daily life. Mostly, however, the governing council was integrated with Iraqi expatriates, among whom one, Ahmed Chalabi, was the Pentagon's favorite. Programs were initiated to train an Iraqi constabulary and to build an Iraqi army from scratch.

The US military claimed some victories that on the surface appeared spectacular. Hussein's sons, Uday and Qusay, who had the reputation, justified or not, of being daddy's torturers and executioners, were killed in a rocket barrage at the house where they were holing up. The word was that their landlord had betrayed them. Whoever did was awarded the $10,000,000 on their heads, no questions asked. Another to fall was Ali Hassan al Majid, the notorious "Chemical Ali".

These relatively meager catches were more than counter-balanced by the scale and the audacity of Iraqi attacks. It was the media, which at first went along with the military talk of flashes of terrorism, that began to speak of "insurgents" and of an "insurgency". For it was indeed between July and December that the Iraqi resistance, perhaps because of the occupiers' initial smugness, perpetrated some of its most ominous attacks: the first downings of helicopters killing their unwary crews in various places in Iraq; practically unhindered bombings and killings in Baghdad, including the death of a governing council member; rocket fire on the hotel in which Paul Wolfowitz, the under-secretary of defense many considered the greatest anti-Hussein hawk, was staying; even the mortar shelling of the Baghdad headquarters of the supreme commander, Gen. Ricardo Sanchez. The Iraqi attacks also demonstrated a savagery and indiscriminateness, such as slitting American soldiers' throats and killing Red Cross personnel, that made it seem as if all hell had broken loose.

(2) Bush goes back to the UN and France tries to collect an unpaid bill

A part of the mayhem might just have given the occupation military an insidious sense of encouragement. Hussein was a Sunni Arab, although as a Baathist implicitly not religiously inclined. Historically, Iraq was an Ottoman formation in the sense that it consisted of three provinces centered on Mosul, Baghdad, and Basra (including Kuwait), ruled by a Turkish governor in Baghdad. The Ottoman sultans doubled as caliphs and the caliphate was a Sunni institution. Territorially most of Iraq, including Mosul, the province that governed the Kurdish population, was peopled by Sunni. Hence, political power in Ottoman Iraq had always been in the hands of Sunni. But the Shia population, which lived mostly south of Baghdad, outnumbered the Sunnis, and it did not have a significant share in governance.

The American attack and invasion of Iraq had been counting on Shia support. There was no actual evidence that such would be the case, but during the initial phase of the insurgency there were some devastating bombings in Shia Iraq which were presumed to be the doing of Sunni terrorists. If a civil war was in the offing, then American forces could expect to have Shia backing to counter Sunni resistance. These hopes were soon to be dispelled.

The Bush administration should have rethought Iraq from scratch. But it didn't. One obvious measure was that optimistic evacuation plans were shelved. Bremer later argued that the invasion of Iraq was undermanned. He and Sanchez did not get along. Sanchez once declared that the successful subjection of Iraq could be achieved only if the political will to do so did not falter, as it had in Vietnam. It was an unfortunate comparison. But it is not clear whether he agreed with Bremer that he did not have sufficient troops to do the job. Sanchez appeared to believe that he did. He was in fact assigned an impossible task, which he and his superiors probably thought was possible. In any event, the Pentagon, where Rumsfeld believed in the biggest bang for the minimum buck, was not moved by the argument of American under-strength. When Rumsfeld was informed of the damage to Iraq's cultural heritage, he answered, "Stuff happens". In due time, the damage was not to be counted in terms of pillaged archaeological sites but in the growing toll of American soldiers. But there was to be no significant increase in the American occupation forces.

In lieu of that, other options were exercised. The US exerted itself to internationalize the situation in Iraq. It obtained small contingents from many countries for occupation duties, so that it could be said that militarily Iraq was not occupied by American and British troops alone but by "coalition forces" and the occupation was called the "coalition provisional authority". The main contributors to the American occupation were Spain, Japan, South Korea, Italy, and Poland.

Bush initiated a tentative rapprochement with the UN, but for this France collected an unpaid bill. The French proposed an UN-certified international force for Iraq, which Bush did not reject outright but insisted that the US would not turn over supreme command. This was not acceptable to France and Germany. UN representatives in Iraq also insisted that the US relinquish military authority. But the Americans were adamant. They showed it by excluding companies from countries that had opposed the war from work in the reconstruction of Iraq, which was mainly awarded without bidding to Halliburton, the company of which vice-president Cheney had been CEO.

The connection between the Iraqi war, Halliburton, and Cheney seemed too pat to be true. The worst that muckraking could come up with was that Halliburton was frightfully over-charging the occupation authorities. However, in May 2004 *Time* magazine affirmed that vice-president Cheney had a hand in awarding the Halliburton contract.

(3) Was "self-rule", which they had under Hussein anyway, what the Iraqis wanted?

The US strategy for Iraq was not unaffected by the events that were taking place under the occupation regime, but it was not essentially modified. Wolfowitz had stated that Iraq could expect an undetermined period of American military presence. Bush requested from Congress and got approval for $87.5 billion for mostly military expenses in Iraq and Afghanistan, mostly in Iraq. In sum, the American occupation was to continue indefinitely. But the plans for transition to Iraqi "self-rule" were speeded up and divided into two phases: the substitution of the occupation authority by an interim government to take over on 1 July 2004 and the implementation of a policy leading to elections for an assembly early in January 2005. The implementation phase required the pacification of Iraq.

The American occupation got a boost of sorts when on 13 December 2003, Saddam Hussein was dragged out of a crawl-in hiding place in a farm outbuilding in the middle of nowhere west of Baghdad. A favorite theory among US military was that the insurrection was the doing of Hussein. In this, the supreme military commander was presumably aiding him in his government, Gen. Izzat Ibrahim. As in the case of his sons, Hussein was probably betrayed for a reward of $30,000,000. The price on Ibrahim was only one-third of that. Hussein, who was photographed being treated as a common felon, disclaimed any responsibility for the insurgency. As if to disprove the American theory, following Hussein's capture there were attacks in various parts of Iraq, including Baghdad, that left at least five GIs and four Bulgarian and two Thai soldiers dead. Helicopters were flying patterns to avoid SAMs, as the Soviets had been forced to do in Afghanistan.

The governing council was lettre morte, except for a charter which came into effect in March 2004, but which was mainly the doing of Bremer, so much so that the future interim government was expressly denied the authority to modify legislation decreed by the occupation administration. One exception to this injunction was that the ban on Baathists for government service later was lifted. In October, the UN Security Council gave its approval to the occupation of Iraq, about which it could do nothing except encourage American steps to grant self-rule. But was "self-rule", which did not exclude the American military presence, what the Iraqis wanted? Since almost everywhere reporters turned in Iraq there was execration of the USA, it seemed that most Iraqis were supportive of the insurgence and opposed to anything short of total American disengagement.

(4) America was "what-if" safe while in other places terrorism seemed to be eating its own tail

If the Second Iraqi war was part of war on terror worldwide it did not seem to be making much headway. A rash of terrorist bombings targeting foreigners occurred in Saudi Arabia. In Casablanca, Morocco, suiciders killed 29 victims in different sites. Jakarta was the scene of a terrorist bombing at a hotel. The situation in Afghanistan instead of simmering down went for a while into a crescendo of violence that peaked during one week in August 2003, which left sixty dead. Afterwards, there were sporadic attacks on foreign military. In the year to August 2004 US soldiers suffered some 30 fatal casualties.

Bombs rocked Istanbul in November 2003. President Musharraf of Pakistan escaped two assassination attempts in December. There was an outbreak of terrorism in Uzbekistan, which was attributed to al Qaida. Since the Uzbek police is detested for its habitual shake-downs of ordinary citizens that was probably just a cover. In Thailand, of all places, there was an incipient Muslim insurrection in its provinces bordering on Malaysia. Government repression was ferocious. In a particularly shocking instance, over 80 prisoners suffocated when they were crammed into overloaded prison vans. The insurrection has not been suffocated.

Where terrorism was really having a field day was in Russia because of rebellious Chechens. From May to August 2003 terrorists caused over 200 deaths. There was a pause in the violence during which the Russians felt confident enough to allow elections for a handpicked president for Chechnya, Akhmad Kadyrov, who was assassinated by a huge bomb. Worse was to come. Nevertheless, much of this scattered terrorist activity (except in Russia and Chechnya) seemed purposeless and un-coordinated, as if terrorism was feeding on itself, and the perpetrators were usually either killed or caught.[1]

By Bush's wide definition of terrorism embracing "evil states" and WMD, the Second Iraqi war had actually had the reverse effect sought by war on terror. North Korea had already asserted it was enriching uranium in a secret location. No one knew whether it did or did not have a bomb. American intelligence was inclined to believe it, as was Mohamed ElBaradei, the director of the IAEA. The Chinese, in a better position to know, were not. Whichever way it was, North Korea, no longer bound by the stipulations of the non-proliferation treaty, said that it was processing spent uranium nuclear rods, which could be used for the manufacture plutonium bombs.

In August 2003, Iran let it be known that it had bomb-grade uranium, but that it intended to use it for nuclear-energy generation rather than for weapons. In October, the Iranians affirmed that they were also processing plutonium, but were disposed to allow inspection by IAEA. There was later a hardening of the Iranian position and the IAEA declared it wasn't getting cooperation from Tehran. Russia was the main provider of nuclear technology for Iran. To ratchet up tensions, Iran announced that it was capable of mass-producing a missile with the range to hit Israel.

In America, but also in developed countries in general—except, as we shall see, Spain—terrorism was in abeyance. The draconian internal measures adopted by the USA after 9/11 seemed to be working, although it was hardly to be expected that another attack of that magnitude would be stepping on its heels. Air travel was supervised rigorously. Eavesdropping by any means on potential terrorists was legalized. The debate about ethnic profiling was off the table. Few raised objections. Prosecution was once started against a white, middle-class American Muslim. It was quickly

1. May 2003: At least ninety die from blast in Riyadh foreign compounds. The Saudis arrested five militants. August 2003: Marriott hotel blasted in Jakarta (10 dead). November 2003: Car bomb in Riyadh razes foreign housing (mainly of Arabs); at least five killed; al Qaida link seen. January 2004: Suicider blast in Kabul kills a British and a Canadian soldier. May 2004: A bomb (possibly detonated by a suicider) kills ten at a Shia mosque in Karachi, Pakistan. September 2004: A probable action by the Jamaah Ismailiyah, a bomb explodes in front of Australian embassy in Jakarta. Many wounded, mostly Indonesians. October 2004: Two bombings kill dozens at a Sunni rally in Pakistan.

reversed. But the grounds, or lack of grounds, on which it began were like a warning that Muslims had to watch their steps. The concept of "material support" was broadened by the Justice Department to include even the suspicion of even accidental association with anything or any one having to do possibily or remotely with terrorism.

Whether these measures prevented anything from happening belongs in the realm of what-if. But they raised the question of why 9/11 in the first place. Already in July 2003, an independent report had faulted the government for lack of vigilance. This and related questions would soon become the subject of intense investigation and recrimination. Before this happened, a legal issue concerning war on terror reached the bar Supreme Court.

(5) The shock of 9/11 made "theoretical" torture an option

In the shocked aftermath of 9/11, people in the upper tier of the Bush administration, especially in the Pentagon, went to the marrow of issues on how to deal with the terrorists that were sure to fall into the hands of American authorities. War on Afghanistan was inevitable. The search for Osama bin Laden and his accomplices was already scouring the world. Catching the principal culprit was objective number one. Dismantling Al Qaida was of the essence. For either end, information was indispensable. Any one who possessed any knowledge whatever that would permit wreaking vengeance and making America more secure had to be squeezed dry.

Two questions were paramount: what legal rights did these people have, if any, and how were they to be interrogated? Some of the answers provided became American policy. Others were in an ambiguous terrain and could be read in different ways. There was no equivocation on the status of terrorists and suspected terrorists. Into this category was prejudicially thrust any one caught resisting the American War on Afghanistan.

The Taliban regime had soldiers. No one denied a state the right to recruit foreign troops. Whichever way you looked at the question, War on Afghanistan was waged against soldiers resisting invasion. The Bush administration decided that such was not the case. Military prisoners were not a priori "lawful combatants". Thus, they were to be held under the authority of the chief executive of the USA, who could do with them what he wanted, and that was to place them under indefinite detention by the military.

Since detainment facilities in Afghanistan were inadequate, this was ruled out, as was most emphatically detention of prisoners in the USA, where a swarm of lawyers would have been on their cases as soon as the planes carrying them landed. The Guantanamo base, American physically but not legally part of America, was an ideal place of imprisonment, which incidentally conceded Castro's claim that its occupation by the USA was illegal. Some 680 persons captured in Afghanistan were flown to Guantanamo.

In Guantanamo, the prisoners would have no right to a hearing in court. Nor could they appeal in any way against their detention. They were to be dealt with by "military commissions". Presumably in time they would be charged as terrorists inside the American legal system. Before this happened they would be subjected to intensive interrogations that would hopefully provide clues to capture Osama bin Laden and his henchmen. A dubious precedent for the policy of surrendering judicial powers to the military was found in a World War II measure approved by President F.D. Roosevelt for a summary trial of a group of German infiltrators who had been caught after landing from a submarine.

The doctrine of indefinite detention of prisoners of war in a legal limbo was in violation of the Geneva conventions, but it accorded with the opinion of legal eagles of the Bush administration who felt that America was already too disposed to give in to international norms.[2] As the USA had not ratified various important international agreements but still subscribed to the Geneva protocols, their attitude was consistent but hardly justified. The principal promoters of the doctrine were vice-president Cheney and secretary Rumsfeld, but ultimately it was President Bush who signed and approved it.

The question of methods of interrogation was not addressed directly, but the present attorney general, Alberto Gonzalez, then a legal advisor to the presidency, was the author of a memo in which torture was contemplated. Gonzalez had argued that a "new paradigm of terrorism renders obsolete" the Geneva accords. In June 2004, Gonzalez claimed that torture was a theoretical issue and was never offered to President Bush as an option.

2T he first Geneva Convention (1864), promoted by Henri Dunant, founder of the Red Cross, concerned the humane treatment of the wounded in war. The convention was ratified by all major states. The convention on the treatment of prisoners of war was adopted in 1929. In 1949, four Geneva conventions were elaborated :elaborated: (1) for the wounded and sick in time of land warfare; (2) extension of (1) to maritime warfare (first accorded in 1907); (3) on the treatment of prisoners of war; (4) on the protection of civilians in wartime. The proliferation of insurgencies led to a protocol in 1977 extending the conventions to non-official armed groups with some claim to political recognition. The 1949 conventions were generally accepted. The 1977 protocol was not recognized by the USA.

The dawning realization of the failure of the Iraqi occupation was already a matter of controversy. Issues on the way war on terror was being carried out were no longer debarred from debate. In Guantanamo, there was the additional complication that one of the detainees in the Afghan war was an American, a renegade but an American nonetheless. Also, other detainees were Muslims from developed countries and pressure was bearing down on the USA to give them a hearing.

Towards the end of 2003, a legal battle was looming and the first salvo came in November when the Supreme Court agreed to hear a case regarding the situation of Guantanamo prisoners. A federal court in New York ruled that terrorist suspects could not be held without access to defense even in cases involving national security. In December, a federal court in San Francisco declared unconstitutional the argument of "material support" of terrorism, which in the official view could be practically any Muslim organization, as being too vague and subject to abuses.

(6) Torture at Abu Ghraib could be traced to Rumsfeld but the buck stopped with the prison guards

By then, the risky policy that 9/11 justified any means to combat terrorism had resulted in a major scandal at the military prison of Abu Ghraib, in Baghdad, through photographs taken in January 2004 in which American soldiers appeared mistreating Iraqi prisoners. Instances of sexual humiliation of Iraqi men involving at least one female American soldier were revealed. One detainee died of blows to the head in the prison. The lower ranking personnel involved were to be court-martialed. One of them, the photographer in the group, Jeremy Sivits, was quickly tried and sentenced to one year in prison after describing the abuses. An army investigation concluded that the perpetrators at Abu Ghraib had not been properly trained in prison duties and that within the prison there had been a break down in command. Presumably, the soldiers, all enlisted, were inventing prison methods as they went along. The female soldier involved insisted that she acted under orders.

As the Abu Ghraib affair developed certain revelations surfaced. Initially, it was claimed that the abuses began in October 2003. Then, it was revealed that the mistreatment of Iraqi prisoners, including generals, had begun in April 2003. It had been going on even before the Second Iraqi war was "officially" over and it was not localized but widespread. The Red Cross witnessed the abuses at Abu Ghraib and reported them in November 2003. The army only responded in December. Gen. Sanchez claimed he only learned of the Red Cross complaint in January. An officer at Abu Ghraib affirmed that Sanchez was present at interrogations.

The intelligence unit that supervised Abu Ghraib also operated a detention center in Afghanistan where in December 2002 two detainees had died after being "chained to the ceiling" and "kicked and beaten by American soldiers in sustained assaults".[3]

When the dust more or less settled, there was a vague consensus that Abu Ghraib could be traced ultimately to the suspension of Geneva protocols before the War on Afghanistan. As the Guantanamo detainees had not been particularly prolific in the information that American intelligence needed to capture Osama bin Laden, secretary of defense Rumsfeld in December 2002 had authorized "harsh" methods of interrogation. How was "harsh" to be understood? An anecdote was told at the time that Rumsfeld approved making them stand for long periods of time under the sun, because he himself usually worked at a stand-up desk top. Was the use of growling dogs, a practice in Abu Ghraib, OK? That too. How about roughing them up? Again, how did you define that?

(7) The Supreme Court takes a stand but the administration does not exactly stand down

An internationally illegal policy that had been approved for Afghanistan in the wake of 9/11 was carried over into the Second Iraqi war. And why not as both wars were part of the same war on terror? President Bush in some form scolded defense secretary Rumsfeld, who was also reprimanded in Congress. Rumsfeld expressed his horror at the goings on at Abu Ghraib. Bush's reprimand of Rumsfeld was in May 2004, but it is possible the president himself might have known of the abuses in January, which was when the army had put a stop to them.

The affair was reminiscent of the famous test in which a subject was told to apply a current supposedly not being felt by a victim strapped to a chair simulating extreme pain and the subject on orders from the experimenter went on increasing the voltage even though the person at the receiving end writhed and screamed. The tortures that were applied in Guantanamo and in Iraq were not Gestapo-type although they were indisputably torture. One FBI agent witnessed strangulation and putting lit cigarettes into a detainee's ears. Another wrote: "On a couple of occasions, I entered interview rooms to find a detainee chained hand and foot in a fetal position to the floor, with no chair, food or water. Most times they had urinated or defecated on themselves and had been left there for 18, 24 hours or more." The prison guards indicted

3 Douglas Jehl, "Army details scale of abuse in Afghan jails", NYT, 12 2 detainees died from GI assaults, reports say", IHT, 14 March 2005.

for the mistreatment of prisoners were tried and in some cases convicted to prison terms.

These regrettable incidents and the growing disaster in Iraq might have influenced the June 2004 decision of the Supreme Court on the Guantánamo prisoners which stated that the executive does not have the right to detain persons without giving cause or allowing them access to legal counsel. Some of the justices spoke of oppression and of an assault on fundamental democratic values. The Supreme Court was so appalled that in a book review John Shattuck could write: "A full measure of the court's rebuff can be found in the concurring opinion of Justice Antonin Scalia, rarely a critic of presidential power against a competing claim of civil liberties. Perhaps best known for his role in guiding the court's decision on the 2000 presidential election Scalia upbraided the president he had voted to install."

Although not referring to Iraq, the court's decision had evident implications for the status of prisoners there. The administration responded with the adoption of a process expediting the review of the cases of the remaining 595 Guantanamo detainees to determine whether they were prisoners of war, hence subject to Geneva convention rules, or unlawful combatants, or for that matter simply those that got caught while the more nimble got away, a possibility that became a likelihood as a trickle of improbable terrorists was released.

(8) The Bush approach combines "torture-lite" with its sanctimonious denial

If Mark Bowden and the various sources he cites did their homework or told the truth, the Abu Ghraib affair and the entire torture controversy was something of a charade.[4] In an abundantly researched article, Bowden affirmed that torture had been standard practice for the USA armed forces and the CIA for decades before 9/11, with a toning down in the 1970s because of Watergate and the moralizing influence it had on American society. Specifically, he cited, from research by others, a 1963 CIA digest on interrogation called the *Kubark Manual*, in which methods such as sensory deprivation, enforced sleeplessness, solitary confinement, mock execution, and a range of pain-inducing procedures, what an intelligence official covered with the graphic but mild expression of "smacky-face", were described. The bodily side of torture, as different from psychological means for softening up suspects, was also called "moderate physical pressure" and "external techniques". The whole methodology was labeled "torture lite".

4 Mark Bowden, "The dark art of interrogation", in *Best American Crime Writing, 2004 edition*, originally published in The Atlantic Monthly, October 2003.

Some of the incidents narrated, however, were not so light. Michael Koubi, the former chief interrogator of Shabak, Israel's General Security Services, hinted at the rough edge of his profession, which some Palestinians interviewed described as Gestapo-type or deeply painful torture. A Marine captain told of how he attached "alligator clips" connected to a generator on a Vietcong prisoner's scrotum, which he made sound anti-climatic and sort of harmless in that the victim started talking even before the preparations were finished. A Special Forces officer told Bowden: "I'll tell you how to make a man talk. You shoot the man to his left and the man to his right. Then you can't shut him up." One CIA operative, nicknamed "Captain Crunch", part of a covert group called "knuckle draggers", assured the author that he had the man who masterminded the blowing up of the American embassy in Beirut in 1983 and that he got him talking with hoses and bats. The CIA man said Lebanese "interrogators" assisted him and that after he was off the case the detainee had died.

Bowden insists that physical torture is less effective than good interrogation in the hands of experts such as Koubi and others he interviewed. He agrees entirely with the approach adopted by the Bush administration, which combines torture-lite with its unctuous denial by the president himself. He accepts the argument that there are the pre-9/11 and the post-9/11 periods, with different sets of security conditions and requisites. After 9/11, as an intelligence operative put it, "the gloves were off". Among other bits of information Bowden remits are: that the *Kubark Manual* was re-issued in 1983 as the *Honduras Manual* (actually the *Human resource exploitation training manual*); that the CIA ran a torture course in a place called The Farm, in Williamsburg, Virginia; and that Guantanamo is known as "Camp X-ray". Other known detention centers are Bagram, the air force base near Kabul, and the island of Diego Garcia, a British possession in the Indian Ocean. What Bowden does not add is that Guantanamo so far has not "x-rayed" any one to the extent of a trial. Also, it is also possible that Bowden was just "talking tough", which is a professional hazard among crime writers. There is evidence that the American military, after Abu Ghraib, have gone out of their way to punish offenders among their members and that they are extremely watchful to prevent the repetition of the atrocities that were characteristic of the Vietnam War.

(9) Bush's axis of evil did not include the worst possible terrorist nightmare

The most sensational result of the war on terror was the revelation that for at least twenty years Pakistan, America's ally against the Soviet invasion of Afghanistan and a linchpin in the War on Afghanistan, had been the world's greatest perpetrator of nuclear proliferation, which was the ultimate form imaginable of a potential terrorist threat. War on terror was beginning to seem like the Edgar Alan Poe story in which inmates had taken over an insane asylum.

In October 2003, the USA intercepted a ship carrying centrifuges for uranium-enrichment to Libya. The shipment was initially traced to Malaysia, but further back to Pakistan. In 2001 (so it was reported), president Musharraf had removed the scientist Abdul Qadeer Khan, the mastermind of the Pakistani nuclear bomb, as head of Pakistan's Kahuta atomic research laboratory. Following the Libyan incident, Khan admitted that he had been selling nuclear-weapons technology to North Korea and Iran since the mid-1980s. It had been suspected that the deal with North Korea involved the compensatory transfer of rocketry expertise. President Musharraf was instrumental in making Khan the scapegoat and then pardoned him, but it would be delusional to believe that Khan's deals were personal and did not have the approval of the Pakistani government up to and including the period after Musharraf took power.

Libya, which was already spent as a promoter of terrorism, so much so that Bush had not included it in the axis of evil, came completely clean and opened wide to international inspection to show that it had dismantled all its programs for acquiring WMD. The USA started citing Libya as an example of the success of the war on terror and began gingerly to normalize relations with the Libyan dictator Muammar al Qaddafi.

In March 2004, Bush raised Pakistan to the status of a major ally of America. But the questions that were left up in the air were extremely perplexing. In principle, Pakistan should have been the number one member of the axis of evil. So how had American intelligence let such a dangerous country escape its mesh? What good were the multiple American intelligence-gathering agencies? Supposing they hadn't been fooled one bit by the Pakistanis, then how could any one evade the question that the USA itself might have been complicit in nuclear proliferation? But involving North Korea and Iran? Had Bush been misinformed when he went after the axis of evil? Or was it perhaps that his informants didn't know any better? Since the Pakistani connection went back to Reagan, had the USA preferred kicking the Soviets in the shins to preventing lesser enemies from acquiring nuclear weapons? One version which probes the extremes of the absurd is that the CIA actually knew what Khan was doing but did not try to obstruct his activities, including possibly obtaining Chinese blueprints for a nuclear weapon, because it wanted to keep him under surveillance. Apparently for the sake of it.[5]

Anything was possible in the topsy-turvy world that America was sponsoring, perhaps even that the USA was both for and against nuclear proliferation or that it knew and did not know that nuclear proliferation was going on. These enigmas to this day have not been solved and it seems that officially (or publicly anyway) nobody is keen on asking questions. One explanation is that America has too many intelligence-gathering agencies acting independently of each other. But the inescapable conclusion to which the Pakistani affair led was that war on terror was a sham, which in turn raised questions on how fit was America to lead a unipolar world. Whatever the answers, if there were any coherent answers, the hopes that were so vibrant when the world was on its brief roll from 1989 to 1991 were finally and definitely rotted in their graves.

(10) With the waning of the Intifada, Sharon was ready to spring on the world his own "roadmap"

Powell's roadmap for peace in Israel/Palestine was torn up before any one had a chance to get bearings from it. The roadmap provided for a Palestinian state on condition that Arafat reined in terrorism. Was this in his power given the state of political disarray, which Israel was promoting among Palestinians? Since Sharon refused to talk to him, Arafat named Mahmoud Abbas prime minister to act as interlocutor. Abbas was considered a moderate. He was also an Arafat loyalist. Here was another conundrum of the war on terror. But it was really only apparent. The give-and-take that was supposed to underlie the roadmap included that Sharon dismantle some West Bank settlements. Almost in the same breath Sharon refused to restrain Israeli settlements and accepted the roadmap with reservations. Bush and Powell did not find this unreasonable.

Sharon also went on building the defensive wall in defiance of UN and general world condemnation. Bush called it a "problem" and gave Israel a tap on the wrist by rescinding something like 10% of multi-billion dollar loan guarantees for the settlements. Abbas had offered that he would restrain the terrorists.[6] Sharon and Abbas met and a few hours later a Hamas suicide bomber killed seven Israelis in a bus in Jerusalem. Abbas was reluctant to carry on the semblance of negotiations and Arafat replaced him with Ahmed Qurei, which was an empty

---

5 William J. Broad and David E. Sanger, "The bomb merchant", NYT, 26 Mystery enevelops a Pakistani nuclear web", IHT, 27 December 2004.

6 "Abbas vows end of terror against Israel", IHT, June 5, 2003.

gesture for the PA no longer existed. In the midst of the American invasion of Iraq, Israel had de facto nullified it when it bulldozed Arafat's compound in Ramallah leaving him barely room in which to survive, which as it later transpired was not for long.

From August 2003 to January, the Intifada had a resurgence and suicide bombings picked up. There were deadly attacks in the West Bank, Jerusalem, Tel Aviv, and Haifa. But they were sporadic. There were two incidents in October, but in general the carnage from Palestinian terrorism was hit-and-miss. Terrorist attacks were like small leaks in the barrage that Israel was building against them. Israel on the other hand was applying a straightforward system of containment, which targeted Palestinians at will, at any time and anywhere.

A pattern was clearly visible. Hamas was the target to destroy and Gaza was the battleground. For each Palestinian strike, there were, apart from the immediate reprisals, at least ten Israeli counter-attacks. The figures in this lopsided struggle were never accurate. The Israeli military came up with either suspiciously exact figure, as that Hamas had taken 243 Israeli lives, or vague body counts in which it seemed as if Palestinian terrorism was more deadly than it really was. The 3 to 1 ratio of Palestinians to Israelis dead was adopted as a propaganda ploy, for it was obvious that the Intifada was dying. This did not mean that resistance was over or that terrorism was totally under control. It meant that the Palestinian objective of making Israel suffer was unreachable. Sharon was ready to spring his own "roadmap" without the niceties of the Powell version.

(11) Fallujah was the nearest the Americans first came to an Iraqi frontline

The insurrection in Iraq during the first half of 2004 became extremely complex because, as in conflicts of this sort, there was no battle line across which adversaries confronted each other. Two things became very clear: one, that the insurgents were constantly active; the other, that the USA did not have enough military forces to subdue them. Events followed upon each other in such a widespread and diverse manner that it was difficult to establish a coherent sequence, but it was nevertheless possible to shift from one focus of violence to another. It was also possible to determine what the targets of the insurgency were. The Americans had one and on one sole objective, which was to pacify the country, for which they accelerated their efforts to create Iraqi surrogates. In this concrete sense, they were active in various directions: forming an anti-insurgency Iraqi force, creating the interim Iraqi government to which the occupation would devolve administrative functions, and doing their best to prevent the violence from spilling over into areas, such as Kurdistan, which were in relative peace.

From the start the Iraqi insurgency was concentrated in central Iraq with Baghdad as fulcrum extending north along the highway to Mosul. Most of the attacks occurred roughly in these areas, but they were happening all over Iraq wherever targets presented themselves as they did in the Basra area and along the border with Syria. As one of the occupation's crucial tasks was to create an Iraqi police and an Iraqi army the places where such activities as recruiting, training, and quartering occurred were principal targets of the insurgents. So were soft targets such as contingents from other countries that were willing to collaborate with the American occupation. The Iraqis made no distinctions between Americans and other foreign troops.

Another indication of the way the conflict would go was that, after Baghdad, the city most recalcitrant to the occupation was Fallujah. It was there that it would be demonstrated just how difficult it was to create a local military force. In Fallujah the resistance was active and aggressive, the closest the Americans were encountering to a frontline. The American post nearest to it came under fire during a visit by Gen. John Abizaid, the commander of all US forces in the Middle East. When he expressed surprise at the welcome he got, a fellow officer told him: "General, this is Fallujah".

(12) Potential allies, the Shiites defrauded American hopes by launching an insurrection of their own

American troops were taking hits daily. When President Bush declared the Second Iraqi war "over", American fatal casualties were less than 200. By January 2004, they stood at over 500. By November, prior to the battle for Fallujah, they were around 1200. As was to be expected, the greater number of dead was among Iraqis themselves. The highest single day's toll during the insurgency occurred in March when 169 Shiites were killed in attacks during the commemoration of a religious festival in Karbala and in Baghdad. The obvious inference from this was that Sunni and Shia were heading towards a confrontation.

American intelligence had already another theory to hand, which was that the Iraqi resistance was being led by Abu Musab al-Zarqawi, a Jordanian infiltrator sympathetic to Al Qaida. A price of $10,000,000 was placed on his head. This was the equivalent of making Osama bin Laden the only enemy the USA had in the Muslim world and deliberately ignoring the USA-Israel alliance as one of the causes of 9/11. It was also inherently improbable that al-Zarqawi could be made responsible for the national insurrection in Iraq. But it followed the if-only pattern of Bush's war on terror, which consisted in the reasoning that if you killed or captured this or that person or persons the war would be over. In fact, the American high command in Iraq was mystified and, even as it kept on blaming al-Zarqawi for the violence, it also kept alive the speculation that Ibrahim was the leader of the national resistance. The expectation of a Sunni-Shia conflict in which Americans would be the arbiters of peace for a country perverted by Saddam Hussein was quickly dissipated.

The most respected of the Shiites clerics in Iraq was the ayatollah Mohamed Husseini Ali Sistani, who was willing to go along with the occupation's plan for the eventual restoration of Iraqi self-rule. The word "ayatollah" itself conjured memories of Khomeini and this made Americans chary. Sistani would turn out to be the occupation's most valuable asset. But the lack of full support for Sistani from Bremer and his occupation administration resulted in that a considerable segment of Iraqi Shiites staged an insurrection of their own which was as intense as anything that American forces were facing in Sunni areas. It was led by the young cleric Moktada al-Sadr, the son of a charismatic Shiite leader in Baghdad, where a huge area, usually described as a slum, was named Sadr City. The son inherited the father's ascendancy over Shiites and in April he launched a violent resistance movement in Sadr city, in Kufa, and particularly in Najaf, the latter with Karbala one of the holiest of places for Shiites.

(13) Terror strikes Madrid and Spain goes back on its commitment in Iraq

While these events were taking place in Iraq, elsewhere the war on terror took a turn for the worse. In March 2004, a spate of bombings in Madrid trains and railroad stations left over 200 dead. The government rushed to blame terrorists of the ETA Basque separatist movement. This was impulsive and evidently intended to exonerate Spain's military presence in Iraq, the largest after America's and Britain's.

Elections were coming up and, even though Aznar's government backtracked before the evidence that it was Muslims and not Basques that had caused the carnage in Madrid, Spaniards voted the conservatives out and elected the socialists, whose leader, Jose Luis Rodriguez Zapatero, had promised to bring Spanish troops from Iraq. Bush fleetly distanced himself from Aznar, whom he had feted in his Texas ranch, but Rodriguez Zapatero did not go back on his pre-electoral commitment and ordered the Spanish contingent back, not before it had to bear the brunt of the Shiite insurrection in Najaf.

This could have been interpreted as that Spain was giving in to terrorism if it weren't for consistent poll results that Spaniards had been opposed to the war long before Aznar got his country involved in it, and that what the incoming government did was to keep its promise and respect Spanish public opinion. Spanish authorities, with strong international cooperation and support, were soon on the trail of the Madrid perpetrators, who were mostly apprehended.

(14) In some of its excesses, Iraqi terrorism showed it was certainly not Islamic jihad

Hostage-taking and the sabotage of contractors for Iraqi reconstruction, especially its oil industry, had already begun on a large scale. This type of resistance was merciless and grisly. It was repugnant to see tapings of pleading hostages and of beheadings, usually aired on the Al Jazeera TV network in Qatar, which was used by Osama bin Laden and Iraqi terrorists to communicate their messages. One particularly lamentable execution was that of Margaret Hassan, an Irish humanitarian, married to an Iraqi, who was working for CARE (Cooperative for American relief everywhere). Bin Laden's appearances on Al Jazeera were the irrefutable evidence that he was alive. The USA tried to have Qatar censor Al Jazeera, the closest in the Arab world to an outspoken media outlet. It was rebuffed and in the process it showed that its commitment to democratic practices in the region was subordinated to its strategic interests.

Perhaps the most deplorable of all the terrorist acts committed by the Iraqi resistance was the killing on camera of twelve dirt-poor Nepalese workers in September 2004. Fellow Muslims from Turkey and Pakistan working in Iraq were not exempted from terrorism. This was proof that the Iraqi insurrection was closer to exacerbated nationalism than it was to an Islamic jihad, which American reports tried to play up as evidence that resistance to the occupation was the doing of foreign interlopers rather than of resentful Iraqis

On the use of crude terrorist methods, insurgents could argue that in Iraq it was war to death. For reasons that can only again be called "faulty intelligence"—to some more like an arrogant refusal to admit they were in the wrong place for the wrong reasons—Americans did not want to admit that what was happening in Iraq was tantamount to a war of independence in which the resistance saw itself as facing a ruthless and powerful enemy. For the insurgents, every means to fight it, however foul, were therefore justified.

It couldn't even be said that it was only terrorists who hated America's guts. The populace itself was quite inclined to lynchings if they could get away with them. It got a chance in Fallujah where four American contract workers were waylaid, burned alive, and literally pieced into limbs, which were hung from a bridge. The American military now had a dilemma: occupy Fallujah with all necessary force or concentrate on Najaf, where the Shiite insurrection was in full spate.

The Fallujah incident so incensed the occupation authority that it was given priority. But American forces were thin on the ground and when they tried to take Fallujah they encountered block-by-block resistance so fierce that the number of casualties was considered prohibitive. Still, not willing to lose face, the American military, alleging the likelihood of high collateral losses, accepted a truce by which the Marines were allowed to enter Fallujah and hand over peacekeeping to Iraqi troops it had trained and were under the command of former Iraqi army general Mohammed Latif.

This was the first test of the efficacy of the American training program for Iraqi collaborators. Even though President Bush called the Fallujah insurgents "thugs and killers", the American forces had backed off and the situation eased up somewhat. This allowed concentrating on an assault on Najaf. This was to go on for the following weeks during which other events occupied center stage in Iraq.

(15) The UN intervenes to sanction Bremer's transition project

The occupation authority had proceeded with its plan to devolve internal administration to an interim government. Bush's appeal to the UN and the UN's approval of the American occupation on the condition of its termination in a reasonable lapse of time, set to the end of 4005, resulted in that an UN representative, Lakhdar Brahimi, was sent to Iraq to supervise the transition.

Basically, Brahimi was given a project by Bremer, which he then approved. Chalabi had fallen out of America's graces. He had been undergoing criticism for misinforming the Bush administration on the situation the Americans would encounter on the ground in Iraq. This amounted to placing intelligence failures on his shoulders. Chalabi was being blamed for not having foreseen the insurgence, although the specific accusation that brought about his disgrace was that he had been feeding the Iranians classified information. As it was unlikely that he was privy to decision-making in Bremer's office, he could hardly be in a position to do any such thing, but out he went and in came instead Iyad Allawi, who in the end of June was installed as prime minister and Bremer departed.

(16) When Sharon unveiled his "roadmap", even the Americans suspected that it was probably an excuse for more land grabbing in the West Bank

Without specifically saying that he had his own "roadmap" for Israel/Palestine, Sharon announced in February 2004 a plan that contained three basic points: Israel would dismantle the settlements in Gaza and evacuate the territory, the defensive walls in the West Bank would be continued and completed (they had only been built to one-third their intended length), and, basically, there would be no more concessions to Palestinians. Implicitly, a Palestinian state could be constituted from these premises although Arafat would not be recognized as an interlocutor by Israel.

Surprisingly, the Americans, possibly Powell, were alarmed. Sharon's move could be construed as an outright disregard of the American roadmap and it might have been feared that the abandonment of Gaza could signal more land grabbing in the West Bank. Even the American government apparently had its misgivings about the lengths to which Sharon would go. He showed that soon enough.

The Israeli army initiated a massive offensive against Gaza with the objectives of neutralizing Hamas and of sealing the porous border with Egypt through which weapons were being smuggled. Sharon really did mean business. The Gaza battle went on with unrelenting intensity in the following months. This time there were no limits to Israeli military reprisals.

A missile killed the paraplegic founder of Hamas, Sheikh Ahmed Yassin, as he was leaving a mosque. His successor, Abdel Aziz Rantisi, was killed the same way almost before he had time to say that Hamas was indestructible. The attacks on anything resembling resistance in Gaza were continuous, deadly, and often indiscriminate. The Palestinians were able to mount a few terrorist attacks, one particularly devastating in Egyptian resorts frequented by Israeli tourists. The pathetic suicide bombing of a 16-year old Palestinian girl elicited the equally pathetic comment from some Palestinian spokesman for a terrorist group that resistance was still alive. Arafat was being blamed for social chaos in Gaza whereas the Israeli offensive demonstrated that the only say that counted there was Israel's.

Sharon's "roadmap" encountered two blockages. One was a pushover. Bush's misgivings were allayed after Sharon visited him in April. Bush gave Sharon's plan his blessing. Sharon's own Likud party was another kettle of fish. An assembly of a minority of potential delegates turned it down. Jewish extremists mobilized to oppose the dismantling of the Gaza settlements. There were insubordinations within the Israeli cabinet. Sharon had a lot of placating to do.

His first announcement was that Gaza would be vacated before the year was out. This was probably a bargaining stance. In the end, he got support for a phased evacuation over a period lasting until the end of 2005 requiring government approval at every phase of the withdrawal. In fact, as in Oslo and as in Camp David, the Israelis were making promises that they probably had no intention of keeping. Sharon perhaps might have, but Likud extremists were probably calculating that they could sabotage the process along the way. In any event, Sharon's plan was approved in the Knesset in October.

When Arafat died in November, there were no reasons for changes in Sharon's plan. The Israeli leader had never taken the so-called Palestinian Authority into consideration. Besides, it was a recurring Israeli refrain that things would be much better with Arafat dead. That wish was now realized. Would Sharon's plan and Arafat's death finally bring peace to Israel/Palestine?

(17) Sistani brokers a truce, which permits the American to turn their sight on Fallujah

With Fallujah quiescent, so to speak, the American military turned on Moktada al-Sadr, who had been declared an "outlaw" by the occupation administration before it ceded authority to Allawi. The Shiite leader was causing troubles in Baghdad with his so-called Mahdi army, but there was no chance that city would fall to Iraqi insurgents and mobs. But Najaf was different for there the city was already in the power of the Shiite recalcitrants.

It was decided to give the Iraq auxiliary forces a go at the Shiite fighters in Najaf. The American surrogates in Fallujah had been ineffectual and parts of the city were being bombarded by air on a permanent basis. As in Fallujah, the Iraqi soldiery could do little to dislodge the insurgents in Najaf. A truce was arranged, but when it broke down, the Americans went in with armored vehicles. They fought their way to near the city's Imam Ali mosque, which the insurgents occupied but which American troops were under orders to respect because of its sanctity to Shiites. Through ayatollah Sistani's intervention the fighting finally stopped with the agreement that Najaf would be handed over to Iraqi police. This happened in August 2004 and there was a good chance that Shiite southern Iraq would have a respite from fighting, though not necessarily from insurgent terrorism. Now, the Americans were ready to take on Fallujah but certain previous changes and preparations had to be made.

(18) It began to seem that the Second Iraqi war had been a choice and not a necessity

While these events were transpiring in Iraq, in the USA there was an intense debate over, essentially, President Bush's war on terror. There were various circumstances that contributed to the controversy. One was of course that no WMD had been found. David Kay, chief US weapons inspector in Iraq until 23 January 2004, declared that Iraq had no stockpiles of chemical or biological weapons. He recommended an enquiry on why no WMD were found despite pre-war intelligence. He suggested that Bush had been given "gappy" information.

Former UN inspector, Scott Ritter, wrote that he and others had told the government that Iraq was not a weapons threat. The CIA had produced a report in October 2002 to the contrary. George Tenet, head of CIA, recognized in a speech that there were gaps in the intelligence that supposedly led the USA to attack Iraq. Basically, he admitted that the CIA exaggerated Iraq's work on nuclear technology. Finally, the president himself had to admit that Iraq did not possess WMD. These admissions alone made the Second Iraqi war and its consequences unnecessary. But it was possible that president Bush had been misled. Besides, he and his entourage still insisted that the struggle in Iraq was part of the war on terror.

There was another important circumstance. With the stringent security measures taken by the administration after 9/11, America felt less threatened by terrorism. Even before the Second Iraqi war, a commission had been formed to investigate how 9/11 had been possible at all. As the situation in Iraq got more complicated, the 9/11 panel, as the commission came to be known, had been widening the reach of its investigation to encompass the reasons behind the Second Iraqi war. This was justified because it was al Qaida that had been responsible for 9/11 and the administration had been assuring the public that Saddam Hussein and Osama bin Laden were partners in terrorism. This implied that president Bush had acted against Iraq on the strength of reliable information.

Since president Bush had included Iraq in the axis of evil before 9/11 took place, there existed the suspicion that he might have been intending to wage war on Iraq all along and that 9/11 gave him the opportunity he needed. In other words, the Second Iraqi war might have been undertaken not because Iraq was, as Bush asserted, a real terrorist threat to America but because he was determined from the start to invade Iraq and get rid of Hussein. Hussein had indeed been eliminated but the cost of doing so was an increasingly futile war of occupation during which terrorism had multiplied a hundred fold, and this certainly could not have been part of the package he offered his country.

The possibility of the Second Iraqi war had been declared by the Bush administration not because it was necessary but because it was wanted gained credence through public testimonies from unexpected sources. Paul O'Neill had been briefly Bush's secretary of the treasury. Now he came forward to say that he had been amazed at the insistence—he spoke of an "obsession"—with which the question of Iraq was raised by Bush and the people closest to him. Another former administration functionary, Richard Clarke, an anti-terrorism advisor, also used the term "amazement", specifically when, immediately after 9/11, Bush personally sought confirmation for an Iraqi link, which Clarke considered preposterous.

(19) Had Bush been misinformed or was he the principal promoter of misinformation?

On 9/11 itself, the panel concluded that the American intelligence services had received multiple warnings and leads not just about a possible terrorist attack on America but about an attack specifically involving plane hijackings. The Germans communicated their findings on the suspicious activity of an al Qaida cell in their country. The FBI and the CIA received reports about the movements of two terrorists implicated in the attack on the USS Cole in Aden. Most damningly, it was known that Muslims with dubious backgrounds were training in simulators at American flying schools. One of these trainees had even taken a course on flying large jetliners but had omitted lessons on how to land them. The panel faulted the American intelligence system and proposed that reforms be implemented to break barriers between them and make them more centralized.

But the conclusion that had the greatest impact was that the investigators found no evidence for the reputed Hussein-bin Laden link. This undercut the fundamental stay of Bush's claim that Iraq was a terrorist state. Hussein might have used terrorist methods in Iraq, but there was no basis to Bush's claim that he was a terrorist threat to America. Given the importance that the 9/11 panel gave to intelligence failures, president Bush did not emerge from the report as having lied or deceived the public but as himself having been misled by government's spies. However, there existed also abundant and trustworthy reports that if the intelligence services had given the president the wrong picture, it had been because the administration had encouraged reports that could be used to back its case against Iraq. The intense desire to wage a justified war on Iraq had been, in fact, self-fulfilling.

(20) The body count "strategy" used in Vietnam was irrelevant in a country that had possibly suffered 100,000 civilian deaths

In Iraq, the preparations for the battle of Fallujah were under way. Sanchez had proved inadequate to the task of pacifying Iraq. The facts belied his optimism. His reference to Vietnam evoked bad memories of Gen. William Westmoreland, the hubristic hawk whose claims of imminent victory had been shot down one by one. Apparently, the only lesson the American military carried over from Vietnam to Iraq was not to rely on a body-count strategy. Yes, there were occasional announcements of the killing of insurgents, but this was not taken as an indication of a forthcoming defeat of the insurgency. Besides, what did body counts matter when a respected British medical journal estimated civilian losses in Iraq as a result of the occupation at 100,000, which had not dampened Iraqi recalcitrance? The possible involvement of Sanchez in the Abu Ghraib scandal was an albatross around his neck and he was replaced as head of the USA military in Iraq by Gen. George Casey Jr., former vice chief of staff.

A summary of the over-all situation in Iraq in August and September 2004 was not conducive to optimism, although there was some indication of progress. A report from the coalition command recognized that that attacks from Iraqi insurgents had been escalating from some 650 in March to 2700 in August. According to a survey by a private security company, during September there had been 2368 anti-coalition attacks. In a detailed map, it appeared that the majority of these attacks were clustered around Baghdad as far west as Ramadi and south towards Karbala, although attacks in southern Iraq were much less numerous due to the truce in Najaf. The highways between Baghdad and Mosul and Kirkuk showed high concentrations of insurgent actions, as did those cities themselves. There was a significant cluster of attacks in the British-occupied Basra area. There were virtually no incidents in Erbil and Kurdistan in general. The types of attacks in order of importance were: homemade bombs, mortar and rocket fire, small arms fire, rocket-propelled grenades, hand grenades, and land mines. The hopeful sign was that the Shiite insurgency led by Moktada al-Sadr had been contained and there was even talk that Moktada himself was disposed to take part in normal electoral politics. But this had occurred in August and the attacks in September, if these reports were to be believed, had not diminished significantly.

The US military had a plan to reverse the deterioration of the efforts to pacify Iraq. In a document titled "U.S. National Strategy for Supporting Iraq", the Pentagon outlined a project to neutralize centers of resistance one at a time. These objectives were classified in terms of the threat they pose to the stability of the country and to the process envisioned to culminate in the January elections. As the US operations proceeded, they would result in the turning over of control to the Iraqi army. If the strategy worked, the US could start reducing its military commitment in Iraq in the course of 2005.

The first objective was the reduction of Fallujah and its hardcore insurgent forces. Sectors of Fallujah had been for weeks under constant aerial bombardment. US forces encircled the city. The civilian population had mostly fled to refugee camps and to Baghdad. As a prelude to the attack on Fallujah, Ramadi, another center of Iraqi resistance, had already been taken, although it wasn't clear how firmly it was under control. Before the battle of Fallujah, something occurred in America, which in effect put an end to the debate about President Bush's controversial leadership.

(21) Kerry was burdened by a "Jane Fonda complex"

Concomitant with international developments, the campaign for the American presidency had been undergoing a crescendo of confrontation and intensity. The Democratic candidate, Sen. John Kerry at first did not appear to be aggressive enough despite the ammunition that the 9/11 panel and the failure of war on terror put at his disposal. Polls did not show that Americans were antagonized by Bush's strategic gaffes. There was no collective perception that he had deceived the nation. America after all was not Iraq, and there at least the containment of terrorism was a success.

Kerry was burdened by two heavy loads: first, he had not opposed the Second Iraqi war when he could have, and second, even though he was a decorated combatant in Vietnam, after his military service he had publicly and vehemently opposed the Vietnam War. During the campaign this showed in a sort of "Jane Fonda complex" that prevented him from forthrightly attacking Bush's misguided war on terror. On the contrary, his argument was that he could be better at fighting terror than Bush.

Kerry's challenge to Bush came alive during the presidential debates, in which Kerry showed skill and steadfastness while Bush flip-flopped. The president acted at first as if his record was unimpeachable. Then he waved his arms. Then he went back to the friendly, smiling, loose-and-easy style that was the undoing of Al Gore. Kerry was cool throughout and, though there were still ambiguities in his position on the Second Iraqi war, the points he did harp on discredited further Bush's hollow re-iterations. If the debates had decided the election, Kerry would probably have won. As it was, the contest, which in the polls had been favoring Bush, became much closer. Although Bush retained a slight advantage, it looked as if it was really neck-to-neck.

The Democrats began harping on Florida where they had lost the previous national election by some 500 votes. At the time there were accusations and rebuttals of electoral shenanigans. The votes of blacks had supposedly been undercounted. This time around the Democrats were determined that they were not going to be shortchanged. There was a miscalculation in this approach.

(22) Floridians did not relish being considered nincompoops

Which way would Florida tumble? A good many Floridians were probably being made to feel as if they were nincompoops who did not even know how to vote. They might have wanted to dispel that impression and re-affirm their backing for Bush with a really indisputable majority. This could be the doing of white, middle-class, Protestant voters (still there the majority, as in the rest of America). Blacks would again vote nearly 100% for the Democratic candidate. Cuban-Americans were divided. Bush made a bid to put them on his side by tightening the screws on Castro. But Americans of Cuban descent are probably by now resigned to Castro and they are more concerned with relatives in Cuba. Bush's anti-Castro measures had made it more difficult for them to help those they left behind. The Cuban-American vote would probably behave this time as it did then, that is, not significantly inclining towards one side or the other.

There remained the substantial "Jewish vote". An estimate put it at 4% of eligible voters in Florida. This was surely undercounting. The Jewish vote, whatever this exactly means, was possibly as high, in the aggregate, as one quarter in cities such as Miami, Fort Lauderdale, the Palm Beaches, St. Petersburg, and Tampa. This vote had Israel on its mind. Kerry had not manifested that his attitude towards Israel was different from Bush's. He has Jewish ancestry.[7] However, the reasoning that could prevail on the trend of this vote might be that a Bush in hand was better than a thousand Kerry-type birds. No president in history

7 Before emigrating to America, Kerry's paternal grandfather, Fritz Kohn, an Austrian Jew, renamed himself Frederick Kerry and adopted Catholicism. He committed suicide in a hotel in Boston. See Michiko Kakutani's review of *John F. Kerry: the complete biography by the Boston Globe reporters who know him best,* by Michael Kranish, Brian C. Mooney, and Nina J. Easton. IHT, 10 May 2004. Kakutani's review, incidentally, calls Kerry "lugubrious", "ambitious", and "stilted", and says of him that he is "a man of contradictions", "trailed by a reputation for political opportunism" (a verbatim quote from the authors), and "a man who was known for his diffident aristocratic manner".

has been more pro-Israel than Bush. Jews might or might not be more Liberal than the rest of Americans, but their liberalism stopped at the borders of Greater Israel. Jews could have gone foursquare for Bush.

Another possible miscalculation was that towards the end of the campaign, possibly on the advise of ex-president Clinton, was that Kerry neglected the national security issue and the whole war-on-terror imbroglio and concentrated on the state of the economy, with Democrats claiming that not since president Herbert Hoover back in 1933 had an administration overseen a net decline in jobs and Republicans countering that in the previous year 1.6 million new jobs had been created.

When the voting ended, Florida left no doubt that it wanted to keep Bush in office. The Jewish vote in Florida went to Kerry, as it did in the states where it is especially strong (New York, Connecticut, New Jersey, Illinois, and California), all of which Kerry won. The focus shifted to Ohio where the race was close and whose electoral votes could have made the difference between victory and loss for either candidate. But there Bush's advantage was not 500 but 150,000 and in addition the national vote was favoring Bush by over two million votes. The Democrats were tempted to wait for the final count in Ohio, that is, mainly absentee votes, but the odds were stacked against them and Kerry finally had to concede.

How did Bush, running on such a blemished record, defeat Kerry? One indication was a large exit poll that showed Americans were so-so on economic issues and primarily interested in national security. Paradoxically, Iraq came very low in voters' concerns, which implied either that they believed the place did not exist or that war on terror had become irrelevant. Wider perspectives on American elections could provide some historical explanations on why Americans voted as they did.

(23) The incumbency factor

The American presidency is still the bully pulpit it has always been and the person in office has a big initial advantage. Out of 25 incumbents during the 20th century only four were not re-elected and in each of these cases there were extraordinary circumstances.

Theodore Roosevelt challenged Howard Taft and the Republican vote divided. Roosevelt was probably the most credible third party candidate in the history of American bipartisan politics. His challenge sunk Taft's re-election campaign. The Great Depression sandbagged Herbert Hoover. A president who resigned rather than be impeached designated Gerald Ford. Ford's presidency was undistinguished but even so he was defeated by a margin that was not large. Jimmy Carter had to face the Iran crisis. He had staked his presidency on a humanitarian foreign policy and when he tried to use force to rescue the hostages in Iran the attempt failed and his re-election bid went down in flames.

American voters especially do not usually remove from office a president in time of war. Woodrow Wilson led America into the First World War during his second presidency but America's hostile attitude towards Germany had grown during his first administration to the point where war might have seemed as nearly inevitable. The USA was at war at least with the German submarine fleet. Had Americans wanted to avoid war, they would have voted Wilson out of office. F.D. Roosevelt was elected to four terms because America was either near or at war. The daring step was going for a third term in 1940 when war with the Axis was not just likely but imminent because of Japanese imperialism. Roosevelt's fourth re-election happened in the midst of war.

The Democrats were voted out of office during the Korean War. But Americans chose a soldier, Dwight D. Eisenhower, who promised to negotiate peace but whom every one thought of, reasonably enough, as some one who knew how to conduct a war. Lyndon Johnson was re-elected as America became entangled in Vietnam. When the choice was between a liberal, Hubert Humphrey, and a Republican, Richard Nixon (up to that time much more a loser than a winner), Americans did not hesitate in going for the Republican, who was seen as more likely to persevere in Vietnam.

Nixon was re-elected while the Vietnam War was still on. True, negotiations to end it for America had begun, but Nixon defeated George McGovern, who said unambiguously that he would end the war. When it is alleged that the USA abandoned Vietnam and that it lost the political will to fight, it must be kept in mind that Americans chose Nixon when they could have chosen McGovern, which meant that it was more likely than not that war would go on. The American electorate, in point of fact, never actually and explicitly voted against the war in Vietnam. Countless anti-Vietnam activists still believe, as does, for instance, the newspaper writer Carol Pogash, that they "stopped the war in Vietnam", but this is an impression not borne out by cold political facts.[8]

(24) The war factor

As to the war on terror and the involvement in Iraq, Bush's triumph probably was also conclusive in the sense of showing that America is not the peace-loving giant that in the past it has reveled in proclaiming. Here too history had lessons to impart.

8 "Romanticizing the revolutionaries", IHT, 15 December 2004.

315 The Iraqi Insurrection and the Re-election of G W Bush

The first war the USA fought was its prolonged but intermittent conflict with the Barbary States of northern Africa. Even as the Barbary Wars were going on, the USA invaded Canada and initiated the War of 1812. It attacked Mexico and annexed the major part of what today are the western American states. The Barbary wars were not much of a political issue. But the War of 1812 and the war against México had decided popular support.

The American Civil War was a war of survival and the northern states gave it nearly total political backing. The USA waged war against Native American "savages", although this only occasionally engaged regiments and hardly qualifies as a real war. As it was pure and unjustified American aggression, the Spanish-American war is a misnomer. The war was imperialistic and aroused the same enthusiasm in America as the Boer war did in Britain. It was, as Theodore Roosevelt put it, a "splendid little war". Bush the younger is an admirer of Roosevelt's speeches, which he had on a coffee table in his Texas ranch house. American went into the two world wars eyes open.

The Post-War wars were not all waged to contain aggression. The Korean War was seen as necessary by President Harry Truman and there is little doubt that the public was with him. The Vietnam War is more often judged to have been aggressive rather than containing. Reagan's proxy wars and his invasion of Grenada (not to mention his challenging of the Soviet "evil empire") occurred during his first administration, and Reagan was re-acclaimed for a second term. The proxy war in Afghanistan was against Soviet aggression, but Nicaragua and Grenada could hardly have been considered threats to America.

In 1989, President George H.W. Bush invaded Panamá to overthrow its dictator Manuel Noriega, suspected of drug trafficking. Panamanians probably did deserve to be taught the rules that were to apply upon the return of the canal. A dictatorship was not in itself as objectionable as exporting drugs to America. The evidence against Manuel Noriega was not that strong but capturing and convicting him showed who the ultimate decision-maker in Panama was. In 1991, the USA organized and led a multinational (but overwhelmingly American), UN-sanctioned coalition to liberate Kuwait.

Bush the younger was a president without a real electoral mandate. He began his presidency on the cocky note of the "axis of evil". Al Qaida attacked the USA and Bush retaliated with war and invasion of Afghanistan. With Pakistani help, this war was brief and to the point. But with no provocation at all, Bush launched all out aerial warfare against Iraq, which culminated with invasion and the subsequent occupation of the country.

This makes in all fourteen major and minor, declared and undeclared, states of war in the last two centuries. By way of comparison, during the same period Great Britain, the greatest imperialist power in history, fought the Napoleonic wars, the War of 1812, the Crimean war, the Boer war, World War I, World War II, the Falklands war, and the Second Iraqi war. In all there were eight formal states of war, although there were also two undeclared Afghan wars plus countless other colonialist operations. The Afghan wars were fought with Indian troops. The other conflicts were generally minor. The Great Indian Rebellion, which started as Indians against British, was converted into an Indian civil war. Prussia/Germany, an aggressor state par excellence, fought six formal wars: as Prussia, the on-and-off wars against Napoleon, war against Denmark, war against Austria, and war against France; and as Germany, World War I and World War II. If double and triple counting is eliminated—the Napoleonic wars, the War of 1812, the two world wars—it appears that America fought more wars on its own (11), often of its own making, than the UK (5) and Germany (3) combined.[9] No war has ever been politically detrimental to an American presidential incumbent. The 2004 elections amply ratified that perception.

(25) The "it's the economy, stupid!" myth

On the issue of the economy, Kerry and the Democrats were way of the mark. The American business cycle can be disconcerting. Even though in the details no solid correlation can be found between specific cyclical events and electoral results, the over-all trend of the cyclical process itself has been largely determinant of basic American political attitudes since 1929. In the third quarter of that year, Wall Street was brought low by the Great Crash and an economic recession began that lasted until the first quarter of 1933, in all 43 months, or over three and a half years.

This was one of the greatest recessions in American history, not so much because of its duration as because in it America had gone from a time of giddy prosperity to a period of profound depression with a quarter of the active population unemployed. It is still not clear why the market crash preceded such a prolonged depression (and not the other

9 The UK was at war continually with France from 1793 to 1815 with only the brief interlude of the Peace of Amiens (1803). So for the UK there were only two formal Napoleonic wars. By way of comparison, Prussia declared war on France three times during the Napoleonic period. Although Britain participated in the Korean War it did so on a minor scale. An instance of double counting is the War of 1812 and of triple counting are the world wars.

way around), whether there was a cause-effect relation or a mere convergence of circumstances. But there is no denying that this was the great crisis of capitalism in the 20th century, affecting its American citadel but spreading all over the world.

Before the presidential election of 1932, America had been a largely conservative country where successful politicians who were not pro-business or anti-union were a rarity. The Republican Party was the party of business par excellence. Wilson, the last Democrat to be elected president before Franklin Roosevelt, had edged into the office. Before Wilson, another Democrat, Grover Cleveland, had been president in two non-consecutive terms, a real political feat, but his administrations were indistinguishable from those of Republicans before, between, and after his.

Wilson was an idealist. His devotion to his foreign policy objectives made him extremely unpopular and nearly even killed him. The extent of his incapacitation by a stroke to this day is not fully known. He left office in a wheelchair and he died three years later. Franklin Delano Roosevelt entered the White House in a wheelchair but the only incapacity he suffered from was in his polio-blasted legs.

The previous Republican president, Herbert Hoover, a humanitarian who had saved millions of Russians from a communism-induced famine, would probably have lost the election whatever he did. But he did not contribute to his chances by refusing to do anything to alleviate America's economic pains. His conservative approach abhorred fiscal deficits, which he sought to cover with a sales tax (instead of increasing progressive income taxation), and he stood by the principle that the best remedy for economic depression was to let the business cycle run its course. This was very much a 19th century view out of place in a society where the accumulation of wealth was so immense it did not seem possible, or ethical, that there could be so much misery.

(26) America's penchant for liberalism did not extend to eggheads

Although at first wary of deficits, Franklin Roosevelt shed his qualms about over-spending if this contributed to ending the economic and social crisis. He also spoke over the radio to the distressed masses and in general his New Deal was like a national pep rally. The economic indicators had in fact started improving when Roosevelt was sworn in. His administration probably contributed to the weak momentum, which peaked during his second administration. Unemployment remained double-digit, but Americans appreciated the efforts, apart from accepting government aid that did not make them feel like beggars.

The economy started picking up very sluggishly after June 1938. Economic historians are agreed that the New Deal did not rescue the USA from the Great Depression, but few social historians would disagree that Roosevelt, who never doubted the inherent virtues of American capitalism, turned a majority of Americans into Democrats and liberals, not in the 19th century British sense of laissez faire—liberalism from the Latin liber or free—but in the sense of supporting a compassionate, activist state, or what conservatives later took to calling "bleeding hearts". Government spending to increase demand did not turn the American economy around, although it certainly made Germany flourish. In the USSR, the problem was not lack of work but how to make people work with virtually no material incentives. The Stalinist answer was to force them to work. The alternative was to starve.

Hitler was making the world unstable with his territorial demands, which were a disguise for designs so inconceivably inhuman no one before him had even entertained them. America knew where it stood in relation to Nazism and to Japanese aggression. When it entered the war, during Roosevelt's third term, the timid economic recovery very quickly became a boom, which lasted until November 1973 (34 years) with unemployment rates far below 10% and six recessions which lasted on average less than ten months (five years in all).

Americans were so overwhelmingly liberal that it took one of their greatest war leaders, Dwight D. Eisenhower, to unseat the Democrats, and then in large measure because he was pitted against Adlai Stevenson, a man everyone described as an egghead or intellectual, and Americans' penchant for liberalism did not stretch that far. Eisenhower won despite a previous economic expansion that carried well into his first administration. The business cycle was so mild that it had no effect on the election. American liberalism was strong enough to break in favor of Democrat John F. Kennedy a reputedly powerful prejudice against Catholic politicians, although whether this was real or just political myth-making is not clear.

(27) The stagflation scare

With the oil crisis of 1973, things began to seem seriously bad, for there was high inflation, which would normally accompany expansion, with stagnation, and this, called stagflation, was so mysterious to analysts that it evoked fears of another Great Depression. There were also political complications of all sorts.

The Soviet leader Nikita Khrushchev once told Richard Nixon, then Eisenhower's vice-president, that the USSR would bury America. He did not mean a nuclear attack, which would have been extremely incautious, but that through peaceful economic competition communism would outlast capitalism, whose corpse the communists would then bury, presumably out of common decency. It turned out that it was the communists themselves in the USSR who buried communism. But in 1973, the USA had given up the struggle in Vietnam and President Nixon himself was under political siege. Oil scarcity, which provoked frighteningly high gasoline prices and long waiting lines at service stations, had been caused by third-world oil producers albeit with the obvious connivance of the large, mainly American oil multinationals. Communism had been gaining ground in the third world. An economic crisis was coinciding with a looming constitutional crisis in America and Marxists were gloating about a capitalist endgame.

Faced by imminent impeachment, Nixon resigned. President Ford lost the election to a real bleeding-heart liberal, Jimmy Carter, who might not have relished the label but who fit the description perfectly. Ford lost even though the economy had come out of the doldrums during his administration. The upswing peaked with Carter but the recession that followed was the shortest on record (six months).

(28) As residual fears of another Great Depression dissipated, Americans went back to their conservative ways

Americans by then had had it with the past. They wanted out of the Vietnam tunnel, which lingered like a nightmare will after wakefulness, and in particular they were done with residual fears of another Great Depression. Liberalism no longer had an economic leg to stand on. Some said it hadn't even at the height of Roosevelt's popularity. An audience was growing for conservative economists who argued that the 1930s American economy could have recovered on its own to 1920s levels if it hadn't been for the New Deal. As deficit spending had not fueled inflation and it had restrained somewhat the downtrending cycle, this wasn't a very likely supposition. But Americans were now, for the first time since 1929, overwhelmingly conservative again, and proud of it, which they showed by electing Ronald Reagan in a landslide and re-electing him four years later. Their conservatism had unbeatable results: the Soviet empire undone, communism collapsing, the USSR dissolving, all in the wake of the president who had called a spade a spade and under whom a boom had begun which lasted through the George Bush administration and the two Clinton administrations, until it suddenly ceased in March 2001.

The recession that ensued was short-lived. By December America was out of it. Employment did not pick up and financial markets remained stagnant but in a steady-cycle pattern within reasonable ranges that do not exclude future surges. If with Clinton there had been inklings of an American return to its old liberal leanings, Bush's re-election showed that liberalism carried little weight. It could even be argued that Bush's victory indicated a definite return to the way America behaved electorally before the Great Depression. A very long historical cycle had finally been closed. Reagan and Bush the elder were not deviations from the norm but representatives of a firm trend and the Clinton years were if anything an anomaly, perhaps because of the president's charisma and flexibility and the dullness of his Republican rivals.

(29) Fallujah encourages Bush's high spirits

Shortly after Bush's electoral triumph, American GIs and Marines reinforced by Iraqis (mainly, it seems, mopping up in the rear) began the battle for Fallujah. On 14th November, US forces declared Fallujah taken, with maybe still four or five days to go for flushing out die-hard fighters. On a videotape, American soldiers appeared to be enjoying killing wounded Iraqis. In reality, they were fearful of booby traps, but a dialogue made them seem like Hollywood action heroes. One Marine said: "Hey, this guy is faking his dead", and, after a couple of shots, another Marine answered: "well, he's dead now". In the battle actions described by the embedded reporter Dexter Filkins, writing for the IHT/NYT, the Iraqis were fearsome, tenacious, and wily fighters. The capture of Fallujah coming on the heels of Bush's re-election was giving the media a bad case of triumphalism. It shouldn't have.

On the day the Fallujah offensive started Iraq had been unstable in other ways: Mosul had routed an Iraqi police attempt at pacification--worse, it was suspected the US-trained constabulary might have had more than a foot on the insurgent side--and the Americans had taken casualties; a senator from Rhode Island, Jack Reed (albeit a Democrat), declared that the insurgency was becoming "more pronounced in many parts of the country"; the third Blackhawk in a week was downed near a place called Taji, north of Baghdad; in Baghdad itself, there had been three American casualties, one fatal; gunmen shot a top policeman in the yard of his own house; when firemen arrived on the scene, they were also shot; the house of a provincial governor was burned. The police chiefs of Mosul and Samarra had been dismissed. Even before they had finished their job in Fallujah, some American troops were rushed to Mosul.

The attack on Fallujah itself had been facilitated by the transfer of British troops from Basra to Baghdad, where three of them were promptly killed in an ambush. As in Afghanistan, where Osama was the man who got away, in Fallujah it was Zarqawi. An estimate of American casualties in Fallujah was a quarter of the soldiers engaged, of which 12% were fatal. As command had committed a division, it was possible that the war and occupation of Iraq was costing American forces upwards of 1300 dead out of a total occupation strength of some 135,000 soldiers.

Nothing however was dampening Bush's high spirits and assertiveness. For obvious reasons, he did not manifest the militarist, devil-may-care swagger of his first months in office. Perhaps this portended good. John Ashcroft, the Bible-thumping attorney general from whose department had emanated a favorable judicial opinion on torture, resigned. The NYT editorialized: "The investigation and prosecution of domestic terrorism cases have produced little since 9/11 except dismissed charges, misidentified suspects and minor convictions of minor figures".

In Guantanamo, the 550 remaining prisoners were being subjected to "combatant status review tribunals", which was the administration's answer to the Supreme Court's injunction that all detainees under whatever circumstances had a right to appeal. These strictly military "tribunals" were basically confrontations of prisoners with some of the evidence the military had against them. Not one of the Guantanamo detainees had yet been brought before a lawful court. A federal judge in Washington, James Robertson, ordered that the ongoing process of a prisoner under review be halted because it did not meet standards of the Geneva Convention on the treatment of prisoners of war. The Geneva rules require a full court-martial, not just a "status review", to determine if a prisoner is or is not a lawful combatant. The administration planned an immediate appeal.

(30) There was no dancing and prancing over Arafat's death

Morbid though it might sound, the death of Yasir Arafat on 11 November should have been the silver lining in the Israel/Palestine storm. British PM Blair had given his personal assurances that he would give this issue priority. The Israelis had always said that Arafat was the major obstacle to a solution. An American columnist, Jeff Jacoby of *The Boston Globe*, blamed Arafat personally for the killing of 21 children on the terrorist attack on Ma'alot in northern Israel in 1974. The author of the NYT obituary, Judith Miller, accused Arafat of ordering the killing of the nine Israeli athletes during the Summer Olympics of 1972 in Munich. Miller was so partial in her reporting on Bush's policies that she went to jail to protect a government source who tried to discredit an administration critic and had even given a blanket approval to being identified. In one of those eye-popping mei culpae that at times make American freedom of the press and reportorial veracity seem incurably hypocritical, the IHT, which had published the Jacoby libel, also published a note saying that there was no evidence to link Arafat to the Munich killings. So why was Jacoby's stronger defamation printed? Nevertheless, the monster was dead. So why wasn't there dancing and prancing?

When Arafat's illness was first reported—it was a blood infection that later caused a mortal stroke—a London-based Palestinian journalist said that Israel might rue not having Arafat as a potential interlocutor. Arafat's death at first seemed to be making the situation in Israel/ Palestine cloudier. His successors (Abbas as president of the PLO), all described as moderates, did not begin by condemning violence or terrorism. In his last years, the main Israeli accusation against Arafat was that he did nothing to suppress anti-Israeli violence. At least Arafat condemned the killing of civilians. The moderates that were to take his place initially at least did not even go that far. So was Arafat really the monster that serious English-language dailies depicted? In its obituary, the *Financial Times* carried this characterization to the physical level by saying of Arafat that he had an "unprepossessing physical appearance" and a "shifty appearance", which made the article in essence grotesque.

When all is said and done, the condemnation of Arafat comes down to that he was willing to wield terror against Israel in the name of the Palestinian cause. Curiously, he is also condemned because the PLO adopted as its goal the creation of "a democratic society in Palestine where Muslims, Christians, and Jews could live together in complete equality", which is not an unfair characterization of Theodore Herzl's vision for a Zionist state. Israeli strategy against Palestinians has become notorious world-wide (except in the USA) for its use of terror. So who started what?

In the web, you can find sites that will provide equally long lists of Israeli and Palestinian children victims of terrorism. An Israeli historian, Benny Morris, made a reputation for himself by collecting evidence that in 1948-1949 the Palestinians that fled had mostly been chased from their homes by Jews. Later, Morris used that reputation for fair scholarship as a podium from which to blast Arafat and Palestinians in general. Three Israeli PMs—Begin, Yitzhak Shamir, and Sharon—had at one time or another been committed terrorists.

Some have criticized Arafat for not having been sufficiently accommodating with Israel, a state that in 1967 annexed and occupied Gaza and the West Bank and the least it wanted was to have as neighbor an independent Palestine. He reputedly missed the boat in the successful 1978 negotiations between Egypt and Israel at Camp David, to which he had not been invited and in which any direct Palestinian intromission would have been rejected. Aside from the fanciful and the extreme, there were some concrete accusations against Arafat. The one every critic seems to share was his presumed responsibility for the failure of the 2000-2001 Camp David talks. We shall get to that shortly.

(31) Basically, Arafat was blamed for being a "loser"

The negative balance of Arafat's leadership was that he had not achieved a Palestinian state and on his death had left an impoverished, divided, and quarreling Palestinian population. His first strategic mistake was to try to act as if he ruled in Jordan. There is no doubt that Arafat was opportunistic and he always tried to grab as much as he could, in lieu of which he would put up a bold front. Arafat had co-opted the PLO after the Six-Days war showed that Arab states were powerless to advance Palestinian interests. As before that, with the exception of Jordan, these states had also shown very little disposition to integrate Palestinians into their societies, Arafat and the PLO had cause to branch out on their own.

They tried again to act tough in Lebanon, but the accusation that the Israeli invasion in 1982 was solely because of Arafat is untenable. Syria was installing missiles in the Bekaa valley and Hizbollah was already in the frontline against Israel in southern Lebanon. Sharon reputedly once said that the biggest mistake he had made in his life was not to kill Arafat when he could have during the invasion of Lebanon. In fact, if he was willing to allow Falangist Christians to massacre Palestinians in Sabra and Shatilla, the only reason why he didn't kill Arafat then is because he could not lay his hands on him.

Arafat is accused of dissembling in his 1988 recognition of Israel and in his renunciation of terrorism. It is usually argued that this came about at the time that Arafat and his organization had been ejected from Lebanon and the PLO's fortunes were at their lowest ebb. He is blamed for having supported Iraq's annexation of Kuwait.

There is no evidence that Arafat was at any time unwilling to negotiate with Israel after he took the momentous step of formally abandoning the objective of destroying Israel, to which most Palestinian extremists were still committed. The consequences of Arafat's 1988 commitment were the Oslo accords of 1993. And on the Gulf war, Arafat would have betrayed his constituency if he had not backed the one state that at that point was willing to go the distance in support of Palestine. Once the military preliminaries had been disposed of, the civilian occupation of Kuwait by Iraq was in part a Palestinian operation. Palestinians took over the Kuwaiti oil industry. Eyewitness accounts tell of European and American technicians escaping from Kuwait in SUVs over the desert between Iraqi tanks parked on the border with Saudi Arabia. USA tanks would have blown to bits any object moving between them in any direction. The Iraqis knew that Palestinians were manning their rearguard.

(32) Arafat probably owed his personal survival to international opinion

Somehow, Arafat is not given much credit for Oslo, which anyway is not made much of by pro-Israeli observers. Paradoxically, Arafat critics tend to emphasize the controversy that Oslo produced among Palestinians and the execration that Arafat got from extremists, particularly from Hamas. *The Economist* described Oslo as a "thicket". But the facts on this question speak clearer than they ever have on the Israel/Palestine problem. After Oslo, Arafat was not fomenting violence. If violence there was it came about not because but in spite of Arafat. The Nobel Prize would not have been awarded to some one over whom there hung even the hint of double-dealing and terrorism. The obverse is that Israel procrastinated.

When an Israeli fanatic assassinated Rabin, the Oslo process scrunched against a rock field. After Peres' interim tenure as Rabin's successor, Israel voted for Netanyahu, who had made no secret of his opposition to Oslo. Israeli distrust and obstruction were the obstacles that Oslo could not overcome. Except for the Second Iraqi war, if ever in contemporary history there is a patent example of international deception, it is the one perpetrated by Israel on Arafat and Palestinians over Oslo. It is true that Arafat made empty threats about an unilateral Palestinian declaration of independence, but he knew, or he was mad (which he wasn't), that he had only the very abstract backing of world opinion behind him. During the Sharon years, Arafat probably did owe his personal survival to his international renown, but that wasn't getting him much more than that.

The last important act of the last diplomatic drama in which Arafat played was the 2000-2001 Camp David talks. Just as Oslo is downplayed, so his critics overblow this Camp David. This is probably because it is so obvious that, Intifada or no Intifada, suiciders or no suiciders, since 2001, Sharon held all the cards and Arafat had virtually no role. You could make anything you wanted of Arafat. He was a loser. Since the least he had was co-responsibility for the failure at Camp David, then losing was his own fault. Sharon was on top and he could do what he wanted, including pose as a statesman. Grant him bravery and generalship, but on the Palestinian issue he can only be described as a bully.

Bush the younger's years in office coincide exactly with Sharon's. Among his priorities in the White House was to wean the Jewish vote away from the Democrats. Maybe, like the FT, he also thought that Arafat looked shifty. Bush is an ordinary type of guy apart from his extraordinary political talent. Ordinary Americans would tell you that Arafat looked like a terrorist. Bush and Sharon converged entirely on their takes on Arafat and Palestinians. For Bush, who has proven he most definitely is no statesman, Sharon was a statesman. The two created a tiny but powerful mutual admiration society.

(33) The ideal scenario for Palestine would be for Israel to thank Sharon and dismiss him as incapable of achieving lasting peace for his country

Nobody really knows what went on in Camp David during Clinton's lame duck presidency. Since Arafat is now dead—he was dead politically for a long time before his physical death—whatever is argued on this event will have a missing link. Clinton is a good starting point. Shortly after Camp David, he leaked to the NYT his frustration over Barak's intransigence. It is said that Clinton "owned" the Jewish vote. He certainly went over big with Jewish celebrities. His wife Hilary was elected senator from New York with Jewish support. New York State has 18 million inhabitants. Some 12 million of these at least live within the metropolitan area of New York City. Anybody who underestimates the importance of the Jewish vote in NY is either a liar or a doofus.

When Clinton wrote his memoirs, he said that Barak's offer to Arafat could not be improved on. Some say that Barak went as high as 97% of the West Bank. Clinton mentions 91%. Just prior to Camp David, *The Economist* gave a word of warning to the incautious: Barak had awarded in his less than two years in power more construction permits in the West Bank than any previous Israeli PM. Again as per Clinton, Palestinians were also offered some vaguely advantageous deal on East Jerusalem. In 1996, Palestinians in East Jerusalem were an electoral constituency, so they weren't getting anything especially new here. It is entirely within the likely that, with Oslo behind him, Arafat might have been mistrustful and was expecting guarantees of some sort. Clinton gets off the hook of seeming too pro-Israel by saying that he might not have made it clear enough to Arafat that the last offer he communicated from Barak was the best he would ever receive from Israel.

Arafat is accused of secretly supporting the suicide bombings during the Second Intifada. But the same chorus that blames him for not curbing terrorism in Gaza is the one that in 2004 cried that Arafat could not keep Gaza in hand. By this time, Arafat had been bulldozed to a fraction of his Ramallah compound. When Sharon won two elections in a row, what Arafat should have done was resign. This would have been capitulation. But would that have stopped the terrorism or shamed Sharon into assuming a less aggressive stance on Palestinians?

Arafat did indeed fail. Hussein also failed. Iraq is a maw for Marines. Has Israel ensured its security for the future? Sharon has removed the Israeli settlements in Gaza, but it is unlikely that Israel will ever discontinue its military "supervision" of Gaza, and that for some powerful reasons: Gaza is a Petri dish of despair; despair breeds violence; suicide bombers are, as an Israeli officer put it, the ultimate intelligent weapon. Israel is trapped in a bad circle. It wants security; to get security it thinks it must act in a manner which makes Palestinians powerless, and poorer; but the more misery it spreads the more likely it makes it for terrorism to continue indefinitely.

There is a less dismal scenario for Israel/Palestine. Perhaps fearing a loss of prestige, which is the usual anti-Arafat interpretation, but more likely because he wasn't likely to be obeyed, Arafat never made an upfront call to end the Intifada. After a brief period of cautious hesitation, his successor, Abbas, has. Palestinians are being made grandiose offers of international aid. Social terrorism, no matter how powerfully motivated, cannot be kept up endlessly. Hamas is still capable of striking at Israel, but there are indications that Hamas is no longer of one mind. Its West Bank leadership appears to be accessible to Abbas' call. The trouble is Gaza, which has been harrowed by Sharon. The ideal resolution in this scenario would be that Sharon went once more to the electorate and Israeli voters, grateful for his services but conscious that he is not the person to achieve lasting peace, turned him out of office. This is a long shot, but it is possible.

(34) Putin's Russia

The world terrorism situation is muddled. Osama bin Laden is still on the loose, and what is worse there are many "osamas" in many places. These however do not have the financial resources or the fierce hatred of the original. Historically, no matter what angle you take, jihad is a losing proposition. It was never a majority view of Muslims and its excesses cannot have gained it many new adepts. As during the Cold War, when America feared groundlessly that individual states could not contain the impetus of communist subversion, so today the countries that have been hit by terrorism have shown that they can contain it, if not uproot it at least capture and try its perpetrators.

Perhaps the country most vulnerable to terrorism is Russia. Putin might have become over-confident despite the assassination of Russia's handpicked president in Chechnya. He might have thought that the problem was contained to Chechnya itself. What happened in Beslan, in North Ossetia, next to Chechnya, is a horrific reminder that Russia lags far behind America in safeguarding its internal security. Some thirty Chechen terrorists there seized around 1,200 hostages in a school. In the assault to rescue the hostages 338 died, mostly children. The survivors described the kidnappers' behavior as barbarous. The Chechen rebel leaders Shamil Basayev and Aslan Maskhadov were accused by Russia of having planned the terrorist action, which came after the downing by suicide bombers of two Russian airliners flying out of Moscow and a subway bombing in Moscow itself. Basayev recognized that he was indeed responsible for the Beslan atrocity.

Putin has become a bete noire of the American media. He is accused of leaning to Soviet-style political dictatorship.[10] Like Arafat and Fatah, Putin is seldom mentioned without reference to his work for the KGB. The jailing of Mikhail Khodorkovsky was the occasion of "for shame" cries even though Khodorkovsky was easily the wiliest of the operators during the shameful Russian privatization process. Putin is accused of having him jailed because he posed a potential political threat. What is not usually emphasized is that Khodorkovsky was an economic loose cannon. He had too much economic power and he had no scruples about selling stakes in Yukos to foreign partners. One of the reasons why privatization in Russia was so inequitable and messy was that the government preferred its home-grown tycoons to foreign interlopers. What Putin has done with Khodorkovsky and Yukos is to nationalize or "re-statize" the Russian oil industry. This may not be acceptable to indignant globalizers, but it could be pointed out that Putin was only following Jeffrey Sachs, the American "genius" of privatizations, who denounced Russian privatization as scandalous.

After Beslan, Putin did a Japanese-style self-criticism. He also proposed constitutional measures that had foreign democracy advocates chanting

10 An American commentator wrote this astounding observation: "Many of the men and women who wield power in Russia—especially former KGB operatives like Putin—have inherited the mind-set that regards all politics as a naked struggle for power." Serge Schmemann, "The eternal suspicions of the Soviet mind-set", NYT, 9 Peering into Putin's mind", IHT, 10 December 2004

Jeremiads. He said he favored the appointing of provincial governors by Moscow rather than their local election. This should have been put in the context of the countless articles written during the conversion of Russia to democracy in which the quirks of elected local governors were set up for Western ridicule. That Putin might just be trying to streamline Russian democracy and increase national security, is corroborated by his further exhortation to his countrymen to form real parties, and not the ad hoc affairs that the new Russia has had since its beginning, for which he offered to implement the electoral system of proportional representation, all of which would be unthinkable in a ruler trying to reinforce his powers by the history-hallowed means of dividing the electorate. Russia, in sum, does not present such a dismal panorama even if its president has shown that he can be very clumsy. Another of his self-criticisms concerned his meddling in Ukraine, which he tempered by adding that Russia could get along with whoever was elected there and by making sport of America's world crusade to create sham, unconvincing democracies, as in Afghanistan and Iraq.[11]

(35) Globalization is on the ropes but not out of the fight

It is not only in Russia that globalization is on the ropes, though hardly out of the fight (somewhat like Muhammad Ali used to do in his day as the King). The weak dollar is probably skewing financial markets all over the world. It could even be behind recent sharp rallies in Wall Street, and capital that flows there is capital that is not going to emerging markets. This is of course highly debatable. What few are debating nowadays is that the problem of world poverty is taking precedence over the promotion of globalization, in part because the latter has not turned out to be the panacea that it seemed to be in the 1990s. In other words, growth per se is no longer the first priority in international economic conclaves.

The World Health Organization announced recently that for the first time more than half the population of the planet has water piped to their homes. Not long after that, in fact by a difference of weeks, the UN Food and Agriculture Organization informed that hunger was increasing in the world. In 2003, there were 55 million more chronically hungry people in the world (852 million) than in 2000. From 1990 to

---

11 In 25 November, in Ukraine, Viktor Yanukovich, a candidate for PM whom Russian president Putin had actively backed, won fraudulently over Viktor Yushchenko. In the wake of the Ukrainian electoral controversy, the constitution was reformed to give the Rada (parliament) greater power. On 29 December, in an electoral re-match, Viktor Yushchenko won the presidency of Ukraine.

2000, the incidence of hunger had decreased from 823.8 million to 796.7 million. On the step of those figures, the International Labor Organization informed that 1.4 billion human beings were subsisting on less than two dollars a day. It seems that war on terror, if it ever was anything but hollow American sloganeering, has to cede in urgency and importance to other more realistic and humanitarian wars. Just because President Bush, and America in general apparently, disdain them, the Kyoto protocol and environmental causes are not losing but gaining momentum. America might prefer to spend countless billions in the useless Iraqi intervention, but the rest of the world thinks that money might have been better employed in other pursuits.

(36) The one thing war on terror achieved is that America will never again be what it once was, or seemed to be, to the rest of the world

It would be different naturally if war on terror had been a success, but the fact is that it is not only mythical but that it is a myth that is acquiring an extremely deleterious reality. Before the Iraq fiasco, Bush had only to deal with the "axis of evil". Bush, Cheney, and Rumsfeld (the order here is not historically clear) thought they had a great idea by taking on the pushover in the group. The way it turned out is that they created from themselves and their countrymen a real triangle of mischief. The chronic instability in the Middle East is now worse than it ever has been with the looming nuclear threat from Iran. It is not likely that a nuclear-armed Iran would immediately bomb Israel out of existence, but nuclear proliferation is not a welcome development under any circumstances. Israel started the nuclear arms race in the Middle East, but it did not know what it was getting into. Every one now knows that Israel and America miscalculated, the latter for the umpteenth time in the region. The ironies start popping up here again like mushrooms. For the pains of invading Iraq, a trivial threat, the USA is faced in Iran with a nuclear problem it can do nothing about.

North Korea had accepted to freeze its nuclear-weapons program long before Bush came along and started bandying moral epithets, which make no sense in the relations between states. North Korea is not a country any one would choose to praise. It has been sinking into misery for decades under the rule of a megalomaniacal dynasty. But it too has become a nuclear threat, and it has done so while America was blabbing about terror and sticking both its feet into its mouth. Like Iran, North Korea would use nuclear power at the risk of national suicide. But a Kim Jong Il with nuclear weapons is not something any one relishes. Unfortunately for America, it has precious little leverage either in Iran or in North Korea. In dealing with Iran it has to rely on Europe and in dealing with North Korea it has to rely on China. This is a sorry condition for a state that a few years back was still the world arbiter and that for decades had an informal world empire.

The saddest part of this story is that not only did America create a world in which nuclear proliferation, the greatest terror imaginable, has become real, but that it is mired so badly in Iraq that it can only look aghast at its own mistakes. It is only in America where a second Bush administration can be a cause for celebration, and even there it should be a cause for lamentations. The USA is still taking hits in Iraq. This country is slowly and painfully coming alive again, but its prospects are not encouraging. It will be for the foreseeable future a land divided, its people walking along the edges of an interminable civil war. The cost of securing the suburbs of America from the terrorizing hordes of Saddam Hussein has been the creation for America of an Israel/Palestine-like situation but on a vastly larger scale. Sooner or later, America will have to disengage. But it will not have furthered anything of value in Iraq, whose redemption can only be achieved from within itself. Bush's war on terror becomes more curious and more tragic the more you dig into it. One thing it achieved is that America will never again be what it once was, or seemed to be, to the rest of the world.

9

A World-Historical Surge of Relativism

Individuals do not make history. Individuals are part of processes. Alexander's empire left behind an artistic legacy in Asia, but politically it was brittle and fragmented into territorial states. Ancient Greece had already been coalescing into states before the rise of Alexander. It was the formation of the first really powerful Greek territorial state, Ancient Macedonia that gave Alexander a base for his conquests. Christianity spread in the Roman Empire among Jews. Christ himself was part of Jewish tradition. There are many theories on the Christianization of the Roman Empire, but none involve Christ as a person. The Carolingian empire, like the Mongol empire and the Turkic empire of Timur, did not outlast its founder by long. It was built on the nuclei of emerging European nations (in the sense at least of peoples who spoke different proto-languages).

Luther was the culmination of a political process within the Holy Roman Empire. His doctrines had been proposed before, by John Wyclif in England among others (the Hussites, for example). Luther's protest prospered because German princes shared it. Luther himself could defend it because he was under the protection of the Elector of Saxony. Napoleon was a byproduct of the French Revolution. When he returned from his failed invasion of Egypt the French republic's generals were already victorious over France's enemies. The architect of French military power was Lazare Carnot, the inventor of conscription. The French European Empire that Napoleon built was the briefest in history until that time. Even Hitler, who is often accused of single-handedly perverting Germany, fitted nicely into an ultra-nationalist strand in German society that found in him its ideal personification. Were Germans as a nation then responsible for the Holocaust? Yes, if we give the Holocaust its proper dimensions, which embrace the near-genocidal occupations of Poland and much of European Russia apart from the specific persecution and slaughter of Jews.

(1) One act of injustice suffices to bring down the idea itself of justice

If this argument is valid for these towering figures of history, then it would be foolish to say that history is about ordinary mortals. History as process has in a very wide sense been trending towards the appreciation of individual human lives, but in general history is indifferent to the fate of individuals and it does no make room for anything resembling any possible notion of justice. A nearly impotent state, Tibet executed foreigners basically on whim just prior to the arrival in Lhasa of a small British expeditionary force led by Francis Younghusband. In his novel *Farewell to arms*, Hemingway described how, during the Italian retreat from Slovenia after the battle of Caporetto, military kangaroo courts executed any one in the files who even breathed a word of discouragement. The accusation was defeatism and the sentences were carried out immediately. The Taliban were killing any one they suspected of religious infidelity when the Americans were about to capture Kabul. One act of injustice suffices as a denial of justice. Mortality stands in the way of any attempt at justification. Artistic representation is the closest human beings come to rescuing the past and its ignominies. At best, history is about the survival of humanity and its evolution towards some situation in which poverty and violence are not so pronounced as they are now.

The actors in modern history are states, for whom moral considerations come very low in a list of priorities. Nevertheless, there are states and states and America is one that seems to confer an incalculable value on the lives of individuals. It is not and it never has been the case that the individual is above the state. The individual must first submit to the state and the state will do its utmost to protect him and to commemorate him as being, like the state itself, a part of history. Even for the Vietnam War, which the USA could have done without and tried in many ways to put behind it, America built, what it had not done for World War II veterans until recently, a special monument on which were inscribed the names of all the fallen in that conflict. This was in part to show it did not regret what it had done in Vietnam, but also to emphasize the value it gave to each individual combatant. It was in this symbolic way that America finally dispelled the lingering Vietnam darkness.

In America, concern for individual life extends to the time before it is actually independent self-sustaining life. A majority of Americans consider fetuses to be as alive as newborn babes. Abortion is legal because some forms of conception raise serious moral concerns, but if very conservative Americans had their way abortion would be banned the way liquor was during Prohibition. The ban on liquor did not stick. Neither would a ban on abortion. Many of those who voted for Prohibition probably drank socially with a clean conscience. Even some pro-lifers, as the enemies of abortion are known, might in certain extreme cases, like rape by an illegal alien, consider abortion an option. Despite the hypocrisy that moral rigidities make inevitable, America is emphatic about the absolute value it places on the life of the individual. America is either eccentric or exceptional. There are other grounds for the thesis of American exceptionalism. Today there are also important reasons for doubting it.

(2) Land of opportunity

The USA has always called itself the "land of opportunity". This means that it is a country where becoming rich is not only an inalienable right but as well an irrevocable, attainable goal. America has the largest economy in the world and it is, after Luxembourg, the most prosperous country that ever was. As the concept of GDP in itself entails, America's economic bigness has inevitably to do with the size of its population.[1] But when we consider certain aspects of American economic might, it does not seem as muscle-bound as it appears to itself. There is, for example, the matter of international comparisons on bigness, or more appropriately, hugeness. In absolute terms, the USA has the largest GDP of any other individual nation, but the combined GDP of the EU is only slightly behind it. If measured by purchasing power parity (PPP), the difference is even lower. The figures, from the World Bank to September 2004, show that, in absolute terms, America's GDP is $10,881,609 millions and for the EU, $10,621,601 million. In PPP terms, the figures (rounded) are $10,871,000 millions for the USA and $10,735,000 for the EU.

A single European consortium, Airbus, is at present the biggest builder of commercial aircraft in the world despite facing the competition

1 William Grimes, in a review of *An empire of wealth: the epic history of American economic power,* by John Steele Gordon, writes: "The United States occupies 6 per cent of the world's land mass and has 6 per cent of its people, but accounts for nearly a third of the world's gross domestic product and leads in nearly every category of economic competition." (IHT, 14 December 2004) Another recent book on American economic exceptionalism is *Saving the sun: a Wall Street gamble to rescue Japan from its trillion dollar meltdown,* by Gillian Tett, reviewed by Sharon Reir in the IHT, 28-29 June 2004

of Boeing, which not only builds commercial airliners but is also an important defense contractor. In the transatlantic debate on subsidies, which a mention of Airbus usually evokes, the Europeans might have the better case, for Airbus is possibly now self-sustaining—it is subsidized mainly by soft commercial loans—and American military spending, which is the bread-and-butter of American airplane manufacturers, has not emerged unruffled from the Second Iraqi war. Among the welter of recriminations, investigations, disclosures, accusations, and so on that the Second Iraqi war churned up was the nearly incredible story of the woman in the Pentagon who was second in charge of contracting for air force weaponry and who at the same time that she was handing out contracts to Boeing was wangling jobs in that company for herself and for her daughter.[2]

(3) In some devious way 9/11 might have had a more than symbolical impact on American economic might

Hugeness is not everything, of course; more important than size is competitiveness insofar as it is the womb of growth. Americans are famous for their productivity as are their manufactures for their quality. When quality or efficiency falters, Americans have no hesitation about going for imports, as for a long time happened with Japanese cars. America, it is said, is the best plowed field for start-ups and small- and mid-cap enterprises, and this, in the final analysis, is what economic opportunity is all about. But any one who knows the history of the Post-War is aware that the country that built its economy on the prosperity of small businesses is Italy, and Italy cannot have been that much different from other European countries. Today, Spain might have a better claim than Italy on successful small entrepreneurship. China could be eclipsing or has already eclipsed parameters established in Europe. Start-ups in America were the growth engine during the computation and internet revolutions. But that time is past and the downfall of NASDAQ proved that much of that growth was bloat. According to the World Economic Forum, the leading country in competitiveness today is Finland, followed by the USA, closely tailed by Denmark, Sweden, and Taiwan.[3]

America still is indisputably the land of opportunity, but mainly for Latinos escaping from misery in their countries to poverty in the USA. In 2004, it was reported that 25% of blacks in America lived below the poverty line. The figure cannot be much better for Latinos if it is better at all. This means that between the two groups alone there are over 20

---

2 Leslie Wayne, "A growing military contract scandal", NYT, 8-10-2004

3 www.weforum.org.

million poverty-stricken Americans, which is like saying that the USA harbors in its midst as many poor as a good-size third world country. And getting poorer if figures from the U.S. Census Bureau, which show the real income for the bottom 20% of earners decrease in 2004 to 1990s' levels, are correct. What the American economy has become notorious for is the concentration of capital and the overblown salaries and recompenses of its CEOs. Except for middle-sized corporations in some areas of manufacturing, you will seldom find in the USA that a company, even with a name haloed by age, is not owned by another. The sum of the emoluments of the upper quintile of the highest, best-paid American executives is probably superior to the combined budgets of a majority of countries in a very low-development category. President Bush, who in his first term reduced tax rates on large personal incomes, has pledged to make permanent those cuts in his second term.

But can you take away from the USA its well-earned crowns in science and technology? A rapid inventory is in order here. Even though American scientists, native-born or naturalized, have won more Nobel prizes for physics than the physicists of all European countries combined, Europe has attained some crucial technological and scientific achievements in the last half-century. The transistor was invented by a German working in Paris. The first jetliner was the British Comet. A Briton and an American made the discovery of the structure of DNA in England. Sputnik was the first artificial satellite of the Earth. With the construction of the accelerator CERN, Europe is probably on a par with America in particle physics. It was at CERN that an American and a Frenchman first devised the www protocol language that opened the Internet to the general public. America outspends Europe on science and technology by a wide margin, but Europe seems to have made a more productive use of its resources than America. Even in America there are discouraging voices about the state of American technology. The American Electronics Association declared: "We are still in the lead, but it is a precarious one. Already other countries are challenging us in key technological arenas. If we don't act now to maintain our competitive edge, we should not be surprised if the next wave of breakthrough technologies is created abroad." In the article in which this warning appeared it is conceded that America's supremacy was due to the inflow of talent, which now is threatened by widening opportunities elsewhere and by restrictive American immigration policies. More telling was the admission that China and the EU are training more engineers than the USA by entire multiples rather than just percentages.[4]

4 Robert Weisman, "U.S. is warned it is losing competitive edge in technology", IHT, 24 February 2005.

When the euro first circulated, expectations were that it would either stay on a par with the dollar or eventually lose ground to the US dollar. In a relatively brief lapse, the euro first dipped and then started overhauling the dollar. It got to be worth almost 25% more than the dollar and it has recently begun to get stronger again though not as impetuously as in the recent past. Alan Greenspan, the president of the Federal Reserve System and a man American media call indistinctly a genius or the greatest economist alive, believes the euro is not going to come down any time soon. Americans, who feel macho about their currency, are being offered the consolation that commercially a weak dollar works to the advantage of the USA and to the disadvantage of the EU. But it is not as simple as that.

The USA has been running a trade deficit for decades, which has been compensated by a favorable current account (capital flows). At present, the USA has a budget deficit so large that the current account no longer overhauls the trade deficit, because the USA has to borrow by selling treasury bonds abroad, which means it is borrowing and making payments in its own currency, devaluing it in the process. These are facts that have arisen under the Bush administration. The principal buyers of USA treasuries are Asian central banks (China, Japan, and South Korea), which are in effect sustaining the value of the dollar. There is a logical way out of this circle and that is for America to raise taxes and reduce the budget deficit. This would improve the current account compensating for the trade deficit, which, under present conditions, it is almost impossible even to prevent from growing.

Greenspan, who is beginning to seen more like a political animal than a super-brain, also defends lower taxes, which in general benefit the rich more than the middle classes.[5] The Bush-Greenspan thesis is that budget cuts have to be made. And here there looms a huge discrepancy: while the administration prognosticates that the budget deficit will not grow beyond a reasonable level to the year 2010, the Congressional Budget Office points out that the administration is not taking into account in its figures costs such as the extension of the Bush tax cuts, other administrative projects (particularly a controversial overhaul of the Social Security system), and military expenditures in Iraq and Afghanistan. The situation of the dollar is so fraught that the slightest hint from Asia of selling dollar-denominated assets causes immediate jitters and hand wringing and not incidentally waves of speculation. Paradoxically, the USA has been pressuring China to make the yuan a less competitive currency, which involves selling dollars, thus further weakening the American currency and making it less attractive as a

5 Edmund L. Andrews, "Greenspan defends his support of tax cuts", NYT, 16 March 2005.

reserve currency. In a situation like this, even small investors might prefer to buy euros rather than artificially sustained dollars. In a not so oblique manner, the attack on the WTC as a symbol of American power might have had a quite unsymbolical effect on America's economic standing in the world.[6]

When all is said and done, economics is about behavior and America has not done anything recently to inspire confidence in its behavior. On the other hand, there is no basis for resuscitating Marx's more than shopworn ideas on the mechanics and the fate of capitalism. And America is still the world's largest economy, and growing.

(4) The professor who doubled as child pornographer and the hack who committed suicide

American exceptionalism is also based on a legendary tradition of freedom of expression that more than once has risen to the defense of pornography. A recent case can illustrate this extreme.[7] An outstanding law professor in New York City was not long ago caught with literally a cache of child pornography in his computer. The material included rape and other acts of disturbing sexual violence. The discoverers were two technicians the professor had called in to repair his machine. They did nothing on their own but report what they had seen and it was the university that felt legally bound to go to the public prosecutor's office and inform on what was by any standard a type of criminal possession. The professor was eventually charged but his case raised issues among the faculty, presumably composed of legal experts, concerning privacy and freedom of expression. One professor described his delinquent colleague's collection as a "victimless crime". The contracting company under real or feared pressure from the university fired the technicians that made the discovery.

---

6 William Pesek Jr., "The dollar may be a casualty of U.S. foreign policy", IHT, 21 December 2004; a more conventionally economical view of the dollar's weakness appears in "The passing of the buck?", *The Economist*, 4 December 2004: "The requirements of a reserve currency are a large economy, open and deep financial markets, low inflation and confidence in the value of the currency. At current exchange rates the euro area's economy is not much that smaller than America's; the euro area is also the world's biggest exporter; and since the creation of the single currency, European financial markets have become deeper and more liquid. It is true that the euro area has had slower real GDP growth than America. But in dollar terms the euro area's economic weight has actually grown relative to America's over the past five years."

7 Otto Penzler and Thomas H. Cook, eds., *Best American crime writing* (2004).

Another feature often cited, as being characteristic of the scrupulous American respect for freedom of expression is the circulation and the survival in print of any theory or any concoction however discredited by the facts. An event contemporaneous with the case of the porno-obsessed law teacher was the fate of a hack writer with a criminal record. The man had been on the verge of a turnabout in his career from churning pulp to respectability through a contract with a major publisher for a biography on then presidential candidate George W. Bush. The writer already had an advance when the deal was cancelled.

Between taking it in the chin by going back to his usual writing fare and salvaging the Bush project, the writer chose the latter course, but through the dubious expedient of claiming that he had found out from Karl Rove, Bush's elections manager, that the Republican contender had once been arrested for cocaine possession, which was an invention. There was the matter of the writer's rap sheet, which contained three incarcerations, and when this came out again the publisher definitely dropped the book. Still panting for a best-seller, the writer went to a Bush-hating basement operation, which did indeed publish the prevaricating manuscript. The small-time publisher might at first have believed the story, but even when confronted with the evidence that it was an out-and-out lie he went ahead and published the work, which has by now gone through various printings making it a minor best seller. Its author committed suicide and Bush was of course controversially elected president in 2000, in part perhaps because he had been the victim of a patently libelous accusation.

(5) Revisionism and freedom of the expression

Closer to the mainstream of history, exemplary American freedom of expression concerns veracity and objectivity rather than pornography and defamation. The facts often contradict what can be called the "official version". Freedom of the press, as the traditional exemplar of freedom of expression, is the right to print what an honest reporter or investigator believes to be the facts whatever the government says the facts are. It is remitting the obverse of the official version without having to fear being denied due process or sent to a concentration camp.

The USA is not the only country where this is possible, or where this has been possible consistently in the past, but it is perhaps the country in which advocating contrarian views has always had permanent legal status and where there are no limits to how far you want to go as long as you do not stray into some arcane national security mine field. The Mordechai Vanunu case, in which an Israeli technician was kidnapped by the secret police and tried and jailed for revealing that his country was producing atomic bombs, is inconceivable in America, where any federal or state project however blanketed in secrecy is not just an opening but more likely a magnet for enquiry and broadcasting.

When President Bush was about to go to war against Iraq, he said something to the effect that his conscience was clear and that he left debate on the correctness of his actions to "revisionists". He surely wasn't but he could have been referring to D.F. Fleming, a Canadian professor who wrote a two-volume work titled *The Cold War and its origins* (1961), in which he contradicted every official American stance on the USSR and on communism. The tour de force in Prof. Fleming's monumental effort was his attempt to prove that South Korea, with the backing of America, might have provoked the Korean War, rather than the latter being a gratuitous communist aggression.

Fleming was not wrong on every point he made. His balanced views were on the whole edifying. He belonged to the group of what were once called fellow travellers—if he was not actually a crypto-communist—and fellow travelers were noted for their idealism and good intentions. The thing about Fleming that pertains to freedom of expression in America is that he built his meticulous arguments on what he found in a spyglass perusal of American newspapers, in particular *The New York Times*. He had no truck with the headlines, in fact it was the headlines he wanted to refute, but he went through every page and checked every item however minute that might have a bearing on his suspicions.

Another significant characteristic of mainstream freedom of the press in America is its willingness to recapitulate the past and revisit every incident that normally a nation would rather expunge from collective memory. American newspapers have virtually exhausted the mine of events through which American governments or organizations, legal or illegal, have committed atrocities or have inflicted injustices or the semblance of injustices against other nations or social minorities or even individuals. The accused or the condemned who could make a plausible case for their innocence have been particularly privileged. Thus, Alger Hiss was given the benefit of the doubt on his conviction as a Soviet spy until decrypts of Soviet coded messages, called Venona, not long ago were found to contain references which sustained a consensus on his culpability.[8]

American freedom of the press can be said to reach its acme in its willingness, past and present, to gather and divulge facts however offensive to authority, as in debunking the Vietnam War or forcing President Nixon to resign. If we string together revisionism, national self-criticism, and insistence on veracity and objectivity, then the case for America as the paradigm of freedom of expression is strong indeed. But let us do what could be called a factual revision of revisionism.

---

8 Joseph E. Persico, *Roosevelt's secret war: FDR and World WarII espionage* (2001), pp.391-392.

(6) Pressures, prejudices, and parti pris

The objective facts are that the press in America (and everywhere) twists and distorts the news every day through the inevitable ways in which the news is presented. These twists and distortions do not necessarily falsify the happenings that are reported and least of all are they deliberate lies. It is just that objectivity is impossible because every newspaper has to choose what it publishes among many real events and it has to decide what importance to give to events. Finally, and most perniciously, even when presenting a total picture that is in essence factual, reporters and editors slant the presentation of the news through a prejudicial use of language, which is not necessarily in itself promoting or expressing falsehoods.

Apart from the obvious, which is the featuring of events and the headlines that these events are given, on which, obviously again, pressures, prejudices, and parti pris have crucial influences, there are at least three particular instances in which subjectivism is flagrant. They are: book reviews and reporting on judicial redress and on police brutality.

Some big dailies have weekly literary sections where many books are reviewed, but on a day-to-day basis the books that receive specific attention from reviewers are strictly a matter of subjective judgment to say the least, for the worst conceivable but plausible inference is that "subjective" here could be interpreted as deliberate slanting. When America was on its post-Afghanistan jag before the anti-Iraq aggression, there was a cascade of reviews on books that debated, usually favorably, America's role as that of a necessary world imperial arbiter or gendarme.[9]

---

9 Niall Ferguson, in *Empire: the rise and demise of British world order and the lessons for global power*, called the USA "an empire in denial" and "an empire that dare not speak itself". One could hardly describe two successive wars in Asia, the second one unprovoked, as "denial". The concept of empire, Ferguson insists, is more valid than ever. He takes the British Empire as exemplar. But the very idea that the British Empire can be used as a model for the contemporary world is preposterous. To be a world-empire now, the USA would have to drag China and Russia along when it cannot even persuade France and Germany. If anything, what the USA suggests today is imperialism gone haywire. Another author in the same general tendency that believed in the rightness of American imperialism, Walter Laqueur, in *No end of to war: terrorism in the 21st century*, contended, not originally, that Islam has always been anti-West and only time would change it. It is almost trite to believe that Islamic fundamentalism cannot go on eternally defying common sense with doctrines such as that women are only truly good inside burqahs. But as to the eternal hatred between Islam and the West, the evidence can be loaded for or against.

When Iraq turned into a fiasco, reviewers shifted their attention to books that questioned the honesty or the competence of the Bush administration's war on terror. By then war on terror had become more or less meaningless, but the expression was used currently as if it were an indisputable reality.

America has a self-built reputation as a country where judicial redress is always possible. But how valid is it? For the press, the case can be made through news items in which plaintiffs get hearings in courts for justified or unjustified grievances. Normally, such items are not the stuff for front-pages or even for inside-pages' headlines, but the cumulative effect of so many instances of courts acceding to hear challenges against the powerful from what can be called collectively "ordinary citizens" or "John Does", combined with those instances which, usually because of the principles or the money involved, gain special news treatment, give the impression that America is indeed the land where the powerful are obliged to toe the line and the weak cannot be stepped on with impunity.

In the same informative category is the frequent coverage of cases of abuse of authority, which in a majority of instances is about "police brutality", to use the common expression. Since the 1970s, when Hollywood sensed that the national mood sanctioned it because of the strong backlash against the Vietnam War, films began to proliferate in which ordinary people could get away with treating cops as if they were their equals. This is a fantasy, which still lingers. For every real-world case in which police brutality and abuse of authority are documented or merely reported, there are innumerably more cases, which pass unmentioned by the press. Likewise, the cases in which courts refuse to hear plaintiffs' complaints vastly outnumber the cases in which they give them the opportunity to air them publicly.

What it comes down to is basically a "lottery effect". In America's judicial system, as in that of any democratic society, if your number comes up, you are news, but if it doesn't, and the odds are necessarily against you, you will just be another member of the legions who tried and failed. In America, it is probable but not assured that eventually every important legal issue will have its day in court, but this is not a sufficiently strong argument for claiming that American society is indeed the paragon of "justice" that its media like to present.

(7) The ups and downs of front-page news

In the very recent past any one who wanted could observe how the American press hierarchizes information. During more than the first half of the year 2004, events in Iraq were regularly featured as front-page news. Even though nothing had changed in Iraq, the focus gradually changed to the presidential campaign, particularly during and after the Bush-Kerry debates. This is understandable as how Americans voted would have to have an effect on the Iraq problem, apart of course from the fact that any American presidential election has to be the center of attention for newsgathering while the electoral process is going on.

The election came and went. Bush won. Iraq was unchanged. The battle for Fallujah could not be ignored and it was highlighted side-by-side with the preparations for Bush's second term. But a subtle change then occurred. The taking of Fallujah was inevitable given the correlation of forces. It was presented as a significant victory in the occupation of Iraq. A seemingly vindicated Bush displaced Iraq from front-page headlines. The pre-election denigration of the president ceased. A man who before was habitually being called a liar suddenly could do no wrong. During October, Iraq was still big news because it was there that American forces were embattled. By mid-November, although the battle to pacify Iraq had not abated, Iraq became and has remained mostly inside-pages material.

Most importantly, there is the slanting of the news, for which also recent events are a good showpiece. As the USA stumbled its way to the Fallujah confrontation, Sharon in Israel was doing exactly as he pleased with the Palestinian problem. The Intifada was if not finished very nearly under control. We shall return to the way the press treated this process, and here we shall just point to a reporting habit that had become as ingrained as the use of "war on terror" as a knee-jerk tag for something that no longer had any rational justification.

If Israel unsurprisingly had triumphed and Palestine was a castaway of power politics, America had no cause to feel that there was anything amiss, because the Israel/Palestine problem was simplified in daily reporting as a conflict between Arafat, the founder and leader of the terrorist Al Fatah organization, and Sharon, the Israeli PM who was only trying to protect his country against terrorism. Conversely, it was never stated that Sharon once was condemned—and stands accused in the bar of history—as the artificer of the slaughter of Palestinians in Beirut. As a matter of Pavlovian routine, the mention of Al Fatah, whatever it was, triggered the idea of unfettered terrorism. Even when the Israelis said that Hamas was the main terrorist Palestine organization, press reports seldom mentioned that Hamas was opposed to Arafat because he had accepted the creation of the weak PA. Also, this simple fact was never cited when it was said untiringly that Arafat was deliberately tolerating Hamas terrorism.

(8) Has freedom of expression really confronted America's dark past?

If we go over the evidence on America's exceptional freedom of expression, what stands out is that it is not so much about objectivity, veracity, or fairness, but about the quantity of information that the press remits. Here again we must cite the NYT, arguably the most informative daily in the world, the unwitting source, as we saw, for Fleming's vast tirade on American responsibility for the Cold War.

A simple comparative judgment permits the inference that the choosing, the prioritizing, and the slanting of news easily beats quantity of news in influence over public opinion. Freedom of expression has little significance if it is not also a commitment to fairness of information. Nevertheless, freedom of the press in America is unhindered and you can find if you search in American newspapers all the news that you will ever want to have on current events and politics. But does this fulfill the constraint that freedom of expression is not "actual" if it is not also truly objective? The privileging of freedom of expression in America over freedom of expression anywhere else is that it is indeed "potentially" there in a newspaper such as the NYT. So what is "actual" as against "potential" freedom of expression in America and its influence on the public's view of the unfolding of history?

An undeniable actual is America facing its past as an overtly racialist country, not much different from what South Africa still was when America had legally dismantled institutional racism. This is often contrasted with Europe in relation to its past. A good example is France.

Any time that some story surfaces there about the collaborationist pro-Nazi Vichy regime, American papers routinely remark that France has never "faced up to its past". No mention is made of the historical fact that the Post-War French Fourth Republic was led by politicians, Charles de Gaulle foremost, that had no links to Vichy, or if they had once had, as was famously the case of president François Mitterand, they had turned against Vichy long before the Normandy invasion made the defeat of Germany a matter of time. France has faced its past. Collaborators were tried. French Gestapo henchmen have been sentenced decades after the end of the Nazi occupation.

In America, a similar facing of the past would require the active denunciation, at least, of every state administration that ever tolerated or was complicit with the KKK directly or indirectly. Indictments should have been handed down when there were still survivors to every identifiable participant in racial lynchings. A confirmation of this historical remissness came about when the U.S. Senate in June 2005 apologized to the victims of lynchings and surviving relatives. Even so, the Senate vote was not unanimous.[10]

The worst burden on Europe from its past is Nazism and in particular the Jewish Holocaust. American dailies seldom miss any news item that might indicate that Europe is still potentially anti-Semitic and Holocaust-prone, in other words, that unlike America, France and Europe generally (except Great Britain) has still not "faced the past". But have Americans really faced their past in all its terror-filled dimensions? Does freedom of expression really take the many dark sides of America's past into account? Try a gedanken here and imagine the carnage that would have ensued had a black terrorist killed a white politician at the height of the lynchings era.

The American Civil War is generally a matter of pride rather than of shame, despite the knowledge that no 19th century war in Europe attained the degree of brutality of the war between the states, in which destitute Irish immigrants were paid to serve as cannon-fodder in place of the well-off and during which, arguably, the ritual lynching of Negroes began not in the South but in New York city. Has America been made to understand through freedom of expression that nearly the entire post-Civil War period in the South was one long, unmitigated reign of terror for blacks? This turning away from history would be justified if racial prejudices no longer existed, but in America the recurrence of police brutality and the passionate espousal of capital punishment, both of which fall disproportionately on blacks, are more than enough proof that such is not the case.

And has actual freedom of expression in America led to the recognition that My Lai was not the only atrocity committed in Vietnam but that there exist sufficient testimonies to the effect that the entire war was blemished by constant and incorrigible atrocities?[11] The sum of the Civil War, the Indian wars, and the Vietnam war, without going any further, makes the issue of facing the past not a recommendation but more likely an indictment of America's "exceptional" freedom of expression. As we said, one act of injustice is a denial of justice and, in strict ethical terms, a difference between thousands and millions of victims is not tenable. The American respect for the sanctity of life may

10 Sheryl Gay Stolberg, "A split over when to say 'sorry'", IHT, 20 June 2005

11 To cite one case, in the pages of the Toledo, Ohio, newspaper *The Blade*, a Vietnam veteran admitted that he lost count of the civilians he had killed. In 1967, his elite army unit killed thousands of Vietnamese and the army opened and closed an investigation without indictments. Other members of the same unit confirmed the story of unpunished war atrocities.

be exceptional but mainly if it's towards the lives of Americans. Iraq shows daily that, as an American cartoon put it, "the rest are just Arabs".[12]

(9) Soviet revisionism was done by people who seemed to be hanging on to lightning rods in the middle of a heavy thunderstorm

Often in reading American dailies one gets the impression that the Cold War is not over and that Stalinism is still alive and well in Russia. As to China, the American freedom-of-expression keynote is Tianamen. Let us look at these cases.

It was not the USA that forced Nikita Khrushchev to denounce Stalin's crimes. The voluminous biography of Khrushchev by the American historian William Taubman has as its underlying leitmotif that his subject was practically as guilty as Stalin himself. What would Taubman, who sounds so authoritative on moral issues, have done had he been in Khrushchev's shoes or had he merely happened to be born in the USSR? Was the denunciation of Stalinism in the 20th Congress of the CPUS not perhaps the most remarkable act of facing the past in our times? The only process that comes close to de-Stalinization in daring and courage might be Gorbachev's dismantling, first, of the Soviet empire, and then, of the constitutional basis of Soviet tyranny. And is there any doubt that Gorbachev was a direct political heir of Khrushchev? American freedom of expression faces the past practically from an armchair. Facing the past in the USSR was done by people who seemed to be hanging on to lighting rods during a heavy thunderstorm.

No one knows how many people were killed during the suppression of the pro-democracy riots in Tiananmen Square in Beijing in 1989. The usual figure is "hundreds". The certitude under American freedom-of-expression rules is that Tiananmen is a synonym for tyranny and brutality.

China today is hardly an American-type democracy. It is, if political realism counts, a communist-type democracy. People at the top get there through elections, not by a general electorate but by the large electoral base that is constituted by membership in the Communist

12 A interesting item on "facing the past" that surfaced in the NYT in October 2004, was that a professor at Southern Methodist University in Dallas, Benjamin Heber Johnson, had unearthed archival evidence that the Texas Rangers had probably been responsible before 1919 for the "evaporation" of up to 5,000 Mexicans in the Rio Grande valley to make way for American settlers. Substitute "desparecidos" for "evaporation" and what do you get? Chile under Pinochet comes to mind.

Party of China, a country that by any economic touchstone is no longer communist but the most dynamic capitalist economy in the world today. Is it not reasonable to presume that if the democratic protesters in Tiananmen had been "empowered" in some miraculous manner China might not have arrived at where it is now? Lee Kwan Yew, the founder of Singapore, who was often accused of being an authoritarian prime minister but never of having usurped power undemocratically, affirmed that Chinese leadership did the right thing in restoring order in Beijing against what were basically riotous students.

Would American capitalism have developed as phenomenally as it did if the authorities had not prevented the propagation of the violence and disorder in manifestations such as the Haymarket riots and the Pullman strike? Is preventing social disorder in a democracy more valid than preventing social chaos in an authoritarian society? And where does American freedom of expression get the right to promote the imposition of the American democratic model, in which the foundational principle of majority rule can legally be disregarded, on the rest of the world? Of course American democracy has worked now for well over 200 years and of course it is preferable to tyranny in any guise, but unexceptional American freedom of expression cannot claim for it that it is indisputably exceptional.

(10) The apotheosis of Sharon

We dealt with slanting the news briefly before. We would like now to expand on that crucial issue for freedom of expression. In May 2004, the NYT circulated a letter among its staff criticizing the readiness with which its reporters and editors accepted extravagant claims about the existence of Iraqi WMD. As it was already evident at the time that whatever claims made about Iraqi WMD were per se extravagant, the correct reading to put on the letter was that it constituted an incitement to more caution and balance in the weighing of sources and in the presentation of the news. Any reasonable interpretation of it should have included the truism that the official version is not on the face of it necessarily trustworthy, or that, as the saw goes, might does not make right. As children are taught this, presumably news professionals were simply being reminded of something that they should already have known.

By August 2004, Israel was literally calling the shots in Palestine and Sharon was at the summit of his power, a summit that extended almost without indentations during the following months. The Israeli PM could do no wrong. He had smothered the Intifada. He had made the West Bank settlements secure. He was practically dictating American foreign policy in the Middle East. If the biggest gainer from the destruction of

Iraq was Israel, then Sharon had not just shown the way he wanted the American government to go, but it could be argued that he had benefited from the election of president Bush as much as the American president himself. The futility of the Second Iraqi war for America could be used as a demonstration that it had been undertaken as much with Israel as with war on terror in mind. Here was a case, if there had been one, in which a reporter or an editor did well to keep his/her eyes peeled and to look for the underside. The NYT threw caution to the wind and did exactly the opposite.

A spread on 16 August in the IHT, which is the NYT abroad, Sharon appeared in a photograph sitting at a table looking as pleased as Punch surrounded by bodyguards and politicians. The piece was titled "Shaper of modern Israel: Sharon the warrior". What else could the man want? It was his apotheosis, unfortunately marred by lies and inaccuracies, which the reporter, James Bennet, must have intended and his editors had let pass. To dissect the entire article would be repetitious. To start with, if the shaping of modern Israel was the doing of a "warrior" who hated Arabs and had an iron grip on Palestinians, then it wasn't Sharon at all but Jabotinsky, the man Ben-Gurion vilified as "Validimir Hitler", who had planned it over 80 years before. Not too far into the article one came upon this whopper: "When the Palestinian uprising brought his view of reality back into fashion, Sharon was ready." The fuse of the Intifada had been lit by Sharon and, as the principal promoter of land grabbing in Palestinian territory, he had placed the explosives as well. As to the vogue of extremism in Israel, Sharon had been preceded as PM by Benjamin Netanyahu, who was his equal as hardliner though his inferior as politician. Clearly, the Second Intifada was not what made Sharon's stance "fashionable": Israel was receptive to it before the Intifada in great part because Sharon himself had done all in his power to promote Israeli receptiveness. The IHT/NYT article was an unalloyed case of putting the cart before the horse.

(11) The discrediting of Arafat discredited the exceptionality of American freedom of expression

The completion of Sharon's labors of Hercules, after the scuttling of the peace process and the emasculation of the PA, was the moral and political discredit of Arafat. Politically Arafat was already nearly finished. Now all that was needed was the complete soiling of his reputation. Three days after Sharon's "deification", Arafat obligingly admitted that he had made some indeterminate mistakes. Arafat had indeed made many mistakes in his life. But the self-evident prejudice in the relatively brief piece was present in its lead, which assumed that he was corrupt and qualified Arafat's admission as "rare". How many times had the Associated Press, the source of that jewel, heard such admissions from Sharon or from the greatest blunderer of all, president Bush the younger?

On 17 September, Gregg Myer was not as slavish as Bennet on Sharon when he wrote that Powell's roadmap had "collapsed amid continuing violence after it was introduced in June 2003". The roadmap had not collapsed because of the violence. The violence was there before. Arafat was perfectly willing to accept a roadmap or anything to rescue what at that point was only a caricature of authority. Arafat had once said that he would wear down his archenemy Sharon. But he controlled nothing when Powell was insisting that he control terrorism. It was Sharon who blasted the roadmap in September because, as he had the situation in hand, he did not need it and he had already in mind an alternative for it.

That it wasn't only reporters but editors also who were skewing things at the IHT was obvious from the quality of some of the articles published as op-eds. On 1 October, Gerald Steinberg argued that it was not a double standard for Israel to have nuclear weapons and to do all it could to deny them to its Muslim neighbors. His argument in essence was that Israel, a country which had defeated with conventional weapons all its Arab neighbors and which struck at will from the air any target around it that it chose, needed nuclear weapons because it was only a sliver of land on a map of the Middle East. In view of the history of the region, Iran could have argued that it had the right to have nuclear weapons because it was the only way it could force Israel to negotiate. The footnote in the article did not specify that its opinions were the author's as was the case of an article very critical of Israel, which had been written by another Jew.

Henry Siegman, a former executive head of the American Jewish Congress and of the Synagogue Council of America, had some arguments about Sharon that went against the grain of his representation as a statesman. He wrote, and we quote: "Sharon is not about to agree to the most minimal conditions for viable Palestinian statehood. His unshakable resolve to avoid dealing with the Palestinians—even to prevent chaos in the wake of the promised withdrawal from Gaza—and to widen Jewish settlement activity throughout the West Bank gives the lie to such wishful thinking." What Sharon, in Siegman's view, seemed to be pursuing was a "political disengagement from the Palestinian population [of the occupied territories]...The South African government also 'disengaged' from the Bantustans that it had set up as homelands for the black majority. [Sharon and his supporters] seem not to understand, or not to care, that it is precisely South Africa's 'disengagement' that defined its racist regime and that disengagement will do the same for Israel if it persists in following the South African model." Siegman added: "Sharon and Israel's right wing represent a radical departure from the dominant sensibility of the founders of the Zionist movement, such as Theodore Herzl, Max Nordau, Chaim Weizmann, and others."

The past is the past and Sharon was not alone. He had the support of a majority of Israelis and the backing of President Bush, who cannot be accused of racism. Nevertheless, Siegman argued, "if Sharon—with the support of Israelis, world Jewry and the United States—leverages his promised withdrawal from Gaza into an Israeli presence in the West Bank that it is impossible to dislodge, a racist enterprise is surely what his policies will produce." But didn't Israel have to defend itself against Palestinian terrorism? "The Palestinian national struggle and terrorism resorted to in its name, has created major security problems for Israel. But these security concerns cannot be invoked as a pretext for policies that bring apartheid rule to the West Bank and Gaza. It is not true that Palestinian violence represents an existential threat to the state of Israel. More to the point, whatever the seriousness of the threat, it can be dealt with by Israel at least as effectively from Israel's pre-1967 borders as it has under conditions of occupation." For Israel, then, it was a choice between racism, the doctrine with which Hitler tried to exterminate Jews, and accepting the political rights of Palestinians. The Jewish lobby made sure that next to Siegman's credentials was written: "This is a personal comment". Presumably, or his computer activated itself and wrote without his knowledge and consent.

Obviously, there was in the IHT room for opposing views, but the balance between them was noticeably skewed. On the question of what exactly is the "Jewish lobby", a simple answer would be a group of highly paid public relations people advancing specific "Jewish causes" in Washington. But there are no "specific Jewish causes" and a PR person making the case for Israel to a congressman would be like telling an extremely thirsty person next to a water cooler: "Drink! Go on, drink!" A brief and not inaccurate (but not complete) answer is that the Jewish lobby is constituted by the American media themselves, or at least that its power is manifest there better than anywhere else.

On 4 October, Steven Erlanger wrote a piece, which outdid Bennet in turning the facts about. It said that the Second Intifada had begun as a "popular insurrection" which had become "low-intensity warfare" and had convinced the Israelis that the Palestinians were unreliable. "One result", he continued, "was the election of the hawk Ariel Sharon as the Israeli prime minister", which sounded critical if it had been true. Israelis had elected Netanyahu in 1996 and he was clearly convinced, five years before the Second Intifada, that Israel could not, and indeed should not, negotiate with Palestinians. The statistics that Erlanger used remitted the Israeli wheeze that for every Israeli three Palestinians were killed, which was preposterous as Palestinian bombs at the worst of times had gone off sporadically and Israel had then been attacking Gaza continuously for months with almost complete impunity. By November, the NYT/IHT had the dying Arafat profiled as a thief with an empire which in one paragraph was estimated at between $3 billion and $5 billion and in the next was down to a "few million".

These articles are only selections, and not even of the most exaggerated examples of anti-Palestinian and pro-Israeli bias in the NYT/IHT. Apparently the internal letter the NYT had circulated either did not apply to the problem of Israel/Palestine or it was deliberately or unwittingly ignored. The slanting of the news on that issue by the premier among the elite of American dailies, to boot a newspaper with a reputation for extreme liberalism, could leave no doubt that freedom of expression in America as commitment to veracity and balance was far from exceptional.

(12) How smart is American intelligence?

The opposite of freedom of expression is intelligence gathering in which secrecy is the norm. No one disputes that this should be so and what is expected in this terrain is not openness but efficacy. There was a time when America's CIA was considered practically infallible. It knew everything and it could undertake successfully any covert operation it chose. In Latin America in particular leftists believed that the CIA was everywhere and had infiltrated any organization, from governments down, it wanted to subvert or subject to its wishes. The CIA is another expression of American "exceptionalism" on which the Second Iraqi war has imposed a re-appraisal.

"Intelligence" in a government or a military context usually involves not just information but the actions determined by what is finally defined as "information". "Smart intelligence" is not a redundancy but the real reliability of information, which is not necessarily what "official" intelligence decides information to be. With these touchstones, it turns out that the intelligence of the greatest, most powerful, most democratic, and most just-about-anything nation on earth has a remarkably poverty-stricken record.

There is much more than the CIA to the American "intelligence community", but for the sake of not being short of accuracy we shall avoid delving into any specific intelligence service, except for this brief historical prologue: that the CIA proper was not founded until 1947, that before World War II there existed intelligence services and especially decryption departments in the different branches of the armed forces, that Franklin D. Roosevelt made a hotch-potch of American intelligence, and that after the CIA was created it was often assigned "operations" in Latin America.[13] It must also be kept in mind that after World War II and until 1991 the defeat of the USSR was America's number one priority, that after 1991 USA government intelligence gradually became a watchdog against terrorism and nuclear proliferation, and that after 9/11 it was oriented exclusively to capturing Osama bin Laden, destroying Al Qaida, overthrowing Saddam Hussein, and subduing Iraq.

The first notable intervention of the CIA in Latin America was the overthrow of the leftist government of Gen. Jacobo Arbenz in Guatemala. The operation was successfully carried out with one or two P-38s and a couple of bombs. Arbenz was deserted by the Guatemalan armed forces, which from the 1960s to the 1990s caused hundreds of thousands of deaths against agrarian insurrections it never managed to quell. The covert American intervention in the Guatemalan civil war, repeated in El Salvador, constitutes further evidence that for Americans it is individual American lives that matter and not the ideal per se of the value of individual lives.

The next Latin American deed of the CIA was the organization of the invasion of Cuba to overthrow Fidel Castro, whom incidentally it had previously misjudged as a paladin of democracy. The planning for this expedition was initiated under president Dwight D. Eisenhower and approved by President John F. Kennedy. In many respects, it was not very intelligent. To start with, it wasn't very subtle. The Cuban regiment that was to knock Castro out trained in Guatemala in full view of any one who cared. In fact, it was believed that it wasn't even necessary for the invaders to get to Havana before Cubans rose up as one man and expelled or imprisoned Castro. The landing was on Playa Girón, a sandy stretch with one road through a crocodile-infested swamp. Castro made short shrift of the invaders.

The only really successful undertaking in Latin America by the CIA was the overthrow of the Chilean Socialist Salvador Allende, but there are some quodlibets here. For one thing the role of the CIA in Allende's overthrow is debatable. The military led by Pinochet were intent on doing it and the CIA did not need to buy or train them. And two, if the CIA did contribute to Allende's overthrow, it must bear the responsibility for the tens of thousands of people who in Chile were tortured or killed during the savage period of the Pinochet dictatorship. The reason the Allende operation can be considered a success is because

13 Persico, op. cit. See, among other passages, pp.181-187, pp.248-250, and pp.446-448.

Chile today is Latin America's most prosperous country, which, who knows, might have happened without the butchery. Incidentally, Nicaragua was another "success story" if we assume that post-Sandinist Nicaragua is indeed a success.

It was in the third world in general and not just in Latin America that the CIA had a free run. Its most renowned intervention was in Iran where it backed Shah Muhammad Reza Pahlavi to the hilt and managed to enthrone him as a pro-American dictator. Reza Pahlavi tried to modernize Iran but used a very heavy hand. When a Muslim national insurrection forced the Shah to flee, the opprobrium for all that had been done during the dictatorship was placed on the USA. There followed the sequestration of the American embassy with its diplomatic personnel in Tehran and the chasm that still separates the USA and Iran.

(13) Gorbachev left Kremlinologists out of work, which in a sense let American intelligence off the hook

The American intelligence record against communism is patchy, not to say lamentable. When Vietnam was divided into a communist north and a capitalist south, South Vietnam began organizing itself to resist communism under President Ngo Dinh Diem, appointed by the last Vietnamese king, Bao Dai (whom Diem deposed later). Diem had considerable support in his own country. Buddhists monks, with at best dubious motivations, were putting pressure on the Diem regime. But in general South Vietnam was fairly stable.

Domino Theory, the futility of which we have already described, was a concoction of American intelligence. It was from its wrongheaded premises that the USA decided to intervene militarily in Vietnam with 12,000 "advisors", a force that in seven years had grown over forty times. No sooner were Americans arriving in large numbers than American intelligence, coached by ambassador Henry Cabot Lodge, began intriguing against Diem, who basically was thrown by the Kennedy administration to the South Vietnamese military dogs and assassinated. After that, South Vietnam became very politically volatile. Stability was achieved under Gen. Nguyen Van Thieu, but by then Americans were calling the tune, which made any South Vietnamese president seem like a straw man.

During most of the war either the intelligence was lacking or it was disregarded that USA-fronting governments were doomed. When the USA finally did hand power back to the South Vietnamese it was to a demoralized military clique that soon caved in to the communists. Domino Theory also led to the deposition of the competent, neutralist King Norodom Sihanouk and the imposition on Cambodia of a feckless military regime that crumbled before the homicidal Khmer Rouge boy-soldiers.

But it wasn't in poor, backward countries only that American intelligence got it wrong. The USA was caught flat-footed by the invasion of Egypt by Israel, Britain, and France. Intelligence services might have fomented rebellions and dissent in the Soviet empire but not one of those that occurred—in East Germany, in Hungary, in Czechoslovakia, and in Poland—was foreseen. Obviously, the gift of accurate prediction is not given to any individual or even to a conglomerate of the best and the brightest. But it is striking that, when the USSR began its sharp economic decline during the feckless, pompous Brezhnev regime, the estimates for Soviet economic performance emanating from American intelligence sources gave no inkling of the straits the Soviets were in.

Perhaps this had changed somewhat by the time Reagan was elected president and it could only have been through a very downbeat assessment of Soviet economic and military capabilities that Reagan dared to challenge the USSR with the SDI, the anti-missile shield which, if quickly erected (and it wasn't feasible then), would have been like inviting a Soviet pre-emptive attack. But the crumbling of the Soviet empire, despite Gorbachev's manifest reformism, caught the world and American intelligence by surprise. And the dissolution of the USSR left Kremlinologists out of work—temporarily because they are back in business again—which in a way leaves the American intelligence community off the hook as it proves that Western academics and pundits are also wrong most if not all of the time.

(14) America won in the Post War but it is in danger of losing the post-Cold War

Having won the Cold War, the USA had an interest in maintaining the world status quo. President George H.W. Bush showed it during the First Iraqi or Gulf war. World stability required that nuclear proliferation not be tolerated, and this highlights one of the greatest conundrums of American intelligence.

The exact dates for the nuclear-proliferation network established by Pakistan are not known. But it is almost certain that by the mid-1980s, when the USA and Pakistan were already fast allies against the Soviets in Afghanistan, Pakistan was busily supplying Iran with nuclear technology and exchanging the latter for rocketry expertise with North Korea. To say it briefly, America became friendly with Pakistan precisely when Pakistan was behaving as perhaps the world's greatest purveyor of technological terror. These alternatives are, then, inescapable: either American intelligence knew about Pakistani nuclear proliferation and winked at it, or it had no idea that Pakistan was a nuclear proliferator, in which case it was worthless.

The inferences become wilder and wilder. But still remain inferences. American intelligence had to know it was dealing with fundamentalists in Pakistan and in Afghanistan. When Donald Rumsfeld established a cooperative relation between the USA and Iraq it was to foil anti-American fundamentalism in Iran. American analysts knew that Saddam Hussein was a Baathist. They knew, or had to know, that Baath was a laicist party indifferent if not antagonistic to religion. Ergo, it was OK to use Iraq against Iran. So American intelligence in one part of the Middle East at large was palling around with fundamentalists and in another it was making anti-fundamentalist friends. This was cynical but acceptable. After all, intelligence is about mutual benefits, not about love marriages. What astounds is that America should have been surprised by Iraq, the Baathist state, making a grab for fundamentalist Kuwait and firing off Scuds against Israel with as much gusto as the Taliban would have done if they had had half a chance. It was as if it ignored what is as palpable as the fingers of a hand, which is that the bridge linking all Muslims is hatred of Israel.

American intelligence still hadn't demonstrated its full capacity for blundering. During the Clinton administrations, intelligence was relatively focused if on occasions erratic. It sent Tomahawks flying against Sudan and Afghanistan. It was wrong about Sudan—how did it miss that fundamentalism in Sudan fell out of favor when its defender, Hassan Turabi, was jailed?—but it was spot on in singling out the Taliban as a menace, which was more than Bush the younger could see. Some have argued that the USA bungled in causing bin Laden to decamp to Afghanistan, where he could do more mischief than in Sudan. But bin Laden's movements could not be controlled. The USA stumbled in taking on Somalia, but got out of there quickly when it realized there was no point in staying. This had the tragic consequence that when the Hutus in Rwanda massacred their Tutsi neighbors in the hundreds of thousands, America was in the forefront of developed countries that refused to intervene in what amounted to a real attempt at genocide.

(15) American intelligence never had a clue and still has no clue of why or whom it is fighting in Iraq

Once Bush the younger assumed office things took a decided turn for the worse. American intelligence became schizoid. It also seemed to have lost its power of concentration. The president and his closest advisor were intent on attacking Iraq. There was no justification whatsoever for this policy but Iraq was made the suspect that American intelligence was forced to track. While this went on, intelligence was getting information on a regular basis on what was going to happen on 9/11. From different sources it was known: (1) that fundamentalists were planning a big strike against America; (2) what means were going to be employed (airplane hijackings); and (3) even who some of the intended hijackers were, including Mohammed Atta, the leader of the 9/11 attack. In brief, one part of American intelligence was on a wild goose chase while the other knew or suspected where danger lurked but had no listeners in the highest sphere of government. When 9/11 happened, President Bush's anti-Iraq stance became so obsessive that it dragged American intelligence agencies along. The personality split was healed. But American intelligence was set to sink to historical lows.

Lies were concocted about Iraq. A so-called mission to save the country from a savage dictator was invented. The supposedly sensible Powell told Bush to beware of taking over Iraq, as if any serious intelligence analysis could propound that he could do any such thing. As in the case of Cuba and Kennedy forty years earlier, Bush and his court were told what they wanted to hear: that Iraq would receive Americans with open arms and that peace would break out after the war. In other words, haywire policy determined what intelligence said. It was the total perversion of the function of government intelligence. The most incredible part was that Bush actually did seem to believe the lies that he wanted to believe in. He had to know he was lying but he somehow imposed on himself the conviction that he wasn't.

Bush declared the Second Iraqi war over when no sane intelligence analyst would have concurred. Immediately, all the lies started coming out, so the "historical mission" thing was trotted out. But even that part of the intelligence community that had gone along with Bush's fantasies dropped out of the circle of lies. Even Bush had to admit that the part about invading Iraq to find WMD had turned out to be wrong. Still there was the "mission". But what indeed was the "mission"?

Apparently it was a double mission. One was to restore democracy to Iraq. Bush's intelligence apparatus didn't know, or didn't bother telling him, that no country enjoys being "liberated" for whatever higher purpose by another country. Iraq was up in arms. All intelligence appraisals had proven wrong. Not only did Iraqis reject the American occupation, but the intelligence that said that America's presence in Iraq would be welcomed by the Shiites, who had been systematically excluded from power by the Sunni, turned out to be literally dead wrong: the Shiites were as hostile against America as the Sunni. The Kurds were about the only Iraqis—and they are Kurds first and foremost—who weren't resisting the American occupation.

The ultimate in the duck-soup universe in which American intelligence exists is that it never had a clue and still has no clue of why or whom it is fighting in Iraq. At first it was believed that Saddam Hussein was leading the resistance. This theory came a-tumble when Hussein was caught. Then the Sherlocks started following the foot tracks of Sunni and Shia clerics, although the Hussein hypothesis, in the person of Izzat Ibrahim, was not entirely abandoned. For a time all eyes were concentrating on Zarqawi, but the snoops at first had no idea if he was a creature of bin Laden or out of where he had come. With the taking of Fallujah it was believed that Zarqawi had been knocked flat, but as the insurrection showed no signs of abating, the betting was again on Ibrahim, this time implicating Syria, basically for lack of any really trustworthy information.

It could be argued that American intelligence has been efficacious where it most counts and that is in the war on terror in America itself, which it certainly appears to be winning. But, without intending to subtract merits where they are deserved, this particular win is probably due mainly to ethnic and religious profiling. Muslims are a tiny minority in America and when they act ostentatiously Muslim, a neighborhood or a building gossip is as good as any CIA operative. A remarkable example of Islamic profiling was first published in the 5 January 2005 edition of the IHT as a half-page in which a NY district court called on some 400 individuals and organizations to answer for deaths, damage, and injuries occasioned by 9/11. Osama bin Laden was naturally included but a third or more of the list was made up of organizations from a cement factory to the "charities" which the CIA has made notorious as presumed conduits for terrorist funds. These accusations may be justified or not but the list as it stands transmits the implication that Muslims, individuals or corporations, are per se suspect.[14]

Despite this critique of the performance American intelligence, the fact remains that the USA won the Cold War and that intelligence was crucial in avoiding nuclear Holocaust. But history does not stand still. In the last sixty years there have been two post-wars. There was the post-World War II, in which America was victorious. But now we are in the post-Cold War and in this one America is not winning and it is not winning because, even though American intelligence has always been flawed, at this juncture it is evident that it has been deliberately perverted by a tiny group of arrogant incompetents.

---

14 This suit was on top of the fund which distributed to 18 November 2004 $7 billion to the families of those who died or were injured on 9/11. The pattern of the awards was a reflection of American society: those who already had got more than those who had less. One of the beneficiaries already had $10,000,000 in insurance and benefits. The 25 wealthiest victims received an average of $6.3 million. There were 2973 possible death-compensation claimants but 2880 actual death-claims. There were also 2680 injury claims. Of the dead, 61% earned less than $100,000; 66% were males; and 37% were in their 30s. The fund was included in an airline subsidy package as an alternative to litigation, the American inclination to which was obviously not dampened.

(16) Summary on American exceptionalism

Let us do a summary on what it is that we mean with our case against American exceptionalism. To start with the concept itself of American exceptionalism, where did it originate? We have taken the thesis for granted basically because it is America that considers itself exceptional. America is not the only nation that has such warm feelings about itself, but Americans did have some grounds for extreme national pride. If we except minor or brief examples from the recent past of Europe—some Italian city-states, the English commonwealth, a period during the inception of the Netherlands as an independent state—America was both the first republic and the first true democracy in the Western world. Britain had achieved a degree parliamentary democracy during the 18th century, but it was also anti-democratic in many ways. By the 1820s, and before any other advanced state, universal white male suffrage was the rule in America.

During the 19th century, and indeed to our days, America was the land of refuge for millions seeking a better life. In one century of independent existence, America had become a power among powers in all-significant respects, especially economic development and military potential. It was America that tipped the balance during World War I and it was America who did its utmost to make the world better after the war. America even helped Bolshevik Russia to overcome the depths of misery to which it had fallen by its own doing. America saved the world from Nazism and from barbarous Japanese aggression during World War II. America, the country who had turned its back on the League of Nations, practically created the United Nations. It was America who drew the line against Stalinism and communist totalitarianism. Whether America peacefully defeated the USSR or the Cold War was declared over by its protagonists, it was America who emerged from it stronger and incomparably wealthier. Even before this happened, any fair assessment had to admit that what America had achieved and had to offer the world was far superior to what communism represented. In the 1990s, when and where America led the world followed, and no one seriously disputed American world leadership, which was not an imposition but as often as not a role it was asked to assume.

Our previous impugnment of American exceptionalism is not intended as a denial of America's greatness but as a correction of exaggerated claims and misperceptions by America about itself. There exists in the world at large at present a situation that makes such a correction not only justified but also necessary. On the trio of categories that we chose—valuation of individual human life, land of opportunity par excellence, and freedom of expression as a full commitment to veracity—America had been quite unexceptional before the Second

Iraqi war. But a powerful denial of America's perception of its exceptionalism required the triggering device that this war provided.

Most emphatically, this is not to advocate Hussein's murderous regime or the needless, arbitrary, and shocking cruelness of kidnappers and executioners among Iraqi insurgents. Each piece of the present world-historical pattern must be placed in its right place. Even the Palestinian cause, which we have championed in this work, is not exempt from serious criticism, particularly as it has been used by Arab states and in it is over-reliance on the expedient of social terrorism. What we have engaged in is the sort of revisionism that Bush himself recommended for historians. His "this is reality now" challenge contained the curious implication that somehow contemporary events are not history. But nothing that happens can be yanked from historical appraisal even as it is happening. History is much wider than Bush envisions it.

(17) Being out of sync can be damaging to America's prestige and influence

What is striking about America today is how much it is out of sync with the rest of the world, and not just with Arabic and non-Arabic Muslim societies. Ironically, in the matter of religious fundamentalism America often seems to be on a par with Iran, one of the vertexes of Bush's "axis" of evil. There is nothing in America manipulating democracy like the theocratic Council of Experts does in Iran. But there is hardly a difference between the claims of American fundamentalists and those of Iranian fundamentalists. Both say that god is with them, like the inscription "Gott ist mit uns" on the German Iron Cross. But what has God to do with international relations? And on social issues, even though American fundamentalists are far less conservative than their Iranian counterparts, they are insidiously gaining so much ground it is not inconceivable they might attain something close to the objectives of pro-lifers, although the pressure now is on for "intelligent design", a seemingly respectable theory that would disqualify evolution and discredit science in favor of religion.

On capital punishment, another issue on which American Christian and Muslim fundamentalisms are of one mind, America defies universal European disapproval. China is prodigious in its application of death sentences. America generally is heedless about its demonstrated inefficacy and unfairness. In terms of basic attitudes, China and the USA are not dissimilar, although a very large allowance must be made for the fact that in America there is debate on capital punishment whereas in China, so far, there is none. Also in America, debate sometimes leads to action, as when Gov. George Ryan of Illinois emptied Death Row by lawful decree. However, the abolition of capital punishment in America is not at present even a remote political option.

No one anywhere likes taxes and America has by far the lowest of any developed country. This of course makes America very exceptional, but is it necessarily exceptional in a good way? Perhaps again the correct appraisal is that America is moving out of step with a global trend. This becomes more pronounced when America's tax largess is placed next to the signs that American democracy has a marked plutocratic bent and that it is willing to put up with the persistence of remarkable poverty in the midst of extremely ostentatious wealth. In this general area must also be placed America's idiosyncratic democracy, which clings stubbornly to an outmoded and unfair system of electors in presidential elections and in which voter absenteeism is still an acceptable social habit. Again, let us make our point clear. America is free to choose however it wants to be democratic and no one has the right to tell it what it must or must not do, but America's choices and preferences also can place it outside the mainstream of history as it unfolds worldwide and especially in countries that are in the same category of development.

The single most deplored example of America's go-it-alone stance is its exaggeratedly stubborn refusal to sanction the Kyoto environmental-protection protocol, which all other industrialized nations have accepted and ratified.[15] As Kyoto is a gradualist and flexible commitment, it is not even quite clear why President Bush, who turned it down cold, is so opposed to it. His rejection is based on that it would hinder American economic growth, but UN statistics show that, with comparable levels of economic performance, Europe and Japan had not increased carbon dioxide emissions from 1990 to 2002 whereas the USA had increased them by about 20%. China was way above the Kyoto emission targets,

15 In December 1997 representatives from 160 signatory nations to the UN Framework Convention on Climate Change had attended a meeting in Kyoto, Japan, and reached an agreement, called the Kyoto Protocol, to reduce global emissions by about 5.2% by 2012. The European Union (EU) agreed to reduce emissions by an average 8% below 1990 levels, followed by the U.S. (7%), Japan (6%), and 21 other industrial countries that would reduce emissions by varying amounts. Binding commitments were not required of less-developed countries (LDCs). Shortly before the meeting in Kyoto, it was reported that the World Bank had prepared a scheme, called the Global Carbon Initiative, which would allow developed countries to pay for low-cost, energy-efficient projects in LDCs. The saving in greenhouse-gas emissions could then be credited to the binding emissions target of the donor countries under a system called 'joint implementation'." Concerns that a reduction could have serious economic repercussions led to doubts over whether the U.S., which accounted for 20-25% of the world emissions total, would ratify the protocol; by the end of 1998, the U.S. had not yet done so." "The environment", in *Encyclopedia Britannica* (2004). In 1998, President Bill Clinton did not count with sufficient support in Congress for a ratification of the Kyoto Protocol.

but Russia had decreased its rate of contamination significantly, perhaps because of the closing down of old, inefficient Soviet factories. China pulled the legerdemain of being exempted from Kyoto strictures because of its developing status. One result is that commonly it is impossible to see China from the air due to a permanent haze part of which must be due to industrial pollution.

America's anti-Kyoto position could be another gesture of irrational defiance of anything smacking of internationalism and specifically of the UN, which sponsored and promoted the treaty. This impression of irrationality is re-enforced by America's refusal to accept the International Criminal Court, which like the Kyoto agreement has been accepted by a vast majority of all other states. The American argument is that it cannot accept a jurisdiction that does not grant immunity to the members of its armed forces, and the International Criminal Court was created with the specific purpose of trying individuals. Since the new tribunal is not in the hands of America's enemies but of eminent judges mainly from developed countries or with impeccable judicial backgrounds, the American refusal to recognize it prompts suspicions that it is motivated by the awareness in the USA itself that it is not the blameless and well-meaning superpower it publicly claims to be. Furthermore, it undermines the credibility of America's sincere efforts to eradicate the excesses of its own military, which is crucial to the role the USA is trying to fill as the world policeman against terrorism.

On the issue of Israel/Palestine, America is not just out of sync with the rest of the world: it often stands completely alone. That America and Israel constitute a syzygy in world affairs entails that there are two sides to the issue and the problem is that, while most other states see both sides, America and Israel are agreed that there is only one side, which is not realistic. Here again, the Second Iraqi war is a crucial piece of evidence that America is out of sync. If such is the case, then America's once undisputed leadership role in an unipolar world is finished. The least that can be said is that the gratuitous attack on Iraq, to which now must be added the re-election of Bush, makes America unfit to be the policeman of the world and that it cannot even be trusted to stick to the facts. This is what we mean by the downsizing of America. If this is indeed happening, it is a relative phenomenon. American military might is uncontestable. The problem is its constraining military predicament in Iraq. America, which has lost prestige and can no longer claim a monopoly on the high ground, may also not have at its free disposal the means to impose a pax Americana where it chooses, and this would probably still be the case if America disentangled itself from Iraq, which is bound to happen sooner or later.

(18) The multipolar world need not exclude American leadership

The downsizing of America means that we are living in a multipolar world. This is the thesis that the president of France, Jacques Chirac, has been insistently proposing. So what exactly is this multipolar world?

Here we can only do a summary. Russia has already been downsized, but it is still a world power, the only nuclear rival of America. The world is tending towards the formation of regional organizations, some more coherent than others. Chirac may have mainly in mind the gradual emergence of the European Union as an international entity different from its component members. It is generally agreed in Europe that the French rejection of the EU constitution does not portend the disintegration of the EU itself. Though far from having yet a clear profile, there is the Organization of South East Asian Nations. India by itself constitutes an important pole in the multipolar world. Conclusively on multipolarity, there is the economic rise of China, which is already a permanent member of the Security Council. China is not on a par with America, but it intends to be and it has the potential for getting there.

The multipolar world is also recognizable in the concrete issues that it is facing and will probably be facing in the immediate future. In the Far East, the "taming" of North Korea is out of America's hands. When it is finally achieved it will almost certainly be the doing of China. The economic importance of Japan can only be sustained in the future through its commercial relations with China. It will be the growing influence of China that will draw the nations of South East Asia into closer relations among themselves. France, Germany and the UK have taken the initiative in negotiating with Iran over its nuclear program. American media speak of President Bush's threats aimed at Iran, but if America cannot control Iraq and in trying to do so has been alienating all Muslim countries, what can it do about Iran? Perhaps Bush has not learned a thing from his awful gaffe in Iraq, but Russia would not stand back if there were the slightest indication, and there is none, that America planned to intervene in some manner, in whatever manner, in Iran. Russia will oppose American encroachment on the former members of the USSR, the Baltic republics not excepted. Putin's intervention in the Ukraine's elections was cackhanded, but it was not totally ineffectual. In Brazil, which we have not mentioned, Latin America has a pole in the multipolar world. Brazil managed to convince the EU to start phasing out "all forms of agricultural export subsidies", which not long ago was an unthinkable.[16]

16 "Round-the-clock meetings produce 'historic' breakthrough", meeting summary 31 July 2004, www.wto.org

So what then is left for Bush's America to do? America today should have been leading a unipolar world. That it can no longer do. But America is still America and it cannot be discarded that it could become the leader in a multipolar world. Taiwan, for instance, is an issue on which China, just as America on Israel, does not admit that there are two sides. America here could be an honest broker. But for America to regain its footing and once again lead the world as it did in the 1990s, it has probably to start by accepting that there exists a multipolar world and that this world looks askance at its complicities with Israel. On the Palestinian issue, America and Israel might sooner or later have to accept some kind of international mediation.

The UN is theoretically in a position to do so, but America so roiled the organization with its unilateral war on Iraq that the UN itself it now in a condition of uncertainty about how to reform itself so that in future crises it can once again act in a consensual manner. The origin of this uncertainty is traceable to America's cavalier attitude towards the authority of the Security Council. The specific issue is the expansion of its permanent members, but any modification of veto power within it is not being contemplated. So exactly where the UN is now headed is just another element in the crisis which it is experiencing.

Republicans in Congress tried to ignite a movement to remove secretary general Kofi Annan for declaring that the Second Iraqi war was illegal. America got away with dismissing former secretary general Boutros-Ghali and placing Annan in his place. Annan is now being accused of having mismanaged the UN-approved oil-for-food program in Iraq. It was true that Iraq under Hussein sold more oil in the international market than the program contemplated, but that was not within the brief of the UN, which was to supervise the way the income from the legally sold oil was spent. Impartial observers argued that America and Britain were in a position to curtail those under-the-table deals and had done nothing about them. The American media, in another demonstration of its slavishness before the official version, tried to make an outcry, but, surprisingly, the White House put an end to that by saying it had nothing to reproach Annan.[17] This seems to be the doing of a more humble Bush, aware perhaps of America's diminishing influence in the world.

---

17 Judith Miller, "Scope of Saddam's scam widens: U.S. Senate doubles estimate of illegal oil-for-food gains", IHT, 17 November 2004; Warren Hoge and Judith Miller, "Annan's post at the U.N. may be at risk", NYT, 4 December 2004; Hoge, "U.S., in public statement, backs Annan in his U.N. post", NYT, 10 December 2004

363 A World-Historical Surge of Relativism

Even from a very short-term perspective, history takes some remarkable turns. Bush started his first administration on an off-putting assertive keynote, especially after an election that he won by the skin of his teeth. It was as if the French Revolution had begun with the decapitation of Louis XVI. Bush's brash projects for America seemed to obey a need to assert an empowerment the electorate had not given him. Bush's lack of caution gave an impression of national arrogance on the loose.

The 9/11 tragedy should have at least induced some sense of his fallibility, but instead, as in the Sophocles play, it encouraged hubris and more complications than he could foresee. Bush was Oedipus and his advisors, Donald Rumsfeld and Dick Cheney, unlike those of the Theban king, did nothing to dissuade him from recklessness. Later, the electorate was like a chorus telling him: "Go on, Oedipus, do your thing whatever the consequences."

Bush attacked Afghanistan, for which there was cause, but he did nothing to encourage negotiations in Israel/Palestine and he went and foolishly attacked and invaded Iraq. Oedipus blinded himself for his folly. These chastening experiences might have induced Bush to see the real world with clarity he did not have before. Unfortunately, his second administration, which does have a substantial electoral backing, appears intent on vindicating the errors of the previous one, with the significant difference that before America went on a wild militaristic spree and now it is reduced to making empty threats.

(19) Cultural relativism

There is an aspect to multipolarity that president Chirac might not have been envisioning. It involves a surge of cultural relativism. During the 1920s, multipolarity referred to balances of military power. Thus, at the Washington naval conference, the recognized "great powers" were assigned ratios of capital ships: the USA and Britain equal at 5, followed by Japan with 3, and by France and Italy with 1.67. At the time, Western culture, because of its political and military strengths, was unchallenged the world over. Nobody was claiming that Japan was anything but mimetically Western. At no time in the history of mankind were so many treaties, agreements, and conventions for peace and against war made as in the inter-war years. Germany's part in Western Civilization was illustrious. The so-called Weimar republic was a cultural dynamo.

When Hitler and the Nazis usurped power they came on determined to withdraw Germany from the West. On the surface, it did not seem to be so. Wagner was still staged in Bayreuth. Fürtwangler conducted Beethoven in Berlin. Richard Strauss composed Tondichtüng. The philosopher Martin Heidegger went up in the academic world. There were also book-burnings, derision and persecution of "degenerate" art and artists, and especially murderous anti-Semitism. A fine writer like Ernst Jünger could still publish works under the Nazis. As a Wehrmacht officer in occupied Paris, Jünger called Hitler the "Golem" in his diaries, but his illumination came too late.

The work *The Gestapo: a history of horror*, by the French historian Jacques Delarue, gives a historical onlooker an unnerving sense of the political claustrophobia that the Nazi regime created in Germany. Delarue's work was published in 1962, but the essential historiography of Nazism has not varied much since then. Delarue submits to the now generally doubted theory that the Nazis set the Reichstag fire that brought them to power. He is also vague on the issue of when the "final solution", or the extermination of Jews, began. Also, Delarue is of the "banality of evil" school and there are grounds for believing that Nazi Germany was born not out of the dark tunnels of the human mind but in concrete German background conditions.

Discrimination of Jews had been decreasing in Europe over the centuries. The French Revolution was a turning point. There was still plenty of anti-Semitism about during the first decades of the 20th century, but if you read a cosmopolitan author like Georges Simenon you find that there were also anti-Slavic and all kinds of "anti" sentiments between European peoples at the same time, so that anti-Semitism wasn't such a remarkable phenomenon. In New York, of all places, as recently as the 1950s the New York Athletic Club reputedly did not have Jewish members. Hitlerite anti-Semitism went with genocide and that was definitely part of the German renunciation to Western Civilization. Balance of power was also a Western invention. Hitler tried to alter that radically.

The world before World War II was politically and militarily multipolar and several of its poles were anti-Western at a very basic level. In some cases anti-Westernism also had Western roots, such as Nazism being a whelp of social Darwinism. Like all civilizations, the West had its own caricatures and deformations within itself. Nazism was a distillation and exaltation of the worst teratomorphic products of Western Civilization.

The Post-War was the triumph of the best values of Western Civilization. The Nuremberg Trials were a denunciation of Nazism but under adversarial and evidentiary conditions: the accused got a far better shake than they ever gave their victims. The 1990s consensus was a direct descendant of the political philosophy and the rules of Nuremberg. The current resurgence or re-appearance of multipolarity is not associated with radical anti-

Westernism. Multipolarity today is a result of the spread of Western Civilization. But it is not the triumph of the West. It is Western Civilization but with so many tweaks and twists that it can only be described as a World Civilization built on the foundations of Western Civilization. It is Western Civilization as, for instance, re-interpreted by Shanghai. Multipolarity plus is the West plus. What is involved in World Civilization is the greatest historical surge of relativism within a certain range of values.[18]

(20) Moral relativity

There is, to start with, moral relativity. Western ethics have been called Judaeo-Christian. The West inherited the Biblical commandments. Kant resumed ethical behavior as doing what you would have others do unto you not out of fear or convenience but because that's what reason enjoins. Somehow this argument seemed very rational, but as reason has no driving force to propel it other than itself, Kant freely admitted it was also hopelessly circular. Islam too has commandments. Unlike the West, it does not seek philosophical justifications for them. A Muslim visitor to the British Parliament in 1799 wondered what all the fuss was about when what needed knowing was down in black and white in the Koran, which ironically had been first printed in Turkey only long after the start of the 18th century. He was both wrong and right from a Western point of view: right in believing in moral commandments but wrong in closing his mind to casuistics or debate on issues of right and wrong.

In other Asian cultures commandments are superfluous: doing what's right consists in obeying the laws of society. Hindus and Chinese do not lose sleep over ethics. Religion is about the gods and how to worship them so that they will give you a hand. Society instills rules of behavior for its own preservation and for avoiding conflicts. If you traffic in drugs in many Asian countries, you risk hanging for it. This goes back to the time the British forced the Chinese to consume opium. Westerners should remember this when they are caught with a packet of marijuana and are shocked at being sentenced as if they were Latin American drug lords.

The time when the Ten Commandments were the absolute truth to be spread over all the nations is long past. It does not do much for

18 Cultural relativism is nothing new in history. Before the West became hegemonic in the world, indubitably in the course of the 18th century, the different world cultures were on a par militarily and some were above the West in cultural, technological, and scientific achievements. China was generally ahead of the West until it began to stagnate during the Ming period (1368-1644). During the early Middle Ages, Islam was more appreciative of classical Greek learning than Europe. Urban planning under the Aztecs had nothing to envy Spain. And so on.

Western ethics to witness the unseemly wrangling over the Holocaust millions. Who are being punished? Who are being rewarded and for what? Who is benefiting from one of the greatest crimes in history? The Holocaust has become trade and speculation. In an IHT piece, Philip Shenon writing on the development of a Jewish legal suit informed that lawyer' and other fees were $40 million compared to $15 million for claimants. Even among Jews, the Holocaust is sometimes treated as a term of reciprocal insult as happened when a group of American reform rabbis were praying together with their wives at the Wailing Wall and Orthodox Jews, who enjoin sex segregation at religious places and functions, shouted that they should go to Germany and be exterminated. The time might come when the Holocaust will lose the ability to inspire hatred of evil.[19]

(21) The view from the Pudong tower

There is also political relativity. Democracy is the one political dogma that humanity shares. Everybody is for it and nobody is against it. And this means "everybody" and "nobody" without exceptions. But what democracy are we talking about? Before, we had the opportunity to point out the subtle democratic quirks that can distort the "will of the people". Our criticism of American democracy stands on two pylons, to which we have pointed time and again: the system of electors for choosing presidents and voter absenteeism. It is a bad model.

In Russia democracy came with the greatest spree of economic hooliganism the world has ever seen. Outright fraud and robbery by a tiny minority were made "institutional" so that the oligarchic media could sway Russians for a man whom they detested weeks earlier. When Yeltsin quit he somehow had the knack to choose the person on whom an overwhelming majority of Russians almost immediately put their trust. This sounds definitely odd until you consider the alternatives: return of the communists or rule by those who, like Mikhail Khodorkovsky, defrauded the nation with the blessings of the World Bank, the AID, the IMF, Harvard, and the LSE.

But it is not just in Russia that corruption and democracy go together. Disciplined and prosperous Japan is basically a one-party state in which the ruling party in the past as often as not has been led by corrupt politicians. So when the case of democratic/undemocratic China comes up, how far can you carry condemnation? How undemocratic are

19 "Moral audit", *The Economist*, 27 November 1999; "Holocaust claims panel reported in turmoil", IHT, January 26, 2002; Deborah Sontag, "Yeshiva students in Israel jeer U.S. reform rabbis", IHT, February 2, 1999

single-candidate elections? How distorting are they of the popular will? After all, it is not as if there weren't elections. And as post-communist Europe has demonstrated more than once, the same people that climbed the ladder of political success under communism would probably have done so under any other set of political coordinates.

Finally, there is what can be called the view from Pudong tower. The Shanghai Bund was like a section of Manhattan transported to the left bank of the Whampo River, the last important tributary of the Yangtze before it flows into the China Sea. Across the Whampo today there is Pudong. It is modern Shanghai and the Shanghai of the future: a vast expanse of immense, mostly desolate boulevards; it has a maglev train to and from its huge airport; and it is dotted with the quirkiest high-rises in the world. Any ornamental whimsy is valid in Pudong: buildings in all imaginable patterns, shapes and forms; extravagant decorative motifs unrelated to functionality; huge cylindrical towers surmounted by inclined, spoked wheels; sharp-edged or angular slabs that resemble some far-out cartoon fantasy; hues out of the palette of an Italian or a Swiss expat churning out Alpine vistas in a tropical country; an Eiffel-tower-inspired television structure but made of concrete with plastic bubbles up its sides and rising at intervals to a crowning finial (the Pudong tower). In comparison, Moscow's Stalinesque skyscrapers are classics of sobriety, just a mite on the Baroque. In fact, Moscow looks the better for those buildings. It was what the Soviets thought the city of the future would look like. Little could they imagine Pudong.

But Shanghai has much more to show for itself. It is the most Western city in China. It was Western long before Canton became Guangzhou. Or before Beijing transformed itself into a monster of huge concrete edifices, with blocks ten times the size of football fields, city highways that snake in and out of the city grid, and traffic-light queues that can last an hour. You can watch ballet in Shanghai. The dancers know all the classical steps: entrechats, jetées, fouetés, but they do them with the precision of acrobats, like watching the Swan Lake in a four-ring circus. The music is almost extraneous. A metronome would probably do. Shanghai also has fashion shows and walkways with tall, hip-swaying, ice-cold Chinese models. The fashions they exhibit would be hilarious if one didn't sense, know in fact, that it was all actually a mockery of the same Western routines, as if Chinese communist-capitalists wanted to show the West that they can do what it does and do it with more panache and in the same process show that they do not really give a damn about Western standards. It is said that imitation is the highest form of flattery: it can also be the most sophisticated and devastating form of burlesque.

India stands in a middle ground between this subtle defiance of the West and the upholding of traditional values, between emulation and commitment to traditions. Unlike China, it is a full democracy in which English functions as a lingua franca across the Indo-Aryan north and the Dravidian south. Its attachment to its civilization is as strong as China's, perhaps stronger, but in many ways India is closer to the West than China will ever be. India is now on the runway to the economic take-off that countries in transition aspire to. If it doesn't yet have China's economic clout it is because it chose to develop according to practices which excluded political authoritarianism. In this sense, India could become the world pole to which the West will turn for support in defending its political values. The USA and India recently signed a vague but ambitious agreement on military and nuclear cooperation. India's role will surely be increasingly important in the future and if it maintains the rates of growth that it has recently attained it will rival China in global economic influence. In fact, if in absolute terms China's GDP is well over twice India's, in PPP terms India ranks fourth, below only the USA, China, and Japan.[20]

(22) Madame Butterfly in a tailleur and Pinkerton in a kimono

For the moment China is occupying center stage. If it does become the world economic fulcrum in the future, it will also be Asia in general that will be setting social and cultural standards. One thing that will go out like the dodo is the value of the antique. The Michelin Green Guides for Europe were meticulous about including and star-rating mainly those monuments whose antiquity could be authenticated. There were exceptions of course. Sacré Coeur in Paris, however architecturally outmoded, was a landmark that couldn't be ignored. Then there came the guides for New York and other parts of America, where real antiquity is rare and often irrelevant.

In New York City, you can do a course on the history of Western architecture by seeking out official landmarks that are self-confessed

20 The figures (rounded), according to the World Bank, are: USA $10,871,000 millions; China $6,436,000 millions; Japan $3,583,000; India $3,096,000 millions. India beats the four largest European economies: Germany, France, the UK, and Italy. Russia at $1,318,827 millions is in 10th place below Brazil ($1,371,355 millions). PPP refers to the rate of exchange of any currency for the dollar adjusted for what that currency can buy of a certain amount of basic goods. The resulting ratio is applied to GDP per capita in absolute terms, which multiplied by population figures gives national GDPs at PPP. In absolute terms, Japan has a GDP of $4,326,444 millions, China (including Hong Kong and Macao) $1,575,213 millions, the SEATO countries (south east Asia minus Myanmar) $672,000 millions (rounded), and India $598,596 millions.

imitations. In fact, you can even compare the imitations to judge, which are the more "authentic". The imitations go by the name of their original styles and it is understood that, as with the Platonic ideas, the original models are in themselves "superior". A frequently used style along the Central Park segment of Fifth Avenue is Beaux Arts, which is what gives Paris much of its charm. It is late 19th century, hence the age difference from one city to the other is not as pronounced, as it is, say, between Paris' Notre Dame and New York's St. Patrick's cathedral. Between America and Europe, as between Buenos Aires and Barcelona, there are obvious disparities in time, but basically the same standards of artistic judgment hold.

In the East in general, the antique per se is not that important. Ironically given its pre-British history of political disunion, India has the utmost respect for its authentic cultural riches, which are on display in many regional museums. The archaeology of India has not been pillaged by Europe in the massive way that occurred with the remains of other ancient civilizations. In India the antique is not only fully appreciated but considered part of nationhood.

In China and Japan the value of the antique is variously appreciated. Lines at museum entrances are evidence of admiration for ancient calligraphy and painting. Even amateurs can tell when other amateurs deface the Great Wall of China. But in Japan, where the art of woodworking has probably been taken to its most intricate manifestations, there is a temple that is torn down and rebuilt every fifty years. It looks exactly as it did one thousand years ago. The ceremony is part of a Shinto ritual, which is more important than conserving the original building. Japanese wooden joints and fittings can be admired equally well in the Brooklyn Botanical Garden as in Nara.

Traditional Chinese architecture was more or less standardized by the Ming period. Imperial constructions did not vary at all until Emperor Qianlong commissioned an European-style Baroque folie from the Jesuits for his summer palace outside Beijing. Lord Elgin, son of "Marbles" Elgin, destroyed this building during the siege of Beijing, much to the consternation of "Chinese" Gordon, who was there as an officer. To replace the Old Summer Palace of Qianlong, the stubborn and scheming empress-dowager Cixi built a New Summer Palace, in another huge suburban Beijing park, in accordance with strict Ming canons. It is as part of this project that she had a small lake dotted with marble boats, near the time when the Japanese crushed on land and on sea antiquated Chinese forces. Many Chinese today think that Cixi's buildings are older than Qianlong's ruins.

Any one who has seen a Tang semi-glazed pottery horse or camel will be sure to recognize any other one. What many ignore is that the Chinese have carried the art of replicating Tang statuettes to such perfection that it is difficult to tell them apart from the originals and many that are seen in museums are probably modern fakes. The tendency to undervalue the antiquity of art might have had to do with the ease with which Mao Zedong encouraged young Chinese to vandalize their artistic heritage, including the destruction of Confucius' tomb. During the French Revolution, the Romanesque church at Cluny, once the largest in the world, was dismantled by a stone contractor, but in general French revolutionaries knew how to distinguish between the function of edifices (as in that a church is just a church) and their historical and artistic merits.

When the French and the Dutch started restoring the great cultural monuments in their South East Asian colonies, they adopted the technique called anastylosis, which consists in putting all the stones around ruins back in their original positions. Thus were rebuilt the Prambanan temples in Java—to great controversy among Western scholars (some would have preferred leaving the stones strewn about)—and much of the ancient city of Angkor in Cambodia, which in places was in relatively good condition and did not require extensive reconstruction.[21] When Japanese experts were retained to restore a part of the Bayon complex in Angkor Thom, they did it by constructing a totally new building in the style of the rest of the site down to the finest detail.

None of this is to imply that there are no Oriental antiquaries or that there aren't countless Chinese and Japanese who appreciate the importance and the value of antiquities. Head per head, and given similar social backgrounds, the number of Westerners who don't give a whit for antiquity is probably about the same proportionately as that of Orientals with the same insouciance. What it does mean is that the

---

21 From the first century CE, Java came under the influence of India. Indian culture and commerce led in the 7th century to the creation of the Sumatran kingdom of Sri Vijaya. The Sailendra dynasty ruled in both Sumatra and Java and was responsible for the construction of the magnificent Buddhist monument of Borobudur in central Java (8th-9th centuries). Sailendra rule was undermined in Java by the Hindu Mataram kingdom, which built the rival temple complex of Prambanan, also known as Loro Jonggrang or Slender Maiden (9th-10th centuries), not far from Borobudur. Cambodia's independence from the presumed Javanese suzerainty of the Sailendras was ritually proclaimed by Jayavarman II (802-850), founder of the Khmer Angkor state. The greatest achievement of Suryavarman II (1153-1150) was the construction of Angkor Wat, the largest religious edifice in the world, dedicated to Vishnu although Shiva was not neglected.

standards of Western Civilization are not going to be in the future the measure of all measures. Pudong skyscrapers, however garish, will be the equal of New York's grander and older and more elegant towers. The concept of elegance will probably vanish from the vocabulary except to signify economical solutions to scientific problems. In sum, elegance will mean Ockham's razor.

Opera productions could become a blend of East and West, like Madame Butterfly in a tailleur and Capt Pinkerton in a kimono. This was already prefigured in the film *M. Butterfly*, in which a fatuous French diplomat falls for a Chinese theater female impersonator. Appreciation for the history of Western painting will surely decrease as Oriental art (genuine or fake) floods the markets. The great buildings of Europe will draw big yawns from international travellers accustomed to theme parks, which could become in time the main attractions for tourists the world over. The ideal blending of insouciance about the real past and theme-park mentality is perhaps what a Beijing real estate developer, Zhang Yuchen, came up with in his Château Zhang Laffitte, a perfect duplicate of the 17th century French Château Maisons-Laffitte with additions (also perfectly replicas) from Versailles and Fontainebleau, the whole surrounded by a moat and serviced inside by liveried former peasants.[22] Hopefully in this new world of perfect fakes, John Wayne will no longer be a world touchstone for moral rectitude, but don't count on this as Hollywood's grand productions, from the likes of *Jurassic Park* to *The Lion King*, will probably go on captivating world audiences, in some sad way making up for the lost lusters of Western Civilization. Whatever happens in the end, relativity looks like becoming the inevitable norm.

(23) A concluding reality check

Let's at this point, however, have a realistic stocktaking. What exactly is it that we are arguing, because it obviously cannot be that Western civilization is coming to an end because the USA invaded Iraq? This is what we are saying. History is relentless. Every historical act has consequences. Afghanistan could not get away with giving refuge to a dangerous, fanatical terrorist issuing fatwas to kill Americans. But the USA embarked on a useless and ill-conceived "war on terror". War on Afghanistan the world could understand and sympathize with. But war on Iraq was incomprehensible when there were alternative means to deal with Saddam Hussein. The USA acted as if it was on track in pursuit of revenge for 9/11. The truth is that it still appears not to have

22 Joseph Kahn, "China's elite learn to flaunt it while the new landless weep", NYT, 25 December 2004.

a clue on Iraq: why the country is up in arms and what it intends to do there and for how long. The USA may still be the destiny of choice of misery-blighted refugees. But as a nation it has never in history been more politically isolated than it is now, and not, as in the 1920s, through its own choice but because it is provoking international disquiet and distrust.

The unipolar world that was the accepted norm in the 1990s went down the tubes. In that time, America had the chance for a shot at a truly "new world order". At present, America as keeper of the flame of Western Civilization (politically if nothing else) is deeply compromised. The trend towards world cultural relativity was well advanced when the USA took it upon itself to rid the world of terror. It is doubtful that the West, in the concrete form of the USA, will recover the influence it has lost through imperialism that seems more irrational than effective in the grand British sense. With the prestige that always envelops conquerors, America for a time could quieten things down somewhat in Iraq. But the rule that historical acts have consequences will not be put in abeyance indefinitely. Neither America nor Israel seems to be aware that the rest of the world does not judge their acts in the same manner that they judge them. There is a disproportion here that is not merely a minor manifestation of political or moral relativity.

The chance of a world civilization under the guidance of Western Civilization came and went. What we have now is a world whose basic principle is relativity. Multipolarity is a military and political concept. Relativity is a cultural phenomenon. The world civilization that is emerging is based on multipolarity. It is not the multipolarity of pre-World War II. The most momentous war in history, World War II has left a lasting mark. The events and the sequels of World War II determine today's multipolarity. This means that the multipolar and relativistic civilization that is opening for humanity will operate under certain constraints.

The world will not organize itself under the guidance of America. More's the loss. But it will not be a dog-eat-dog affair. The multipolar world will probably be a curb on the lust for power. No country will be imposing itself on other countries as a matter of course. No nation will have its unimpeded way anywhere at any time. Hopefully, we shall see as a matter of course the swelling of the international solidarity that the frightening December 2004 earthquake and tsunamis in the eastern Indian Ocean spontaneously provoked. Beyond these modest expectations, present population trends might indicate that the world could become more racially homogeneous over time. If the third world sometime in the unforeseeable future—estimate one and a half century—comes to an end, World Civilization will truly have been a triumph for all of humanity.

Epilogue

After 21 January, when George W. Bush was inaugurated a second time, the USA had a new *Weltanschauung*. It had done nothing wrong in the world at large and it could do nothing wrong. There were concomitant developments. This is the way Roger Cohen, who didn't necessarily subscribe to the new triumphalism, described it: "The Middle Eastern Berlin Wall has fallen, democracy is dawning in countries from Iraq to Egypt, political ambition is supplanting the ideal of martyrdom, mass demonstrations are pushing Syrian troops out of Lebanon, a culture of hope is replacing a culture of death."[1]

The part about the wall is misleading because the only wall of note was the one Israel was completing in the West Bank, which had definitely encircled East Jerusalem putting it out of bounds (except for some access points) to Palestinians. The PA's hopes of having it as its capital were out of the question.

As to Syria, the Americans considered its open border with Iraq to be a major battleground against the insurrection. After Najaf and Fallujah, it became the object of the third major offensive of the occupation. Rafiq Hariri, a former anti-Syrian Lebanese primer minister, was killed by a bomb and all eyes were looking at Damascus. After a massive surge of opposition, even with a huge Hizbollah counter-demonstration, Syrian troops evacuated the country. An international investigation pointed at the head of Syrian state security as the likely author of Hariri's assassination.

The most remarkable transformation was that of Bush from ugly pupa to butterfly. Bush's "achievements" during his first administration were

1 "A Middle East moment of ineluctable motion", IHT, 5-6 March 2005.

incomparable. He had destroyed Iraq, causing widespread devastation, misery, and deaths for American troops, all on the basis of lies, which he knew he was telling. He had propitiated a culture of torture within the American military and intelligence services. He had buffeted America's alliances, revived the nuclear spectre, brought back to life Cold War alignments, and undermined the UN. His tax cuts for billionaires were generating fiscal deficits that threatened the world monetary system by devualing the dollar as the standard reserve currency of central banks.

After this trail of failures, he was transforming himself from the man of the war on terror into the paladin of freedom. The media went along as meekly as they had been doing before. What freedom though? If war on terror was an absurd, freedom is one of those clichés America swears by. But a cliché is a term or phrase that denotes lack of originality in speech but has some grounding in reality and freedom is a cliché that means next to nothing. The closest it comes to some meaning is democracy, which is also a debatable concept.

America itself is closer to plutocracy than to democracy. It was so before Bush, but Bush has done more than any American president in our times to enshrine this doctrine. In America, it is currently accepted that low taxes are the key to its prosperity. But this is a misperception. America was prosperous before Reagan inaugurated supply-side economics, which is economic jargon for giving the rich tax breaks. The most conspicuous result of supply-side economics are the scandalous rewards that American CEOs assign themselves. With much higher income-tax rates, Europe has done as well economically as Bush's America. The strength of the euro is not likely the product of a set of transitory circumstances. It might be part of a cycle, and it has already declined from the heights it reached, but it is not likely to weaken to the level where it was expected to be when it was first issued.

However, America's low rates of taxation have worse consequences than merely making the rich richer, which in itself, as long as others are not affected, is not necessarily bad. As it happens, America's reluctance to tax and spend is having palpably deleterious results, regrettably if pertinently enough during the last two administrations. One is in the area of national security, as shown spectacularly by 9/11. Among the welter of hindsights, it was reported more than once that the CIA had neglected counter-terrorism for other priorities. Just the fact that there should have been "priorities" in this sector is prima facie evidence that curtailing fiscal outlays is not per se a good thing. The destruction of the Columbia on re-entry was due, at least in part, to the underfunding of NASA. As if to make up for lost luster Bush promised that Americans would return to the moon, another copy-cat routine, this time of John

F. Kennedy after Sputnik, which has the ridiculous undertone of making the moon a sort of symbolic substitute for war on terror and the promotion of democracy world-wide. NASA later announced that just to keep the shuttles in operation for the next ten years would require $10 billion more than its budgets contemplated. Then Katrina came along and New Orleans, one of America's urban paradigms, was partially destroyed and so depopulated than to the moment of writing 80% of its inhabitants have not returned. The cause of why some levees gave way to the flooding has been a matter of much debate, but it is unavoidable to think that somewhere along the line there must have been some skimping on spending. How many more "New Orleans" America's tax largesses could produce in the future is now more than just a question of crystal ball gazing.

Returning to the political issue, the worst that can in honesty be said is that America is a plutocratic democracy. The question then arises: is this the model that Bush as the champion of freedom is peddling? Let's forget the plutocracy part and stick to the voting. After all, even on the admittedly controversial assumption that America is indeed a fully fledged plutocracy, it still has the most successful economy in history, and in fact, estimates made in July 2005 were that the expected fiscal deficit for the year would be $100 billion less than a previous estimate of $427, no matter that many analysts pointed out that federal spending was still on the rise, significantly because of the on-going conflict in Iraq.[2]

Bush, then, is no longer engaged in a war on terror but in the right of peoples to vote. But here we have another problem: is voting the answer to the world's problems? Americans certainly deplore the way Latin American countries have been voting into office anti-globalist heads of state. When Venezuela's Hugo Chavez was deposed for a couple of days by a cabal of bunglers, Washington rushed to recognize the "new government". Chavez, already strongly leftist, was understandably miffed and has become more radical and a declared enemy of "American imperialism". The American reaction, again followed by the media, has been to mischaracterize Venezuelan politics and to adopt the "banana republic" option. On a Latin American tour Rumsfeld deplored that Venezuela was acquiring 100,000 assault weapons, which is probably less than US citizens buy in their country in one year. Secretary Rice has been talking of "authoritarianism", ignoring, or pretending to ignore, that Venezuela is the oldest democracy in Latin America and that Chavez himself has won something like six consecutive elections and referenda. It suggests that for America democracy is relative to what America

2 Edmund L. Andrews, "Sharp increase in tax revenue will pare U.S. deficit", NYT, 13 July 2005

chooses to consider it to be and not to the vaunted right to free elections and other minutiae.

The US media keep calling Putin, the freely elected president of Russia, a KGB agent in disguise. China is today America's number one capitalist rival. Has the fact that it is only a semi-democracy—Chinese communist hierarchs, no matter what is said to the contrary, are elected—crippled its economic growth? Israel is as democratic a society as you could want, yet it has voted at least three times against concessions to Palestinians, who have been subjected since 1967 to a most undemocratic Israeli occupation regime.

Bush's credentials to being the knight in shining armor of democracy are the elections in Afghanistan, Iraq, and Palestine. Cohen included Egypt as a "dawning" democracy. Yet all that can be adduced here is that president Hosni Mubarak promised to amend his country's constitution to allow multi-party presidential elections and then went and celebrated one in which he won as usual by a huge margin. Not much here. Let's look at the other cases.

Afghanistan is officially a democracy. In the Afghan presidential elections American bayonets permitted that the provisional president they had been sustaining, Hamid Karzai, won. What sort of elections were celebrated in Afghanistan no one can really say. But there is widespread fear that Afghanistan is once again the world's leading producer and exporter of opium poppies. The Taliban at least had curtailed that. Does this make them preferable to the present situation? Not at all. But to shout to the world that Afghanistan is a democracy is a bit much. Ironically, as when the USA backed the Taliban, who later thanked it by providing the platform for 9/11, Afghan democracy might require America's Drug Enforcement Agency (DEA) to spend as much money as was invested in overthrowing the Taliban, apart from the fact that as of June 2005 Taliban guerrillas were still active and capable of downing an American helicopter. When subsequently elections were held for a Jirga or national assembly, Afghans chose mostly Islamist and warlord candidates.

Now, let's have a look at Iraqi democracy, which is after all what most counts in Bush's new global perspective. There too there were elections for an assembly, which were held against the obstinate opposition of the insurrection, whose movers probably erred in trying to prevent them through the use of suiciders. Whatever these could achieve, the voting was going to take place, but also whatever the results, elections in which an identifiable, substantial, and essential constituency was going to abstain had to be spurious. The violence in Iraq, no longer headlined in front pages (except when more than 50 persons or so are killed), has not abated. Gen. John

Abizaid, the supreme American commander in the Middle East, told Congress that, under Iraqi democracy, the insurgency has not decreased from the intensity it had attained before the elections. A table of statistics on Iraq to January 2005, compiled by a group of American researchers, showed, among others, the following results: oil production declining, Iraqi civilian casualties up to 450,000, a growing majority of Iraqis favoring the near-term American evacuation.[3] On the basis of the legislative election, Iraqis haggled about the formation of a national government and finally a constitution was hammered out, another election was celebrated, and again a fragile majority was mustered to approve it. Since the constitution contemplates the possibility of partial secession from central government authority, it is doubtful that Iraq is a nation any longer. Arab Sunnis and the Baath party, who kept it together, are not being allowed into the halls of power. The Kurds are not going to settle for less than the wide autonomy they enjoy now. The alternative seems to be a Shiite dominated Iraq. Iran next door is also Shiite. America loves Shiites in Iraq and hates them in Iran. Here's another how–de-do. Is Iraqi democracy a working proposition? More to the point: is Iraq itself viable at all?

The one issue on which, as one headline put it, events were going "Bush's way", was Israel/Palestine. With Arafat in his grave, Abbas and Sharon shook hands in Sharm el Sheik, Egypt, about carrying on a serious peace process. A few days later a suicider killed five Israeli civilians in Tel Aviv. Sharon blamed Syria but sent Abbas a word of caution about keeping to the straight and narrow. Abbas has put some muscle in Palestinian police and even Hamas has agreed to participate in the Palestinian democratic process. In this respect, an anecdote by a former Palestinian who spent time in an Israeli jail may be pertinent. He said that when inmates asked for reading and writing materials, the Israelis took away their mattresses. When the mattresses were returned, the inmates were grateful and forgot their previous demands.

Even before Arafat's death, the Intifada itself was dying, but not unsurprisingly it seems now to be spasmodically coming alive again, after the Israeli pull out from Gaza. So far Israel has only agreed to cede Jericho to the PA, which it did before and then took it back. The Palestinians have been offered generous aid by the USA and the EU. This is basically charity. Israel has asked the USA for $2.2 billion in compensation for giving up the sea-side villages settlers built in Gaza. Militarily, there is not the slightest indication that Israel will give up the right of intervention in that unpredictable territory. The chasm between Israelis and Palestinians is still there. No solid bridges have been built.

3 Adriana Lins de Albuquerque, Michael O'Hanlon, and Amy Unikewicz, "The state of Iraq: an update", NYT, 21 February 2005

Sharon, like Bush, is remaking himself. He is now the generous man of peace. It takes a lot of believing to swallow this. Between unmet Palestinian grievances and Israeli denial that Palestinians have valid grievances, the Israel/Palestine peace process is still under intense pressure. If Israel starts ceding this and that, it must go on doing so. Social terrorism has limits also on the side of restraint. As it does with its Palestinian prisoners, Israel will only give when Palestine gives more than it gets. The situation, in sum, is unstable. The future of Israel/Palestine is still very much a question mark.

There is one point on which the NYT, at least, has been hounding the present avatar of Bush as inseparable from the former war-on-terror Bush and that is on the question of torture. Some fundamental facts are known and we have mentioned them: Gonzales proposed that the Geneva conventions be suspended in Afghanistan, the administration concurred, and the Justice Department approved a "narrow" definition of torture (in effect sanctioning the abuse of prisoners); Rumsfeld allowed torture-lite (narrow definition of torture) in Guantanamo. The Afghan rules were extended to Iraq. Abu Ghraib made the gangrene public. As some Guantanamo detainees were handed by American authorities to be tortured in other countries, this practice, called rendition, was traced directly to the authorization given to the CIA by Bush himself a few days after 9/11. To put it bluntly, it was the president who made torture an official American policy. Of the some 680 original Guantanamo detainees 100 at least ended up in the hands of torturers in Egypt, Syria, Saudi Arabia, Jordan, and Pakistan.[4]

The reports on torture came not only from the victims themselves but from investigations by the FBI and the CIA. In January 2005, the Justice Department revoked torture-lite and it was reported that 137 American soldiers had either been reprimanded or were being tried for engaging in it. Yet in March 2005, when "freedom Bush" was all the rage in the media, rendition was still being applied, at about the same time that the State Department publicized its annual list of countries that violated human rights, including of course those to whom the Americans were "rendering" their captives.[5] China and Russia publicly scoffed at American hypocrisy. As to Guantanamo, the accounting is vague but of the original 680 the number has decreased to some 500 or slightly less who are still being held without trial. All of this could be cited as another admirable example of American freedom of expression. It could also be read as the "lynch the bastards and apologize later" American tradition.

4 Douglas Jehl and David Johnson, "Bush gave CIA wide authority to send suspects abroad, aides say", IHT, 7 March 2005.

5 Scott Shane, "Judge bars U.S. from moving some detainees", NYT, 13 March 2005.

The issue of torture had become so notorious in America that the prestigious journalist and NYT editor Joseph Lelyveld decided to do some stock-taking which he published on 12 June 2005. First, he summarized what he knew. Although there is a theoretical difference between torture and abuse, the American public, judging by letters sent to Congressmen, is not particularly interested in making it and prefers to keep things "blurry". Lelyveld himself seemed somewhat vague on the distinction and appeared to consider water torture—called "waterboarding", in which a prisoner is, basically, made to feel as if he were drowning—a form of abuse. Apparently, Americans have been applying this form of torture to foreigners since at least the Filipino insurrection of 1898-1899. As to the present prevalence of abuse/torture, he said he had no idea, but that it probably became widespread spontaneously after 9/11. Then, Lelyveld went to the crux: is abuse/torture justified? For this, he did a lot of research in Israel, where he found out—big surprise!—that abuse/torture or torture-lite has always been a common practice of Israeli intelligence against Palestinians. He got a lot of arguments about its efficacy, which he frankly doubted. Notwithstanding his scepticism, he sort of accepted the plain fact that "democracies threatened by terrorism" will never shrink from using torture. His insistence that torture is generally not applied in America itself, though certainly indisputable in present world conditions, seems much too wide a generalization.

America under Bush the younger is basically living in never-never land. Bush is still a pupa and not a butterfly. The world is now even less amenable to American dictates than it was with "war-on-terror Bush". Do Bush and Rice know where they are going? In the American media, it is made to seem as if the USA has more say about the way Iran will go than it does. The Bush administration is pushing the preposterous idea that Iran shouldn't be allowed to develop nuclear energy even for peaceful purposes because it is an "evil state" that needs to be segregated. The USA is behaving in this sense as if Iran was a classic case of a "banana republic", an offensive phrase Americans are very fond of. This can only be described as a delusion.

China has placed a man in space. It is planning a space station. The biggest American trade deficit with any single nation is with China. There is little in the way of technology that China does not know now or cannot acquire in the short-term. After the Tiananmen events, the world's most powerful democracies imposed a ban on the sale of arms to China. This ban is near expiring and the EU is not inclined to re-impose it. China has carried out joint military exercises with Russia. Bush and Rice are intent on the silly goal of having the ban on arms sales to China maintained because it will upset the balance of forces between China and Taiwan. Bush and his country in general at this stage are being delusional about themselves and about the world in which they have to live in whether they like it or not. The more American media insist in taking seriously Bush's bluster the more they make their country seem like "The little plane that could", a cartoon about a talking Piper who carried the mail against incredible odds over the cordillera between two "banana republics".

There is, to close, a very curious recent development. The "coalition" that Bush built up for the occupation of Iraq has mostly disintegrated. The only presence that gave it some substance was that of Britain. The British are not going to evacuate Iraq, but PM Tony Blair is not the same man who went to war unconditionally on America's side. On 7 July, London was struck by four terrorist bombs which caused over fifty deaths. The American media made a big to-do about "British stiff upper lip" but it was also pointed out that the British had only themselves to blame for not being tougher on home-bred Muslim fundamentalists. While obviously deploring and condemning the carnage—in a bus and three underground trains—Tony Blair also declared that it was crucial to remove the causes of terrorism and he specifically mentioned the Israel/Palestine problem. These were the words of a statesman. Certainly, Blair seemed to be out of Bush's orbit. It was one more piece of evidence, subtle but real, of the downsizing of America, even by the ally Bush has for too long been taking for granted.

In May, the Labor Party won national re-election with only 37% of the popular vote. But before this relative rebuff, Blair had already been using another style of discourse. He admitted that the only justification for the Second Iraqi war was to get rid of a despot. Of more significance, he made a personal pledge to orient British policy towards an equitable settlement in Israel/Palestine and towards a global effort to alleviate poverty, particularly in Africa.

When Blair visited Bush in June, there was already agreement among the G-8—the world's biggest economies plus Russia—to condone the international debts of the eighteen poorest nations. But when it came to the plight of Africa, Bush let loose on "big talkers" who offer and don't keep their word whereas America was giving twice as much in aid to Africa as the next biggest donor.[6] Blair sat through that stoically. A NYT editorial put Bush's bragging in context by pointing out that the

6 The reporter put it this way: "Bush also criticized 'big talkers' who speak of doing more for Africa but who have not given as much as the U.S., which has increased aid to Africa since 2000 and now gives roughly twice as much as any other donor." By remitting without quotes and out of context the Bush claim, it made it sound like real, uncontestable information. IHT, 9 June 2005.

USA is providing only 0.18% of its gross national income to aid for poor countries, far below the 0.7% standard concretely proposed by Britain, France, and Germany.

In a long historical view, what has president Bush achieved in his two administrations? He came to office offering America invulnerability, even as his fiscal policies undercut funding for counter-terrorism. After 9/11, he went and declared an unwarranted "war on terror". America is still occupying Afghanistan and it is promoting democracy in that most backward-looking of countries. This achievement is commendable, but fragile. At first, Bush was not quite sure about who was America's most wanted enemy was, but after 9/11 it had to be Osama bin Laden. As the latter proved elusive, for reasons that, to say the best for them, are still "obscure", he went an invaded Iraq. The example of Israel/Palestine, which should have been foremost, was ignored. If he did anything with the intractable Palestinian issue was to encourage Israel's hard anti-Arab policies.

Iraq was dismantled. But America is still engaged there in a conflict that parallels the one in Israel/Palestine but vastly more deadly and complicated. Reconstruction is moving at a snail's pace and disengagement, which would have to be decisive and quick, is probably not an option for America at this point. Rather than bring terrorism to bay, the attack and occupation of Iraq unleashed a Tsunami of international terrorism. It is so prevalent now that it is hard to imagine the less unquiet world that prevailed when Bush was elected. And to this must be added that America's hubristic foreign policies have emboldened its enemies to pursue nuclear policies, which before they would not have dared to even contemplate. In conclusion, war on terror turned out to be the greatest historical stimulus terrorism has ever received in history. Such a monumental failure means that America's stature is much diminished. And here's where the misperceptions that this book is about played a part. Bush, and Americans in general, had an oversized estimate of America's power. They had the erroneous notion that, because America was so powerful, it either was not a just another historical player or it was above historical circumstances. On no account was any of this true. To close briefly and to the point, America under Bush—perhaps Bush himself in a dim way—is having to face the reality of its un-exceptionalism. Whatever myths it has entertained in the past, the hard facts are that it is a country like all others, on occasions better than all others, normally on a par, in recent years a historical under-performer. This is basically all that the downsizing of America means.

Chronology

12th century

Reynald of Châtillon was a Holy Land adventurer who became prince of Antioch through marriage. Captured by Muslims, he was kept him in chains for fifteen years. When he was ransomed, he became master of the krak of Moab, again through marriage. Despite his advancing age and his experience in Muslim dungeons, Reynald on his own incursioned into the Red Sea and the Arabian coast although he didn't have the means to do much damage. After the battle of Hattin, Saladin allowed Sufis and other holy men in his camp the privilege of killing each a knight of the orders of the Hospital of St. John (Hospitallers) and of the Temple (Templars). Among the prisoners was Reynald, of whom Saladin had about had his fill. Reynald knew what awaited him and when he was faced by Saladin he did not whimper but said he had acted in the manner of a loyal Christian vassal, which was not true at all for the only vassalage he owed was to terrorism. Saladin himself loped off one of Reynald's arms and let his officers finish the job of cutting him up.

1453

Portuguese musketeers from Goa intervene to defend Christian Ethiopia from Muslim invasion.

1578-1648

The Netherlands gradually detaches itself from Spanish dominion and its independence is recognized.

1800-1812

The Barbary wars

1817-1821

Final phase of Venezuela's war of independence

1835

Independence of Texas

1845

Texas is admitted as an American state.

1846-1848

American-Mexican war

1839-1842

First British-Afghan war

1869

The Dominican Republic fails in its attempt to be accepted into the American union.

1874

Conference of Berlin or the scramble for Africa

1878-1880

Second British-Afghan war

1885-1912

Reconstitution of the Spanish African colonial empire

1897-1901

Subjection of the Philippines

In 1897, Emilio Aguinaldo organized resistance to Spanish authorities in the region south of Manila. Spain had built barely 1,000 kilometers of roads in all of the Philippines and so was hampered in trying to put down this insurrection. A truce was signed in December and Aguinaldo took asylum in Hong Kong. The truce was not entirely observed and there was sporadic fighting, but the decisive event was that in April 1898 the USA declared war on Spain and a flotilla under commodore

George Dewey quickly put the obsolete Spanish ships out of commission (Manila Bay). However, the Americans did not yet have the troops necessary to take Manila and transported Aguinaldo to lead Filipino attacks on the Spaniards. Aguinaldo interpreted this as American willingness to grant independence, but it is more likely that Dewey was humoring and using the Filipinos. On June 12, Aguinaldo declared the independence of the Philippines in the town of Kawit or Old Cavite. By August, the USA had landed sufficient troops, under Gen. Arthur MacArthur (father of the more famous Douglas), to take the intitiative on land against the Spaniards, whose situation was obviously desperate and quickly surrendered. In September, Aguinaldo, at a convention in a town north of Manila, promulgated a constitution and formed an independent Filipino government. In December, Madrid and Washington signed the Treaty of Paris by which Spain ceded the Philippines for a compensatory payment of $20,000,000, which obviously meant Americans were going to occupy the islands. Operations to do so were going on during 1899 in the Visayas and in Mindanao. Aguinaldo resisted in north Luzon until he was captured in March 1901.

1914-1918

World War I

1915

During World War I, the Anatolian Armenians favored the Russians and in 1915 the Ottoman reacted with what is often described as the Armenian holocaust: the systematic killing or ejection of Armenians from their ancestral lands. The toll in lives is placed at between 600,000 and 1,500,000. Turks respond that Armenians were victims of famine as were millions of Turks. Be that as it may, the large Armenian community in the Ottoman Empire mostly disappeared.

1937-1945

World War II

1944-1954

Guatemala goes leftist under Juan Jose Arevalo (1944-1951) and Jacobo Arbenz (1951-1954). With CIA backing, Arbenz is overthrown by Carlos Castillo Armas.

1944

During August-October of 1944, the Dumbarton Oaks conference, in Washington, D.C., was the prelude to the UN. During April-June of

1945, the UN was founded in San Francisco. The Security Council became its executive core with the USA, the USSR, Britain, France, and China given veto power over all military actions.

1945-1946

Vietnam declares its independence

1945-1949

Germany was divided into four occupation zones. Berlin, which was engulfed by the Soviet armies, was also divided into four zones.

1946

Jordan (originally Trans-Jordan) becomes independent.

Jewish terrorists explode a bomb in the King David hotel in Jerusalem, where the British had their military headquarters. There were 91 dead, mostly British.

1946-1954

France faced a nationalist-communist insurrection in Indochina after the war. It lost the battle of Dien Bien Phu in 1954.

1947

India and Pakistan are partitioned and possibly 500,000 are killed in savage fighting, in Punjab mainly, between Muslims, on one hand, and Hindus and Sikhs, on the other.

1947-1949

Greek communist insurrection and declaration of the Truman doctrine

War over Kashmir between India and Pakistan

The Baath party was officially founded in Damascus.

1948

Communists take over in Czechoslovakia.

Tito rejects Soviet tutelage.

1948-1949

Berlin is blockaded by the Soviets. The Berlin airlift annuls the effects of the land blockade.

During the first Arab-Israeli war (Israeli war of independence), Egypt retained the Gaza strip and Jordan the West Bank. Israel was immediately recognized by the USSR and the USA.

1948-1952

The US-financed Marshall Plan spends $13 billion (equivalent to around $100 billion today) for the reconstruction of Europe.

1949

Mao Zedong establishes communism in China.

The western powers pooled their zones into the Federal Republic of Germany, capital Bonn, and the Soviets followed suit by creating in their zone the German Democratic Republic (East Germany), capital East Berlin.

A Soviet atomic bomb is tested.

The North Atlantic Treaty Organization (NATO) is created.

Indonesia becomes independent under the leadership of Sukarno.

1950-1953

Korean War

1951-1953

In 1951, there began a tug-of-war between, on one side, the nationalist Prime Minister Muhammad Mussadegh, and on the other, the young Reza Shah supported by the western powers. Mussadegh nationalized the oil industry and was removed in 1952. He returned and Reza Shah had to leave the country. American secret services were openly conspiring against Mussadegh, who was finally ousted and Reza Shah brought back in 1953.

1952

America's first fission or thermonuclear device (hydrogen bomb) detonated on Eniwetok atoll.

1952-1954

The monarchy is overthrown in Egypt. One of the defenders of Gaza, Gamal Abdel Nasser, becomes dictator and a powerful symbol of Arab nationalism.

1953

Stalin dies (5 March). Applying liberal policies, the chief of the Soviet secret police Lavrenti Beria tries to take power, but is arrested and executed. Nikita Khrushchev becomes first secretary of the Soviet communist party (September).

The USSR tests a hydrogen bomb.

An anti-communist popular rebellion is put down in East Germany.

During the Lebanese government of pro western president Camille Chamoun, American forces land in Beirut.

Cambodia becomes independent.

1953-1961

President Dwight D. Eisenhower

1954

At the Geneva Conference, Vietnam was divided along roughly the 17th parallel. The north became the communist Democratic Republic of Vietnam, capital Hanoi, and the south a pro-western state, capital Saigon

The South East Asia Treaty Organization (SEATO) included Pakistan and New Zealand.

Laos becomes independent.

1954-1962

Algerian war

1955

Warsaw Pact is formed to counter NATO.

The anti-communist Baghdad Pact is formed extending from Turkey to Pakistan. The latter country was also a member of the SEATO (1954).

The Afro-Asian summit is celebrated in Bandung, Indonesia. The over-all trend was for neutrality between communism and capitalism.

1956

Ngo Dinh Diem, who deposed "emperor" Bao Dai and declared the Republic of Vietnam, suspended elections in South Vietnam. This was the signal for renewed hostilities, which were carried forward by the Vietcong (Vietnamese communist guerrillas).

In his so-called secret speech, Khrushchev denounced Stalin before the 20th Party Congress.

Soviet tanks quash Hungarian rebellion.

Nasser nationalizes the Suez Canal. British and French paratroops land in the Suez Canal area with the excuse of a pre-arranged Israeli invasion of Egypt. Afrer strong condemnation by American President Eisenhower, the invasion was called off.

Anastasio Somoza is assassinated in Nicaragua.

1957

The USSR launches Sputnik, the first man-made satellite of Earth.

Khrushchev defeats "anti-party group" (Molotov, Malenkov, Kaganovich).

The European Economic Community (EEC), whose goal was the achievement of a common market based on a customs union, and the European Atomic Community, form integrated with France, the Benelux countries, Italy, and the Federal Republic of Germany.

1958

In China, Mao decrees rapid industrialization through the Great Leap Forward, which fails catastrophically.

A military conspiracy in Iraq is led by Abd al-Karim Qasim. King Faysal is overthrown and killed. A republic is declared. The Baghdad Pact becomes Central Treaty Organization (CENTO), with its headquarters in Ankara, Turkey.

Venezuelan dictator Gen. Marcos Perez Jimenez is forced to leave the country. Venezuela becomes the first of existing Latin American democracies.

1958-1969

Gen. Charles de Gaulle, President of France

1959

Fidel Castro enters Havana.

The violent anti-Israel organization Al Fatah is founded by Gazans in Kuwait. Yasir Arafat, Egyptian by birth, was a founding member and soon rose to be its leader.

1960-1961

The Soviets pull out thousands of advisers and cancel projects in China. The USSR breaks with China.

1960-1978

The Belgian Congo becomes independent.

1961-1963

President John F. Kennedy

1961

The United States formalized its support for the Saigon government by treaties signed in 1961 and the following year there were 12,000 American soldiers in Vietnam.

The Russian Yuri Gagarin becomes the first man in orbit.

Soviets bring down the American U-2 spy plane. Khrushchev denounces Eisenhower at Paris summit.

The Berlin wall is built.

Revolutionary Forces defeat the CIA-planned Bay of Pigs (playa Girón) invasion of Cuba by exiled Cubans. Cuba goes fully radical.

The USA creates the Peace Corps and the Alliance for Progress, the latter specifically for Latin America.

India annexes Goa. The Chinese attack India to annex the part of Ladakh through which they had built an illegal road.

Kuwait becomes independent. Iraqi leader Qasim claims Kuwait.

Organization of Petroleum Exporting Countries (OPEC) is founded.

Conference of non-aligned countries is celebrated in Belgrade.

1962

Cuban missiles crisis

1963

The American ambassador in Vietnam, Henry Cabot Lodge, regularly sent negative reports on Diem and his government. When the American presence in Vietnam was increasing, General Duong Van Minh staged a coup in which Diem was killed.

John F. Kennedy is assassinated.

The US, the UK, and the USSR sign a nuclear non-proliferation treaty.

Baath takes over in Syria. In Iraq, Baath and the military overthrow and execute Qasim.

1963-1969

President Lyndon B. Johnson

With French technology, Israel builds the Negev Nuclear Research Center, ostensibly for de-salinization, but in fact to develop nuclear weapons, which it had by around 1963. The USA demanded on-site inspections, which were granted but usually announced before hand. The inspections were suspended in 1969.

1964

Sponsored by the Arab League, the international organization of Arab states, the Palestine Liberation Organization (PLO) is founded in East Jerusalem to reclaim former Arab lands in Israel.

1964

Khrushchev is removed and succeeded as first secretary of the communist party of the USSR by Leonid Brezhnev.

1965-1966

Vietnamese Air Vice Marshal Nguyen Cao Ky came to power in Saigon in 1965. Vietcong units were regularly defeating the South Vietnamese army. The US military presence was boosted exponentially under the overly optimistic Gen. William Westmoreland. By the end of the year there were 200,000 American soldiers in Vietnam and by the end of 1966 the figure was 400,000.

1966-1976

Chinese Cultural Revolution

1967

After Nasser occupies the disarmed Sinai and threatens to interdict access to the Israeli port of Eilat, Israel unleashes the Six-Day War and establishes the Bar-Lev line of occupation near the Suez Canal. The entire West Bank is annexed by Israel. The Golan Heights is taken from Syria.

The Popular Front for the Liberation of Palestine (PFLP) was founded in Jordan by George Habash, a Greek Orthodox Christian from Palestine. It was secularist and Marxist.

late 1960s

China might have been giving nuclear warhead designs to Pakistan. Both countries had in common their enmity with India.

1968

The liberalizing Prague Spring, led by Alexander Dubcek, provokes a Warsaw Pact invasion of Czechoslovakia.

In Iraq, Baath definitely takes power. A Kurdish rebellion, led by Mustafa al-Barzani, has Iranian support.

Arafat's Al Fatah fighters repel an Israeli army attack in Karameh, Jordan.

1969-1974

President Richard Nixon

1969

Neil Armstrong lands on the moon in the Apollo 11 mission. In all, there were eight moon landings and seventeen Apollo launchings.

Secret bombing of Cambodia commences with the fairlessly hopeless aim of disrupting the Ho Chi Minh Trail, the system of jungle paths through which North Vietnam conveyed supplies to South Vietnam.

Yasir Arafat becomes head of the PLO.

Iran contests Iraqi sovereignty over Shatt al Arab.

1970

Chinese-Soviet diplomatic relations are restored.

Nasser dies and is succeeded by Anwar el Sadat.

Gen. Hafez al-Assad comes to power in Syria.

The Socialist Salvador Allende is elected president in Chile with communist support.

1970-1972

In elections in 1970, the Awami League won by a landslide margin in East Pakistan, gaining an over-all majority in the national assembly. President Yahya Khan sent troops to the east. The Awami League set up headquarters in Calcutta. In Chittagong, Major Zia ur-Rahman resisted the regular army. Millions began to flee the country and an alarmed India invaded in December 1971. Bangladesh came into existence under Mujibur Rahman, who offered a secular state.

King Hussein of Jordan declares martial law and launches a military operation to expel the PLO from his country. The PLO's combatants move to Lebanon. Arafat establishes offices in Damascus. The terrorist group Black September is formed.

Britain, Germany, and the Netherlands agree to build centrifuges for atomic energy, which leads to the formation in 1971 of the Uranium Enrichment Company (Urenco).

1970-1975

King Norodom Sihanouk of Cambodia is overthrown by Gen. Lon Nol. Cambodia fell to the Khmer Rouge, whose barbarous Maoist regime not only killed its own people but was invading Vietnam in the name of Cambodian irredentism over the Mekong delta.

1971

With the advent of normalization of relations between China and the USA, China is given Taiwan's seat in the Security Council.

1972

MAD (mutually assured destruction) became "official" with the signing of the Anti-ballistic Missile Treaty (ABM).

Three pro-Palestinian terrorists from the Japanese Red Army attack the Lod airport, Tel Aviv, and assassinate 27 persons. The Israeli commando unit Sayaret Macal, created by Ehud Barak, killed the terrorists. During the Summer Olympics in Munich, the terrorist organization Black September killed nine Israeli athletes.

1972-1974

President Richard Nixon was forced to resign as a consequence of the Watergate affair, a burglary at the Democratic Party National Committee's headquarters in the Washington Watergate apartment and office complex.

1972-1975

The Pakistani scientist Abdul Qadeer Khan, an expert in metallurgy, works for Urenco in Holland and obtains plans for centrifuges to enrich uranium to weapon-making quality.

1973

America pulls out of Vietnam.

In Chile, Gen. Augusto Pinochet overthrows Allende.

The right-wing anti-Palestinian Likud party is formed in Israel.

1973-1974

The 1973 or Yom Kippur war provokes an Arab oil embargo.

1974-1977

President Gerald Ford

1974

The UN recognizes the PLO as legitimate representative of the Palestinian people. Yasir Arafat addresses the General Assembly.

1975

When the communists launched a coordinated offensive in north and central Vietnam, Thieu evacuated the Northern provinces and his government collapsed. In the month of April, Saigon fell to the army of North Vietnam and the Khmer Rouge captured Phnom Penh, the main political beneficiaries of the useless bombings of Cambodia.

Pathet Lao takes over in Laos.

Iran-Iraq agree to share the Shatt al Arab. The Kurdish insurgency in Iraq ceases.

The long-time Spanish dictator Francisco Franco dies.

The General Assembly of the UN declares Zionism to be a form of racism.

1975-1991

The Lebanese civil war

1976

Pakistan inaugurates the Kahuta nuclear enrichment plant run by Abdul Qadeer Khan.

Mao Zedong dies. Hua Guofeng succeeds him.

Israeli commandos liberate Jewish hostages from a hijacked Air France airliner deviated to Entebbe in Uganda, whose ruler, the brutal and unstable Idi Amin, was an accomplice of the pro-Palestine terrorists.

SEATO liquidated.

1977

Egyptian president Anwar el Sadat visits Israel and addresses the Knesset.

1977-1981

President James Earl Carter

1977-1983

Menachem Begin, Israeli PM, gives impulse to Israeli settlements in Palestinian lands.

1977-1978

The USA negotiates a treaty with Panama for the reversion of the canal. It was approved with the Panamanian engagement to keep it open to all nations under all circumstances.

1978-1979

The Vietnamese, under harassment by Cambodia, retaliated and in 1979 routed the Khmer Rouge, although they did not destroy them.

An underground Sandinist movement comes out fighting in Nicaragua, where the Somoza family still held power and takes over in 1979.

1978-1982

Camp David I: Talks are carried on between Sadat of Egypt and Begin of Israel under the auspices and the pressure of President Carter. Sadat and Begin sign a peace treaty (1979) by which Egypt recovered the Sinai (1982). Dissident soldiers assassinated Sadat (1981). President Hosni Mubarak, who stuck by the terms of the treaty, followed him.

1979-1990

Margaret Thatcher, British PM

1979

After losing a power struggle in Kabul, Babrak Karmal fled to the USSR, which, at his behest, invaded Afghanistan.

Full diplomatic relations are established between China and the USA.

1979

The European Monetary System (EMS) is created contemplating the ECU (European currency unit), eventually the Euro.

Saddam Hussein takes power in Iraq.

1979-1981

During the theocratic revolution in Iran, its leader, Ayatollah Ruhola Khomeini, encouraged the take-over of the US Embassy, whose personnel (66 persons) were held hostage by Islamic guards in retaliation for the American visa granted to the former Shah for health reasons and later cancelled. A botched rescue attempt probably cost President Jimmy Carter the election in 1980. The hostages were finally released early in 1981 after the Shah's death in Egypt the previous year.

1980

Gorbachev enters the presidium of the CPSU supported by Mikhail Suslov.

1980-1988

Iraq-Iran war

1981-1995

François Mitterand, president of France

1981-1989

President Ronald Reagan

1981

In China, the liberalizer Hu Yaobang displaces Hua Guofeng.

Reagan's proxy wars: the USA backs the Contras in Nicaragua; the USA and Pakistan act against the USSR in Afghanistan.

Reagan offers the USSR not to deploy Pershings if it dismantles its SS-20s. The USSR rejects the offer. Nevertheless, START (Strategic Arms Reduction Talks) begins.

Israel strikes at Ossirak, the Iraqi atomic plant.

1982

Pershings and cruises deployed in Germany.

1982-1985

Yury Andropov resigns at KGB (since 1967). Brezhnev dies and Andropov succeeds him as secretary-general. Andropov dies (1984) and Konstantin Chernenko becomes secretary-general of the CPSU (Communist Party of the Soviet Union). Chernenko dies (1985). Igor Ligachev helps deliver the central committee of the CPUS and Mikhail Gorbachev becomes secretary-general. Boris Yeltsin from Sverdlovsk is named head of the party apparatus in Moscow.

Israel invades and occupies Lebanon as far north as Beirut. The massacres at the Sabra and Shatilla refugee camps occurred in 1983. Israel terminated the invasion in 1985, but left in place a buffer zone in southern Lebanon.

1983

Reagan announces plans for a Strategic Defense Initiative (SDI), an anti-ballistics shield in outer space.

Terrorists target American and French troops in Lebanon.

Tamils launch a separatist movement in Sri Lanka.

1983-1984

Yitzhak Shamir, Israeli PM

As special envoy of the Reagan administration, Donald Rumsfeld, meets Saddam Hussein. He later said he warned Hussein about the use of chemical weapons, but foreign minister Tariq Aziz described the visit in glowing terms. On March 1984, the USA condemned Iraq's use of poison gas. Rumsfeld was sent back to re-assure Hussein of America's good will.

1983-1985

In 1979 Maurice Bishop led a leftist coup in Grenada. Castroist extremists in the army overthrew and executed him in 1983. With regional support, the USA occupied the island from 1983 to 1985, when democracy was re-established.

1984-1986

Shimon Peres, Israeli PM

1984-2004

Mordechai Vanunu, a technician at the Dimona nuclear plant, reveals to the British journalist Peter Hounam that Israel has nuclear weapons.

For that, Mosad pursued him to Italy and brought him back to Israel and jailed. He was released in May 2004. The estimate of Israel's nuclear arsenal varies from 100 to 200 weapons.

1985

Boris Yeltsin becomes member of the Politburo of the communist party of the USSR.

Libyan bombs are detonated in Athens and Vienna.

ca1985

The Pakistani scientist Abdul Qadeer Khan was organizing a nuclear proliferation network, which, it is believed, supplied nuclear technology to Iran and North Korea.

1985-1991

The Gorbachev years

1986

The Chernobyl nuclear plant in Ukraine suffers a catastrophic meltdown.

Shuttle Challenger explodes on liftoff.

Iran-Contra affair

Gorbachev and Reagan meet in Reyjavik, Iceland.

Accused of planting a bomb in West Berlin, which killed an American soldier, Libya is bombed by the USA.

1986-1992

Shamir is PM again. Jewish settlements in the West Bank involve a population movement of over 150,000.

1987-1993

First Intifada

1987

At the Washington summit between Reagan and Gorbachev, the Intermediate Range Nuclear Forces treaty (INF) is signed. In the Moscow summit between Gorbachev and Reagan, the INF is ratified but Reagan makes no promises on the SDI.

Yeltsin is removed from his Moscow post and from the Politburo.

Zhao Ziyang replaces Hu Yaobang.

Mohammad Taha and Sheikh Ahmed Yassin launch Hamas (Harakat al-Mukawama al-Ismailiya or Islamic Resistance Movement) in Palestine, initially with Israeli tolerance as a potential rival to the PLO. Hamas was an offshoot of the Islamic Brotherhood, an Islamic organization with independent existence in many Muslim countries.

1988

An on-board bomb downs a Pan Am liner over Lockerbie, Scotland. Libya was suspected as the perpetrator in retaliation for the USA bombing in 1986, in which one of Qaddafi's daughters was killed.

Gorbachev initiates glasnost and perestroika.

1989

Gorbachev is elected president of the USSR.

The Soviets abandon the fight in Afghanistan, which fragments into warlordships.

The Tiananmen Square pro-democracy demonstrations in Beijing are quashed by the military. The liberalization process in the USSR probably influenced the democracy movement in China. Deng Xiaoping, who as head of the military committee had been the Chinese power behind the throne since 1981, removed Zhao Ziyang, who had adopted a conciliatory attitude.

Khomeini dies of a heart attack. A theocratic Assembly of Experts elects Sayyed Ali Khamenei as spiritual and effective political leader of Iran.

The PLO recognizes the right of Israel to exist.

Yugoslav president Slobodan Milosevic deprives Kosovo, where Albanian agitation had been going on, of all autonomous powers.

Carlos Saul Menem, president of Argentina, applies liberal economic program.

1989-1991

The Soviet empire collapses.

1989-1993

President George H.W. Bush

1989-1990

In 1989 a military dictator, Manuel Noriega, whom Americans suspected of being also a drug smuggler, ruled Panamá. In 1990, American forces invaded. There was some scattered resistance but Noriega was captured, tried and convicted in the USA.

1990

First Lithuania and then Estonia declare independence from the USSR.

Capitalist "shock therapy" is applied in Poland by American economic advisors. Subsequently, Polish voters elected reformed communists.

Germany is reunified.

1990-1991

Gulf or First Iraqi war

Relations between the USA and Iraq were friendly. Iraq had been expecting the Saudis and Kuwaitis to condone its war debts, which was not on the cards. Alleging a flooding of the oil market, Iraq invaded Kuwait (2 August 1990), abolished the local regime, and proclaimed Kuwait's annexation as Iraq's 19th province. The UN Security Council and the EU voted for an oil boycott of Iraq. The Arab League and the Security Council approved measures to make the boycott stick. Led by the USA, a large military alliance was formed. Hussein was served notice to evacuate Kuwait by neighboring Arab states—only Jordan, for commercial reasons and out of political prudence, maintained relations with Iraq—and by the USA and the members of the alliance. On 29 November, the Security Council, with China abstaining, gave Iraq until 15 January 1991 to comply. When there was no compliance, Iraq was bombarded heavily and an USA-led multinational force of 690,000—510,000 ground troops of which all but 10,000 were Americans—easily vanquished Iraqi forces (army and reserves estimated at 1,060,000), but not before Soviet-designed Iraqi Scud rockets in the hundreds were flung at Israel and at Saudi Arabia. Resistance collapsed when a high-tech American bomb was aimed so perfectly that it penetrated the air vent of a bomb shelter for Iraqi officials and their relatives killing all its hundreds of occupants. However, American President George Bush restrained the invasion short of Baghdad and Hussein remained in power through a stronger repression of opposition than ever before.

1990-1997

John Major, British PM

1991

The USSR is dissolved.

The Berlin wall is torn down.

1991-1995

The dissolution of Yugoslavia and the Bosnian war

An attempt by the Serbs to co-opt the Yugoslav presidency in 1991 led to the secession of Slovenia and Croatia. Macedonia seceded in 1992. Serbia and Montenegro formed a new Yugoslav federation. The status of Bosnia and Herzegovina, which was divided into Muslim, Serbian, and Croat communities (sometimes separate, often mixed), were still indecisive. When Bosnia and Herzegovina attempted to go independent under prodding from the Muslims (who constituted a small absolute majority of the population), Serbia unofficially intervened. War broke out and the Serbs, who applied "ethnic cleansing" in the areas they controlled, besieged Sarajevo. Serbs tried to gain control of Krajina and Slavonia, both part of Croatia. In 1994, Croats and Muslims agreed on a Bosnian government. The Serb re-started their attacks on Sarajevo. In 1995, in operation Deliberate Force, NATO forces intervened with effective air strikes that made the Serbs back down. On the ground UN troops were positioned in "safe zones". The air offensive allowed Croats to recover territories occupied by the Serbs. The Serbs captured Muslim Srebrenica and perpetrated a massacre of their male inhabitants that shocked the world as a throwback to Nazi barbarism. Estimates are that around 7,000 male Muslims were killed. At the trial of two Serb Bosnian officers in The Hague, the accused admitted with convincing and harrowing details that the massacre, carried out in the nearby towns of Bratunac and Zvornik, were deliberate and planned under orders from the commander of Serbian forces, Ratko Mladic. Subsequently, Serb defences crumbled and in November 1995, all parties signed accords in Dayton, Ohio, in which Bosnia and Herzegovina were divided into a federation including Muslims and Croats (51% of the territory) and a less federated Serb republic, Mladic and Radovan Karadzic, the leader of the Bosnian Serbs, have been declared international outlaws.

Economic shock therapy was applied corruptly in Russia with Anatoly Chubais as minister for privatization. Russia transits from a centrally controlled economy to a chaotically, de-centralized (though hardly liberal) one.

1991-1996

Under P.V. Narasimha Rao, PM of India, finance minister Manmohan Singh introduces economic reforms.

1992-1995

Yitzhak Rabin, Israeli PM

1992-1993

By the Maastricht treaty, ratified in 1993 by all member states, the EEC becomes the European Union (EU). The common market becomes a single market.

1992-1994

America intervenes in Somalia.

1992-1997

Boutros Boutros-Ghali, secretary general of the UN

1993-2001

President Bill Clinton

1993

On 21 September, Yeltsin unconstitutionally dissolved the Congress of People's Deputies. A quorum of deputies of the Supreme Soviet, whose authority emanated from the dissolved parliament, defied Yeltsin. Gen. Pavel Grachev, minister of defense, backed Yeltsin. On 4 October, the Russian parliament was taken. In December, a new Russian constitution was approved.

Oslo accords (officially "Declaration of principles on interim self-government arrangements") are signed in Washington between Israelis and Palestinians. The bridge-builder was the Norwegian foreign minister Johan Jorgen Holst. The principle of two contiguous independent states, Israel and Palestine, was accepted, although the accords mentioned the "Palestinian side". A transition to the two-state solution would be made through the Palestinian Authority (PA), to which Israel would gradually cede sovereignty over the West Bank and Gaza.

Muslim fanatics attempt to blow up the foundations of the World Trade Center in New York.

1994

Kim Il Sung of North Korea dies.

Yasir Arafat arrives in Gaza and immediately forms the PA with jurisdiction initially in Gaza and Jericho (in the West Bank).

Mass killings in Rwanda of minority Tutsis by Hutus leave over a million dead. Uganda-backed Tutsis invade and take over Rwanda. The new government prohibits all mention of ethnicity (Hutus and Tutsis speak the same language). Burundi is still in the grip of Tutsi-Hutu ethnic hatreds.

40,000 Russian troops attack Chechnya. Grozny, the Chechen capital, is destroyed.

1995

Jacques Chirac won the presidency of France and was re-elected in 2002.

US armed forces office building in Riyadh, Saudi Arabia, is bombed.

November: Israeli Prime Minister Yitzhak Rabin is assassinated. His successor, Peres, calls for elections.

1996-1999

Binyamin Netanyahu elected Israeli PM in June. He soon lifts ban, imposed by Rabin, on the construction of Jewish housing in the West Bank.

1996

Yasir Arafat is ratified by dodgy elections in Gaza and the West Bank as head of the PA.

Former-Gen. Aleksandr Lebed, a Yeltsin aide, closes the first Chechnya war (80,000 dead).

Yeltsin is re-elected president.

Jose Maria Aznar is elected Spanish PM.

A terrorist attack on the Khobar tower barracks for American personnel, near King Abdul Aziz Air Force Base, in eastern Saudi Arabia, is blamed on Hizbollah, the Iranian-backed international fighting organization.

The Taliban, led by Mullah Mohammed Omar, gradually take over most of Afghanistan. The Uzbek north is not entirely reduced. Osama bin Laden moves to Afghanistan and starts organizing al Qaida.

1997

The Kyoto Protocol is scheduled to come into effect in 2005. Over 120 states have signed it.

Deng Xiaoping dies and is succeeded by Jiang Zemin as leader of China.

Tony Blair becomes British PM.

Kofi Annan becomes secretary-general of the UN.

Ayatollah Mohammad Khatami is elected president of Iran.

Swiss government agrees to compensate relatives of victims of the Holocaust.

1997-1998

The PA rejects an offer by the Israeli government of 9% of the West Bank. The Israeli government rejects a proposal by the PA for a cession of 13% of the West Bank. Arafat threatens to declare independence unilaterally. Israel offers to "redeploy" troops in the West Bank but after terrorist attacks in Gaza cancels plans.

1997-2003

Jiang Zemin, secretary-general of Chinese communist party

1998

Gerhard Schroeder, German chancellor

There are bombings in American embassies in Kenya and Tanzania. Tomahawks fly against Sudan and Afghanistan.

Osama bin Laden emits fatwa to kill Americans.

Iraq expels UN arms inspectors.

1998-2004

Atal Behari Vajpayee, PM of India

1999

The US Senate approves by a vote of 97 to 3 a bill to partially re-activate the SDI (Space Defense Initiative), aimed this time at attacks from "rogue nations" rather than as a full-scale anti-nuclear missile defense system such as the one originally envisioned by President Reagan with the USSR in mind. President Clinton supports the initiative.

May: The Oslo accords expire. Ehud Barak is elected PM of Israel. Not much later, his government was allowing 2,600 new homes in the West Bank settlements. The outposts permitted by Netanyahu were also approved. In October, Israel transferred 7% of West Bank, including Ramallah, to the PA. Also, Israel approves a controlled land link between Gaza and the West Bank. In December, negotiations for a further 5% transfer of the West Bank to the PA fail.

Slobodan Milosevic applies brutal ethnic cleansing in Kosovo, whose Albanian inhabitants were forced into refugee status in Albania and Macedonia. Milosevic was warned off by NATO but persisted and in the first purely airborne war in history, mostly aimed at Serbia, the Serbs were forced to back off. The UN approved an international administration for Kosovo. The Kosovo peacekeeping force (KFOR) was activated. Montenegro proposes transforming its association with Serbia into that of a very loose federation.

The Czech Republic, Hungary, and Poland join NATO.

Islamic irregulars, with Pakistani army connivance, occupy the heights of Kargil, in Kashmir, and are dislodged by India with considerable losses.

When Pakistani Prime Minister Nawaz Sharif tries to meddle with the army hierarchy, Gen. Pervez Musharraf overthrows him.

Pinochet is arrested in Great Britain.

1999-2002

Formation of East Timor

1999-2004

Argentine is struck by economic crisis. After a period of belt-tightening, the country was flourishing again in 2004.

2000

Vladimir Putin is elected president of Russia.

10-3-2000: NASDAQ peaks; 21-3-2000: recession in the USA. December: Recession officially ends in the USA, but unemployment still growing. The economy improved noticeably in 2004-2005.

Israel evacuates southern Lebanon.

Palestinians spontaneously begin the Second Intifada.

George W. Bush is elected president with a minority of popular vote.

The *USS Cole* is attacked in Aden harbor.

2000-2001

In a final failed stab at peace, lame-duck President Clinton brings together Yasir Arafat and Israeli PM Ehud Barak for peace talks called Camp David II. Both sides distrusted each other and were afraid of the reactions of their respective constituencies. Arafat and Barak never met alone.

2001

The Taliban destroy the Bamian Buddhas.

President Musharraf reportedly removed Abdul Qadeer Khan as head of Pakistan's bomb-building nuclear laboratory.

Junichiro Koizumi is elected Japanese PM.

Ariel Sharon is elected Israeli PM. Suicide bombings surge. Eighteen bombings kill eighty Israelis, the largest one-month toll during the Second Intifada. The worst attack killed 29 persons in Natayah. Sharon implements the policy the state assassinations.

Israeli gunships bombard Arafat's headquarters in Gaza city. The PA moves its offices to Ramallah, north of Jerusalem. Arafat's bodyguard unit, based in Deir al-Balah, Gaza, is decimated.

9/11

War on Afghanistan

Afgfhanistan refuses to hand Osama bin Laden to the USA. September: CIA starts financing Mohammed Fahim of Northern Alliance east of Kunduz. October: CIA identifies ground targets; bombing starts; Kunduz falls. November: Mazar-i-Sharif falls. Taliban abandons Kabul. December: Kandahar, home of the Taliban, falls. A central government is installed in Kabul headed by President Hamid Karzai, but regional warlords prevail. The USA rounds around 680 al Qaida and Taliban militants that might have been involved in or have knowledge of the 9/11 attack and imprisons them in the Guantanamo naval base, in eastern Cuba, out of the reach of the American legal system. Many of them are non-Afghans. There is an Australian and an American among them.

In view of the gravity of the attack on America, the government considers special criteria to apply in the case of prisoners in anti-terrorist war and other operations.

End of 2001-early 2003

Twelve major offensives in Afghanistan against Taliban and al Qaida recalcitrants

2002

January

North Korea admits that it is in the process of making nuclear weapons at a secret plant. In November, the USA and allies cut supply of fuel to North Korea.

White House legal counsel Alberto Gonzales advises that the Geneva conventions did not apply to prisoners in Afghanistan but that they be held by executive authority and judged by military commissions rather than normal courts. The presidency took this advice to apply in principle to al Qaida but not to Taliban fighters.

April

Operation Defensive Wall: Israel starts building walls to fence off Israeli settlements in the West Bank from Palestinian areas. The Israeli army launches an offensive on Jenin, deep in the northern West Bank.

Second half of 2002

Accusing Iraq of possessing or in the process of manufacturing weapons of mass destruction (WMD), President Bush and the highest officials in his administration were busy making their case to potential allies and to critics, not only abroad but also at home, because support in Congress was not unanimous.

August

Alberto Gonzales, who had requested judicial orientation, obtains a Justice Department memorandum with a narrow definition of torture in the sense of pushing out the limits on physical duress applicable to prisoners.

October

A White House-Congress deal authorizes limited use of force in Iraq contingent upon a UN resolution approving it.

November

The physical Euro (the name finally adopted for the ECU) in the form of bills and coins begins circulating as the sole currency of most of the members of the EMU (Austria, Belgium, Finland, France, Germany, Greece, Ireland, Italy, Luxembourg, Netherlands, Portugal, and Spain). UK, Denmark, and Sweden opted out.

In the congressional election, the voters give the Republicans majorities in both houses of Congress, which is a virtual go for war against Iraq.

According to UN Resolution 1441, arms inspectors, headed by the Swede Hans Blix, were to go to Iraq. War would ensue only if it was reported that Iraq either possessed or was concealing a program or programs for the development of WMD. The deadline for the report was set for 17 March 2003. On 7 November, the UN inspectors arrived in Iraq and in general found no obstructions to their task.

Suicide attack kills eleven on Jerusalem bus, 48 wounded. Arafat condemns attacks on civilians.

December

As the rule of indefinite detainment of combatants excluded from the protection of the Geneva Convention is not producing any concrete results, defense secretary Donald Rumsfeld authorizes a harsher treatment of Afghanistan-war prisoners and terrorism suspects, very close to outright torture.

2003

The UN International Criminal Court, empowered to try individuals for atrocious crimes, is set up.

February

Shuttle Columbia burns on re-entry.

Labor suffers a crushing defeat and Sharon's Likud gains seats.

The Commission on terrorist attacks on the United States (better known as the 9/11 panel) is formed to investigate the events leading to 9/11.

March

In Pakistan, al Qaida leader Khalid Shaikh Mohammad, possible planner of 9/11, is arrested.

Russia will veto Iraq war.

Secretary-general Kofi Annan declares that war on Iraq without UN consent would violate the charter of the world organization.

Bush states that Iraq is a direct threat to America.

Given an ultimatum to leave Iraq, Hussein refuses. UN weapons inspectors withdraw.

Under international pressure but mainly because he has no access to the Israeli government, Arafat approves the office of Palestinian prime minister for which he names Mahmoud Abbas.

The Second Iraqi War started on March 19. President Bush declared the war officially over on 1 May, when the fatal casualties of the coalition forces stood at 190. Marines plan to leave Iraq by end of August.

April

North Korea withdraws from the Nuclear Non-proliferation treaty.

May

The "roadmap", the American plan for peace in Israel/Palestine, is delivered. Purposefully snubbing Arafat, Powell urges Palestinians to disarm militants. Sharon rules out restraining Israeli settlements, of which, as per the roadmap, those built starting in March 2001, when Sharon was elected PM, would have to be dismantled.

54 die from blast in government offices in Znamenskoye, northern Chechnya.

June

Hamas had taken the most Israeli lives (243), according to Israeli army sources. Powell demands that Hamas be neutralized. The Israeli wall goes up, says Sharon, though Bush called it "a problem".

Belgium scraps universal human rights law under which Sharon had been accused for the massacres at the Sabra and Shatilla Palestinian refugee camps in Beirut, Lebanon.

July

US-appointed governing council for Iraq meets. It includes Kurds, Shiites, Sunnis, and Iraqi exiles.

August

UN headquarters in Iraq are bombed, killing at least 20 dead, including the head of mission, Sergio Vieira de Mello. Annan declares that security in Iraq is an American responsibility.

North Korea gives approval to multilateral talks about its nuclear program (the two Koreas, Japan, Russia, USA, and China). The talks start in Beijing.

Terrorist bomb carried by truck-suicider targets a military hospital in Mozdok, Russia, near Chechnya, killing at least 49. There had been eight suicide attacks since mid-May—four in Chechnya; two in Mozdok; two in Moscow—leaving more than 150 dead. Three bombs kill three persons in Krasnodar, Russia. Dozens die in a terror blast in north of Chechnya. Woman suicider kills five in a hotel near Red Square Moscow.

September

Sharon blasts the roadmap. Two suiciders kill two Israelis. A suicider in central Jerusalem kills 20, including many children. Hamas and Islamic Jihad claimed the attack. Israelis kill a senior Hamas leader. Powell calls on Arafat to use force on militants. An Israeli attack kills four members of Hamas in Gaza. Suiciders kill 15 Israelis in Jerusalem and Tel Aviv. Sharon cuts short trip to India. Abbas resigns and is replaced by Ahmed Qurei, who names a cabinet.

Bush requests $87.5 billion for operations in Iraq and Afghanistan; approved by the House the following month. It is estimated that the wars in Afghanistan and Iraq, including reconstruction expenses, would have cost the US $166 billion to the end of 2004. There were 127,000 US troops in Iraq; 9,800 in Afghanistan.

October

UN Security Council authorizes US occupation of Iraq.

US officials see Saddam's hand in attacks on GIs in coordination with General Izzat Ibrahim, the second-ranking member in Hussein's former government.

Hanadi Jaradat, a young woman from Jenin, explodes herself in Haifa killing 15 Israelis, including four Israeli Arabs. Israel strikes at Syria after blast in Haifa. Bush backs Israel over defense of homeland. In the House of Representatives sanctions against Syria are approved. Another suicider killed two Israelis in West Bank. US vetoes Syrian-sponsored UN resolution at Security Council condemning Israeli walls. Britain and Germany abstained. Gaza road bomb hits US diplomatic convoy. Eight Palestinians killed in Israeli attack on Rafah in Gaza against arm-smuggling tunnels. Israel vows not to ease pressure as raids kill ten in Gaza. Three Israeli soldiers killed in West Bank. Rockets are fired from the Gaza strip; Israeli counter-measures kill a dozen Palestinians. Three Israeli soldiers (one a woman) killed at Gaza settlements.

UN assembly asks Israel to raze West Bank wall.

The USA intercepts the ship BBC China carrying uranium-enrichment centrifuge parts to Libya. The shipment was traced to Malaysia, but further back to Pakistan

China lifts astronaut Yang Liwei to orbit on a Senzhou 5 rocket. It becomes the third country to do so and is making plans for a space station. China posts its biggest surplus ever in trade.

Russia's richest man, Mikhail Khodorkovsky, is arrested on charges of tax fraud and other derelictions, of which none, according to observers, could have been attributed to any other Russian tycoon.

November

Twelve suiciders kill 29 people in Casablanca, Morocco (hotel, Jewish center, Spanish club, Belgian consulate).

Bomb attacks on HSBC bank and British consulate in Istanbul leave at least 25 dead.

December

The American government announced that companies from the countries that had opposed the war would not be considered for the task of reconstructing Iraq. The biggest contactor was Halliburton, a company in which vice-president Cheney had been CEO.

Saddam Hussein is captured by US troops in a crawl-into hiding place.

Libya gives up nuclear, biological, and chemical weapons programs. It hands over Pakistani blueprints for nuclear warheads.

Israel kills seven Palestinians in invasion with tanks of the Rafah camp on Gaza-Egypt border after two Israeli officers were killed in the area. In a month, at least 25 Palestinians have been killed. Four Israelis killed in suicide bombing near Tel Aviv. There have been over sixty bombings since the Intifada began.

2004

January

Resistance to the American occupation becomes intense in the Sunnni areas of Iraq with Fallujah, west of Baghdad, as the center. Iraqi use of SAMs forces US Helicopters flying low to take evasive measures. Scores die in two blasts aimed at Iraqi Kurds. Iraqis collaborating with the occupation authorities either in the police or in training for the army are also targeted. Roadside bombs are the weapon of preference of Iraqi insurgents.

February

Sharon announces plans to evacuate 9,000 Israeli settlers in 17 settlements in Gaza. In all there were around 230,000 Israeli settlers in Gaza and the West Bank. US urges talks on the Israeli pullout.

March

Suicide bombers killed at least 169 people in a series of attacks on Shia Muslims marking the religious festival of Ashoura in Karbala and in Baghdad. The chief suspect of the USA occupation authorities was Abu Musab al-Zarqawi, a Jordanian admirer of al Qaida, known to be active in Iraq, with a $10 million price on his head.

Train bombs terrorize Madrid with over 200 dead.

Intense fighting breaks out in Gaza. Israeli raids usually include helicopter-fired missiles. Israeli missile kills Sheikh Ahmed Yassin, the paraplegic leader and founder of Hamas, on his way out from a mosque in Gaza. Abdel Aziz Rantisi substitutes him.

Richard Clarke, ex-antiterror adviser, faults Bush's response to warnings about al Qaida threat. The 9/11 panel cites further unheeded warnings to Bush. The White House admits that it initially sought to link 9/11 to Iraq without any evidence.

In Russia, Putin gets 71% of vote for a second term.

April

The young Shiite cleric Moktada al-Sadr, leader of a resistance force called the Mahdi army, launches an insurrection against the American occupation. The Shiites' centers of resistance are the huge Baghdad sector known as Sadr City (2.2 million of Baghdad's total population of 5.5 million) and the cities of Najaf and Kufa, south of Baghdad.

UN approves the plan to substitute the US-appointed Iraqi governing council with a caretaker body to be installed on 1 July.

After a bombing in the port of Ashdod, which caused ten fatalities, the Israeli military assassinate Abdel Aziz Rantisi, the new leader of Hamas, with a helicopter-fired missile.

The bipartisan 9/11 panel finds that, when the intelligence agencies did not turn up a connection between 9/11 and Iraq, the Bush administration, and the Pentagon specifically, turned to a team headed by Douglas Feith, which by the end of 2001 had prepared reports vaguely linking Iraq with all Arab terrorist groups.

May

The military prison of Abu Ghraib, in Baghdad, becomes a major scandal through photographs taken in January in which American soldiers appear mistreating Iraqi prisoners.

The US-named governing council dissolves itself as the prelude for the handover to the interim government on June 30.

The Ezzedin al-Qassam brigades, dependent on Hamas, fought a large Israeli incursion into Gaza destroying two armored vehicles and killing 11 Israeli soldiers. Israeli fire killed 26 Palestinians. The purpose of the Israeli raid was to close tunnels to Egypt and destroy arms workshops. Subsequently, Israel attacked Rafah with tanks and helicopters, demolished over 100 houses, and killed more than 40 Palestinians. Rafah grew out of a Palestinian refugee camp on the border with Egypt. Bush expressed support for Israel.

In India, which had shown a sensational rate of economic growth in 2003, it was expected that the ruling Bharatiya Janata Party would win easily. Elections in India are a three-tier process. By its middle, it seemed that Prime Minister Atal Bihari Vajpajee's government was in trouble. At the end of polling, Indian voters had turned it out of office and had given instead a plurality to the Congress party led by the Italian-born Sonia Gandhi, widow of former PM Rajiv Gandhi, son of Indira Gandhi. The markets in India fell precipitously, especially as in order to form a government the Congress party might have to seek a coalition with the political left in the national parliament. Sonia Gandhi ceded the post of Prime Minister to Manmohan Singh, a reformist economics minister in the previous Congress-party government (1991-1996). Towards the end of the year, the Mumbai stock market was booming.

Terrorists kill five foreign oil workers—two Americans, two Britons, and an Australian—and a local policeman in the Saudi Arabian oil port of Yabu on the Red Sea, immediately producing the departure of other foreigners, mainly Americans, in the industry. Oil prices began trending upwards.

A bomb kills the Russian-backed president of Chechnya, Akhmad Kadyrov, at a celebration in a stadium; 29 others also die.

June

The UN envoy in Iraq, Lakhdar Brahimi, chooses Iyad Allawi as future Prime Minister of the provisional government of Iraq after consultations with Bremer. The ceremonial office of President goes to Ghazi al-Yawar, a Sunni. Unanimously the Security Council of the UN approves the transfer of power from the American occupation authorities in Iraq to a provisional government. The UN resolution also approves the presence of a 160,000 multinational troops force, mainly American (140,000), in Iraq, with a mandate until the end of 2005. The top Shiite cleric in Iraq, grand ayatollah Mohamed Husseini Ali al-Sistani, gives his approval to the plans for the provisional government.

In contradiction to President Bush and vice-president Cheney, the 9/11 panel concludes that there was no collusion between Saddam Hussein and Osama bin Laden. The panel uncovered that the CIA did not give the White House specific authoritative information that Iraq did not possess WMD. But it did repeatedly tell President Bush that, contrary to his belief, there was no Iraq-Al Qaeda link. But the panel's conclusions tend to ease the burden of responsibility for the Second Iraqi war on President Bush. Its basic recommendation is that the American intelligence agencies should be re-structured to make them more cooperative. Those agencies are principally the CIA, attached to the presidency; the Defence Intelligence Agency, the National Security Agency, and the National Geospatial-Intelligence Agency, attached to the Pentagon; and the Bureau of Intelligence and Research, attached to the Department of State.

A revised Israeli "roadmap" is approved by the cabinet: the withdrawal of settlers and troops from Gaza is postponed for nine months and then it will be done in phases each one requiring cabinet approval. Later it transpires the evacuation will not occur until 2005.

The expansion of Israeli settlements in the West Bank goes on at the rate of 10,000 new residents every year. It is reported that there have been 60 new settlements in the West Bank since March 2001, when Sharon was elected prime minister.

The Supreme Court rules in relation to the Guantánamo prisoners that the executive does not have the right to detain persons without giving cause or allowing them access to legal defense. Some of the judges speak of oppression and of an assault on fundamental democratic values. Although not referring to Iraq, the court's decision had evident implications for the status of prisoners there. The administration responded with the adoption of a process of review of the cases of the remaining 595 detainees in Guantánamo to determine whether they were prisoners of war, hence subject to Geneva Convention rules, or unlawful combatants.

The International Atomic Energy Agency (IAEA), an UN body, rebukes Iran for lack of cooperation.

Chechens make a surprise night time attack on Ingushetia, neighboring Chechnya on the west, resulting in 92 deaths, 67 of them on the government side.

July

Gen. George Casey Jr., former vice chief of staff, takes over the US military command in Iraq from Gen. Ricardo Sanchez.

American planes bomb Fallujah, where it is reported that Abu Musab al Zarqawi has bases. Earlier, a "senior official" of the dissolved American occupied authority said that it was "hard-core Saddamists" that led the Sunni insurrection. He speculated that Iran might have been financing the Shiite resistance leader Moktada al-Sadr.

The International Court of Justice, sitting in The Hague, Netherlands, considers that the Israeli walls are illegal and that the UN should try to have them removed. Israel answers it will only heed its own supreme court. The UN General Assembly votes by 150 to 6 in favor of the international court's decision. The lopsided majority included all members of the EU. Poland, a EU member, has a contingent in Iraq.

August

A truce in Najaf with the Mahdi army of Moktada al-Sadr breaks down as US bombs the city and fighting resumes. Care is taken to avoid damage to the city's Imam Ali mosque, holy to Shiites, although the insurgents resist from the huge cemetery next to it. An US chopper is downed. American armored vehicles advance inside Najaf to within 800 meters of the Imam Ali mosque. Ayatollah Mohamed Husseini Ali al-Sistani brokers a deal by which the insurgents cede the custody of the mosque to Iraqi police.

September

Some 30 Chechen terrorists seized around 1,200 hostages in a school in Beslan, North Ossetia. In the assault on the school 338 are killed, mostly children.

President Putin recommended constitutional changes towards greater centralization of power but also for the strengthening of political parties through proportional representation.

October

A massive attack involving 200 tanks is launched by Israel on the Jabaliya refugee camp producing the death of 33 Gazans. Previously a rocket attack had killed five Israelis, including two children. In the following days the Palestinian toll reached 64.

Hamid Karzai wins the elections for president of Afghanistan. The elections were celebrated in an orderly and non-violent manner.

The Qatari TV network Al Jazeera receives and partially airs a tape in which Osama bin Laden threatens the USA with more terrorist attacks. Bin Laden says in it that the idea to attack the WTC towers came to him in 1982 after the invasion of Lebanon by Israel.

The Israeli offensive on Gaza eases up.

Towards the end of October it was estimated that over 150 foreigners had been abducted in Iraq and more than 30 killed since the campaign of kidnappings had begun in 2004.

November

President George W. Bush defeats his Democratic opponent John Kerry by a clear popular-vote majority of 3,500,000 in the highest electoral turnout for a presidential election in American history. The Republican Party increased its majorities in the Senate and the House of Representatives.

A division-size force of GIs and Marines operating with about a quarter of that size of the best available Iraqi troops starts the battle for Fallujah, where an estimated 5,000 insurgent fighters are entrenched. The scenario presented by the press was that Iraqi Prime Minister Ayad Allawi had given the municipal authorities in Fallujah an ultimatum for handing over the resistance fighters and he had ordered the attack when they failed to respond. The same day it was reported that the vice mayor of Fallujah had been killed by the guerrillas. One of the principal immediate objectives of the attack was a hospital, for two reasons: fighters had been reported inside it and it was giving out high civilian casualty figures. No fighters were found in the hospital. Resistance elsewhere in Fallujah was reported to be intense.

Mosul stages its own insurgency in support of Fallujah. The Mosul police fail to cope with the insurgents. A brigade of occupation troops is rushed to Mosul to quell growing anarchy.

Iran announces that it is capable of mass-producing a missile with a range to reach Israel.

Yasir Arafat dies.

Occupation forces declare Fallujah occupied, although some sporadic resistance remains.

Mahmoud Abbas is chosen leader of Al Fatah to succeed Arafat as president of the PA. He favors participation in elections to be held in 9 January for the PA, whose incumbent PM was Ahmed Qurei.

The IAEA did no refer the case of the Iranian nuclear program to the Security Council, as the USA wanted. Iran is in the process of negotiating with Britain, France, and Germany. Iran has barred inspectors from the military bases where it is reported that it might be working on the manufacture of nuclear weapons.

The USA will increase its troop strength in Iraq to 150,000.

December

Congress approves Bush's intelligence services bill creating a central office for coordinating 15 intelligence agencies and branches with an aggregate budget of $40 billion and 200,000 employees. The major part of the money is managed by the Pentagon and spent in satellites. The new post is called the national intelligence director.

Russian authorities "auction" Yuganksneftegaz, the core of Yukos, the biggest Russian oil producer, to collect back taxes for more than $20 billions. The winning bid for Yuganksneftegaz was $9.35. Yukos, whose owner, Mikhail Khodorkovsky, remains in prison for unpaid taxes of his own, was put together for much less. However, the fair value of the auctioned company was estimated by foreign bankers as much higher. The Russian government oil company Rosneft was the buyer of Yuganskneftegaz, the main asset of Yukos.

Mahmoud Abbas calls for an end to the Second Intifada.

A suicide bomber manages to penetrate a mess tent in an American military base north of Mosul and kills 22, including 18 Americans. The highest toll of fatal military casualties on a single day was on 23 March 2003, during the Second Iraqi war itself, when 29 troopers were killed.

A 9.3 magnitude earthquake off the northwestern tip of Sumatra produces huge tsunamis. By January, the deadly toll of the tsunamis stood at 150,000 with millions homeless. In Sri Lanka, it is estimated that over 30% of fatalities were children. The final figure exceeded 250,000, the majority in the provinces of the Atjeh region (northern Sumatra). The Asian catastrophe stimulates the largest outpouring of aid in history.

2005

January

The Justice Department formally rescinds previous narrow definition of torture.

A large majority elects Mahmoud Abbas president of the PA with two-thirds of 1.8 million eligible voters in the West Bank, Gaza, and East Jerusalem participating.

A well-planned Palestinian attack at a border crossing in Gaza kills six Israeli civilians and three Palestinian assailants. Mahmoud Abbas orders Palestinian security forces to border areas with Israel.

Hamas obtains an overwhelming electoral backing in local elections in Gaza.

Despite the highest number of insurgent attacks since the start of the Second Iraqi war, elections are held in Iraq. Numerous suicide bombings take place in voting places. However, extraordinary security measures taken by the USA occupation forces allow most Iraqis who wanted to vote to do so, which they did in large numbers in Shiite areas and in Kurdistan. Muqhtada al-Sadr, leader of the clandestine Shiite Mahdi army, did not participate in the election, which had the backing of ayatollah Ali al-Sistani and the political organization he managed, the United Iraqi Alliance. Results in the Iraqi elections give Shiite parties 48% and a Kurdish alliance 26% of votes. Sunni participation in the election was virtually nil.

February

Mahmoud Abbas and Ariel Sharon meet at Sharm el-Sheik, in Egypt, and agree to a truce in the struggle between Palestinians and Israelis. Egyptian President Hosni Mubarak and Jordanian King Abdullah II were present. Later, in an interview, Abbas said that he hoped that Israel would release Palestinian prisoners, approximately 8000, and that Hamas and Islamic Jihad would evolve into political parties. He asserted the Palestinians' rights to compensation for lost property now in Israel.

North Korea announces it is withdrawing indefinitely from multilateral talks about its nuclear program.

Rafik Hariri, a former Lebanese anti-Syria prime minister, is assassinated in a bomb attack. Syria denies involvement but all eyes look to Damascus, and an international investigation later points at the Syrian head of state security. Demonstrators in Beirut demand the withdrawal of the Syrian military presence, some 14,000 soldiers, in Lebanon. Soon afterwards, Syria started evacuating Lebanon.

The Kyoto protocol on the curtailing of the emission of greenhouse gases comes into effect. China and India are exempted. The USA has not subscribed it.

Sharon obtains cabinet approval for the Gaza withdrawal.

A suicider kills four Israelis in a Tel Aviv disco. Islamic Jihad claims the act. The Israeli government blames Syria but also sends a word of warning to Abbas.

Russia agrees to supply fuel for Iran's Bushehr nuclear power plant.

The Israeli security walls in the West Bank are two-thirds built and enclose 7% of the West Bank.

March

Hamas announces that it will participate in the Palestinian parliamentary elections.

Bush names UN-basher John Bolton as American ambassador to the UN. His nomination instantly awakens stiff opposition. During a congressional recess, Bush appoints him by decree.

Israel plans to expand the Maaleh Adumim settlement, east of Jerusalem, the largest of the settlements in the West Bank (30,000 inhabitants), by urbanizing with 3,500 new housing units a corridor from Jerusalem to the settlement, actually an Israeli city for all intents and purposes. The expansion would divide the West Bank along a short but strategic east-west axis. It would also complete the encirclement of East Jerusalem, where elsewhere Israel controls all accesses, thus making unrealistic Palestinian aspirations to make East Jerusalem the capital of a real Palestinian state, itself only so far a distant possibility.

April

Pope John Paul II dies. The Vatican conclave chooses Joseph Cardinal Ratzinger, a close collaborator of John Paul II, as new Pope Benedict XVI.

The Iraqi government is formed with the Kurdish leader Jalal Talabani as president and the Shiite Ibrahim al-Jaafari as prime minister.

May

Israeli forces raid Sida, a Palestinian village in the West Bank, resulting in the death of an Israeli soldier and a Palestinian militant. The PA protested continued Israeli incursions.

Deadly terrorist outbursts against the Iraqi government leave over 100 dead.

Labor wins the British national elections, but sees its previous parliamentary majority reduced by 55 seats. The Conservatives gain 35 seats and the Liberal Democrats 5. The popular vote was 37 for Labor and 33 for the Conservatives. PM Tony Blair is ratified, but he is challenged by leaders of his own party for having eroded its electoral base because of his support for the Second Iraqi war.

France votes against the EU constitution.

June

The group of G-8 agrees to the cancellation of $40 billion in debts by the world's 18 poorest countries.

The US Senate apologizes for the lynchings of blacks in American history.

Violence between Palestinians and Israelis continue, although on a lesser scale as during the height of the Second Intifada. No suicide attacks have been reported. Israel only reluctantly turned over Jericho and Tulkarm to the Palestinians. It offered to return also Bethlehem, Qalqiya, and Ramallah, but has not done so. Israel let it be known that it was resuming its policy of political assassinations, especially against Islamic Jihad militants.

American military officials both in Iraq and in Washington admit that the US forces in Iraq are taking more casualties than ever since the invasion and that the Iraq rebels, rather than giving in, are "building their military skills".

The CIA reports that Iraq has become a breeding ground for terrorism.

Gen John Abizaid, the top USA military commander in the Middle East, admits to Congress that the Iraqi insurgency is as strong as it was six months before. In another context, Gen. George Casey Jr., the American military commander in Iraq, says: "Things in Iraq are hard".

Islamic hardliner Mahmoud Ahmadinejad wins the election for president of Iran. Some Americans recognize him as one of the young Islamic guards who seized the American embassy in 1979.

India and the USA sign a wide military and nuclear cooperation agreement.

In eastern Afghanistan, Taliban guerrillas down an American helicopter killing the 17 people on board.

July

The dismantling of the Israeli settlements in Gaza is proceeding.

American forces in Iraq are subjected to some 60 attacks daily. The official fatal casualties count is 1,735.

London is struck by four terrorists' bombs in a bus and subway stations leaving 53 dead. As the investigation proceeded, it was determined that British Muslim suiciders detonated the time bombs.

Iraqi government declares that from August 2004 and May 2005, insurgents and terrorists had killed an average of over 800 Iraqi civilians and police a month.

China abandons the exchange system that keeps the Yuan at a fixed rate to the dollar.

There are over 90 dead in various terrorist attacks in the beach resort of Sharm el Sheik, Egypt. A so-called brigade of al Qaida claims responsibility.

Two Algerian diplomats are kidnapped and assassinated in Iraq.

The Muslim insurgency in southern Thailand, which began in January 2004, has claimed more than 700 fatalities, of which 200 were mass killings by Thai soldiers.

The recently named Egyptian ambassador in Iraq, Ihab al Sharif, is executed by the insurgents who had kidnapped him.

A Palestinian suicider kills two Israelis in Netanya. Abbas ordered a crackdown in Gaza by the Palestinian police, which resulted in two deaths. There were also Israeli reprisals.

There are over 90 dead in various terrorist attacks in the beach resort of Sharm el Sheik, Egypt. A so-called brigade of al Qaida claims responsibility.

August

The future Iraqi constitution is being debated with representatives of the Shia, Sunni, and Kurdish communities.

American forces open operations in western Iraq, on the Syrian border, to interdict the flow of military supplies and personnel for the insurgency.

Officers in military intelligence declare that the identity of Mohammed Atta, the leader of the attack on the WTC, was well established around January 2000, but the information was not transmitted to civilian agencies.

Israeli military kills five Palestinians in the city of Tulkarm, in the West Bank, suspected of being terrorists. Mahmoud Abbas accuses Israel of endangering the peace process.

Iran starts activating uranium-enrichment facilities in Isfahan. EU mediators react with a highly critical attitude.

Sixty-five American soldiers have been killed in operations in Afghanistan during 2004.

Chinese and Russian troops engage in joint military training maneuvers somewhere along the coast of China.

Powerful hurricane Katrina hits New Orleans and some levees break inundating much of the city, especially lower-income, low-lying areas, in effect forcing the evacuation of the city. The death toll of the New Orleans disaster is estimated in the hundreds.

September

The Gaza withdrawal is completed.

Bomb in Bahgdad kills over 75 as the constitution is approved. The following day various terrorist attacks leave over 150 dead.

Afghans vote for the national assembly. Islamists and former guerrilla fighters win half the seats.

Finance ministers of highly developed countries close a deal forgive $55 billion in debts of the eighteen poorest countries. Involved in the negotiations were the World Bank and the IMF.

The UN International Atomic Agency votes for a future, indeterminate reference of possible Iranian violations of nuclear non-proliferation to the UN Security Council.

October

The Pentagon emits a report from which it can be extrapolated that the total of Iraqis killed by insurgents from 1 January 2004 to 16 September 2005 is around 6,500. Body counting by private researchers places the figure for the same period at some 11,200. The Iraqi ministry of the interior estimated 8,175 killed from August 2004 to May 2005.

Six Marines are killed during the military offensive in western Iraq. Sectarian violence in the rest of the country continues. In Basra, the British occupation contingent is facing Shiite antagonism against which a local limping police force is ineffectual.

After Palestinian gunmen kill three Israelis, the Israeli government breaks contacts with Palestinian functionaries.

Saddam Hussein is brought to court charged with the killing of around 140 men in the Shiite town Dujail, where he had been the object of an assassination attempt. Husseing refuses to collaborate with the tribunal.

Chechen rebels attack Nalchik, the capital of Kabardino-Balkaria, in the same norther Caucasus region as Chechnya. In engagement with Russian forces over 100 die.

The UN commission headed by Detelev Mehlis and charged with investigating the assassination of Rafik Hariri, the former Lebanese primer minister, is following a trail which leads to Asef Shawkat, head of Syrian military intelligence and brother-in-law of president Bashar al-Assad.

Iraqi voters approve a new constitution, which contemplates the possibility of secession from central authority.

A suicider of Islamic Jihad kills five Israelis and Israel unleashes a major offensive against Gaza and a wave of arrests in the West Bank. Sharon does not discard the possibility of a re-occupation of Gaza.

Officially, the count of USA soldiers dead since the start of the Second Iraqi war surpassed two thousand in October.

November

NASA is short by $5 billion to maintain adequately the shuttle program.

Three Iraqi suicide terrorists kill 56 persons in three hotels in Amman, Jordan. The Jordanian terrorist active in the Iraqi insurrection, Abu Musab al-Zarqawi, assumed responsibility as head of a so-called Mesopotamian Al Qaida.

After prolonged haggling, Germany's two major parties, the Christian Democratic Union and the Social Democratic Party, agree to form a disparate coalition headed by Christian Democratic Angela Merkel, the winner by a bare minimum in the previous national election.

Five Marines are killed in the continuing American operation in the Syrian border region of northwestern Iraq.

According to the Associated Press, the American government has detained over 83,000 foreigners since the start of the "war on terror" in 2001.

Ariel Sharon calls for new elections and announces plan to form his own party, which Shimon Peres declares he will join.

Republicans in Congress oppose some of Bush's projected budget cuts which will affect social services while sticking to his tax breaks for upper-incomes tax payers.

December

The Iraqi insurgency is recurring more frequently to suicide bombers.

Chinese militiamen fire on protesting villagers killing over 20. The commanding officer was arrested, but Chinese authorities clamped on further reporting of the incident.

French surgeons perform a partial face transplant on a disfigured woman and provoke an outcry over the ethics of the operation.

Iraqis, including many from Sunni areas, who had abstained in the previous referendum on the country's constitution, participate in the election for the national assembly. The elections were characterized by an almost total absence of violence. Shiites and Kurds voted massively. Results announced in January showed the Shiites and Kurds had not managed to obtain the two-thirds of vote necessary to form a government by themselves due to dissenting Sunni votes.

In Israel/Palestine there is noticeable de-escalation of violence. In Palestine political infighting is reported in Al Fatah, the ruling party founded by Arafat and now headed by Mahmous Abbas.

The NYT reveals that immediately after 9/11 the Bush administration initiated a program of wire-tapping and eavesdropping of doubtful legality.

2006

January

In the elections for the Palestinian assembly, Hamas obtains a likely 35% of the votes to 42% for the ruling Fatah party and prime minister Mahmoud Abbas. The fear of a government including the hardline anti-Israel Hamas, prompts the Israeli government to halt payment of import duties due to the Palestine Authority. Also, Israel obstructs transit from Gaza, where Hamas won overwhelmingly, to the West Bank, where the Palestinian government functions.

During 2005, the USA military suffered 844 fatal casualties, adding to a total since the Second Iraqi war began of 2,178 and 7,989 wounded. January, when conditions were being established for the election to the constitutional assembly, was the bloodiest month with 107 US soldiers dead.

In the course of the same year, the US occupation, through the constituted Shiite dominated provisional government, had recruited over 200,000 Iraqis to oppose the insurgency. However, even as the mostly Sunni insurgency continued, there was a tendency for the Iraqi government forces to fragment along sectarian and tribal lines. The American-sponsored Shiite forces had been unleashing sporadic, but sometimes extremely brutal persecutions of Sunnis. The Mahdi army of the recalcitrant Shiite cleric Moktada al-Sadr was active in Baghdad, Basra, and elsewhere. Al-Sadr tended to place the root of the violence on the American occupation, constituted by 160,000 troops. It was believed that the Sunni had placemen in the oil industry, from which funds were being diverted to stoke the insurgency. There were also reports that there was friction between Al Qaida in Mesopotamia and secularist Iraqi insurgents.

Ariel Sharon suffers a massive stroke that puts him in a comatose state. He is succeeded provisionally by Ehud Olmert, who offers to carry on his predecessor's policies and to continue building the walls around Israeli settlements, of which 300 kms., or roughly half, had already been built.

The IAEA votes to refer Iran's nuclear program to the Security Council but, at the insistence of Russia and China, within lapse of at least a month and including a stricture about Israel's nuclear arsenal.

Insurgents kill eleven American servicemen and some 130 Iraqis.

The IAEA announces that Iran has resumed its nuclear program.

February

The US reports four dead Marines amidst attacks mainly aimed at Shiites.

The Shiite alliance, with the largest bloc of voters in the Iraqi assembly, decides to retain Ibrahim al-Jaafari as prime minister, but there were no immediate perspectives for the formation of a cabinet.

The golden dome of a mosque in Samarra sacred to Shiites is blown up.

March

Sectarian violence kills 75 Iraqis, mostly in Baghdad.

In what amounts to a contemporary diplomatic revolution, Bush, on a visit to India, sanctions a wide-ranging military cooperation and particularly a nuclear deal by which India's fast-breeder or weapons reactors will remains off-limits to inspections but civilian facilities will be monitored in exchange for technology and fuel supplies. In the following visit to Pakistan, Bush offers only encouragement and help in its fight against terrorism.

The Russians offered to sell India nuclear fuel without pre-conditions, while in the American Senate the India deal was expected to spark controversy.

American forces launch a large-scale offensive against the insurgency in mostly Kurdish areas of northwestern Iraq.

Index